THE LIBRARY
ST. MARY'S COLLEGE OF MARYLAND
ST. MARY'S CITY, MARYLAND   20686

D1525353

9780521052641

THE
MIGRANT COCOA-FARMERS OF
SOUTHERN GHANA

To the Memory of
my Grandparents

J. N. K. 1852–1949

F. A. K. 1861–1958

THE
MIGRANT COCOA-FARMERS
OF
SOUTHERN GHANA

A study in rural capitalism

BY

POLLY HILL

Fellow of Clare Hall, Cambridge

CAMBRIDGE UNIVERSITY PRESS

CAMBRIDGE

LONDON · NEW YORK · MELBOURNE

Published by the Syndics of the Cambridge University Press
The Pitt Building, Trumpington Street, Cambridge CB2 1RP
Bentley House, 200 Euston Road, London NW1 2DB
32 East 57th Street, New York, NY 10022, USA
296 Beaconsfield Parade, Middle Park, Melbourne 3206, Australia

© Cambridge University Press 1963

ISBN 0 521 05264 5

First published 1963
Reprinted 1970 1977

First printed in Great Britain by The Broadwater Press Limited,
Welwyn Garden City, Hertfordshire
Reprinted in Great Britain at the University Press, Cambridge

The Syndics of the Cambridge University Press wish to
acknowledge with gratitude a grant from the Smuts
Memorial Fund towards the production of this book.

FOREWORD

by Professor Meyer Fortes

In this book Polly Hill expounds a series of discoveries and observations that will surely delight readers who are academically, professionally or practically concerned with social studies in West Africa and who are not averse to revising some of their most time-honoured beliefs. Miss Hill calls herself a 'field economist' to distinguish her methods from those of the more normal variety of economist who nowadays swoops down upon an 'underdeveloped economy' for a week or a month, peruses the files and the blue books, and presently produces a plan or a treatise. Miss Hill takes a very different course, and the result is a book packed with original data of first-rate interest, accompanied by a sharp and scholarly theoretical elucidation. In the sphere of economics, Ghana is virtually synonymous with cocoa to the world at large. This book treats of cocoa. But not as normal economists do. Their interest lies in the crop itself, in questions of costs and prices and terms of trade. The producer, the cocoa-farmer, comes into their analysis only as a peripheral character; and when he does so it is in a stereotyped form that has hardly changed since it was first invented by traders and colonial officials in the early days of the cocoa-export trade. In extenuation it must be admitted that surprisingly little study has hitherto been made of the cocoa-farmers' way of life in different regions of Ghana. W. H. Beckett's *Akokoaso*, of twenty-five years ago, is still the most authoritative description of the social organization of cocoa-farming available to students.

Miss Hill's book is an opportune first instalment towards filling the gap. But it is a different kind of study altogether from that of Beckett. Where he confined his attention to one long-settled farming village, she ranges extensively over a large area of the hinterland of Accra where cocoa was first established at the turn of this century; where Beckett's interests are those of the agricultural economist concerned with the statistics of finance, production, acreages, labour and marketing, hers are closer to those of the economic anthropologist concerned with such matters as the leadership, enterprise, social composition, legal framework and historical development of cocoa-growers' undertakings. Her principal sources are the people themselves, interviewed, as in anthropological fieldwork, in their villages; but she also draws brilliantly on the scattered documentary material she has been able to ferret out to give the historical depth to her narrative which clinches the case for her main thesis.

Miss Hill's book is concerned with the oldest cocoa area of Southern Ghana, one that has, in recent years, been almost denuded by swollen shoot. Indeed it was the farm maps prepared in the campaign to rehabili-

FOREWORD

tate this area which formed the starting-point for her investigations. When cocoa was introduced to the Gold Coast in the eighteen-eighties this area consisted largely of uncultivated forest. Miss Hill maintains that, contrary to the orthodox view, it was opened up for cocoa not by sedentary peasants who established individual small farms in the neighbourhood of their villages, but by groups of migrant farmers from adjacent districts who operated with tracts of scores and even hundreds of acres. These groups were found to have had clearly defined forms of organization at the time of their inception, often fifty or sixty years ago. What is more, they have retained and perpetuated these forms by inheritance and succession in the changed circumstances of today. Basing her analysis on a collection of striking case histories (summarized in the Appendices), Miss Hill shows how the social organization of migrant farming groups ties in with their systems of land-tenure and land utilization, their economic aims and motives, their living arrangements and their civic status. In the course of this analysis she examines and refutes some of the most time-honoured clichés about such issues as communal land-tenure, the mis-called 'extended family', and the alleged lack of foresight and thrift among tropical peasants.

For my part, however, the special distinction of Miss Hill's book lies in observations that could not have been anticipated by her, but which represent a major contribution to the anthropological study of West African social structures. The novelty of these findings is the more striking to me when I compare them with my own field observations in the cocoa-growing districts of Ashanti in 1945–6. There, migrant farmers established themselves individually in new cocoa areas assisted only by their immediate family members. They held their land on a usufructuary tenure in virtue of an annual payment to the local chief which was more in the nature of an acknowledgement of his chiefdom's inalienable over-right to the land than an economic rent. These farms were mostly so new that few had passed from the original tenants to a later generation, but the indications were that they would devolve to heirs and successors in accordance with the normal Akan rules of matrilineal inheritance or paternal gift *inter vivos* to which reference is made in Miss Hill's book.

This is very different from the group migrations described by Miss Hill, quite astonishingly so in the case of the 'company' system. Miss Hill shows that two forms of group organization were followed by the migrant farmers, though their economic aims and activities were the same. One type was (and is) invariably made up of a group of matrilineal kin, both male and female, acting as a corporate group under the leadership of a senior male who is often also the chief financier of the enterprise. The block of land purchased by the group was and remains corporately owned but it was (and still is) farmed by the members severally in irregular parcels distributed patchwork-wise. When the leader dies his appointed

vi

FOREWORD

matrilineal successor takes over the management, and the individual plots, though completely under the control of the persons who farm them during their lifetime, become 'family' property, matrilineally heritable, on their death. In this way individual exploitation of land is reconciled with the ultimate corporate ownership of the soil, in accordance with principles often described by anthropologists. There is, however, a built-in potentiality of conflict between the urge to establish individual holdings and what Miss Hill calls the 'drift towards family property', and she makes some significant comments on the economic implications of this situation (ch. VII). She argues that in the society she is concerned with, where sale, mortgage and credit are institutions long ante-dating the advent of the modern market economy, corporate land-owning can serve as a spur to expansionary enterprise and as a form of 'banking' resources, and often promotes rather than impedes individual economic achievement. That is why it has persisted and has proved highly adaptable to changing economic and social conditions, in Ghana as elsewhere in the world (e.g. India) where similar corporate family organizations exist. Miss Hill's data strengthen the view held by anthropologists that there is no justification for the assertion, repeatedly and uncritically made by 'development' experts, that the so-called extended family system is 'almost certainly a drag on effort' (Lewis, 1955, p. 114) and a 'serious obstacle to economic progress' (Bauer & Yamey, 1957, p. 66).

There is much more to be said on this subject from the anthropological point of view. For Miss Hill's discussion of the matrilineal land-owning group is unusually instructive by reason of the stretch of fifty years or so to which her records refer. But I must not try her readers' patience by riding my own hobby-horse. Let me turn, therefore, to the second form of group organization described by her. This is the 'company' form by which a group of men from the same community who were friends and neighbours, not kinsmen, clubbed together to buy a block of land for cocoa-farming. In this case the land was (and remains) allocated in strips projected from a common base-line, each member receiving a strip of width proportional to his financial contribution to the purchase price. These strips are individually owned in the strict sense and there is no concept of corporate ownership corresponding to that of the matrilineal group. The strips are freely alienable and pass by inheritance to the owner's sons, not matrilineally. The reason for this is that the 'company' system was utilized exclusively and solely by the communities whose traditional family structure and inheritance rules are patrilineal, not matrilineal. It is this that makes Miss Hill's account of the 'company' system so fascinating and important for the anthropologist. For it should be borne in mind that the two types of community live in close proximity to one another, have many features of custom and social life, including their traditional political institutions, in common, and, of course, basically the

vii

FOREWORD

same economic practices and aspirations. Why they have nevertheless maintained their distinctive forms of family structure is an intriguing anthropological problem, but I cannot pursue it here.

What does emerge clearly is that we have in the 'company' a form of communal enterprise rooted in traditional family patterns but based on a kind of contract, and not on kinship status (to use Maine's well-known formula). We can describe it, perhaps, as a non-corporate collective. There are experts who maintain that contract relationships are incompatible with the traditional African 'extended family' organization and that individual land-ownership is not consistent with communal principles of tenure. We can see from Miss Hill's observations (which are amply confirmed by anthropological studies in many parts of Africa) why this thesis is unacceptable.

The co-existence of these two contrasting systems of family and property relations in the same ecological and economic environment offers material of great interest for comparative sociology. Anthropologists will seize particularly on the rich detail of Miss Hill's records and comments, which are the more revealing because they are often incidental to her main inquiry. We can see how neatly the figures she gives for the acreages held and inherited by members of farming groups represent the relative weight of the claims of different classes of kinsfolk on the common estate. Her findings about cross-cousin marriage, the *guaha* ceremony, and the position of sons who are allowed the use of small portions of the family land during their father's lifetime but must return it to the estate when he dies, fit in very well with what is known of Akan and other matrilineal African social structures. (It is an indication of Miss Hill's sensitive sociological judgment that she notes the corresponding practice in the company system whereby a daughter may enjoy the use of a strip-farm during her lifetime, but it reverts to her brother or his son on her death.) Her description of the inner organization and growth of the company farming groups is, as she remarks, less complete than for the matrilineal groups because not enough is known about the social structure of the patrilineal towns and communities from which they migrated. I suspect, from the inheritance patterns she describes, that corporate kinship groups will be found to be less developed among them than in the matrilineal areas.

I have, I fear, let my professional zeal and personal interest in Ghanaian social systems run away with me. I must therefore emphasize that Miss Hill's book has a much wider scope than the foregoing comments might suggest. Much thought is now being given to problems of social change in Africa. Miss Hill's study bears directly on this subject. On the one side it presents impressive evidence of how tenacious and resilient the basic principles and values of African social organization have proved to be. On the other, it enables us to see how changes were initiated, often

FOREWORD

by venturesome individuals, inspired by new pecuniary opportunities, by family loyalty or by the new ideas that came from missionaries and government officials. Some tantalizing questions arise. For example, would the story have been different if the political structure of the land-selling chiefdoms had been more centralized and the chiefs who sold land without scruple consequently more strictly controlled?

Again, land-tenure comes in for close attention, and Miss Hill draws on her records with very good effect to show how the customary laws of land-tenure have been influenced by the land transactions of the migrant groups and the litigation which soon supervened. There is important material here for the analysis of change and conflict in inheritance and succession laws.

But of course the outstanding feature of this book is the documentation and discussion of fundamental issues in the economic history and the theoretical appreciation of the cocoa-industry of Ghana. As a layman in this field I hesitate to do more than bring this to the notice of the experts. It seems to me, however, that Miss Hill's demonstration of the critical part played by the migrant farmers in creating the cocoa-industry, and more especially of the scale of their operations, must stimulate some new thinking on the subject of economic growth in West Africa. Furthermore, in showing how the earlier trade in palm products and rubber served as a springboard for the move into cocoa, she throws new light on that process. The more technical arguments pursued by her, such as those connecting land-purchase with investment, I must leave aside. But I cannot conclude without expressing my admiration for the absorbing piece of scholarly detective-work unfolded in Miss Hill's reconstruction of how cocoa was first introduced into the Gold Coast. Doubtless there will be some controversy over this, as over some of the other unorthodox conclusions reached by Miss Hill. As she is no mean literary craftsman and has, moreover, a ready eye for unconventional testimony for her thesis (witness her short lexicon of Twi economic terminology), I foresee a lively debate. What no one will dispute is that Miss Hill has given a new slant to African Social Studies by boldly combining the methods and theories of economics, anthropology and history—not to speak of her personal gifts of imagination and ardour—in these researches.

ACKNOWLEDGEMENTS

As usual with work of this kind, my main debt is to the thousands of cocoa-farmers who so willingly volunteered the information on which this study is based. I have no means whatsoever of thanking them—except by writing this book. I should like to emphasize, as have so many before me, that the friendly, forthcoming, painstaking, unprejudiced attitude of the ordinary West African man in farm or street makes fieldwork very pleasurable. 'Informants' do not merely endure the intrusive questions of the newly arrived research worker: they participate actively in the discussion, presumably having an instinctive understanding of the nature of research work.

As I had no paid assistant to help me in the field, I was always dependent on voluntary assistance offered in the numerous places where I worked. Assuming that those on whom I leant so heavily for help bear me no grudge as a result, I must heartily recommend this practice of relying on *local* experts as interpreters and guides, for their knowledge of the country and people so often enables one to go straight to the place, person or point. The list of those who assisted me in all the places I visited runs literally into hundreds, a great proportion of whom were members of the staff of Area Offices of the Ministry of Agriculture, in particular Liaison Officers—many of them with a most reliable knowledge of the farmers, their relatives and their backgrounds—as well, of course, as Area Survey Officers, Drawing Office Assistants and others. As a token list I remember: Mr K. Amoa Ampah (Kofi Pare), Mr W. Gorman (Asamankese), Mr P. K. Bedjabeng (Nankese), Mr N. B. Hammond (Kabu Hill) and Mr S. T. Osabutey (Kwesi Komfo). Their prototype, if he will forgive the expression, is Mr E. M. Addo Akuffo, who as a Liaison Officer at Nankese first conducted me to Obomofo-Densua, making me aware of the potential usefulness of the farm maps; we spent many days walking round the farms in that district and later on Mr Addo Akuffo's other identity, that of migrant cocoa-farmer, came into play when he introduced me to many migrant farmers in Akropong, his home town. Among all the other people who assisted me in the Akwapim home towns, very special mention must be made of Mr Eugene Ohene Walker of Larteh, elder brother of the late Benkumhene of Akwapim, for his wonderfully constructive help and encouragement over a long period—his work in connexion with the bridge at Mmetiamu is acknowledged in the text. Among others who assisted in Akwapim were: Mr J. J. Obeng (Aburi), Mr A. Larbi Ayeh (Mampong, now a Local Court Magistrate elsewhere) and Mr E. L. Asa-Anakwa (Mamfe). I am also very grateful to the Adontenhene of Akwapim (Nana Osae Djan) for most valuable information and hospitality, to

ACKNOWLEDGEMENTS

the Benkumhene of Akwapim (Nana Okanta Obrenti II) who gave much help before his lamented death in 1959, and to the Chief of Berekuso (Nana Adu Mreku Agyeman II). I made few inquiries in the homelands other than Akwapim, but I wish to acknowledge the help of Nene Mate Kole (Paramount Chief of Manya Krobo) and Nana Danso Ntow V (Krontihene of Anum).

Among colleagues, both past and present, at the University of Ghana, I must acknowledge the help of Mr H. J. Bevin, Mr D. Brokensha, Dr J. M. Hunter, Dr W. Manshard, Mr Douglas Rimmer, Dr W. Tordoff and Mr Ivor Wilks—some of their specific contributions are mentioned in the text. I cannot adequately express my gratitude to Dr M. J. Field, a pioneer in this field, especially for the encouragement she gave me at a time when it seemed that hardly anyone else was interested in this work. I am also grateful to Professor Meyer Fortes, Mr C. H. Cooke, Mr S. G. Davies and Dr Michael Young for criticizing parts of the typescript, and to Mr Andrew Opoku for permission to reprint part of 'Across the Prah'. Finally, I must acknowledge the great value of the instruction in the Twi language which I received from Mr S. Nyako-Agyakwa, then a medical student at Cambridge.

This book would not have been written had not Professor Meyer Fortes, who knew scarcely anything of my work, suddenly encouraged me, I think on the spur of the moment, to revisit my home town. I am most grateful to him as well as to the University of Ghana for their trust and far-sightedness in allowing me a year's study leave in Cambridge, and to the administrators of the Smuts Memorial Fund both for awarding me a Fellowship and for other financial assistance connected with the publication of this book.

P. H.

UNIVERSITY OF GHANA
August 1962

CONTENTS

Foreword		*page* v
Acknowledgements		x
List of Illustrations		xv
I	Introduction	1
II	The Company	38
III	The Family Land	75
IV	The Operation of the Customary Rules of Inheritance:	
	I: Company Lands	109
	II: Family Lands	122
V	Akim Abuakwa Land Sales in Relation to Customary Law	138
VI	The Background Economic Conditions	161
VII	Economic Aspects of the Migratory Process, 1894–1930	178
VIII	An Outline Geography of the Migration	219

Appendices to Chapter I

1	The Treatment of the Migration of Southern Ghanaian Cocoa-Farmers in Published Books, Reports, etc.	18
2	Swollen-shoot Disease and the Farm Maps	23
3	Notes on the principal Migrant Cocoa-Farmers of Southern Ghana	25
4	Notes on the History and Ethnology of Akwapim, by David Brokensha	27
5	'Across the Prah', by A. A. Opoku	30

Appendices to Chapter II

1	The Reports of the Reserve Settlement Commissioners	55
2	The Kwesi Komfo Area	60
3	Company Lands in the Nankese Area	62
4	The Kyerepon Company near Nobeso	63
5	The Mamfe/Trayo Company	65
6	The Shai/Nankese Company	67

CONTENTS

7	The Shai Company at Obomofo-Densua	*page* 69
8	The Mamfe/Saforosua Company	70
9	The *Huza* System	72

Appendices to Chapter III

1	Sakyikrom	86
2	An Aburi (Nsakye) Family Land near Krabokese	89
3	Akotuakrom	91
4	The Kofi Pare Family Land	92
5	Kwame Tawiah	96
6	Ahwerease-Akim	97
7	The Omenako Family Land	97
8	The Boah Family Land	100
9	An Akropong Family Land near Bepoase	104
10	An Amanokrom Family Land near Dome (Suhum)	106
11	A small Aburi Family Land near Dome (Suhum)	107

Appendices to Chapter IV

1	A brief Note on the Legal Concepts of Self-Acquired and Family Property	131
2	Gifts and *Samansew*	132
3	Notes on the Larteh, Mamfe and Mampong Inheritance Systems	133
4	Notes on the Aburi and Akropong Inheritance Systems	135

Appendices to Chapter V

1	The West African Lands Committee (with a Note on the 1897 Lands Bill)	149
2	The Apedwa/Apapam Land Dispute of the 1890's	151
3	The Akwapim/Akim Abuakwa Dispute over Jurisdiction	154
4	The Asamankese Arbitration	157
5	The 'Renting' of Land to Strangers in the Asamankese Area	158
6	Documentation of Land Sales	160

Appendices to Chapter VI

1	The Introduction of Cocoa into the Gold Coast	170
2	Annual Gold Coast Exports, 1886–1913	176

CONTENTS

Appendices to Chapter VII

1	The Akwapim Surveys: Statistical Results	*page*	193
2	Companies and the 'Patrilineal System'		199
3	Akwapim Case Histories		200
4	Additional Notes on certain Akwapim Towns		211
5	Cocoa-Farm Labourers		213
6	Linguistic Economics		214
7	Miscellaneous Cocoa Statistics		217

Appendices to Chapter VIII

1	William Adjabeng Quansah Solomon	238
2	'Omanhene the Farmer'	240
3	The Bridge at Mmetiamu (with Notes on the Mangoase and Bibianiha bridges and the access roads to Akwapim)	243
4	The Population of Akwapim, 1891 to 1960	248
5	The Population of 'Stranger-Towns and Villages', Akim Abuakwa	249
6	The Anum Migration to Asamankese	250

Bibliography	252
Index	257

LIST OF ILLUSTRATIONS

PLATES

The plates (all from photographs taken by the author) are bound in
between pages 206 and 207

1 A migrant cocoa-farmer
2 The bridge at Mmetiamu
3 Mr Eugene Ohene Walker on his food-farm
4 Mr Ofosu Appiah on his family land
5 A Shai 'village' near Jumapo
6 The farm-yard on the pinnacle of the mountain Nyanao
7 A typical 'village' inhabited by Shai farmers
8 An Ewe 'hoe farmer'
9 An Aburi cocoa-farmer on his replanted farm
10 Part of a typical small 'village' in the forest
11 A small house in Larteh-Ahenease
12 An old-style 'storey-house' in Larteh-Ahenease
13 Dilapidation in Larteh-Ahenease
14 Sakyikrom
15 A farmer demonstrating the geometry of strip measurement

MAPS

1	The historic cocoa-growing area	*facing page* 1
2	Ghana	*page* 5
3	Holdings of cocoa-land in the Kwesi Komfo area	61
4	Company lands in the Nankese area	62
5	A Kyerepon company land	64
6	The Mamfe/Trayo company land	66
7	The Shai/Nankese company land	68
8	The Shai company land at Obomofo-Densua	*between pages* 71/72
9	The Mamfe/Saforosua company land	*page* 71
10	The Akotuakrom family land	91
11	The Kofi Pare family land	94
12	The Omenako family land	98
13	The Boah family land	101
14	An Akropong family land	105
15	The Dome/Amanokrom family land	106
16	The historic cocoa-growing area showing place-names	266/267
17	The main south-eastern districts in which migrant farmers acquired land	268

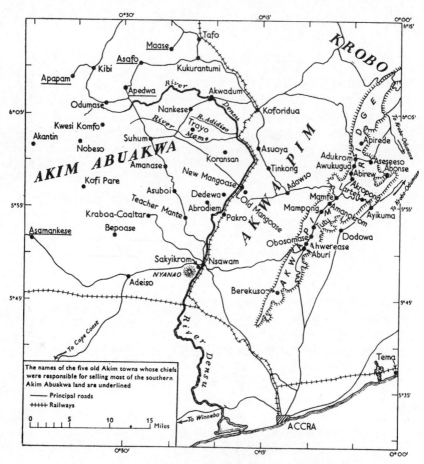

1 The historic cocoa-growing area, in relation to the Akwapim Ridge.

CHAPTER I

INTRODUCTION

Although the migration of southern Ghanaian cocoa-farmers, which began in about 1892 and is still continuing today, was responsible for the creation of the Ghana cocoa-growing industry and was one of the great events of the recent economic history of Africa south of the Sahara, its occurrence has been largely overlooked in the literature.[1] The migration involved individual Akwapim, Krobo, Shai, Ga and other Ghanaian farmers[2] from south of the forest belt, in buying forest land which, at the time of purchase, was hardly inhabited. Although within less than twenty years of the start of the migration the principal Akwapim towns (which are strung along the top of a beautiful, narrow and salubrious ridge about twenty to thirty miles north of Accra) lost much of their resident population, the westward exodus which began as a migration remains a migration today. Despite their long residence in the forest the migrant farmers have lost none of their attachment to their home towns and are always involved in a to-and-fro movement: 'They work on their lands like sailors taking very long voyages.'[3] They build Italianate mansions in their home towns (the antithesis of the week-end cottage) and spend nearly all their time in the forest area, living either in cottages, houses or grouped settlements on the land (which used to be called 'camps' by the earliest mapmakers and for which no satisfactory word has been found since), or in towns, such as Suhum, which are inhabited entirely by strangers and which have grown, usually rather gradually, over the years.

Later in this chapter I shall try and explain why the migration has been overlooked—it is a matter which still surprises me after six years' work among cocoa-farmers; but I must straight away emphasize that it was not superior insight, but the calamity of swollen shoot, which made possible its study today. This virus disease,[4] which became really serious over twenty years ago, destroyed most of the cocoa-trees in the historic cocoa-growing area[5] of southern Akim Abuakwa and north-western Akwapim —and most of the migrant farmers lost all (or nearly all) their cocoa-trees as a result of this disease, which, incidentally, tended to put a brake on the migration owing to lack of finance, rather than to encourage it as is generally supposed. For about fifteen years the Ghana Ministry of Agriculture has been engaged in an immense, and continuing, operation of 'cutting-out' the diseased trees, this being the only means known to the scientists

---

[1] See Appendix I. 1 (p. 18) for documentation of this statement.
[2] See Appendices I. 3 and I. 4 (pp. 25 and 27).   [3] Quoted from a letter from Dr M. J. Field.
[4] See Appendix I. 2 (p. 23).   [5] See maps 1 and 2.

INTRODUCTION

of rendering the land replantable by the farmers. Understandably, the cutting-out operation was originally opposed by many farmers who, stunned by the destruction of the work of three generations, sincerely believed in the possibility of the spontaneous recovery of the trees. Like farmers the world over they were not, at first, at all impressed with the offer of compensation for their 'treated' farms—the farms that had been created by two or three generations of toil and abstention were worth so much more than the income they yielded. As time has gone by and the devastation has appeared complete they have stopped opposing 'cutting-out' and indeed usually welcome 'Agriculture' with open arms. This benign and efficient organization 'Agriculture' has had an immense army of surveyors and draughtsmen at work mapping the devastated farms and it is the existence of these maps which has made the present work possible. Armed with a map and a list of names of farm-owners it is possible, using the method of oral interview, to study with some precision the evolution of a land-holding group over a period of half a century; it is possible to supplement such field studies with inquiries in the home towns and thus to build up a picture, in depth, of the migration.

This migration has many features which, I hope, will be found of general interest to those concerned with 'problems of under-development'. It is usually supposed that when individual Africans become fully embroiled in the exchange economy (caught, as these farmers are, in the mesh of money) they are obliged to extricate themselves from the 'traditional system'.[1] But the present inquiries show that with these farmers this is not so and that, on the contrary, the migratory process derives much of its strength and impetus from the fact that it is firmly based on 'traditional organization'. Jural corporateness and mutual 'insurance' for the whole group are provided by the lineage structure, but there is also enough flexibility in economic affairs to permit of individual enterprise and private 'profit' during each person's lifetime.

Certainly the farmers evolved two types of migratory group which were entirely new to them. One of these, the *company*, was an Akwapim modification of a system of group land-purchase which had been invented some half a century earlier by Ghana's most distinguished food- and oil-palm farmers, the Krobo, for the purposes of acquiring additional forest land for the cultivation of their crops.[2] The other type of land-purchasing group, that which bought *family lands*, had, as far as I can tell at present, no prototype, but developed spontaneously in response to the stimulus of

---

[1] 'The extended family system has tremendous advantages in societies living at a subsistence level, but it seems not to be appropriate to societies where economic growth is occurring. In such societies it is almost certainly a drag on effort. For growth depends on initiative, initiative is likely to be stifled if the individual who makes the effort is required to share the reward with many others whose claims he does not recognize.' (W. A. Lewis, *Theory of Economic Growth*, p. 14.)

[2] See Appendix II. 9 (p. 72).

INTRODUCTION

commercial cocoa-farming. Although each type of organization was new, neither was revolutionary. Ties with the past were not broken and the structure of society in the homeland remained, I think, basically unchanged.

Those readers who dislike the anthropological approach (feeling, perhaps, that its adoption is an insult to a modern society) must at any rate tolerate the fact that field inquiries show that the company system was devised by farmers belonging to patrilineal societies, the family land system by 'matrilineal farmers'. This book is largely taken up with this observed distinction: with the facts that strip-farms are typically owned by those who inherit through their fathers and that the mosaic pattern of farm-ownership on the family land has to do with the nature of matrilineal societies—in which 'blood' is supposed to flow through females only. The strip-farm is the sperm, the mosaic structure the egg—a generalization which some may find useful for mnemonic purposes.

The other main feature of the migration which, I hope, will be found of general interest is the practice, which extends over the generations, of investing a large part of the proceeds of one cocoa-land in the purchase of another—a process which was rudely, though temporarily, checked by swollen shoot. Especially in chapter VII I have sought rather literally to regard the migrant farmer as a 'capitalist', whose primary concern has been the continued expansion of his business. I hope that this book will do something to undo the notion that 'Africans' (an over-generalized term which social research workers seek to avoid) are always apt to lack economic foresight. It is one of the main contentions of this book that the Ghanaian migrant cocoa-farmer has shown himself to be remarkably responsive to economic incentives, remarkably dedicated (within the framework of cocoa-farming) to the pursuit of economic ends. The whole operation was based on *saving* or *accumulation*, by all the various parties involved, and on the long view. The notion of 'getting rich quick' and then going out of business and retiring to the homeland did not exist.

The book may also interest those concerned with the possibilities of the 'inter-disciplinary' approach[1] to social problems in under-developed agrarian economies. Social research in the field in Africa can be immensely exhilarating to Europeans and one of the reasons for this is the constant need to trespass outside one's proper field, owing to the small number of other investigators. One is sometimes forced despite one's better judgment to acquire a rudimentary mastery of other people's approach. At other times, work which had started as an innocent kind of 'nature study'[2] later develops into a field of inquiry which refuses to be enclosed

---

[1] Which I shall henceforth refer to as the 'extensive approach', so as to emphasize the artificiality of the accustomed boundaries.

[2] There is much to be said for the spirit of the old-fashioned naturalist in the early stages of field-work in an unfamiliar and undocumented environment.

3

INTRODUCTION

within the artificial boundaries of the various disciplines. I am sure that many social anthropologists, historians, geographers, lawyers and sociologists will regard this book as deplorably, even intolerably, amateur; I know there are many economists who will explain the undeveloped, unsophisticated and sometimes reckless nature of my economic approach in terms of my inclination to meddle elsewhere. As if this were not enough, I shall be accused, with entire justification, of totally ignoring the agricultural approach.[1] It would be considerably easier to offer a show of defence to all this were I an editor introducing a book by seven experts, each responsible for a chapter in his own field.

However, this book is primarily designed for those who are interested in the recent economic history of West Africa and of Ghana in particular. When, in 1954, I first began to investigate the social organization of Ghanaian cocoa-farmers, I had no intention whatever of approaching the subject historically, but was interested solely in an extensive approach to contemporary economic problems. An element of autobiography must here intrude itself. I had been working for nearly a year, visiting southern Akim Abuakwa and many other districts, before I became aware of the migration. I had never heard the word 'company' (as distinct from *huza*) and vaguely supposed that most of the farmers in southern Akim Abuakwa were native Akim whose social organization resembled that at Akokoaso.[2] Ironically, the first I ever heard of the companies was when I was farthest away from the land of their birth—at Worawora in the Volta Region, where an Ewe farmer described this group system of land-purchase. If, therefore, I seem to be blaming others for their failure to recognize the facts during the past seventy years, at the same time I admit to having been even more blameworthy.[3] And this has been a great incentive.

There are circumstances, then, in which history must be pursued for therapeutic purposes. If we know no history our minds are not blank, but cluttered with half-truths and inventions. As the history of cocoa-farming in the historic cocoa-growing area of southern Akim Abuakwa was so totally at variance with the beliefs of the instinctive 'pseudo-historians' (and in this group I include everybody save the farmers themselves and even them sometimes, for they are great conformists when they get to school), it followed that it was impossible to think clearly about current problems, such as the replanting of the areas that had been devastated by

---

[1] This regrettable deficiency arose, so far as I was concerned, from the need to draw the line somewhere and this seemed the natural place, especially as most of the migrants' cocoa is dead. Readers who require scientific information on such matters as cocoa agronomy, soils and manuring, or diseases and pests, should turn to the massive volume *Agriculture and Land Use in Ghana*, ed. J. Brian Wills, 1962, which also includes an important bibliography of very wide scope.

[2] See p. 76n.

[3] When writing my book *The Gold Coast Cocoa Farmer: A Preliminary Survey* (1956).

4

INTRODUCTION

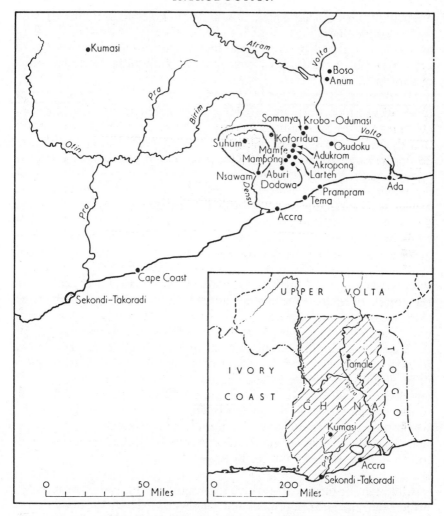

2 Ghana, showing the location of the historic cocoa-growing area.

swollen shoot, until the half-truths and inventions had been swept out by the need to accommodate the new facts. Remote as much that is contained in this book may seem to contemporary problems, I think that it contains something of practical usefulness even at this stage. I think, for instance, that the farmers' traditional unwillingness to finance farm labour employment from 'capital', explains their reluctance to use their swollen-shoot compensation, or their replanting grants, for the purpose of replanting their farms. I think that the work throws much new light on the concept of absenteeism. I am sure that it shows that investigations into the differing rates of replanting in any area should take account of the

INTRODUCTION

origin of the farmers concerned. I should have no difficulty in multiplying such examples indefinitely were it to be suggested that work of this kind has no practical utility. So I hope that those who are concerned with practical problems will at least agree that this is *one* of the necessary forms of approach.

Many other motives have prompted this research and the writing of this book and it occurs to me to list five of them. First, I am concerned, by attacking the problem simultaneously on a number of fronts, to 'prove' that the migration actually occurred: I am concerned to be persuasive. Secondly, I wish to record certain facts before it is too late and to stimulate others to do likewise: the migratory history of individual pioneer farmers may seem dry as dust to some, just as the stone axe-heads preserved in the museums of West Africa do to others. Thirdly, I wish to demonstrate that the recent economic history of West Africa is worthy of study by West African students both in terms of its intellectual content and because it should be a matter of pride to them—and that the conventional approach of the textbooks should be avoided. Fourthly, I offer this book as a sort of African travel book for the mid twentieth century: in this continent where travelling nowadays largely consists in passing from the arms of one public relations officer to another, it is gratifying to discover, one and a half miles from one of the most important tarred roads in Ghana, a splendid contractor-built bridge, paid for by the migrant farmers themselves, the existence of which has not as yet been recorded in print, although it has been standing for half a century.[1] Fifthly, there are iconoclastic pleasures—I am glad to have a hand in destroying the myth of the peasant farmer as the creator of Ghana's cocoa-growing industry, when the reality is so much more interesting. The inclusion of much detail, especially in chapter VIII, results directly from the first, second and fourth of these motives and seems unavoidable.

Although the farm maps, which were mostly compiled quite recently, project the past into the present and enable one to study the operation of the customary rules of inheritance over more than half a century, it is nevertheless true that the main concern of this book is with the expansionary period of the migration which was terminated by swollen shoot, and more especially with the first thirty years—the pre-lorry age. The chief reason for this concentration on the past is a practical one, namely that the farm maps, which are indispensable, exist only in areas where most of the land was acquired, if not planted, in the pre-lorry age. Fortunately, the expansionary process is inherently far more interesting[2] than the

[1] See Appendix VIII. 3 (p. 243). It has been pointed out to me that very careful scrutiny of the one-inch Ghana Survey reveals the existence of the Mmetiamu bridge, though not of that farther north at Bibianiha. See plate 2.

[2] Though, of course, the quality of the investigation has been greatly impaired by the fact

INTRODUCTION

vicious circle of contraction which resulted from swollen shoot—though the latter, also, would be well worth studying. While the atmosphere of 'progress' and 'expansion' conveyed by this book is unfortunate and absurd, considering that most of the farmers lost nearly all their cocoa-trees, the farmers themselves (now that the initial shock has been sustained) have settled down into taking such a long view that *they* will understand, if others do not, that the misfortunes of the past twenty years seem but a passing phase. The migration has been slowed down by this catastrophe but not stopped.[1] Few of the farmers have returned home because of swollen shoot, as the 1960 Census figures show.[2] The large family lands, such as Kofi Pare and Akotuakrom, have throughout continued to sustain large populations of several hundred people, many of whom have come near to reverting to a 'subsistence' standard of living.[3] Pursuing our analogy, the migrant farmers continue on their voyages, even though, for the time being, many of them are obliged to consume all the fish that they catch.

It is the justification of the extensive approach that where social organization is heterogeneous (as with the cocoa-farmers of Ghana) and where one is concerned to pursue one topic, such as cocoa-growing, to the exclusion of others, what one loses in depth, by this procedure, one gains in scope. It is possible, to some extent, to compensate for this loss of depth by adopting a historical approach (such as is often frowned on by social anthropologists)[4] and by undertaking *some* relatively intensive work (though still not intensive by social anthropological standards), such as that on individual companies or family lands for which farm maps exist. But a great degree of superficiality is unavoidable and many horrible lacunae are certain to be revealed when, in the seclusion of one's study, one comes to examine and write up one's field notes. An overwhelming regard for the social anthropologist is apt to inhibit the field economist in Africa, partly because he is envious of the checks and safeguards implicit in the anthropological procedure: the anthropologist's

that most of the cocoa is dead, so that I have had to rely to a large extent on statements about the past, rather than on current observation.

[1] This is true in various senses: the farmers are replanting their devastated farms, they are opening up their hitherto unplanted lands and they are acquiring and planting new lands. It would, of course, be out of the question for the migration to 'stop' in the sense that all the farmers returned to their homelands—there are now far too many of them.

[2] See Appendix VIII. 4 (p. 248).

[3] So that their standard of living is no higher than that of their forebears before the start of the migration. In a sense their situation is worse than was that of their forebears owing to their difficulty in meeting certain expenses which have meanwhile become conventional— such as house maintenance (in the home town) and education. As swollen shoot is always said to be 'under control', in the sense that it is contained and not spreading, and as the farmers are so philosophical, there has been little understanding of their plight. See plate 13.

[4] See E. E. Evans-Pritchard, *Anthropology and History* (Manchester University Press, 1961).

INTRODUCTION

material tends to be automatically checked and rechecked as his work proceeds and if his method is properly applied over a long enough period the main features of an articulated structure are bound to emerge. But with the extensive approach there are few safeguards, other than those implicit in any procedure of asking the same questions time and time again, and there is always a chance of becoming so increasingly obsessed with the importance of certain observations to the exclusion of others, of becoming so one-track minded, that wrong-headedness and error may grow as the work proceeds.

So serious are these difficulties and so multifarious the possible errors that many are inclined to suppose that the extensive approach should necessarily be statistical. Which of us is free from the semi-mystical belief that if you add up enough figures the errors are apt to cancel each other, the total having a significance altogether different in kind from the component figures? For all sorts of reasons, including the fact that it is usually thought improper to ask an author to produce his field notes, there is a splendid unassailable anonymity about the *total* figure—a 'take it or leave it' quality. And as the ability to organize a social survey using mathematical techniques is one of the few 'skills' which the European economist carries with him on arriving in the rural areas of Africa, it is natural that such surveys should possess great prestige and that any extensive inquiry carried out without their aid should appear to be old-fashioned.

I therefore want to emphasize that my decision not to employ the social survey technique (or to use questionnaires, except occasionally to assist myself when taking notes) was conscious and deliberate.[1] There is no need to apologize for this: the social statisticians are flourishing in Africa as never before, especially in the demographic field, and some of their work is even pioneering in the sense that their methods are subsequently imitated in Europe. The point has been reached where it is possible to argue that in a country like Ghana, large-scale surveys should never be undertaken except by the government, which alone commands the resources necessary. Small-scale surveys, on the other hand, may suitably be conducted by individuals, provided the person in charge undertakes sufficient of the interviewing himself to eliminate the bias which is otherwise certain to result from the stereotyped response of the field-worker to the unexpectedness of what is revealed[2]—so that the total is more misleading than its components. Only by being, as it were, *there all the time,*

[1] But at the same time it should be one of the distinguishing marks of the field economist that he plans his work in such a way as to make use of such relevant statistics as already exist and collects figures for himself when opportunity offers—as it did in Akwapim, see Appendix VII. 1 (p. 193).

[2] No criticism is here implied of the Ghanaian field-worker—though it is true that he is usually worse trained than his counterpart in Britain. The point is that his findings are apt to be much more unexpected, so little being known at the outset.

8

INTRODUCTION

can the research worker in charge keep adequate control. And if one has got to be there all the time anyway, it is sometimes better to dispense with field-workers altogether[1] and to make all the inquiries oneself, hinging them perhaps to reliable statistical material, which is a by-product of administration, such as the records held at the Ghana Ministry of Agriculture's Area Offices.

But if the alternative to the statistical approach is the kind of extensive approach used in this inquiry, one is unfortunately faced with a difficulty which has seldom been discussed, namely that a great many of the facts that one collects cannot be checked, are bound (owing to the waywardness of human memory) to be inaccurate *and will at once be perceived to be inaccurate by readers with special inside knowledge.* Whether I have checked my facts sufficiently for the present purpose is obviously a matter of opinion; I can only say that most of my elderly informants and possibly I myself would have been dead long before I had succeeded in submitting all my facts to the kind of rigorous checking which is usually considered necessary for scientific or other scholarly purposes. This being so, I have decided not to be over-inhibited by the certain knowledge that many of my facts are 'wrong', but rather to publish such material as seems to be plausible and reasonably reliable.[2]

Equally important are the omissions: the hit-and-miss methods I have had to adopt result in the omission of the names of many important pioneering farmers. In deciding whether or not to mention a farmer by name, I have followed no very consistent policy, beyond that of concealing the identities of those who might be embarrassed by the facts presented. I now incline to think that I have been too cautious—and that many more farmers would like to see their own or their forebears' names in print. There are others whose identity could not have been concealed without deception—and this I have not resorted to, except for the adoption of false names in two or three cases only. A family land like Kofi Pare is so large (some two square miles) that its location would have to be falsified were concealment the object.

I must make it very clear that in asserting that a large proportion of my facts may be 'wrong' I am blaming nobody—least of all the farmers. One becomes so accustomed to taking the farmers' willingness as informants for granted, so accustomed to assuming that illiterate people are gifted with 'perfect' memories, that even the experienced field-worker may be

[1] 'There are some people who look on statistical studies as the only valid kind of social science. This attitude is as illogical as that which despises statistics altogether. In all investigations involving man, and indeed in the biological world generally, there is a large field for accurate and thoughtful observation of structure, function, behaviour and association; indeed this field ought to be covered properly before measurement and the application of statistics begin... It may be said of statistics, and indeed of experiment, that their value really starts when observation has shot its bolt.' Stephen Taylor, *Good General Practice,* p. 15.

[2] Readers are invited to send corrections and additions to the author.

9

INTRODUCTION

shocked to find (say) that four members of a cocoa-company, formed in 1906, will never agree, if interviewed independently, on the details of membership, numbers of 'ropes' bought and so on. Even when it is possible, which it usually is not, to find each of the four farmers, there will be no way of telling which of them is the most accurate and their information certainly cannot be averaged—so that it is often better to spend the time available interviewing someone else. I have, therefore, followed the policy of believing what I have been told, provided it is plausible, apparently offered in good faith and stands the test of such further questioning as is practicable. Of course such a procedure would have been quite unjustifiable had the scope of the questions not been strictly limited and factual—and had they not always related to the informant personally (and his forebears) and never to third parties.

This warning about the inaccuracy of the material is a general one. It has, for instance, much less relevance to the companies and family lands for which maps are provided, than to the case histories given in Appendix VII. 3 (p. 200): I hope that the material relating to the Boah family land (Appendix III. 8, p. 100) is reasonably reliable on any standard. While I think that most of the dates I have included are correct within a few years, I can vouch for the absolute accuracy of few of them. I hope that in most cases commonsense considerations will indicate the degree of accuracy which the reader is entitled to expect.

I further contend that it sometimes does not matter very much if the facts are incorrect. If a man who belongs to a patrilineal society insists that he was accompanied by his 'real' brother when buying a land, although he was actually accompanied by his father's brother's son, we need not necessarily be dismayed:[1] we are usually not concerned to assess the statistical frequencies of the various possibilities, but rather to establish what these possibilities are. Many of my informants were third-generation migrants who, when speaking of the early days, could do no more than repeat the traditions handed down to them. But as every student of oral tradition knows, such material has its own intrinsic value if handled properly.

Like the statistician, then, one is mainly concerned with trends and tendencies (as well as with matters that are only partly understood) and it is difficult not to overdo the language of probability and uncertainty. I am aware that words or expressions such as *often, apt to be, it is to be presumed, might, could be, probably, sometimes, inclined, impression, said to be, tend, wont to be, there is no evidence* . . . abound on most pages, and that their use does not exactly enhance readability. I am aware, too, that the urge to be rid of this burden of tentativeness is a powerful one—leading at times to dogmatism.

[1] If there is no need in the society in question to distinguish the two types of 'brother', then such a distinction may also be unnecessary for our purposes.

10

INTRODUCTION

As one of my purposes has been to destroy a myth (the myth of the sedentary peasant farmer who, though unfamiliar with the cash economy, nonetheless succeeded in the space of twenty years in transforming the economy of Ghana), so I must beware of installing another in its place. The migrant cocoa-farmer of southern Ghana is not *the* typical Ghanaian cocoa-farmer, for no such person exists. (The social organization of cocoa-farming in Ghana is extremely heterogeneous, reflecting differences in population density, customary conditions of land-tenure, accessibility, soil fertility, etc.) At present more than half of Ghana's cocoa is produced in the region which until recently was known as Ashanti,[1] mainly by Ashanti farmers, and while much migration of Ashanti farmers has been involved, the whole migratory process has differed radically from that of the southern farmers, mainly because Ashanti chiefs seldom sell land outright to strangers, but 'rent' it on some system (the details of which vary from place to place) which at the outset is dependent on the farmer's actual achievement in clearing and planting—boundaries not being fixed before farming begins, as they nearly always are in the south. The nature of the westward migration within Ashanti is in urgent need of investigation; but as swollen shoot was relatively slight there, work such as this on the southern migrants would be impossible owing to the lack of farm maps.

In southern Ghana, too, there are many cocoa-farmers other than the migrants who are the subject of this book. There are the native Akim farmers, nearly half of whom are women farmers in their own right, who live in small towns such as Akokoaso, Asafo, Maase and Apapam, whose farms, of which they ordinarily own several, are usually about one to three acres, the women's farms being somewhat smaller than the men's: these farmers never in any circumstances, even if all their cocoa dies from swollen shoot, contemplate migrating outside their own state. Then in some Akim districts, especially the Anyinam/Kwabeng area of northern Akim Abuakwa, there are native farmers who operate on a larger scale. Farther west, on land which though little affected by swollen shoot is nowadays often marginal for cocoa-growing, are many Fanti, Awutu, Agona and other farmers, some of whom bought, or otherwise acquired, their land, many of whom are natives. This list, as will be apparent, makes no sort of attempt at comprehensiveness.

Since 1911 or so, the migrant cocoa-farmers of southern Ghana have been responsible for a declining *proportion* of Ghana's total cocoa-exports —this being mainly because of the development of cocoa-growing in Ashanti, which started some twenty years later than in the south. Nowadays, owing to swollen shoot, they are responsible for quite a small proportion of Ghana's total cocoa-exports;[2] but taking a long view, as do the

---

[1] Now two regions, Ashanti and Brong-Ahafo.

[2] Even if reliable figures of production by locality were available, which they are not, it

11

INTRODUCTION

farmers themselves, it may be that in twenty or thirty years' time they will again produce a third or more of the total.

When I first started my investigations I was warned that the farmers would be unwilling to talk about land-purchase—that fears and reticences surround the subject, as indeed they surround that of money.[1] But I found that this was entirely untrue—that given a little encouragement most farmers delight in talking about their own and their forebears' acquisitions, feeling no more squeamishness than would a retailer in listing his chain of branches. This, then, is not the reason for the neglect of the great migration in the literature. Nor were all branches of the Gold Coast government or administration always ignorant of it. The history of the Akwapim/Akim Abuakwa dispute over jurisdiction[2] shows that the government was not only aware of the presence of great numbers of strangers in southern Akim country, but sought, especially in 1915, to ease the situation; in the nineteen-twenties the administration of the Eastern Province regarded the associated unrest as one of its principal concerns; the Reserve Settlement Commissioners, most of whose work was done comparatively recently,[3] were empowered to determine compensation payable to stranger farmers whose purchased land lay within newly created forest reserves. There is no need to dwell on the volume of litigation in the courts which resulted directly from the practice of purchasing land. Yet it remains true that all writers on *cocoa-farming*, without exception, have always regarded land-purchase as a newfangled practice; and that many otherwise rather well-informed people consider that the migration developed in response to swollen shoot.

Explanations of why the farmers' activities have been shrouded in such obscurity for so long may be sought at many levels. But I think that they may be conveniently classified under two headings: there are, first, intellectual obstacles, in the minds of many Ghanaians[4] as well as Europeans, which stand in the way of the appreciation of the facts and secondly there is the attitude of the farmers themselves. The main intellectual obstacle is the widespread belief that chiefs who hold land in trust for their people are necessarily prevented by custom from selling the land outright to strangers. Most Europeans find it very difficult to grasp the essence of a land-tenure system such that, in principle, there is 'no such thing as land being without an owner' (Rattray, vol. I, p. 222); having grasped this idea, having learnt something of what Rattray called the 'spiritual associations'

would still be difficult to estimate the proportion at all precisely, owing to the presence of both native and migrant farmers in some areas; one major uncertainty is the proportion of the trans-Volta crop which is produced by southern migrants, other than Ewe.

[1] See p. 184.   [2] Appendix v. 3 (p. 154).   [3] Appendix II. 1 (p. 55).

[4] Ghanaians are just as apt as Europeans to generalize from their own experience—and such is the degree of social heterogeneity that the consequences are often absurd, as every lawyer knows.

INTRODUCTION

of land (p. 223) and having concluded that 'inalienability' is an inherent part of the thought-structure of the forest-dwellers (as is indeed true in most of rural Ashanti), they then become unbudgeable, whatever facts may stare them in the face. They argue that as land cannot be sold it must in fact be cultivated by farmers whose rights were 'immemorially established' and that those who think otherwise lack sophistication.

A subsidiary intellectual obstacle consists of a bunch of prejudices relating to the inability of 'Africans' (especially those who live in rural areas) to behave as economic men, except in the very short term. That farmers are incapable of saving remains a commonplace in the most respectable circles, being associated, for instance, with a very emotional official Ghanaian attitude towards rural indebtedness. (No one ever points out that in a society where nearly all the rural creditors are Ghanaian farmers, indebtedness and the capacity to save are mirror images.) That Ghanaian farmers could have been as responsive, prudent and foresighted as the facts of the migration indicate was unthinkable. Therefore the migration could not have occurred. Therefore it did not occur. Therefore we resort to the myth of the peasant farmer.

The second explanation stems, I suggest, from the sophisticated and cautious attitude of the farmers themselves—particularly of the Akwapim, who stopped being surprised by their achievement over half a century ago, if indeed it surprised them then.[1] The farmers' own attitude is in no wise reflected in this book.[2] Visitors to Akwapim are told, with a wave of the hand, that owing to land shortage it proved necessary, at some unspecified time in the recent past (which might have been yesterday) to 'extend' westwards—'down the hill there'. There is no boasting, no dwelling on history, no reference to land-purchase, and the visitor may well conclude that the 'extension' is a local affair. But the farmer has not intended to mislead. His speech reflects his thought. It has always seemed to him (pursuing our analogy further) that his freedom to sail the seas will be respected provided he takes his rights for granted.

When resident in the farming area the migrant farmer will not wish to conceal the fact that he bought his land and the name of his town of origin will be for ever on his lips.[3] That he comes (say) from Mamfe (not

[1] As pointed out in chapter VI, most of these farmers had a 'mobile agricultural outlook' before cocoa-farming began.

[2] They have never supposed that the facts of the migration are of the least interest to anyone save themselves and in talking among themselves they take much for granted. Educated Akwapim usually share this attitude. It is, therefore, a pleasure to include, as Appendix I. 5 (p. 30), part of a literary narrative, 'Across the Prah', by Mr Andrew Opoku, of the Ghana Broadcasting System, himself the son of an Aburi minister of religion and farmer. Although many Ghanaians are great travellers, they travel despite the fears aroused by the journey—as Mr Opoku so well conveys.

[3] He will regard it as his 'home', irrespective of whether he was born there—a fact which embarrasses the demographers who usually equate 'strangers' with those who were born elsewhere.

13

INTRODUCTION

just from Akwapim) is his 'nationality' so far as concerns his relationship with other residents in the district. No description of him, however brief, could fail to note the name of his home town. At the same time, because he stands in the same relationship to his land as did the original owner (whom he has wholly and for all time displaced) he does not regard himself as a 'stranger', but as a species of 'native'. There is no Twi word meaning 'stranger' which he might apply to himself;[1] and even the Akim, who of course pride themselves on their 'natural right' to farm the land, may do him the honour of referring to him as *okuroni*—fellow-townsman or countryman.

The myth of the peasant farmer has hardened in the past few decades, becoming an essential ingredient of the oral tradition of the educated. This is partly the consequence of *Akokoaso* (see Appendix I. 1, p. 18), though its author, Mr W. H. Beckett, is scarcely responsible. 'Akokoaso', he wrote (p. 3), 'is typical of numerous villages scattered throughout the cocoa-belt in the forest country'—as is indeed true. The stranger-farmers do not inhabit such villages. They live on their land, or in towns like Suhum of their own creation. Akokoaso is typical of the kind of village of which it is typical; and the inhabitants of such villages own a really small proportion of the total area of cocoa-farming land in Akim country.

Because I believe that misconceptions about customary law in relation to land sales partly account for the obscurity surrounding this subject, I have, rather reluctantly, devoted much attention to this matter in chapter v. Because I am sure that the travelling Akwapim farmer is a far more interesting creature than the mythical peasant, I have over-dramatized certain aspects of his behaviour, endowed him (at times) with too much purpose. Although it has been impossible, such is the history of thought on this subject, to disengage from argument, I am yet hopeful that the general outline of this splendid story will find acceptance.

Most of my fieldwork in the farming areas and homelands was undertaken within a period of three and a half years ending in July 1960, when I spent perhaps the equivalent of a continuous year in the field.[2] Working on my own, though helped all the time by local friends and acquaintances, it was necessary to concentrate on certain aspects of this vast subject—and to neglect others.[3] This approach is reflected in the structure of the book which consists of seven essays (each with ap-

[1] Thus the word *ɔhɔhɔ*, rendered by Christaller as 'stranger, foreigner', would never be used of a farmer—it rather means 'temporary visitor'. Akim people sometimes refer to the migrants as *asasetɔfo*—'people who go about buying land'. The nearest Twi equivalent to 'migration' is *atutra*, meaning 'a change of dwelling place', 'a removal'.

[2] Much of the historic cocoa-growing area and most of the home towns happen to be within daily commuting distance of the University of Ghana, so that (as I am an economist not a social anthropologist, and given the extensive nature of the work) I, unlike the farmers themselves, did not often find it necessary or convenient to spend the night away from home.

[3] Social, as distinct from economic, aspects have been largely neglected up to date.

14

INTRODUCTION

pendices[1]) on various aspects of the migration, to which this chapter is an introduction. As most of these essays are largely analytical, I conclude this chapter with the following rather arbitrary and brief catalogue of some of the more salient features of the first thirty years of the migration:

(1) In the early eighteen-nineties Akwapim farmers from certain of the larger towns on the ridge became interested in the commercial possibilities of the new cash crops, coffee and cocoa, but they lacked sufficient land for their cultivation.

(2) Small supplies of coffee- and cocoa-seeds and seedlings had recently become available, especially at the botanical gardens at Aburi (just founded by Governor Sir William Brandford Griffith) and European exporting firms were prepared to handle the new produce if it was delivered to them at the ports.

(3) The Akwapim were familiar with the cash economy, mainly owing to production of and trade in palm produce for export and a fair number of men were able to raise small sums, such as £5, for the purchase of forest land.

(4) Most of the land that was bought during the first five years of the coffee-cum-cocoa migration was in Akwapim, north and west of the ridge where the home towns are situated, and east of the river Densu—some of the land was already in the possession of those who planted it.

(5) In 1896, or 1897, pioneering farmers from several of the Akwapim towns simultaneously started buying forest land for cocoa-growing in various parts of Akim Abuakwa, west of the Densu; some of the areas acquired were very large, running into square miles.

(6) The forests of southern Akim Abuakwa were then scarcely inhabited except by hunters; the land belonged to the inhabitants of a small number of small Akim towns (including Apapam, Apedwa, Asafo, Maase and Asamankese), all far away to the north or west. As the inhabitants of these towns were not, as yet, cocoa-farmers and as, in any case, they would have been able to exploit no more than a tiny proportion of their land, their chiefs were glad to seize the opportunity of selling land outright to the enterprising Akwapim.

(7) The cash received for the land seemed like a windfall to the vendor chiefs and if payment in instalments, following an initial down-payment, was the best the purchasers could offer, such terms were accepted with alacrity.

(8) The land-purchasers, for their part, were obliged to offer such terms (unless they were to hold back and wait, or persuade the sellers to lower their prices), for they lacked the cash to pay in full and foresaw the possibility of meeting part of the cost from future sales of cocoa.

---

[1] Much essential matter has been relegated to appendices in an attempt to enhance the readability of the chapters and to facilitate reference.

15

INTRODUCTION

(9)   Soon after 1900 the desire to participate in the migration became so strong that a scramble for land developed in some Akim districts, where land became a factor which was 'quantified' and bought and sold on commercial terms. The migrant farmers themselves resold much surplus (or second-hand) land to other migrants and many of them developed the habit of buying land 'forward'—in advance of requirements.

(10)   It was at this time that groups of inhabitants of certain of the patrilineal Akwapim towns (as well as Krobo, Shai, Ga and other farmers from south-eastern Ghana who had now joined in the westward march) began to buy land through companies, which were modelled on the older *huza* system of the Krobo people. These companies, which were basically groups of friends (not relatives) from one home town, were land-purchasing clubs which enabled rich and poor alike to buy land for cocoagrowing, each member being allotted a strip of land of a width proportionate to the sum he proposed to contribute.

(11)   The matrilineal Aburi and Akropong farmers had earlier adopted another means of migration, entailing the purchase of family (or *abusua*) lands; the purchaser or purchasers (who were always related by blood or marriage) encouraged or permitted their matrilineal kin to settle on these lands, granting them usufructuary rights (hence the typical mosaic pattern on the farm maps), but retaining large portions for their own individual use, which later passed to their successors.

(12)   From the earliest times it was conventional for the proceeds of growing cocoa on one land to be invested in the purchase of another, and soon most migrant farmers possessed several lands, acquired at intervals as the cash became available. The fact that, under the customary rules of inheritance, individual property was always in process of conversion to family property provided individuals with a great incentive to acquire additional lands, over which they had, for some time at least, unlimited control. There is no evidence that the enterprising individual found himself unreasonably hampered by the demands made on him by members of his matrilineage—or patrilineage, as the case might be; or that inheritance systems underwent any major modifications as a consequence of the migration, although outside observers of the matrilineal scene have never ceased forecasting its imminent collapse.

(13)   In fact the expansionary process involved a constant balancing of the forces of capitalist enterprise (as represented by the individual farmer and his wives and children) against the demands of lineage solidarity (and the need to provide for the very old, the very young, the less enterprising, and for certain stay-at-home women): though the initiative lay with the individual, his less active kinsmen might urge him on. There were many respects in which the migrant farmer who owned several lands came to resemble the travelling manager of a business, with relatives in charge at each place.

INTRODUCTION

(14) Among the Akwapim a small class of 'large farmer-creditor' played an important financial role in the developing capitalistic process, through their willingness and ability to take over second-hand lands or farms from those whose circumstances compelled them to pledge or sell them.

(15) By the end of the pre-lorry age (1918), after which the farmers travelled farther afield, most of the forest land of southern Akim Abuakwa (south of Kibi), as well as some farther north, had been sold to the stranger-farmers, except in the immediate neighbourhood of the Akim towns and in parts of the area controlled by Asamankese; much of this land was, as yet, unplanted.

(16) Total exports of cocoa rose from nil in 1892 to 13 tons in 1895, to 536 tons in 1900, to 5,093 tons in 1905, to 22,629 tons in 1910 and to over 50,000 tons in 1914—when the total export value was over £2 million (f.o.b.). In 1911, when the Gold Coast became the world's largest cocoa-producer, most of the cocoa was grown by the southern migrants.

(17) In the earliest stages the migrants depended on family labour on their farms, though many 'outsiders' were employed as carriers—of whom some, notably the Shai and the Anum/Boso, saved money for land-purchase and soon evolved into cocoa-farmers in their own right.

(18) At a later stage, when the cocoa-trees had started to bear, many (though not all) of the larger farmers began to employ farm labourers who were rewarded with a share of the crop they harvested and who also assisted in the establishment of new farms. By 1910, or earlier, there may have been as many farm labourers as farmers, most of them being Ewe and others from east of the Volta.

(19) Although the stranger-farmers were concerned to be on their best behaviour, were non-litigious in their dealings with each other and as individuals were totally lacking in territorial ambition, the process of land-purchase lacked orderliness mainly because of the indeterminateness of the boundaries between the lands controlled by the various Akim chiefs, so that there was much litigation between them—this, in itself, tending to promote further land sales in order to meet legal costs.

(20) Although they were based on their home towns, most of the migrant farmers were fully resident in the farming area, together with their wives and children. Second- and third-generation migrants who had been born in the farming area still regarded themselves as 'camping' there. The farmers travelled as individuals and their chiefs remained at home.

(21) In economic terms the dedication of the farmers to their crop was almost complete. As time went by it became increasingly conventional for part of the profits from cocoa-growing to be invested in house-building in the home town and part in educating children, preferably at home; but apart from cocoa-buying and lorry ownership, the farmers were little

17

APPENDIX I. 1

interested in other economic activities, such as trading, always ploughing back their surpluses in the purchase of more land.

APPENDIX I. 1

THE TREATMENT OF THE MIGRATION OF SOUTHERN GHANAIAN COCOA-FARMERS IN PUBLISHED BOOKS, REPORTS, ETC.

While this summary does not, of course, pretend to deal comprehensively with the subject, it is hoped that it provides sufficient evidence for the assertion that the migration has been overlooked in official and other publications, except by a handful of writers and that the myth of the small peasant farmer, as the backbone of the industry, responsible for growing most of the cocoa, has tended to strengthen as time has gone by.

Official (Ghanaian) Publications

The migration of southern Ghanaian cocoa-farmers has been consistently overlooked in official publications of the Ministry (formerly the Department) of Agriculture; there was only a passing reference to land-purchase by Akwapim farmers in the Director of Agriculture's *Enquiry into the Gold Coast Cocoa Industry* (W. S. D. Tudhope, Gold Coast Sessional Papers, nos. II and IV, 1918–19), in C. Y. Shephard's *Report on the Economics of Peasant Agriculture in the Gold Coast* (Accra, 1936), or in the interesting periodical *The Gold Coast Farmer*, published in the nineteen-thirties. In official utterances, ignorance of the farmers' affairs has usually been mixed with condescension, the following being typical:

'Until 1930 the price of cocoa was high and credit easily obtained owing to the demand for cocoa and the peasant farmer had therefore neither need nor incentive to save, as the unexpected flow of wealth had not permitted of Government to making plans to educate him to realise the rigours and demands of modern civilisation and the necessity of practising thrift.' (From the draft report of the Cocoa Farmers' Credit Committee, which was set up on 8 January 1946 under the chairmanship of the Financial Secretary.)

'It is generally found that each farmer has several distinctly separate plantations. This is variably due to greed. . . It has also been due to native shrewdness, for . . . in planting cocoa . . . they thought it best to make farms in different locations to ensure some of these being successful. . . All evidence . . . points to their [the cocoa-farmers'] desire to have a lot of cocoa and thus get money quickly without their giving much consideration to the future of the industry.' (Tudhope, *op. cit.*, Interim Report.)

Demographic Statistics

The migration has received scant attention from the Census-takers—see Appendix VIII. 5 (p. 249). The extremely poor quality of the demographic material collected for the rural areas of Akim Abuakwa until 1948 has impeded research.

Mr W. H. Beckett

Mr W. H. Beckett was an official of the Department of Agriculture when he undertook his work at Akokoaso (1932–5) and Koransan (1936–9). The report on the latter, *Koransang: A Gold Coast Cocoa Farm* (Accra, 1945), provides figures of yields and acreages from 1905 to 1943 and contains the only map of a stranger-farmer's farm in Akim Abuakwa to have been published before the Ministry of Agriculture began to map the farms as a result of swollen shoot. In his introduction Mr Beckett

18

asserted that most of Ghana's cocoa was grown on small farms of about two and a half acres and while he recognized that large farms were common in certain parts of the (then) Eastern Province, he did not realize that they were virtually all owned by strangers. Perhaps he thought that the migration was, in general, a new development for, in commenting on the presence of four Akwapim farmers in Akokoaso, he wrote: 'The Akwapim came to Akokoaso from the Akwapim ridge, buying land for the purpose of cocoa planting, a now common reason of immigration from the older cocoa areas to the middle and west of the Colony where land is more readily obtainable.' (*Akokoaso*, p. 5.)

The Typical Small Cocoa-farmer

Mr Beckett's view that most of Ghana's cocoa is grown on small farms of about two and a half acres has been implicitly accepted by virtually all the authorities[1] (though not, be it noted, by the politicians, who tend to fly to the other extreme and to assume that all Ghanaian cocoa-farmers are wealthy).

'... the average size of cocoa farms in Ghana is only 2 to 3 acres...' (From an article on 'Black Pod Disease of Cocoa in Ghana' by A. L. Wharton (W.A.C.R.I.) and G. A. Burge (Ministry of Agriculture), in the Ministry of Agriculture's periodical *The Ghana Farmer*, vol. IV, no. 1, 1960, p. 22.)

'Cultivation is usually, though not always, on a small scale. The average area on each holding is 2 acres...' From W. J. Varley and H. P. White, *The Geography of Ghana*, 1958, p. 152.)

'Cocoa is usually grown on small farms of from one to two acres.' (From E. A. Boateng, *A Geography of Ghana*, 1959, p. 64.)

'... most of the producers [of cocoa in West Africa] are small farmers—indeed, very small farmers.'

'... although ownership distribution is very unequal [in West Africa], normally even the largest farms are small.' (From pp. 16 and 17 of *Cacao*, F.A.O. Commodity Series, Bulletin no. 27, 1955.)

The Conventional Account of how Cocoa-growing developed

'The introduction of a crop exclusively grown for export brought about a great change in the economics of farming by the methods of shifting cultivation. For the purpose of food production to meet the requirements of the family the old system continued, but the fields which formerly had been abandoned and allowed to return to jungle were now required for the young cacao trees originally planted amongst the plantains and other crops. The care of these rapidly became impossible physically to the owner and planter. He had to engage labour and the peasant small-holder, semi-nomadic by inclination and heredity, evolved quite suddenly into a settled and landed working farmer.'

'So great was the extent of the land available and so limited in numbers the indigenous people that practically any unoccupied land could be taken by one of the latter and claimed as his or his family's own by virtue of the right which issued from the act

[1] Of course in some parts of the Ghana cocoa-area most of the farmers are 'small'—thus inquiries made by the Government Statistician's Office in the Oda/Swedru/Asamankese triangle, where native (or sedentary) farmers predominate, showed that about a third of the cocoa-farming *families* produced under nineteen loads of cocoa annually (*Statistical and Economic Papers*, no. 6, 1958). But there are also areas, especially in Brong/Ahafo (see Hill, *The Gold Coast Cocoa Farmer*), where most of the cocoa-farmers are 'large'. Statistical generalization about the 'size' of cocoa-farmers is a matter of bewildering perplexity—see an article by the present writer in the May 1960 issue of *The Economic Bulletin*, Economic Society of Ghana.

APPENDIX I. 1

of clearing. . .' (From A. W. Cardinall, *The Gold Coast*, 1931, pp. 84–5 and 85–6.) 'The reason for the speed of the increase of cocoa growing in much of West Africa is that cocoa was an attractive cash crop which could be established at negligible cost in view of favourable natural conditions. Land was plentiful. It had, in any case, to be cleared for the growing of food crops under the system of shifting cultivation. All that was necessary was to plant cocoa and, when fertility for subsistence crops fell off, to leave the land to the cocoa trees.' (From *Cocoa*, O.E.E.C., 1956, p. 20.)

The Conventional Notion of the Lazy Farmer

'In the field of land utilization . . . two crucial problems confront contemporary Africa: first, how to change from the traditional shifting cultivation to permanent farming, and, secondly, how to rehabilitate land exhausted by food or cacao cultivation. At present African farmers do not have the knowledge, the working habits, or the financial resources for successful attack on these problems. Since rational cultivation involves much more work than the traditional type, the farmer, by means of social propaganda, must be persuaded to place higher values on economic and physical welfare and lower value on leisure. . .' (*Cacao*, F.A.O. Commodity Series, Bulletin no. 27, 1955, p. 21.)

[N.B. This publication does refer to the purchase of land by Ghanaian farmers for cocoa-growing, commenting (p. 21) that the spread of cocoa had 'made land the most important subject of litigation, even before the war'—i.e. before 1939.]

The Lawyers

The lawyers of Ghana have for long been familiar with the fact of the outright sale of land for cocoa-farming purposes—see chapter v. Perhaps the most valiant of all the fighters for truth was Sir William Brandford Griffith (son of the Governor of the same name), at one time Chief Justice. In July 1913 he was grilled for several hours by the West African Lands Committee (see p. 149) who refused to believe in the literal truth of his evidence relating to outright sales of land (which he regarded as 'natural') and who were puzzled by his insistence that courts of law were more familiar than officials with what actually happened:

'. . . the system of individual ownership so far as the cases in the courts go seems so natural to the people; they are so well accustomed to it and you hear them say in evidence: "My grandfather bought this land", meaning by "grandfather" some ancestor long before.' (Griffith, W.A.L.C., *Minutes of Evidence*, p. 489.)

'The tracts of land are rather too large to be called proprietorships.' (He added that he preferred the word 'landowner' to 'peasant'.) (Griffith, W.A.L.C., *Minutes of Evidence*, p. 494.)

The West African Lands Committee

There were few other witnesses who appeared before the Committee who were familiar with the facts relating to land sale. W. H. Grey, chief agent in the Gold Coast for Miller and Swanzy (and a member of the Legislative Council), referred (*Minutes of Evidence*, p. 186) to the very large scale on which agricultural land was sold 'by natives to natives' and he mentioned 'plots' of one to 400 acres. F. G. Crowther, Secretary for Native Affairs, spoke with emphasis on the sale of Akim land to Krobo farmers, scarcely doing justice to the wider knowledge he had acquired of the Akwapim migration before 1906—see p. 145n. The following exchange occurs on p. 354 of the *Minutes of Evidence*:

Q: Have you actually spoken to the chiefs whose land has been thus disposed of and asked them whether they considered they had parted with the land for good and all?

20

TREATMENT IN BOOKS AND REPORTS

Crowther: Yes. I was District Commissioner there five or six years ago. They quite knew what they were doing.

Q: One side thinks it has got the land for good and all and the other side thinks it has ceded it for good and all?

Crowther: Yes.

Q: How do you get knowledge of these transactions?

Crowther: It is very difficult to have the things brought to one's notice. . . I was the first permanent District Commissioner in this district and having very little court work I was able to visit every village in the district and to know the people intimately. I was not bound down by Treasury routine. A District Commissioner ordinarily does not hear of such things save by the prosecution of special enquiries.

Among those who gave written evidence to the Committee was G. Josenhans, General Superintendent of the Basel Mission,[1] who in a letter dated January 1913 (p. 38, *Correspondence and Papers laid before the Committee*), wrote:

'. . . [the Krobo] as well as the Akwapims and other tribes, have very extensively acquired Stool land for private possession and use for growing cocoa, chiefly outside their own country, in Akem and Fantee. Thus extensive tracts of land, formerly stool land, have come by purchase into possession of private individuals and parties and the process is still progressing.'

The *Draft Report* of the Committee, completed in 1917, was not only a dead letter but remained a confidential paper, unavailable in the libraries, for about forty years: it cannot, therefore, be supposed that its authors were in any way responsible for the increased unwillingness to face the facts which has developed since its publication. The report was based on the notion of an antithesis, a false one, between 'the growth of individual tenure' and 'native customary tenure', assuming, as for instance on p. 102, that the growth of the former would necessarily be 'at the expense of' the latter. It was proposed (p. 105), that:

'the rules of native customary tenure with their prohibition of sale and mortgage shall continue in force. . .'

While it was thought that existent rights should be respected yet—

'in future no facilities should be given for the conversion of community or family land by transfer from native communities or families to individual natives or for the transmutation of customary rights into those of individual ownership. . .'

The Krobo System of Land Purchase

Many writers have insisted, or implied, that the Krobo (or *huza*) system of group landpurchase (see Appendix II. 9, p. 72) continued during the cocoa-growing age to be unique and this led them to conclude that companies are mainly associated with food and the oil-palm and that the lands are all situated in Krobo country or in areas of Akim Abuakwa, such as the Begoro district, which border on it.

Dr J. B. Danquah

The well-known lawyer and scholar Dr J. B. Danquah holds a special position in the history of the literature on this subject. As the younger paternal brother (and secretary from 1915 to 1921) of Nana Sir Ofori Atta I (Omanhene of Akim Abuakwa), he passionately deplored the extent of the land-selling by Akim chiefs:

[1] Mr D. Brokensha has pointed out that the annual reports of the Basel Mission and of the Presbyterian Church of the Gold Coast abound with references to the migration, mostly deploring the inability of Christians to attend divine service.

APPENDIX I. 1

'. . . the short-sighted and reckless manner in which lands are disposed of today as if they were so many pieces of common cowries to be had for the asking, cannot pretend to have any historical evidence in support of the practice.' (*Akan Laws and Customs*, p. 212.)

'Let not my sense of responsibility forsake me. But there are overwhelming instances in which stools owning large tracts of good virgin forest lands have sold all away, so that even at this early date some towns are hard pressed for small lots of lands on which the inhabitants are to cultivate their annual foodstuff plantations. It used to be said that lands about three miles away from a town might be safely sold without danger of the inhabitants starving for land. This can hardly be a safe policy. . .' (*op. cit.*, p. 213.)

'I do not like to single out any one Chief as being the greatest culprit in the sale of land, but in order that you may have a concrete example before you of how rapidly mother Abuakwa is being dismembered, I should like you to recall that about 98 % of the land from the Densu at Nsawam to Densuso (Apedwa) has all been sold away absolutely and for all time. . . Lands to the left and right of the Nsawam-Densuso road to a distance of 10–25 miles on either side have been sold. The same tale can be told in the Eastern part of the State on the Krobo boundary; the same tale is now going on in the Northern boundary of the State round about Asuom and you are of course aware that the town of Oda (capital of Western Akim) and surrounding villages are situate on land sold by Akim Abuakwa.' (*An Epistle to the Educated Youngman in Akim Abuakwa*, 1928.)

Although Dr Danquah's books, including *Cases in Akan Law* (to which there are many references in chapter v), have been widely read and appreciated, there have been few to realize the significance of his protests about the land sales.

The Nowell Report

The Report of the Commission on the Marketing of West African Cocoa (the Nowell Report, Cmd 5845, 1938) showed much insight, as the following quotations show:

' "Strangers", whether tribesmen from other districts or more or less de-tribalised people from the towns, have been willing to pay large sums for land on which to establish farms. The custodians of tribal, Stool and family lands . . . have welcomed the opportunity of easy money. With a complete ignorance of mensuration and with no more than an oral indication of boundaries based on impermanent marks, land has been allotted to all comers who had money to offer. . .' (Para. 58.)

'The original conception of the Gold Coast cocoa farmer, still generally held except by those with personal experience of the present situation, is of a peasant cultivator who, with his own labour and the help of his family, grows his food and tends an acre or two of cocoa trees. This picture is no longer true of more than a small minority of farms and these of the smallest size.' (Para. 59.)

'Multiple and absentee ownership is now common. The native small capitalist becomes possessed, either directly by purchase of land . . . or indirectly through the widespread custom of pledging farms for monetary loans, of numerous farms, often widely scattered. . . We heard of one farmer who had in his possession no less than 79 widely scattered farms.' (Para. 62.)

But the report is marred by uninspired guesswork—as, for instance, in paragraph 70: 'But thrift is rare in the Gold Coast. Partly from ignorance, which prevents the majority of farmers from understanding the relation between indebtedness and costs of production and partly on account of the tradition of communal family ownership which gives all members of the family an equal claim on an individual member's

TREATMENT IN BOOKS AND REPORTS

wealth, saving has little attraction for the Gold Coast African. He prefers to spend lavishly, even foolishly, when he has money; and to borrow when he has none.'

Professor W. M. Macmillan

The only writer who has ever emphasized that strangers have been prominent cocoa-farmers 'from the very beginning', is Professor W. M. Macmillan and this Appendix concludes with extracts from 'African Development', by W. M. Macmillan (part II of *Europe and West Africa*, by C. K. Meek and others, 1940):

'From the very beginning the backbone of the Gold Coast cocoa industry has been, not the simple tribal peasant, but in the real sense a "middle" class of traders and entrepreneurs. The dominant even if absentee owners of cocoa-farms are still men from the coastal towns.' (P. 82.)

'The troubles of the industry in the last year should finally have shaken the old assumption that the typical cocoa-farmer is the simple tribesman tilling his share of the tribe's immemorial land. But the most immediate need now is some straightforward *description*. The most elementary facts are still unknown and undiscoverable...' (P. 82.)

'The stress on anthropological study no doubt corrects an omission of the past, but its professors have not so far fixed on the social chaos of tribes in the Gold Coast Colony as a favourable field for their studies... The immense complexities of the situation in the Gold Coast will, I think, best be understood by an economic historian with some thorough and sympathetic familiarity with the conditions and circumstances of our own ancestors' emergence from the open-field system of the Middle Ages.' (P. 86.)

'Cocoa land was naturally in great demand by "strangers", and Stools for their part were very ready to deal in land with any one willing to pay for it, whether by *abusa* [i.e. one-third of the usufruct] or in cash. This has led to the wholesale penetration of the cocoa areas by "alien" natives. The Akim country, in particular, has not only scattered aliens as individual owners but whole village communities of "alien" occupants. In many market towns, of which Suhum is an often quoted type, the aliens are definitely in a majority: land for public purposes (if it were only for latrines) is obtainable only by paying ransom to private owners, most of them alien.' (P. 90.)

APPENDIX I. 2
SWOLLEN-SHOOT DISEASE AND THE FARM MAPS

It is not here proposed to review the history of swollen shoot[1] which was identified as a virus disease in 1939, by which time much of the cocoa in the historic cocoa-growing area had already become infected, so that yields were falling fast. The only means of controlling the disease that is known to the scientists involves the removal, i.e. 'cutting-out', of diseased trees to prevent the spreading of the infection to healthy trees. Unless a farm has been 'treated' it is impossible for the owner to replant satisfactorily, although many farmers have made repeated endeavours to establish what they often call 'appeal' farms (an appeal to the earth to help them) on untreated land.

The swollen-shoot-disease campaign was planned in 1945 to cover 'initial treatment' (i.e. cutting-out) and subsequent reinspection and retreatment of all treated farms. A vast organization based on Area Offices of the Ministry of Agriculture was established and by May 1961 105 million cocoa-trees had been cut out, 67 million of

[1] There is, of course, a very extensive literature on swollen shoot, much of it scientific. The reports of the ten Cocoa Conferences which have been organized since the war by the Cocoa, Chocolate and Confectionery Alliance are the most convenient source of information on scientific aspects and disease-control measures.

APPENDIX I. 2

them in the Devastated Area of the Eastern Region and 31 million in the area of Scattered Outbreak of that Region. The numbers of trees removed would have been far greater had many of them not already died of the disease by the time treatment started. So vast was the task undertaken that the completion of 'initial treatment' in the Eastern Region (where the disease is officially regarded as 'contained', but not controlled) is likely to take at least another decade, and an organization for inspection and retreatment will probably have to continue in existence indefinitely.[1]

Three separate areas within the Eastern Region must be distinguished:

(a) The former Devastated Area, where all the cocoa-farms were mapped by staff of Area Offices of the Ministry of Agriculture;

(b) the former Abandoned Area, where until recently there was no treatment of farms whatever, but where the 'devastated area technique' is now being employed; and

(c) the area of Scattered Outbreak, where the disease is not so severe and where only those farms where 'outbreaks' are found are mapped—so that the maps are useless for research purposes.

All the farm maps included in this book relate to areas which lie within the former Devastated Area, which comprised five divisions based on Tafo and Koforidua to the east, Suhum in the centre, Kibi (including only Apedwa and Amanfrom) and Asamankese to the south west. All the land to the east of the Nsawam/Suhum road and nearly all that to the west (except the areas of Oworam, Mepom, Bepoase, Asikasu, Adeiso and Kofi Pare) lay in the former Abandoned Area where, at the time the work for this book was undertaken, there were no farm maps.

The farm maps are an essential feature of the system under which grants are paid to farmers in respect of cutting-out and replanting. Until 1957 initial grants to farmers were on a 'tree basis'—i.e. based on the number of trees cut out; since September 1957 these initial grants have been on an 'acreage basis'—i.e. based on the acreage of the treated farm. The 1957 scheme has many complications; here it is only necessary to note that the initial grant of £20 an acre is paid soon after the removal of the trees and that a balance of £30 an acre is payable, in three equal instalments, to those farmers who replant their farms satisfactorily and quickly. It is too early to judge the effect of this scheme on the rate of replanting, but it should be noted that until very recently most farmers who replanted their farms did not qualify for the replanting grant, either because they failed to apply for it or because, having applied, their applications were disallowed owing to failure to plant in lines or to fulfil other conditions. (Between May 1945 and May 1961, 47,541 acres of cocoa in the Devastated Area qualified for replanting grant, of which 17,912 acres were certified during one year—1960–1; a total of 86,034 'farms' had been treated in the Devastated Area in this whole period.)

The basic unit for survey purposes is the 'block'. Blocks vary greatly in area according to the terrain, natural boundaries, etc. and are in principle of a size such that one Field Assistant and his gang of labourers may complete the survey in a month. The maps are drawn on the large scale of forty inches to a mile and for most research purposes redrawing on a much smaller scale is necessary. Many company lands extend over several blocks so that to compile a map of such a land it is often necessary to fit the block plans together, eliminating block boundaries insofar as they do not correspond with farm boundaries proper.

The block plans are held at Area Offices, together with lists, for each block, giving

[1] *Postscript.* In mid 1962 the functions of the organization were greatly reduced. Farmers are now expected to cut out their diseased trees themselves and are entitled neither to compensation nor to replanting grants.

24

SWOLLEN-SHOOT DISEASE

the name of the owner of each farm and the farm acreage. It is one of the functions of an official called a 'Liaison Officer'[1] to ascertain the name of the owner of each farm. This official is the link between the administration and the farmer; his duties, which are manifold, include that of being present at the time that the farmers 'point out their boundaries' to the Field Assistants.

The farmers themselves are issued with farm cards, one card for each farm of which they are the registered owner. They are required to present these cards when applying for initial or replanting grants and the Liaison Officer is present at the 'pay out' to identify them as necessary.

These farm maps (and lists of farmers' names) were found to be generally very accurate and their indispensability for the present work has been emphasized elsewhere. With their aid it was possible to study, with some accuracy, the evolution of a land-holding group over half a century. But for a great variety of reasons they must be interpreted very cautiously and this Appendix concludes with a list of some of the difficulties and pitfalls that were encountered:

(a) Swollen shoot itself brought about a substantial degree of redistribution of land-ownership and (an associated point) some farmers took the opportunity of getting the Ministry of Agriculture to draw boundaries where none existed before. Some of the farms would not have existed had the mapping not been undertaken— they were artefacts of the survey work.

(b) Practices naturally vary as between Area Offices—and as between farmers. Some farmers are more inclined than others to register farms in the first instance in the names of their deceased relatives (this practice often reflecting uncertainty as to what will happen to the devastated farm when replanting occurs); and some Area Offices are more tolerant of this practice than others. In all Areas it seems to be common for a resident farmer to be regarded as the effective owner of all those farms for which he holds the farm cards, irrespective of whether his name (or that of his brother, say) is on the farm card.

(c) Farms are sometimes registered in the names of young children, sons and others, when they have not in fact been given to them; usually, perhaps, the owner is intending to express a kind of 'testamentary intention' in this way.

(d) The speed with which changes in ownership consequent upon death are registered is very variable. If treatment occurred some time ago and there had been few outbreaks of disease recently, there may be little occasion for re-registration so the lists may be rather out of date.

(e) Many farmers are known by more than one name, this being reflected in farm registration on different blocks—or even on the same block. When going through the lists of names it is necessary to rely on local advice, especially as a certain amount of mis-spelling arises when, e.g., a Twi-speaking staff is handling unfamiliar Krobo names.

(f) Not all farms were cocoa-farms before swollen shoot—some were kitchen gardens, or food gardens. Portions of some farms were unplantable, being rocky, marshy, mountainous, etc.

APPENDIX I. 3

NOTES ON THE PRINCIPAL MIGRANT COCOA-FARMERS OF SOUTHERN GHANA

(i) The *Akwapim*—see Appendix I. 4, p. 27.

(ii) The *Krobo*. The capital towns of the Yilo and Manya Krobo states are

[1] The present writer wishes to express her gratitude to many Liaison Officers for the expert help they gave her.

25

APPENDIX I. 3

Somanya and Odumase, in the plain south of the forest, not far west of the river Volta. In about the middle of the last century (see Appendix II. 9, p. 72), groups of Krobo began to purchase land on the forest ranges, north-west of the plain, under their *huza* system of land-purchase. Soon after the Akwapim started acquiring cocoa-lands across the river Densu the Krobo, mainly the Yilo Krobo, followed suit. Krobo cocoa-farmers comprise a great proportion of all the strangers in the vast Begoro area which stretches down to the Afram river and they are to be found in great numbers in most parts of the mountain country east of the road from Koforidua north to the Kwahu boundary. (Most of this area is unmapped by the Ministry of Agriculture, this being one reason for the relative neglect of Krobo cocoa-farmers in this book.) As time went by individual Krobo companies penetrated much farther west and in the nineteen-twenties and thirties land was bought in many distant areas. In the early years of the century much cocoa was grown in Krobo country proper, but most of this has now died, food-farming and the oil-palm being the primary concerns. In 1948 the total number of Krobo people in Ghana was recorded as 95,912, of whom about two-thirds were living in the two Krobo states and between a quarter and a fifth in Akim country and Kwahu—part of the boundary between Manya Krobo and Akim Abuakwa remains to this day indeterminate. The Krobo are patrilineal Adangme people.

(iii) The *Shai* inhabit a small area in the plains south of the Akwapim ridge to the west of the Krobo, an area which includes Dodowa, for long an important centre of the trade in palm produce; they formerly inhabited certain small hills in the Accra plain (the Shai Hills), but in 1892 they were removed from these hills by the Gold Coast government and resettled in the plain. The total number of Shai people has never been accurately known. In 1948 the total population of the Shai Native Authority was recorded as 18,446, but this number includes many non-Shai, and most Shai people were presumably resident away from home in the cocoa-farming areas and in Akwapim. Lacking the finance to buy cocoa-land, many Shai people started by working with Akwapim cocoa-farmers; but as early as 1900 there were many Shai farmers in the Mangoase area and they were soon beginning to push eagerly over the river Densu in search of larger lands. The Shai resemble the Krobo in that they are very strongly concentrated in certain cocoa-growing areas (though isolated companies also exist); thus dozens of Shai companies are to be found west of Suhum, but whether each company bought its land entirely independently is not known. No country is too mountainous for the adventurous Shai, many of whom farm the steep slopes east of the main road north from Koforidua—for instance east of Jumapo. Like the Krobo, whose farming methods they closely imitated, the Shai are patrilineal Adangme.

(iv) The *Ga*. The Ga people live in towns strung along the coast from the river Densu, through Accra to Tema. One of the major occupations of Ga men is fishing; another is agriculture, the food-growing hinterland between Accra and the Akwapim ridge having been exploited for over a century by farmers who moved inland for the purpose. Ga farmers sometimes form or join companies for the purpose of acquiring cocoa-land (a large company of Ga farmers bought land near Nankese, for instance), but it is probably more usual for them to acquire land individually. In 1948 the total recorded number of Ga in Ghana was 144,033, of whom 8,372 were resident in Akim country and Kwahu—many of them doubtless in non-farming work. For present purposes the Ga inheritance system may be regarded as basically patrilineal (so that strip-farms pass from a father to his sons on his death, as they do with other company farmers), but see Pogucki, vol. III, chap. v, 'Devolution upon Death'. See also M. J. Field, *Social Organization of the Ga People* (1940).

PRINCIPAL MIGRANT COCOA-FARMERS

(v)   The *Anum and Boso*. The inhabitants of the two neighbouring towns, Anum and Boso, which are situated east of the river Volta, near its confluence with the Afram, are *matrilineal* Guan. In the eighteen-nineties many of them worked with Akwapim cocoa-farmers or were attracted to the Adawso area by the possibilities of other work—they lacked the cash to buy cocoa-land for themselves. Between 1907 and about 1912 many Anum farmers settled in the Asamankese area, where they were encouraged to appropriate land. A little later land-buying started in earnest (for instance in the area south-west of Suhum known as Anum Apapam) and the Anum and Boso farmers are among the most widely distributed of all Ghana's cocoa-farmers, though some of them continue to operate on a very small scale. In 1960 the recorded population of Anum was 4,301, of Boso 2,588 (exclusive of associated villages): there are no figures relating to the very much larger numbers of Anum and Boso who live away from home.

(vi)   *Other peoples*. Among the other peoples who have migrated as cocoa-farmers to Akim country are:

(a)   *Ewe* from east of the Volta; in Akim country they are much more often labourers than farmers (they form the backbone of the rural labour force in southern Ghana), but especially in the Asamankese area individual farmers sometimes acquired land and some labourers, including Ewe from Togo, have evolved into farmers. In recent years many Ewe 'squatters' have been given temporary rights to grow food on the devastated cocoa-lands of southern Akim Abuakwa and Akwapim, usually in return for a portion of the crop; these people are always on the move and are not aspirant cocoa-farmers. (Many Ewe cocoa-farmers have migrated northwards through the Volta Region, especially during the last twenty-five years, to the Kadjebi area where there are many companies of Ewe farmers, as well as individuals—some of whom were given the right to farm in return for a portion—often a half—of the planted area: but this migration lies outside the scope of the present book.)

(b)   *Fanti, Gomoa, Awutu* etc., people from coastal areas south of Akim country; their migration has been neglected in this book, having usually been little more than a casual seeping to the south-western area of Akim Abuakwa only, rather than a sustained process.

(c)   Farmers from a few *Adangme coastal towns*, including Prampram, Ningo and Ada who, usually starting as labourers, have sometimes joined companies basically composed of people from elsewhere.

(d)   *Osudoku* people, from west of the Volta, near Akuse, most of whom have continued to operate on a very small scale. (In Akim country Osudoku farmers are very rare.)

APPENDIX I. 4

NOTES ON THE HISTORY AND ETHNOLOGY OF AKWAPIM

by

David Brokensha

(University of Ghana)

Akwapim is termed one District, yet the Customs and Powers differentiate from one another in each town.[1]

The name 'Akwapim' as used here, refers to the present area of the Akropong Local Council, which covers just over 300 square miles—the traditional Akwapim state is

---

[1] Letter from the chief of Larteh-Kubease to the Commissioner of the Eastern Province, 18 September 1924.

27

APPENDIX I. 4

slightly larger as it includes the Nsawam area to the south-west. The present population of Akwapim is about 80,000,[1] about half of whom live in the sixteen towns (listed below) along the ridge; of the remainder, some 8,000 live in other towns (such as Adawso, Tinkong, Mangoase and Pakro) and the balance in villages, consisting generally of only a few huts. Less than 10 per cent of the total consists of 'strangers' from outside Akwapim, though each town has quarters, or portions of quarters, composed of immigrants from near and far. The more ancient immigrant groups have generally been so successfully assimilated that it is only on rare occasions, such as festivals, that their origin is remembered.

History

Akwapim history may be conveniently summarized in three main periods. In the early period before the seventeenth century, the area would seem to have been occupied by Guan-speaking peoples who were primarily agriculturalists and possessed no formal state organization. The second or Akwamu period, from the early seventeenth century to 1730, was 'characterized by the intrusion from the west of Twi-speaking peoples— Akwamu and Akim—into Guan territory' and 'by the emulation, by some of the Guan groups, of the institutions and customs of the newcomers'.[2] The infiltration of Akwamu and Akim settlers was probably peaceful but it was followed, in the mid-seventeenth century, by the formal annexation of the area by Akwamu. Until 1730 the period was one of lively trade, especially in gold.

In 1729 the original Guan joined with immigrant Akim around Akropong and with some of the Akwamu who had settled near Aburi, in a move to dethrone the unpopular Akwamu king. The rebellion ended in the collapse of Akwamu rule. After their victory of 1730, the rebels held a meeting at Abotakyi and formally inaugurated the new independent state of Akwapim, acknowledging the chief of the Akim settlers at Akropong as Omanhene, Akim Abuakwa having at this time succeeded Akwamu as the dominant power in the region.[3] From then on 'the state was organized in the usual Akan fashion, and existing stools in the area were utilized to provide its divisional (and military) structure'[4]—see below. From 1742 the new state owed allegiance to the Ashanti empire, which sent demands for tribute up to 1872, when the British government concluded a treaty with Akwapim. This period is characterized by a series of external wars and internal crises: in 1919 the Governor reported that 'the Akwapim division has been unhappily notorious for its internal dissensions . . . the history of Akwapim is one of unedifying disputes'.

As might have been expected, the confederation of different peoples did not prevent the operation of fissionary tendencies, which from time to time threatened the unity of the state. In 1770 there was a severe crisis, which was repeated several times in the nineteenth and early twentieth centuries. These disputes included attempted rebellions by Mamfe in 1885–6, the Nifa division in 1893 and 1901–6, Tutu in 1906, Mam-

[1] 1960 Census of Ghana, provisional figures. There are perhaps another 100,000 Akwapim living away from home.

[2] From Ivor Wilks, *The Growth of the Akwapim State: a Study in the Control of Evidence*, forthcoming.

[3] This account is based on Mr Wilks's unpublished article (see footnote 2) and although it differs from the traditional account, as presented by the Rev. C. C. Reindorf (*History of the Gold Coast and Asante*) and others, it is supported by impressive new evidence, mainly from contemporary Danish and Dutch records. It is now clear that there was 'a high degree of continuity between pre-1730 and post-1730 institutions', many of the former having been utilized by the new state.

[4] Wilks, *op. cit.*

HISTORY OF AKWAPIM

pong in 1906, Larteh-Ahenease in 1898 and 1918, as well as combinations of nearly all the towns against an unpopular Omanhene, which recurred periodically. There were also disputes between rival factions for the Omanhene's stool, which often encouraged the Benkumhene or Nifahene to renew attempts to assert their independence. In all such attempts there has been a series of shifting alliances, but the leader has usually been either the Benkumhene or Nifahene.

Ethnic Grouping and Languages

The inhabitants of Akwapim may be divided into four main groups:

(a) The *Guan* inhabit Larteh (which is two towns, Ahenease and Kubease), Mamfe, Mampong (including the former capital, Abotakyi), Obosomase (also known as Asantema) and Tutu. The Larteh people still retain their Guan language (the school children and many adults being tri-lingual, in Guan, Twi and English), but the inhabitants of the other towns are Twi speakers, having probably switched to this language in the mid eighteenth century. The relative isolation of Larteh, on the ridge known as *Akonno bepow*, may partly explain the retention of the Guan language. The Guan have a patrilineal system of descent, inheritance and succession, but there are variations in practices as between the towns.

(b) The *Kyerepon*, who with the Guan were the original settlers, occupy Adukrom (and Aseseeso), Abiriw, Abonse, Apirede, Awukugua and Dawu. They have retained their language, which is very similar to the Guan spoken at Larteh; it is noteworthy that this language should still be spoken at Abiriw which has been contiguous with Twi-speaking Akropong for nearly 250 years. A study of Abonse[1] suggests that the original political organization is less vestigial there than in the Guan towns, perhaps because of its geographical isolation. The Kyerepon, like the Guan, are patrilineal.

(c) The *Akwamu* centre round the town of Aburi and include the inhabitants of Ahwerease (or Afwerase), Atweasin (now part of Aburi) and Berekuso. The original Akwamu settlers arrived in the early seventeenth century and they joined the other groups in the successful rebellion against Akwamu rule in 1730. They speak Twi. They have a matrilineal system of descent, inheritance and succession.

(d) The *Akim* are settled at Akropong and Amanokrom and provide the Omanhene of the state; they, of course, speak Twi. The Amanokrom people arrived from Akim Abuakwa in the late seventeenth century and settled at Akropong. An ancestor of the Ohene, Amano Awua, who is reputed to have been the third of the stool-occupants, is said to have broken away from Akropong after a dispute and to have founded the present 'Amano's town', where an Akwamu group was already settled. The Akim are matrilineal.

Political Organization

As already noted, the political system, as developed after 1730, is basically Akan. The Omanhene lives at Akropong, where he is surrounded by the whole apparatus of the Akan state, with queen-mother, linguists, councillors, stool-bearers and the like. 'Akwapim retains its traditional and typical Akan system intact in structure, though greatly diminished in function'[2]—many of these functions having been taken over by the central government.

[1] Emmanuel Ampene, 'The Political and Social Organisation of a Guan Community', unpublished M.A. thesis.
[2] From Ivor Wilks, *op. cit.*

APPENDIX I. 4

The state is organized into four divisions (corresponding with ethnic groups), the heads of which are directly responsible to the Omanhene:

Division	Head	Subordinate towns
1: Adonten (centre) (Akwamu)	Adontenhene (Ohene of Aburi)	Ahwerease, Atweasin (now included in Aburi), Berekuso.
2: Nifa (right) (Kyerepon)	Nifahene (Ohene of Adukrom)	Abiriw, Abonse, Apirede, Aseseeso, Awukugua, Dawu.
3: Benkum (left) (Guan)	Benkumhene (Ohene of Larteh-Ahenease)	Larteh-Kubease, Mamfe, Mampong (inc. Abotakyi), Obosomase, Tutu.
4: Gyaase (administration) (Akim)	Gyaasehene (Ohene of Amanokrom)	Akropong—although it is the seat of the Omanhene it is still a subordinate town of this division.

In addition, the Ohene of Berekuso is the Twafohene—commander of the vanguard. Recently, Mamfe, Mampong and Larteh-Kubease all claimed the Kyidomhene (commander of the rear-guard) title and by administrative decision the title was 'locked away' or made vacant.

APPENDIX I. 5

'ACROSS THE PRAH'[1]

by

Andrew Amankwa Opoku

Departure

There is a popular saying: 'When your neighbours are taking snuff and you do not join them, they say that your finger nails are dead.' In other words, whenever a new fashion comes in, everybody tries to indulge in it. When cocoa-cultivation came, several people embraced it and migrated into the forest belt to make a start. But we Twi know that the starting of a new enterprise is not an easy thing, not the sort of meat an old woman's teeth can chew.

Kwame Antiri also made up his mind that he would go into the forest to try his hand at cocoa and see if he could succeed there. He had a small farm at Krabo, so he decided to wait till after the harvesting season. Besides, the year had not been a good one. His old cocoa-trees had begun to die out. The farm had been seriously attacked by *akate*[2] and swollen shoot. Concern about this alone had forced him to go and 'eat a fetish',[3] in order that he might be protected from any possible enemies with the evil

---

[1] From *Voices of Ghana* (Literary Contributions to the Ghana Broadcasting System 1955–7), edited by Henry Swanzy, Government Printer, Accra, 1958, pp. 24–39. The original being some 8,000 words long, it has not unfortunately been possible to reprint the whole of it here. A concluding section, which has been omitted, relates how the original settlers were joined by a group of relatives who took up adjoining land and how the little village of Oboadakasu was filled to capacity when 'labourers and strangers, traders and hunters' also arrived. Despite the mention of swollen shoot, this fictional journey can be imagined as taking place at any time since the opening of the central railway line in the nineteen-twenties. Mr Opoku wrote the first draft in Twi and then translated it. For the benefit of non-Ghanaian readers he has now provided a few explanatory notes. See also p. 13.

[2] The capsid insect.

[3] Mr Opoku explains that 'to eat a fetish' means 'to be initiated into a fetish cult to obtain

'ACROSS THE PRAH'

eye and who might be responsible for his troubles. Why, he had not realized that season even fifty loads from his farm! But the previous year his first plucking alone gave him over four hundred loads.

One evening in December, Antiri called the head of his clan, his wife, children and other close relatives together, and told them about his plans. He made a long speech indeed. 'Barima Ofori, listen and pass it on to Nana and the rest of the *abusua*, that if I call them together this evening, I do not do so for any evil purpose. The elders have said that if you sit in one place you sit upon your fortune; and because of that, the fortune-seeker does not fear travelling. I am sure you all know that this new cocoa-industry had made travelling a fashion. I do not need to go far to find you an illustration. Not many days have passed by since our neighbour and friend Kofi Tuo and his family moved to Apragya (the other bank of the River Prah) to start cocoa-farming. It is true that no one has followed them there, but it is also true that we have not had any ill reports about them. Perhaps in the words of the tortoise, they are saying, "No one knows what we are doing in our shell."

'Therefore, my Spokesman, listen and tell the old man and all my kinsmen that I too desire to go to the Prah-side, to take up a contract for one-third share. If on arrival there I succeed in obtaining some of the land to buy outright, I shall buy it and settle there. If by the grace of *Tweaduampon*, the Almighty, we are so lucky as to find some benevolent person who will give us charge of his farm, and enable us to make a living, we shall hang on to that till we settle. But if it should happen that we should fail in our attempt, the saying has it, that "when a trap relapses it comes back to its original position". We shall come back to our old home and resume our ancient oil-palm industry. That, I am sure, with your prayers, will never come to pass. Therefore we are met in parting. All that I am asking is your blessing, with which you will usher me and my family forth, so that we shall not go and return as we went, but that we may rather set out and come back one day in fortune.'

'Parting is hard, but what can we do about it? Once we have been born men, our lot will for ever remain the bitter cup. You are yourselves witness that this half-completed house is not large enough for us, we shall one day have to put up a little hut in addition to it. But "Kwakye's thing is nice, it is money that did it", says the proverb. Again, when there is food in the house, we Twi do not say: "Shut the door and let us go out to the bush to hunt for wild yam." I have finished my talk to you.'

Kwame Antiri made up his mind that on the very next Monday he would start. He paid a flying visit to Nsawam to purchase a few things that he would require in the forest. He bought cutlasses, axes, work dresses, gunpowder and percussion caps, salt and some kerosene. When he had finished collecting all these, he said he would go into the valley beyond the Akuapem hills to take leave of his wife's people.

So he met all his relatives at their village and said goodbye to them. They in their turn blessed him and prayed for him to go and return with fortune. As the proverb says, 'When the people of Nsuta eat their fill, then the people of Mampong have peace.' His mother-in-law gave him seeds of the egg-plant and gourds to give to his wife to take along with her, for, who knows, none might exist where they were going. They followed him to the outskirts of the village, and stopped behind a stile as he went

protection against devils and evil designers. An initiate will then have to accept certain restrictions and taboos. Failure to observe these will always provide an interpretation for any illness or ill luck that might happen to the initiate. He must confess and offer sacrifices and make restitutions to propitiate the fetish. If he fails to do this and dies in his sin, as it were, his property is confiscated and he is not given an honourable burial.'

APPENDIX I. 5

along the path. Dusk was approaching when he got home, therefore he found some water for a bath and went to bed. The next day being Sunday, Antiri did not go anywhere; but the family made themselves a sumptuous meal and rested. After that, towards the evening, they went and bade goodbye to their near relatives, in order that none might have cause to blame them later on. Before going to bed, they carried their boxes, pots and pans and all other belongings they would not take along with them, and deposited them in the houses of their next-door neighbours and relatives for safe keeping.

Early next morning, a mammy lorry[1] came to stand behind their house and they loaded their luggage on to it. Relatives and friends came to see them off in proper fashion. They gave away the objects they no longer needed as parting gifts to friends and neighbours. These in their turn gave food for the road and other send-off presents. The driver tooted his horn and pressed the starter. As soon as the lorry had started all one could hear was shouts of 'Don't be long! don't be long!'

And now it was difficult to stand. Sorrow had descended on everyone. Several people had tears welling up in their eyes. It is true, they said, if you don't know what death feels like, you had better liken it to sleep, but travelling is more like death than anything else which men compare it to. A traveller is just like a dead person. As he is going, perhaps he is on his last journey. Perhaps he will not return to find those he is leaving behind, or even perhaps he himself may never return again. So most of the people who had gathered there began to shed tears. As for the children, they wailed aloud and it was some trouble stopping them. Ɔseadeɛyɔ, the one who fulfils his promise, Kwame Antiri, had put into execution what he said in words. If the day dawned on him again, it would be in a strange land.

The Journey

If we were to narrate all that happened during the journey, we should be left with no leisure. Agya Kwame and his people started from Coaltar in the early morning and they arrived at Agona Swedru by mid-day. When they arrived there, they were famishing. So they asked the driver to permit them to go and find something to eat. They bought some bread and kenkey[2] from the hawkers, and brought it to the lorry and ate it and drank water which they begged for.

But when they finished their meal and were expecting to continue their journey, the rain started unexpectedly to pour, and continued until nightfall. When it stopped, the driver informed them that the road was a bad one, and he would not be able to travel on it in the night. They were very much cast down by this news. Agya Kwame said finally that they would go and find shelter, under somebody's roof, somewhere. Even if they had to pay a sleeping fee they wouldn't mind—when day dawned they would start on their journey. True indeed, he said, it is as good to hasten as it is to delay. They were lucky, for their driver knew the house of someone from their own town, and he led them there himself, and they found suitable lodging. In short, their host and his wife showed them so much kindness that they realized that the proverb is true which says that when an Accra man goes to Kumase and meets *Nkramfoa* (a certain fish), he is delighted that he has seen his kinsman, because they both come from the sea.

At cock-crow, the driver drove his lorry behind the room in which they were sleeping, and tooted his horn. The time was Harmattan season, therefore early rising was

---

[1] Lorries are often called mammy lorries (or wagons) because so many of their passengers are women travelling to and from market with their wares.

[2] A food made of maize (corn).

'ACROSS THE PRAH'

not an easy task at all; but, since one does not stop running before the pursuer gets tired, nor do travellers turn their battle against Ɔsɛɛ into feasting on pork, they persevered, and came and boarded the lorry, after thanking their host and his benevolent wife, who had come to see thèm off.

The sun had risen when they reached Akim Oda. Here they hurried to the railway station, bought their tickets, and boarded the train just in time for Mokwaa country. Travel by railway was a new experience for Kwame Antiri and each member of his family, and from the start their hearts were not at ease. What gave them great trouble was the train guard who paraded up and down the train, asking awkward questions of the passengers. When he finally approached them, and told them to present their tickets for inspection, their ill luck was like that of fowls, who are always destined to perish at the end of the knife. The simple family had blundered into a compartment occupied by those who had paid double the fare they had paid. A lot of pleading had to be put on their behalf before they were hustled into their appropriate compartment.

As soon as they entered the correct class, they beheld a fellow-townsman occupying a seat there. Kwame Antiri accosted him with these words: '*Ohunkyɛree*, how do we meet?' 'We meet in peace. Nowadays I am in the Wasa country, working on a little project, but I had a message about a couple of weeks ago saying that a recent storm had blown off the roof of my house and I went to see it. I am now returning to my place in the forest once again, for it is the forest-clearing season, and no labourer has leisure.' They talked on for a long while, with their acquaintance who was called Kwaku Abɛbrɛsɛ. He did not fear the train guards, because he had travelled this way so often that he had got to know them all very well. Because of that, the newcomers cheered up a bit. They had befriended the cub of the leopard: they no longer dreaded to be in the chase.

They chatted on until they reached the point where Kwame Antiri and his people were to detrain. Kwaku promised them that as soon as work slackened a bit he would come and look them up. Then the train started and they waved to their friend till the train was far out of sight.

Alone once more, the family asked for the road to their destination and found a lorry, and packed their luggage on to it. As they came from the town of the Adɔntenhene, in their own country, so they were going to stay in the town of the Adɔntenhene[1] of the Mokwaa land, called Pɛwodeɛ,[2] which lies on the banks of the Prah. They arrived at mid-day, and asked for the house of the chief spokesman to the chief, for they hoped to lodge there. In less time than it takes to shut the eye and open it again, wind of their presence had gone round the entire town, and the news had reached those away in the fields, and even those fishing in the river Prah.

It was afternoon when the spokesman led them to the chief's house to salute the Adɔntenhene and his elders. They were given seats, and remained sitting for some time. It was not very long before the Adɔntenhene came out and sat down on the small dais in the open hall. Now the family rose and the spokesman led them to shake hands with the people assembled. When they had finished, they sat down again and the chief directed that they should be served with a bottle of rum as their 'fatigue-drink', the drink given to strangers on arrival. After this, they poured the dregs on to

---

[1] Mr Opoku comments that 'this practice is not usual, but it could be used to an advantage, especially if the guest knows that his town is held in great esteem by the people of the host country.' (Aburi is the seat of the Adɔntenhene of Akwapim.)

[2] Pɛwodeɛ is a small village on the banks of the Prah river near Twifu-Praso in the Central Region.

33

APPENDIX I. 5

the ground, bowing to the chief and saying, 'Thank you, sir.' Then the Adɔntenhene asked Ɔkyeame Paemuse to ask them their mission. The linguist stood up in the midst of the gathering, leaning upon his stick of office and said: 'My father, this is what the Benevolent One says. He says it is all quiet here, but what brings you here this noontide?'

As soon as he had finished speaking, Kwame Antiri rose up. Baring his chest, he went nearer to where the chief and his councillors were seated, and bowed low. He then began to tell his story, 'Hear, O spokesman, and let it reach the Benevolent One that we do not come in evil. We are Akuapem people who come from yonder in the east. Our original dwelling-place[1] was at Coaltar on this side of the River Densu in the Abuakwa state. Our native town is Aburi which is the *adɔnten* or vanguard of the Akuapem state. We are cocoa-farmers and it is on account of that we are here. We have heard very often about your state, that a vast virgin forest suitable for cocoa lies here. Hence, we said, we will come and see if, through Nana's kindness, he would be pleased to give us a little portion to squat on and work. I may say that some of our kinsmen have preceded us, and from what we have heard, you have received them very generously. If you were to show us the same generosity, we should be extremely grateful. In short, if we are here today, we wish to make it clear that we have come to stay. Permit me to say, we have come to man the forge, we have not come to buy a cutlass from the smith, and return.'

As he finished, the spokesman thanked him, and spoke for *ɔdeneho*, the Independent One, and for the entire state and said: 'That is good tidings for you!' The gathering responded: 'Good tidings is good!' Now the Adɔntenhene told them that they were welcome, and the spokesman and the elders came round and shook hands with them. After that, Paemuse, the spokesman, spoke again: 'We meet you in peace here also. In fact some time has passed since we received word from your kinsmen of your coming. But with the arrival of your message, an evil wind blew over us, and we sent word to you to defer your coming for a short while. It is now that the storm has completely abated, that you have come, to find the state reviving once again to its former status. Indeed, there is a forest here, but a state is built with people and not with trees. That which made the Kumase state a big one was the cry, "add it on, add it on". Therefore the Mighty One says that if indeed you have come to stay, then he receives you with outstretched arms. At present the shades have fallen, the journey cleared by your feet is long, therefore we shall disperse to allow you to go and wash, knowing that when day dawns tomorrow, the Fante nation will still be in existence.'

After the linguist had finished, Ɔdeneho, the Independent One, rose and the assembly dispersed. The strangers followed their host to the house, where he found them sleeping places, and a good bed for their leader.

The Farm Chosen

When day dawned, the chief and his elders assembled early in the morning and sent to inform Kwame and his two nephews who accompanied him that they were waiting to give them audience. When they arrived at the place they saluted them, and they were offered chairs to sit.

The spokesman stood up and once again inquired from them their mission. The Sannaahene (the Treasurer) who was now the patron of the strangers answered for them that they came to hear what reply Ɔkyeame had for their demand of the previous day for some land to farm.

The spokesman asked them again to explain exactly what they wanted. Had they

[1] This 'original dwelling-place' at Kraboa-Coaltar was their first trans-Densu cocoa-land.

34

'ACROSS THE PRAH'

come to buy the land outright or would they hire the land and then give a third share of their cultivation to the owner of the land? Or did they wish to take the land and plant the cocoa till it began to yield and have the farm split into two between themselves and the owner of the land? Or finally would they rather prefer to hire farms? Kwame replied that if they could have land which they could buy outright they would like that best. But if they could not, they would accept anything, since no one quarrels with his benefactor. When you have some corn in your mouth and you roast the rest, you are able to give it full time to boil.

After the assembly had given thought to the matter, the chief ordered that they should place the matter before the old women. The inner council of elders went into consultation and then informed them that the matter had been laid before the old women and they had given their consent. The strangers should be given some land to buy, for who knew, through them some prosperity might one day descend on the nation.

When it ended in this, the Sannaahene led them to thank the chief and the councillors for this favourable reply; and the young men were given three days in which to survey the entire forest, with a view to finding a suitable portion to sell to the strangers.

On the third day after this meeting, the strangers accompanied the elders to the forest, and there they were given a vast piece of land. On the north it measured 40 ropes[1] while the breadth was 45. The southern side which was bounded by the River Prah measured 38.

When they had surveyed the land they measured it up finally, and set up the boundaries, while the assistants asked for rum, a sheep and a delimitation fee. Then the party returned home to bargain for the price of the land. The Mmokwaa people explained that they wished to deal with the newcomers in a neighbourly manner so all they would ask would be for £200, a case of rum and a fat sheep. On the spot, Kwame and his family paid the cost to the last penny, and received a deed of purchase. They then repaired to the edge of the forest, and performed the *guaha* custom, or the customary act of conveyance.[2]

This custom is a sign which provides evidence for future reference in a sale, exchange or conveyance of property. It is done with a leaf, hence the name *guaha*, a leaf used in trade. This is how it is done: the seller and the buyer each put up a child to act in their stead. The children squat facing each other, and pass their right hands in between their thighs. Behind them are lined their sponsors. The elder supervising the sale then hands the two children the leaf of a plant called *kesenekesene*, or a strip of palm leaf. The seller's child holds the stalk end, the buyer's representative holds the tip, and each presses a cowrie under his right thumb on the leaf. Next the presiding elder orders the children to pull the leaf taut, till it snaps. When it snaps, each side takes away their bit of the leaf together with the cowrie, and keeps it somewhere for future reference. Should any litigation arise over the ownership of the land, the witnesses come forward and require either party to bring their *guaha* (torn leaf and cowrie) and they piece the two together, to see if they fit. The reason why children are employed in the performance of the *guaha* is that they will live longer than the grown-up witnesses.

At any rate, Kwame Antiri had his land by both rights. For the rest of the day, you should have been in the town of Pɛwodeɛ to see for yourself. After the townspeople

[1] See p. 43. Mr Opoku explains that the farmers usually have actual twine ropes of the right length which they carry with them when moving into the forest to farm.
[2] See p. 141.

APPENDIX I. 5

had divided the £200, they began to mourn it.[1] The greater part, in fact, as the saying goes, slept on the backs of their mats.

The New Farm

Next morning Agya Kwame Antiri rose up early and roused all his people to accompany him to make a tour of the entire land to find a suitable spot where they could build their settlement. They had decided not to stay in the town, for out of sight, out of hatred. All day they covered the ground, and finally they came upon a beautiful plateau. About two hundred yards below the plateau they saw large flat rocks frequented by flights of birds. From this they concluded that there should be water there. Sure enough, when they rushed to the spot, they discovered a spring which spouted into a box of rock. They drank some of this clean cool water to their satisfaction and named the spring Ɔboadakasu (stone-box-water).

They were too tired to do anything more that day, and, remembering further that the new moon does not emerge the same day and move across the town, they said they would just survey the site and mark it up with signs, and return the next morning to start the clearing. Then they returned home and informed their host and the women, and after they had something to eat, they went to bed.

At the first crow of the cock, on the third day, Kwame and his hosts set off again and since they have already made their tracks, it did not take them long to reach Ɔboadakasu. There they made their fire and began with the clearing. They continued in this manner till they had finally cleared the thorn from the bush. Soon Ɔseadeɛyɔ and his children began to put up the framework of their buildings. The distance from the village to their new settlement compelled them to move into the bivouacs as soon as sufficient ground had been cleared around them.

You would admire them for their courage, when you hear the story of the early days at the settlement. But the Antiri family could not cry as they rightly should, because, they knew, one does not cry when one dresses one's own wounds.

The roofs and walls of the shelters were made of tree bark. When the wind blew, you could hear it whistling through the chinks. When you looked up at night, you could notice the stars piercing through the roofs into your eyes. When it rained, then you had to make sure that you were sleeping in the duiker's place, or else you would never sleep a wink. The black ants too were there to see to it that there was no peace at night. When these left for a bit, other disturbing insects took up their place, and said, 'We don't agree'. Had it not been for the fact that they slept every night with fires burning inside and around their rooms, they would have found life itself very difficult indeed, because they heard the cries of wild animals like the leopard almost every night. They even awoke in the morning sometimes to find the marks of herds of wild cows, close behind their flimsy walls.

It was in the month of January, when the fruits of the *agyamma*[2] plant are ripe, that the family of Kwame Antiri went to live for the first time at the new settlement. When May came round and the corn was mature, they were a bit at ease, because their farms

---

[1] Mr Opoku writes: 'After they had shared the money every one of them went away and got deep drunk. People get drunk, but when you have an entire village drunk it must be the result of a death. In this case the cause of the general drunkenness was the great windfall which they were frittering away—in other words they were mourning the money which they were "killing" or losing in drinks.'

[2] Mr Opoku writes that 'the *agyamma* is a shrub that normally grows in the secondary forest. It spreads out several branches in a very short time and its seeds provide food for birds and squirrels. There are two blossoms, one in May/June and another December/January. The latter gives the farmers the signal to begin clearings for new farms.'

36

'ACROSS THE PRAH'

were beginning to yield and their livestock was also increasing. Until then they had been living on wild yams and cassava, which they got from the forest and other people's deserted farms, or, in a crisis, on foodstuffs from other people.

You would have pitied them indeed in the months before May. You would agree that the meat of the animal poverty tastes bitter indeed. With the yam or corn, and their intestines to feed upon, the women and children made their way to Pɛwodeɛ. As the proverb says, 'If there is something in the house, no one will say "Shut the door and come with me to find wild yams." ' So the women bent under the weight of the heavy loads, and the children were besmeared with clay, their little all-weather cloths hanging from their necks, their skin covered with sores which attracted a swarm of flies. The men, for their part, had gone to the forest with their guns.

At last the settlement was well established. They had made a few compounds of thatched houses, fenced around with bark of wood, because no palm-fronds were to be found in the forest which could be used for fencing mats. Creepers and vines[1] of *ahurukyim, nsurogya* and *odurufee* were very scarce here, so that the only climber used was the thick one called *fra*. All their farms were blooming, and the plantains standing in full strength. If the forest were one that had been farmed before, there would have been no space because of the cocoyam shoots that would have sprung up. For the rains had been plentiful and all crops had made a good start. Cocoa, transplanted or sowed by seed, had all begun to grow branches. As for pineapples and sugar-cane, they had even started selling some. If you had seen their fowls, turkeys, rabbits, goats and sheep, and especially the fatted ones, you would have thought that they had been at Ɔboadakasu quite a long time. The Pɛwodeɛ people were even coming to the settlers to buy strange new foodcrops like cocoyams, Chinese potatoes, *borobe*, garden eggs, pumpkins, spinach, citrus and other fruits.

[1] The creepers and vines mentioned are all for fencing and tying of faggots. Some of them attain girths of a foot or more and are split up into strands before use.

CHAPTER II

THE COMPANY

Cocoa-farming land is rarely sold, in the first instance, by individuals: it is usually sold corporately, through the agency of chiefs whose authority derives from the people whose land they are selling. The buyers of such land, on the other hand, are always individuals.[1] So as to strengthen their bargaining position *vis-à-vis* the corporate sellers and for numerous other practical economic and social reasons, these individual buyers usually associate with others in the act of buying the land. If most of these other buyers are non-kinsmen,[2] the resultant group of buyers is known as a 'company'[3]—an ambiguous and misleading word, which is yet partly appropriate considering the commercial attitude of the farmers to land-purchase.

So important is the role of the company in the history and present development of cocoa-farming in southern Ghana that it deserves a book to itself. But so does the 'family land'. Companies are a form of organization associated with patrilineal peoples.[4] Family lands were established by the matrilineal Akwapim. This book is much concerned with contrasting these two types of migratory organization. This chapter on the company is mainly descriptive, dealing with the general outline of the system and providing facts and figures relating to individual companies.[5] It is

[1] This is a point which has often been misunderstood. In 1915 the Omanhene of Akwapim sought to argue (see Appendix v. 3, p. 154) that it was Akwapim chiefs who had bought land on behalf of their people. Individuals often buy land with the needs of their lineage or descendants in mind, but this is a different point.

[2] Occasionally a company consists of kinsmen only (an example is the Mamfe/Saforosua company, see Appendix II. 8, p. 70); but the members must then be associated with each other on a commercial basis of equality, each paying the proper price for his portion of land.

[3] This interesting word 'company', which is invariably used by educated and uneducated farmers alike, was in general use, probably in Nigeria as well as in Ghana, long before the invention of the cocoa-companies—e.g. in connexion with *asafo* companies, these being 'military' groups of adult males. In *Report upon the Customs relating to the Tenure of Land on the Gold Coast*, 1895, the word is used, in an undefined sense, to denote some kind of corporate land-holding group which is not identical with 'the family'. The nearest Twi equivalent, which is however seldom used in connexion with the cocoa-companies, is *fekuw*, defined by Christaller, *op. cit.*, 1881 edition, as 'any number or body of people forming a company, society, association, club . . .' There has been little study of other types of indigenous economic organization comparable with the land-buying company: obvious examples are long-distance trading companies (which have existed for many centuries) and migratory fishing-boat crews—as well, perhaps, as the form of rotating savings-club known throughout West Africa by the Yoruba word *esusu*, though the word 'company' is never applied in this case.

[4] See Appendix VII. 2 (p. 199), etc.

[5] Krobo cocoa-companies are different in many respects from others and this chapter does not, in general, relate to them. This must not be allowed to obscure the fact that the first Akwapim cocoa-companies were modelled on the Krobo *huza*—see Appendix II. 9 (p. 72).

38

THE COMPANY

concerned with the establishment of the company members on their land rather than with their subsequent progress. The operation of the customary rules of inheritance in relation to company farmers is dealt with in chapter IV and the migratory process, the process which involves reinvesting the proceeds derived from cultivating one strip-farm in the purchase (through another company) of another strip, is considered in chapter VII.

The general outline of the system is very simple. A company consists of a group of farmers who club together for the sole and commercial purpose of buying cocoa-land. Each individual is concerned to buy land for himself and there is never any intention of joint, or communal, ownership or farming. After the land has been acquired from the vendor stool, each individual member is (sooner or later) allotted a strip, measured along one of the boundaries (the base-line), the width of which is proportionate to the sum of money he subscribes. Each member is then free to do whatever he wishes with his strip; he does not even have to retain it for his own use, but may resell the whole, or part, of it to an outsider of his own choice. Obomofo-Densua (Appendix II. 7, p. 69) is a typical company land; the map shows the layout of farms half a century or so after the land had been purchased.

Companies have leaders, whose main functions are to buy the land from the vendor chief on behalf of the members and to collect the subscriptions from each of them. Once these functions have been achieved the office of leader ceases to exist,[1] as is shown by the fact that if, then, the member who held the office dies, no successor is appointed. If, for some reason,[2] the appointment of a successor is necessary, there appears to be no general rule as to who this should be—whether a son (or other relative) of the original leader, or the purchaser of the next largest portion of land.[3] Although on legal documents, such as conveyances, companies take the names of their leaders, it is an interesting and significant fact that in ordinary conversation companies have no names, showing that once the purpose for which they were formed has been achieved, they cease to exist.[4]

Nor is it necessarily very clear who the original members of a company are.[5] In this book an original member is, in general, defined as someone

---

[1] This is not so with Krobo companies.

[2] Special circumstances, other than that the land is unshared or unpaid for, may make it desirable for someone to remain in authority. Thus a Mamfe farmer explained that the receipts from selling timber from a company land, which had proved unsuitable for cocoa, were shared among the members, in accordance with the width of their strips.

[3] The leader himself often, though not invariably, acquires the largest portion of land.

[4] The family group, on the other hand, has a continued corporate existence and this is reflected in the fact that large family lands always have names, many of which appear on the one-inch map, see p. 80. Companies are referred to as: the Mamfe people at Saforosua, the Shai at Obomofo-Densua and so on. If in any locality there are several companies of the same origin, it may not be practicable to distinguish between them without the aid of maps and detailed inquiries.

[5] This is one reason why informants often fail to agree on membership figures.

39

THE COMPANY

who subscribes for a portion of land which he receives at the time of the original share-out.[1] But if such an original member resells his share to somebody else, is such a purchaser an outsider or a member?[2] Possibly the answer depends on whether the strip had been fully paid for at the time of its resale. But surely, it may be asked, such a newcomer cannot be a member if the other members were not consulted (as they need not be) when the land was sold to him? Questions like these appear not to interest the farmers, providing further evidence, if such be needed, of the non-existence of a corporate group.

Although many company leaders who bought land half a century ago were interviewed, the role of the company leader in the early pioneering days has not, as yet, been sufficiently studied. Who were these leaders? It is a general rule that leaders were not chiefs or other office-holders. Certainly chiefs, like everyone else, bought land, but they did this in the capacity of ordinary company members; as they were required to remain resident in the home town they were not in a position to travel to buy the land. Sometimes leaders were exceptionally wealthy members of their community: where this was so the leader might pay for the whole land himself at the time of purchase and then proceed to resell portions of it to the members—an undemocratic procedure not favoured by the general run of farmers, as clearly there is nothing to stop the leader reselling at a profit, though sometimes, admittedly, he might offer land on very favourable terms at his own expense. More often leaders owed their position to their qualities of leadership, enterprise and trustworthiness. It has not been possible to ascertain whether leaders usually paid in full for their portions of land: perhaps, sometimes, their services to the company were rewarded by granting them strips wider than they would have been able to afford for themselves.

So specialized was the work of leading a large company, so skilled the art of negotiating for land, that a successful leader might, in his time, be called upon to form many companies. But leaders do not, like large farmer-creditors,[3] form a class apart. They are primarily farmers, not leaders. A man might happen to lead one company and then, later on, join another as an ordinary member.

[1] But much ambiguity remains. If, as very often happens, it was a father who put up the money, but his son who first occupied the land, perhaps after his father's death, who is then regarded as the original member? This question is especially hard to answer when the father gave his son the money to buy the land for himself.

[2] Most resales probably occur before farming starts, members sometimes being forced to sell by their inability to meet their promised contributions. With voluntary sales it is usually considered unlucky for a farmer to sell the whole of his strip, so that many farmers retain a portion, however small. Those who sell all their land may be objects of contempt, being given such names as 'Empty Kwabena'.

[3] Although these large farmer-creditors usually buy second-hand land (defined in this book as land, whether planted or unplanted, which was not bought at first hand from the vendor chief), they occasionally act as company leaders.

THE COMPANY

In the old days companies seldom had 'secretaries'[1] and it was one of the leader's functions to keep the records relating to the monetary transactions etc.—usually in his head. A secretary is a 'scholar', a man who keeps written records on behalf of the members. Sometimes, though not always, he is one of the company members, in which case he may be rewarded for his work with a free piece of land. Nowadays secretaries, like written conveyances and surveyors' plans, are becoming increasingly common.[2]

When a leader sets out to buy land he may be accompanied by a small nucleus of other company members, who may or may not assist him in defraying the initial expenses.[3] For safety's sake it is desirable for the leader to be accompanied by other members when buying the land, so that in the event of his death before the land is occupied there will be others to establish the company's identity. There is often a long delay of up to twenty or thirty years or more before planting starts, and it is a common complaint of company members that lands which they may never have seen for themselves have been 'lost' owing to the death of the leader and the consequent impossibility of establishing the purchasers' identity.

Many matters relating to the process of land-purchase, the *guaha* ceremony and so forth, are dealt with in chapter v, on land sales in relation to customary law, and it is unnecessary to add much here.[4] The leader, together with his associates, will ask the vendor chief, or his representatives, to show[5] them the land and will make a general inspection. He will take a particular interest in its defects—in stony outcrops, marshes and mountains. Concerned with the possibility of trespass, he will prefer a land with good natural boundaries—no stream, as the maps show, was ever too meandering for this purpose. If there are other near-by settlers he may check the situation with them, especially if there is any doubt in his mind as to the right of the chief to sell the land, or if it is known to lie near the chief's boundary.[6]

At some stage, whether on the first or on some subsequent visit, the

---

[1] An example of an old company which did have a secretary is Kyerepon/Nobeso, Appendix II. 4 (p. 62).

[2] Although this chapter relates, in general, to the pre-lorry age, it may be noted that there is some evidence of the recent emergence of a class of professional secretary—a man who looks after the clerical affairs of many companies to which he does not belong. One such professional secretary in Larteh had many exercise books filled with accounts relating to the expenses associated with buying land.

[3] The downpayment to the chief, transport costs, witnesses' fees, drinks, boundary-cutting expenses and so forth.

[4] The procedure described in 'Across the Prah' (Appendix I. 5, p. 35), has various modern features, but this chapter in general relates to the earlier days when the lands in the mapped area of southern Akim Abuakwa were purchased.

[5] 'Showing' the land (*kyerɛ* is the Twi verb) is part of the symbolic process of alienation. It is interesting that in parts of eastern Nigeria the Ibo word for 'to show' is used in connection with the letting of land for short periods—see M. M. Green, *Land Tenure in an Ibo Village*, Monographs on Social Anthropology (London School of Economics, 1941), p. 29.

[6] Boundaries were often indeterminate: see chapter v.

THE COMPANY

boundaries of the land to be purchased will be fixed; this will be done by means of 'pillars', bottles or other objects placed at corners and other strategic points, if there are insufficient natural features such as large trees or boulders. The point to note is that companies always[1] buy a definite area of land, determined in advance and not to any degree dependent on the speed of clearing and planting.

At some stage it will be necessary for the leader to form an exact idea of how much land he has acquired, so that on returning home he may set about the task of balancing the demand for land (from his members and potential members) with the supply he has available. This question of the 'quantification of land' is a crucial aspect of the farmers' commercial approach. Before it is considered, it is necessary to deal with the general question of who the company members are likely to be.

Whether, after buying the land, the leader returns to his homeland, or to the area where he then happens to be farming, will depend on circumstances. In the earliest days of the migration there were no companies proper and by the time, soon after 1900, that they became the standard means of migration of certain patrilineal Akwapim, nearly all the farmers from these towns were already farming away from home, in the Mangoase/Adawso area and elsewhere. Although many of the companies were formed in those areas, the home town itself has always been a good place for recruiting potential members. The nucleus of the membership of a new company often consists of a few of the members of an old company, but it is rare for companies to reproduce themselves exactly.

Companies are essentially a male form of organization[2] and in the old days, before the arrival of the lorry, their membership was basically homogeneous, consisting mainly or entirely of men from one home town.[3] With old companies it is invariably possible to denote them as Larteh, Mamfe, Shai, etc. companies, in accordance with the origin of most of the members.[4] But as, from the earliest times, companies were apt to be formed away from home and as the farmers (being commercial in their

---

[1] This generalization applies to practically the whole of the historic cocoa-growing area of southern Akim Abuakwa and to nearly all other areas where companies have been in a position to buy land outright. Where, sometimes, it appears not to hold, as for instance on the Afram Plains or (possibly) in Sefwi-Wiawso, this is because usufructuary rights only have been granted. The whole idea of the company is to buy land first and share it afterwards.

[2] Although the inclusion of women members is not unknown, it is sufficiently rare to cause comment among the farmers.

[3] Although from the nineteen-twenties onwards large mixed Akwapim companies, composed of men from several towns, have sometimes been formed, most companies, other than those drawn from the Kyerepon towns, have continued to be basically composed of men from one town.

[4] The existence of outsiders, who bought second-hand land, is sometimes confusing; for some reason, which is not clear, an outsider's town of origin is usually different from that of the member who resold him the land. (From the research worker's angle, this fact is a great convenience, enabling outsiders to be readily distinguished.)

THE COMPANY

outlook) lacked unnecessary sentiment on the question of origin, there has always been a tendency for reliable outsiders, usually known to the farmers because of their residence in the farming areas, to be admitted as members.[1] Sometimes a whole block of land is made over by the main company to a sub-company of different origin, which allocates land to its members—the association of the two groups then resembling the loose association of members within companies.

Much inquiry in the home towns and elsewhere has so far failed to reveal any general tendency for company membership to be recruited on a kinship basis. Companies, it would seem, are typically composed of friends from the home town and certainly the commercial attitude of the members to each other bears this out. But it must be admitted that so little is, as yet, known about the social structure of the principal Akwapim towns, such as Larteh,[2] where the company system first developed, that it is possible that further inquiry may reveal a tendency, in some places, for company members to be recruited on a residential basis.

It should also be added that although, as it seems, companies usually consist basically of friends, it is quite common for two brothers or two paternal cousins each to be a member in his own right.[3] But such relatives always farm independently, though their strips may adjoin, so that it remains true that the company farmers are freely associated in a commercial venture, untrammelled by considerations of kin.

To return to the question of the quantification of land, it is always necessary for the leader to say how much land he has on offer—and at what price. There were (and are) no indigenous units of area in these preliterate (though commercial) communities (see below, p. 46) and the farmers depended entirely on a unit of length. According to the standard procedure one of the boundaries[4] was selected as the base-line and its total length was measured by means of a 'rope' (more often of natural than of manufactured variety) of a certain fixed length. If the total cost of the land was expected to be £100 and the base-line measured twenty of these ropes, then land was offered to members and potential members, at a price of £5 per rope.

Although the length of this unit, the rope, is not nearly as invariable as most farmers tend to assume,[5] a certain degree of standardization has

[1] Thus the Shai/Nankese company (Appendix II. 6, p. 67) admitted members from the coastal towns Ada, Prampram and Ningo, some of whom had formerly been labourers who had worked with the Shai farmers.

[2] Larteh is a particularly complex example as it consists of two towns, Ahenease and Kubease; while Larteh companies may draw their membership from both towns, this is perhaps not usual.

[3] But a father and a son, on the other hand, would never both be members; where this appears to be so, it is because the father has given his son a portion during his lifetime.

[4] Although farmers often hold strong views on whether this 'ought' to be the longer or shorter side of the rectangle, the maps show that there is no standard practice.

[5] Though Dr J. M. Hunter reports, in a private communication, that he is impressed by

43

THE COMPANY

existed for some time, especially among the Akwapim. All the different migratory peoples define the rope in terms of 'arm-stretches' (or 'fathoms'), *abasam* in Twi.[1] Among Akwapim people nowadays it is almost unknown for the rope to be defined, in conversation at any rate, as other than 24 arm-stretches, i.e. 24×6 ft $= 144$ ft.[2] Among the Krobo there is still, and always has been, much variation, though 12 hand-stretches is becoming increasingly standardized.[3] The Krobo rope is usually shorter than the present standard Akwapim rope of 24 hand-stretches. The Shai rope is usually 12 or 14 arm-stretches.

If a company land is reasonably rectangular, then the area of a strip-farm is determined by its width and the farmers' great ambition of achieving 'fairness', as between themselves, is achieved. While it is not in all senses true that uneducated farmers are ignorant of multiplication,[4] it is yet their lack of training in elementary mathematical operations which is associated with their inability to compute area. Because they cannot compute area so no practical end would be served by measuring the length of their strips, and it is a general rule[5] that farmers neither measure, nor take any interest in, the length of their strips. But as practical men they realize that the company lands 'ought' to be rectangular—and occasionally they refer to a sort of ideal shape, a 'matchbox'. The maps show that in some areas, as for example one of the Nankese Areas (Appendix II. 3, p. 62), a fair degree of rectangularity is achieved and that in others, such as the Kwesi Komfo Area (Appendix II. 2, p. 60), it is not. Much depends on topography—streams, contours and so on.

Although farmers know perfectly well that 'size' is not completely determined by one dimension, their whole linguistic approach to measurement is full of pitfalls. Thus even an educated Twi-speaking farmer when asking how large a farm is, is quite likely to inquire '*nhama ahe?*'—literally, 'ropes how many?' It is not, therefore, surprising that nearly everybody insists on *speaking* as though a ten-rope farm (i.e. a strip ten ropes wide) which has been acquired through one company is necessarily more

the degree of standardization in part of the Suhum area, where he has noted the existence of ropes of 12, 22 and 24 fathoms.

[1] Derived from *abasa*, the plural of the Twi noun meaning 'arm'. Christaller (*op. cit.*) defines *abasam* as 'the space to which a man can extend his arms'. (Neither pacing, nor the length of the human foot, is ever used for measurement purposes.)

[2] The actual length of the rope is subject to variations in human stature and thus in arm-stretches.

[3] In Krobo country proper (see Appendix II. 9, p. 72), there has always been much variation in the length of the rope. Dr M. J. Field (*Social Organization of the Ga people*) refers to units of 5, 7 and 12 arm-stretches and other writers have regarded 8 as a standard unit. But the Krobo farmers in Akim country may have been more inclined to standardize the unit at 12 arm-stretches. The Krobo word for the rope is *kpa*, for the arm-stretch *gugwe*.

[4] Thus the uneducated farmer 'knows' the total sum he should receive for x loads of cocoa at £y a load as readily as the educated farmer; and the notion of multiples is fundamental to many ancient crafts such as weaving and the manufacture of gold weights.

[5] To which there are exceptions. This is a conventional matter, bearing little relation to the level of education of the farmer.

44

THE COMPANY

or less the same 'size' as a ten-rope farm acquired through another company—ignoring the relative lengths of the company lands. The most intelligent and sophisticated people will sometimes be prepared to go on arguing like this indefinitely.[1]

Given the built-in processes of thought implicit in the linguistic approach, it is all the more remarkable that the farmers[2] have devised a geometric procedure for ensuring fairness as between company members in cases where, as farming proceeds, the company land is found to taper, or widen, to an embarrassing extent. The procedure involves altering the length of the original rope, as illustrated by the map of the Shai/Nankese land (Appendix II. 6, p. 67); plate 15 shows an uneducated Larteh farmer demonstrating the geometry by drawing with a stick on the ground.

Dr J. M. Hunter has referred to this procedure[3] as 're-orientation *en masse*' and he notes, as has the present writer, that it shows itself on the Ministry of Agriculture farm maps by its 'sharp angularity'. If a land is very tapering and the farmers are very keen, the reorientation may occur several times before the farmers complete the planting of their strips, to the obvious inconvenience of everybody, as the strips may then cross one another.[4] Dr Hunter believes, as a result of his work in the Suhum area, that if a piece of land tapers appreciably companies are often aware of this before they start planting and will cut the base-line along which the strips are measured, on the narrow side, thus:

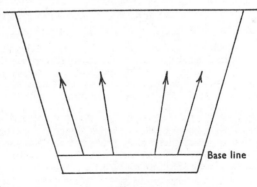

Fig. 1

[1] The sort of thing these people are sometimes saying is that *if* the price per rope for the two companies is much the same, the two investments are of about equal value. Alternatively they are insisting that *if* both the lands are of the ideal matchbox shape, then the two farms are about equal in size.
[2] This procedure is an old one among many migrant farmers: the present writer has observed it on farm maps of Shai, Krobo and Ga companies and has discussed it with Larteh farmers.
[3] In a personal communication.
[4] This may be one reason why, as the maps show, the procedure is not very commonly adopted.

He thinks that as farming progresses it is largely a matter of luck who gains from the progressive widening of a block of land and that it is sometimes those on the flanks and sometimes those in the centre:

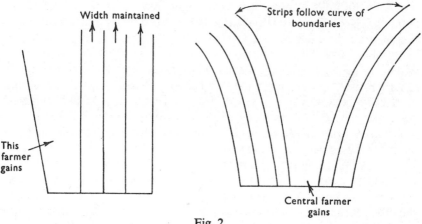

Fig. 2

The farmers, then, have a certain instinctive knowledge of geometry which stands them in very good stead when it comes to carving up awkwardly shaped lands. But it is of the nature of the case that pre-literate people[1] should lack an indigenous unit of area based on multiplication.[2] In English manorial records[3] the acre was defined in terms of the amount of work that could be achieved in a day by a ploughing team,[4] much de-

[1] Such was the lack of educational opportunities, even in Akwapim, that most southern Ghanaian migrant farmers (including many of the most enterprising) have always been uneducated. There has not yet been time for the great expansion in education, which occurred about ten years ago, to affect the general standard of literacy of farmers as a class. However, owing to the work of the Ministry of Agriculture in swollen-shoot areas, there is an increasing familiarity with the 'acre'.

[2] See F. W. Maitland, *Domesday Book and Beyond*, Essay III, chapter I on Measures and Fields. 'The scheme of computation that we know as "superficial measure", was long in making itself part of the mental furniture of the ordinary man.' 'Whatever may have been the attainments of some cloistered mathematicians, the man of business did not suppose that he could talk of size without talking of shape...' (pp. 430–31).

[3] See C. S. and C. S. Orwin, *The Open Fields*. An orthodox 'land' in the open field of a village was one acre—viz. 220 yds (a furlong) long and 22 yds (a tenth of a furlong) wide; but if the soil were heavier, more difficult to turn, the land would be smaller. Strips were made up of one, two or more lands, according to the length of the furlong and the lie of the land generally. While the argument that the system was 'the fairest' (for 'it gave to each member an equal share of the near and of the remoter land, and of the good and of the less good parts of the field if it were not uniform in every part') is of remarkable application to the company farmers, the temptation to draw comparisons between the open field and company systems must be strenuously avoided, so utterly different are all the background circumstances.

[4] See also Macaulay's *Lays of Ancient Rome*, Horatius having been thus rewarded for keeping the bridge:

      They gave him of the corn-land   As much as two strong oxen
      That was of public right   Could plough from morn to night.

THE COMPANY

pending on the nature of the soil and the terrain. In tropical forest country, where man is the beast of burden and the wielder only of axe, hoe and matchet, it is seldom possible to define a standard unit of work in relation to virgin land, so variable are the problems encountered, so feeble the tools in relation to the task. Besides, the company farmers buy the land *before* cultivating it—often indeed taking several decades to complete cultivation—so that no unit based on the quantity of work would solve their problems;[1] and the same would apply to a unit based on fruitfulness,[2] or potential fruitfulness.[3]

Farmers, then, are obliged to *speak* in a very vague way about area and they are certainly apt to allow their imaginations full rein when it comes to answering questions put to them by innocent outsiders about large farms.[4] Even educated farmers, familiar with English units of length and area, may put the distance between two cottages at two miles, when a quarter of a mile would be nearer the right figure—and this not from any wilful desire to deceive.

But despite the disabilities inherent in their approach to measurement, there is evidence that purchasers and also, presumably, land-sellers, are often, in practice, rather good judges of area. Before considering this, it is necessary to conclude the account of how a company land is shared among the members.

The company leader, let it be supposed, has 25 ropes of land on offer. He decides to buy 5 ropes himself, the remainder being taken up by 9 other members whose allocations vary from 4 to 1 rope—farmers much prefer round numbers and it is rare for fractions of a rope to be involved at this stage unless the land be very small.[5] The farmers have to be 'positioned' on the base-line and to avoid future disputes it is very desirable, possibly necessary, for all the members (or their representatives) to travel

---

[1] Akwapim farmers sometimes speak of an apparent unit of area 'the one-pound farm' which is employed in connexion with the clearing, not the purchase, of land and which is an area such that at some time, in the distant past, a contract labourer would have charged £1 for clearing and planting it. The geometry of these units is sometimes based on the square or rectangle, but dimensions vary greatly from time to time and place to place, sometimes with the deliberate intention of cheating the labourer. (See Hill, *The Gold Coast Cocoa Farmer*, footnote, p. 84.)

[2] 'Rents' of cocoa-farms are often based on the usufruct, the quantity of cocoa.

[3] Cocoa being a perennial crop, taking fifteen years or so to come into full bearing, the number of trees is not a good measure of short-term potential fruitfulness—which is one reason, perhaps, why farmers ordinarily do not count their trees. Little has been written about these problems anywhere in Africa, but see Green (*op. cit.*, p. 31) for a definition of an Ibo 'unit of land' the breadth of which was normally five rows of yams, the length not being definitely specified.

[4] They lack watches and their estimates of the time taken to walk round a farm are often preposterously high. On the other hand, in more general conversation, farmers are often most modest, perhaps giving no inkling at all, in the early stages of a conversation, of the large scale on which they operate.

[5] Though fractions may be involved later on when subdivision of the strip occurs, following the original farmer's death.

47

THE COMPANY

to the land to effect a formal 'share-out'.[1] If the company be large and the land distant, it may be a hard task to muster everybody and farmers often shake their heads sadly when asked if a land, which may have been purchased long ago, has yet been divided. However, in the earlier days, with which this chapter is mainly concerned, delays were not so great and as the company is always glad to have its 'representatives' resident on the land in order to prevent trespassing etc., individual members who take the matter into their own hands by installing themselves there and 'farming forward' on a strip of appropriate width usually seem to cause no offence, though they stand the risk of having to relinquish any planted land which is recognized as encroaching on their neighbours' strips when the share-out does occur.

With Krobo and Shai companies there is usually a main path, which runs down the entire length of the land not far from (and parallel to) the base-line, on which all the 'villages' (i.e. individual farmhouses or cottages) are built; such a main path can be seen on the map of the Obomofo-Densua land.[2] Akwapim company farmers, on the other hand, are complete individualists, each building his village at the point on his land which suits him best—this, of course, reflecting the lack of corporate feeling.

When the share-out occurs, *ntɔmmɛ* trees[3] are usually planted to mark the boundaries between farms. There appears to be no general rule as to whether these boundaries are cut, or marked, in advance of farming. Some farmers will say that *ntɔmmɛ* are planted down the whole length of the boundaries which are cut before farming starts. Others insist that they cut their boundaries as they proceed and that they may or may not re-measure the width of their strips. The neatly drawn strips of the Krobo and Shai farmers are instantly distinguishable on the maps[4] and it may be that these farmers are more apt than others to measure their strips throughout their lengths. The members of a large Krobo company with

[1] Although the farmers attach the utmost importance to 'fairness', if it so happens that a member receives an altogether undue share of rocky or marshy land, this is often considered to be unavoidable bad luck.

[2] There is a similar main path on the Kyerepon/Nobeso land—this may be because the strips were measured for the farmers by Krobo people. Even with Shai farmers, topographical factors partly determine the situation of villages.

[3] Defined by Christaller as 'a plant (species of palm) with ensiform leaves, the living stems of which may serve as posts in fences or for landmarks'—see plate 4. The *ntɔmmɛ* is known as *buna* to the Krobo. 'The *buna* is a mean-looking tree resembling an ambitious aspidistra and is often very difficult to find among the other vegetation, but it is tenacious of life and readily takes root when a slip is stuck into the ground' (M. J. Field, *Social Organization of the Ga People*). A company land may have lain untouched for years, following swollen shoot, but the *ntɔmmɛ* will survive, sometimes under other vegetation, sometimes growing high in search of light. Pineapple and jatrophra are other common boundary plants.

[4] Their narrowness is, also, a distinctive feature. It is probable that Krobo strips tend to be narrower from the start than non-Krobo strips (the Krobo rope being shorter), but certainly the distinction becomes more striking as time goes by owing to the common Krobo practice of dividing strip-farms among several sons of a deceased father.

48

THE COMPANY

land near Asikasu said that they measured their strips afresh each year and fixed a maximum length of strip which might be planted by individual farmers in the year—there are supposed to be agricultural advantages to be gained from marching forward abreast like an army.[1] Other Krobo farmers have insisted that this is not their procedure.[2] At the other extreme, many Larteh farmers have said that they do not measure, cut or even mark their strip-boundaries, but just farm forward and trust their neighbours not to encroach on them—the great importance attached to fairness in the original allocation contrasting with this casual spirit when it comes to the actual farming. Certainly few boundary disputes between company members ever reach the courts.

The cocoa-companies came into existence soon after 1900 in response to the realization that the demands of commercial agriculture required a commercial attitude to land as a factor that was bought and sold. In the eighteen-nineties each parcel of land was unique, to be described like a painting or piece of sculpture, in its own terms; there was a scramble for land without being a proper market in land. In the extreme south of the Akim cocoa area, where the Aburi and Akropong farmers bought their large family lands, such a state of affairs continued; but farther north where, for geographical reasons, the companies bought their trans-Densu lands and where the land-selling chiefs had much less land to offer, there is some evidence that land became quantified in the fullest sense—that the price paid by the companies really began to bear some relation to the area acquired,[3] showing that the parties involved in the sale were good practical judges of area. The following statistics, shaky as they are in some respects,[4] suggest that the approximate cost of cocoa-land in the Nankese area in about 1906 was of the order of £1 per acre—and that the variation in the price paid per acre, by the different land-purchasing groups, was much less than would be expected given the farmers' ignorance of mensuration.

[1] That some Krobo farmers follow this practice, at least in Krobo country, was confirmed at a meeting with Nene Mate Kole in Krobo-Odumase in March 1959.

[2] Many Krobo companies bought land near Asafo-Akim and their 'leader', or spokesman (the farmer who represents the companies in their dealings with the Ministry of Agriculture), said that they had never imposed any restriction on the length of strip that individuals might clear and plant in a year. He said, though doubt was subsequently expressed on this in Krobo-Odumase, that all the inter-strip boundaries had been cut before farming started.

[3] As nearly all the land in this area was 'good for cocoa', the question of its quality did not arise.

[4] As leaders die and companies have no corporate existence, the total cost of a land (as distinct from the price per rope) may soon be forgotten. The practice of paying in instalments often means that the sum finally paid is less than the sum originally promised and in retrospect the figures may be confused. Then there is lack of comparability resulting from the inclusion, or exclusion, of incidental expenses—'drinks', witnesses' fees, boundary-cutting, etc. But oral interview sometimes yields reasonably reliable figures when the independent statements of a number of original members, as to the price they paid per rope, are found to correspond.

49

THE COMPANY

The Cost of Cocoa-land in the Nankese Area in about 1906

Land-purchasing group	Total acreage as surveyed by Ministry of Agriculture	Estimated total cost of land (£)	Approx. cost per acre (£)
Obomofo-Densua/Shai	560	600	1·1
Adidiso/Amanokrom	732[1]	1,000[2]	1·4
Boah/Akropong	163	200	1·2
Shai/Nankese	596	672	1·1
Ga/Mame	165	225	1·4
Mamfe/Trayo	990	700	0·7

[1] Including a slight element of estimation.
[2] This figure may be too high.

All the land-purchasing groups were companies—except for Boah/Akropong, which was a family group (see Appendix III. 8, p. 100).

Four of the lands can be seen on the map in Appendix II. 3 (p. 62); the Shai/Nankese land adjoins this area and the Boah/Akropong land lies within about a mile of it. The land-sellers were the chiefs of Asafo and Maase and all the land was sold between about 1905 and 1907. The estimated total cost of each land was obtained by questioning farmers, most of them in the farming area—see further information on some of the companies in the Appendices. Some of the figures are much more reliable than others. The most that can be said for the figures is that they were collected independently, over a period, without any regard to the possibility of a uniform price of land—and that the fact that so little variation was revealed came as a great surprise.

If it is agreed that the figures in this table establish the likelihood that the cost of land in the Nankese area in about 1906 was of the order of £1 an acre, a rough statement intended to signify that the price was nearer to £1 than to (say) 5s. or £4, it is still not known whether such price standardization was typical. Fortunately there exist some more reliable statistics, collected by Reserve Settlement Commissioners (see Appendix II. 1, tables III and IV, p. 58) and these seem to establish that in the nineteen-twenties and thirties there was some degree of price uniformity and an inverse relationship between price and the area of the land bought—the largest lands, as in the case of Mamfe/Trayo in the above table, being the cheapest per acre. Although it is true that when these lands were bought the transactions were sometimes set down in documents, to which plans were attached, there is still no reason to think (see Appendix V. 6, p. 160) that these plans were sufficiently accurate to give the farmers a reliable idea of the acreage they had acquired. Again, the conclusion is that the parties to the transactions were often quite good practical judges of area.

The general outline of the larger company lands in any Ministry of Agriculture Area can usually be seen at a glance on the wall-maps, showing farm boundaries, where these exist.[1] Certain of the smaller companies

[1] Not all Area offices compile farm maps on a scale small enough for the whole Area to be seen at a glance.

50

THE COMPANY

also, especially if they be Krobo or Shai (with their narrow strips), may be picked out. But in order to ascertain the general pattern of land-holding in an Area, a laborious examination of present-day farm-ownership, farm by farm, is usually necessary. Such an examination was carried out for two Ministry of Agriculture Areas, one of them an Area based on Nankese (Appendix II. 3, p. 62), the other (lying about ten miles farther west) the Kwesi Komfo Area (Appendix II. 2, p. 60). Comparing these two Areas, which are different in many respects, the dangers of generalization at once become apparent. Thus, most of the company lands in the Nankese Area are large—half a square mile or more—while most of those in the Kwesi Komfo Area are much smaller.

Many factors (associated and unassociated) are responsible for determining the size of company lands. They include: the wealth of the buyers and their town of origin, the size of the company membership, the price of the land, topographical considerations, the presence (or otherwise) of Akim cocoa-farmers in the area, the willingness of the land-vendor to deal with many different buyers, the accessibility of the land (farmers are unlikely to find it worth while to travel to very small lands in remote areas), the fruitfulness of the land (in marginal cocoa-growing areas company lands tend to be large) and so forth. In the historic cocoa-growing area of southern Akim Abuakwa, company lands are seldom larger than two or three square miles. Areas of a half to one square mile or so seem very common. It is hard to put a lower limit to company area—perhaps fifty acres.

The art of guessing the town of origin of company lands from their outline and farm boundaries on the Ministry of Agriculture's wall-maps is not without fascination. As already mentioned, the Krobo and Shai lands, with their narrow and neatly drawn strips, are easily distinguishable;[1] these lands run through the full range of size, and include some of the very smallest, as it seems that most of the sub-companies which buy second-hand land from individual company members (as e.g. at Mamfe Saforosua, Appendix II. 8, p. 70) are of Krobo or Shai origin. Contrasting with the Krobo and Shai lands are the Mamfe (Akwapim) lands, with their very large and broad farms which are occasionally not strips at all (as at Mamfe/Trayo, Appendix II. 5, p. 65).[2] Very wide strips may signify the presence of Larteh farmers, who have been less inclined than many to subdivide farms on the death of the original farmer. If the original membership of the company was evidently large, then it is unlikely to have consisted of Mampong, Tutu or Obosomase people, who seldom formed large companies in the early days, when most of the land in the mapped area was purchased. If the company land is small and evidently

---

[1] The only lands which might be confused with them were purchased by farmers of Ga origin—but Ga companies are rather rare.

[2] Of course not all Mamfe lands are large.

51

THE COMPANY

not Krobo or Shai, then (though depending on the district) it may be of Anum or Boso (or occasionally of Osudoku) origin—the members having been penurious labourers, or ex-labourers, with little money to spare for land-purchase. (But there are some very large Anum lands—e.g. in the area west of Suhum known as Anum-Apapam.)

There is much material elsewhere in this book touching on the size of company lands. Thus in Appendix II. 1, table I, p. 57, there are statistics relating to forty-six lands, acquired during the nineteen-twenties and thirties in areas which subsequently became forest reserves, the average size of which was nearly 1,000 acres. But enough has, perhaps, been said to illustrate the dangers of statistical generalization.

How large are companies in terms of the size of their membership? This is a subject which is even harder to pursue statistically than that of the size of the land purchased. Whilst the number of separate farms within a company area provides some indication of the number of original members, practices with regard to division of farms, as a consequence of gift or inheritance, vary greatly.[1] Nor, as experience has shown, is this a matter which can be reliably pursued by oral interview alone, without the use of maps showing farm boundaries. The size of the group partly determines (and is partly determined by) the size of the land—at the time the leader negotiates for the purchase of the land he usually does not know the exact number of members, but he will have a fair idea of the possibilities. As already noted, large memberships are uncommon in some towns and common in others. Perhaps most pre-lorry-age Mamfe (Akwapim) companies had no more than eight members. Certainly many Krobo companies had very large memberships, perhaps up to fifty, sometimes organized in sub-groups. Kyerepon companies, too, tended to be large, this being associated with the relative poverty of these farmers. Generalization must, therefore, be in terms of the origin of the farmers. Account must also be taken of the date of formation, for in the lorry age companies grew larger.

Turning now to the question of the area of strip-farms, it is already clear that there is so much heterogeneity that generalizations, or statistical averages, should relate (say) to Krobo or to Mamfe companies and not to all companies. Farm size must, therefore, be studied on an individual company basis—and an historical approach is unavoidable. Such work is detailed and time-consuming[2] and no more than about a dozen com-

---

[1] See chapter IV.

[2] As much of the land in the mapped areas was sold between forty and fifty-five years ago most of the original farmers are now dead and the work involved in ascertaining the relationship of present-day farm-owners to original members is often very laborious, especially when key informants have to be sought out in other parts of the country. When the number of original members was small, as was the case with the Mamfe Saforosua company, the work tended to be less, but the labour of listing all the farms which had been sold to outsiders (who had all to be identified as such) was considerable. Fortunately, though, many of the original farmers still survive—and were usually helpfulness itself.

52

THE COMPANY

panies* have been satisfactorily investigated so far: the figures given in the following table, which is concerned with the original size of strip-farms,† relate to five of these.‡

The Original Size of Strip-farms

	Kyerepon/ Nobeso	Mamfe/ Trayo	Shai/ Nankese	Obomofo-Densua (Shai)	Mamfe/ Saforosua
	(A)	(B)	(C)	(D)	(E)
1. Total acreage	439	990	596	560	759
2. Acreage resold	35	442[1]	60	105	198
3. Acreage retained	404	548	536	455	561
4. No. of original members (approx.)	19	8	34	12	6
5. Average retained acreage per member	21	91[2]	16	38	93
6. Acreage of largest strip					
(a) total	106	274	49	174	224
(b) resold by original farmer	—	84	16	25	52
(c) retained	106	190	33	149	172
7. Acreage retained exc. 6(c)	298	358	503	306	379
8. Average acreage retained exc. 6(c)	17	72[3]	15	28	76
9. No. of original strips less than 10 acres	3	—	12	n.a.	—

[1] Including a small acreage (less than 30) of share v given away to relatives other than sons.
[2] Average for 6 members, 2 members having sold all their land.
[3] Average for 5 members, 2 members having sold all their land.

Notes on Table

Companies For further particulars see Appendices to this chapter. It is here assumed that those who resold the land were all original members.

(A) Nine of the original farmers acquired strips of between 15 and 35 acres.

(B) Two of the original members resold all their land, amounting altogether to 261 acres. The smallest acquisition was 66 acres.

(C) Ten of the 34 farmers acquired strips of 20 acres or more, 12 farmers between 10 acres and 20 acres and 11 farmers between 5 and 10 acres.

(D) The total number of original members could not be determined exactly.

(E) Each of the 5 Mamfe company members gave away most or all of his land to his sons in his life-time; the sixth member, an Akropong man, retained about 40 acres (out of an unsold acreage of 76) for his own use.

* Abortive attempts were made to study a good many more companies, but circumstances beyond one's control, such as the fact that the particular Area Office of the Ministry of Agriculture was too busy to fit in the map-work required, prevented the completion of the work.
† The table on p. 120 relates to the subsequent division of these strip-farms.
‡ These five cases were selected as interesting examples—needless to say there is nothing representative about them.

53

THE COMPANY

1. *Total acreage*   This is the total acreage acquired by the company, excluding any subsequent resales.
2. *Acreage resold*   This is the total acreage resold by members to outsiders.
3. *Acreage retained*   This is (1) less (2).
4. *Number of original members*   The figures are based on an analysis of present-day farm-ownership, the original owner of each farm having been ascertained.
5. *Average acreage retained*   (3) divided by (4).
6. *Acreage of largest strip*   (a) The largest acreage acquired by an individual member, inclusive of any area subsequently resold.
   (b) The portion of 6(a) subsequently resold.
   (c) 6(a) minus 6(b).
7. *Acreage retained*   As (3), excluding 6(c).
8. *Average acreage retained*   As (5), excluding 6(c).
9. *Strips less than 10 acres*   This number should be compared with (4).

The table shows that the total areas of these company lands ranged from 439 to 990 acres—the companies were all fairly large. The number of original members varied between 6 and about 34. The average acreage retained per member lay within the range of 16 and about 93, or 15 and 76 if the largest acreage is in each case excluded—in 4 out of 5 cases the largest acreage made up a quarter or more of the whole company land. With only one company, Shai/Nankese, did any significant proportion of the original strips consist of small strips under 10 acres. The smallest area acquired by a member of the Mamfe/Trayo company was 66 acres; the corresponding figure for Mamfe/Saforosua was 33 acres.

All these company lands lie within ten miles of Suhum and all of them were bought within a period of about six years—between about 1906 and 1912. At that time most of the company members (or their fathers) already owned one or more cocoa-lands; many of them were farming[1] in the Adawso/Mangoase area, east of the river Densu; and some had already progressed over the river. While the Shai and Kyerepon lands may have been divided fairly promptly, some of the larger farmers waited a long time before starting to clear and plant. In general, the Mamfe farmers were in no hurry to start planting these new acquisitions, which had been bought well in advance of requirements—with Mamfe/Trayo there is evidence of much delay. While four of the companies were typical groups of friends, one of them, Mamfe/Saforosua, was a group of close relatives (including a brother of the leader's wife, an Akropong man). Company leaders often buy land expressly for their sons, who may even be unborn at the time of purchase; this was true, to an unusual degree, of Mamfe/Saforosua—only one of these farmers (and he the Akropong man) failed to give away most of his land to his sons in his lifetime. Much land was resold by the Mamfe farmers in particular, always (or nearly always) to farmers from other towns: the present-day pattern of farm-ownership is, therefore, more complex than most of the maps suggest.

[1] A few of the Shai members were probably labourers in that area.

54

REPORTS OF SETTLEMENT COMMISSIONERS

APPENDIX II. 1

THE REPORTS OF THE RESERVE SETTLEMENT COMMISSIONERS

It was laid down under the 1927 Forests Ordinance (as amended) that, when Forest Reserves were established, an official called a Reserve Settlement Commissioner should be appointed as a court to assess any compensation payable in respect of any necessary restrictions on the exercise of rights in the Reserve. After the boundaries of the Reserve had been cut, the Forestry Department proceeded to 'demarcate' all cultivated areas within these boundaries. The Commissioners had powers to 'exclude' all these demarcated areas from the Reserve by permitting continued cultivation therein, and these powers were usually exercised whether the farms had been established by natives of the area or by farmers from elsewhere. The former were not entitled to compensation, but the latter were awarded compensation in respect of any area not demarcated but included in the original purchase, in which future farming rights were prohibited. As the title to the land was not considered as affected by the establishment of the Reserve (if the Reserve were later to be released by government, farming rights would revive in full), and as the various stools tended to assert that mineral and timber rights had not been fully transferred,[1] compensation was not paid in full,[2] but compound interest was allowed in respect of the period that had elapsed since notice had been given of the creation of the Reserve. While it is significant that the Gold Coast government should have thus overtly recognized the rights of stranger-farmers and while the farmers were, most of them, willing to take part in the Commissioners' work, the principles involved have received little general publicity; accordingly, most migrant farmers who lack personal experience of the procedure are unwilling to believe in its existence—and there is, even today, a widespread belief that if the government were to know about the land sales 'they would take the land away'.

The reports of the Reserve Settlement Commissioners were never published by the Forestry Department, but are made available for reference purposes. As the Commissioners constituted single-man courts with powers to call for all the necessary information, and as several of them, in particular Mr C. H. Cooke,[3] went to great trouble to have all the alienation claims surveyed and mapped, often by Forest Rangers, the material collected, relating as it does to acreages, price of land, dates of acquisition, numbers of company members and so forth, is of great general interest. So high is the farmers' regard for legal procedure (and so keen their desire for financial gain), that they will willingly divulge facts in a court of law which, consciously or unconsciously, they consider unsuitable for the ears of a research worker. To the Reserve Settlement Commissioner, but not (spontaneously) to the research worker, they will admit, for example, that land is apt to be paid for over a very long period.

A large number of alienation claims were allowed in the Dede Forest Reserve, which lies between Begoro and the Afram river, an area of some 14,609 acres, of which about two-thirds had been sold before 1937 to strangers by the Benkumhene of Akim Abuakwa whose seat is at Begoro. Although most of these sales had occurred before 1930, in something like a half of all cases payment had not been completed, over a quarter of a century later, when Mr Cooke conducted his inquiry in 1956,[4]

---

[1] It is doubtful whether, in most cases, these rights were, in fact, reserved at the time of sale. It was the fact of the Reserve Settlement Commissioners' inquiries which probably prompted some of the stools to formulate their conditions for the first time. See p. 148.

[2] In accordance with the estimated total value of the land. This estimate was mainly based on the actual purchase price, but was checked by comparisons with prices in other reserves.

[3] To whom the present author is much indebted for information.

[4] That many of the lands had not been planted at all was an unconnected point. In a

55

APPENDIX II. 1

when it was found that at least half of the purchase price was commonly outstanding.[1]

The statistical information culled from these reports relates to at most[2] 87 companies,[3] which had bought[4] land in 16 different forest Reserves established between 1927 (the date of establishment of the Southern Scarp Reserve in Kwahu) and 1954 (the corresponding date for Chai River Reserve, in the northern Trans-Volta cocoa area); most of the Reserves had been established in the nineteen-thirties, the cocoa-farmers having, in all cases, bought their land previously.[5] A quarter of the companies (22 of them) had bought land in the Asuokoko River Reserve,[6] which is situated west of Ahamansu in the Volta region; and another 18 companies (most of them Krobo) had bought land in the Dede Reserve. In no other Reserve did the number of admitted alienations (for which compensation was paid) exceed 6, though the number would have been larger in the Atewa Range Extension Reserve had the original boundaries not had to have been revised owing to the confusion resulting from widespread selling of the same land by the stools of Asamankese and Akantin.

None of the Reserves in which alienation claims were allowed is situated in Ashanti.[7] But in one Ashanti Reserve, the Desiri Reserve, which is situated south of Hwidiem, there was evidence that a mixed company of strangers had bought two lots of land in 1952.[8] The Akwaboahene of Kumasi, who claimed that all the land in the Reserve was attached to his stool and to the stool of the Hiahene of Kumasi, insisted that none of his land was sold, but that those who wished to farm paid him various sorts of tribute. The Hiahene of Kumasi is reported to have said: 'I have let out a lot of my land for farming, but have not, of course, sold any. People who want to farm pay drink money; there is no fixed amount for this and it may be £10 or £20 or a sheep.' Both chiefs insisted that most of the stranger-farmers were Ashanti. At the inquiry relating to the Subim Reserve, west of Mim, the Hiahene had previously said that it would have been 'against custom' for him to sell land. 'If a stranger wishes to farm some of our land he first approaches me with the customary drink money, and I depute an Odikro or elder to show him an area. If the land is for cocoa, a stranger-farmer pays me yearly tribute in cash according to the size of the farm. If the farm is for food crops I do not

private communication to the writer Mr Cooke observed that never, in the course of all his work, had he come across a single case in which the whole area purchased had been cleared for cocoa or food crops—'usually at least half had been left as forest, and often (even when the purchase had occurred 20 or 30 years ago), only a small portion had been made into cocoa farms'.

[1] It was interesting that in two cases payment had been partly or wholly in kind. One group claimed that they had sawn logs for eight years before the Benkumhene said that they had paid sufficient for their land; another that they had built a house for the Benkumhene. Extensive inquiries elsewhere have revealed few similar cases.

[2] Certain statistical information is available for some companies and not others.

[3] While most of the purchasing groups were companies proper, a few of them may have been family groups.

[4] Information on the 'cash renting' of land to strangers was obtained for the Dede Forest Reserve and the farms were demarcated, but this information is not included here.

[5] Claims were in all cases disallowed if it was ascertained that the chief had sold the land after notice of the establishment of the Reserve had been given; some unscrupulous chiefs had been apt to take advantage of the strangers' ignorance of the prohibition on such sales.

[6] The companies were of very mixed origin, including British and French Ewe, Akwapim, Krobo, Shai and Ga.

[7] This had to do with the fact that nearly all the Ashanti Reserves had been set up under by-laws and not under the Forests Ordinance.

[8] The claim was disallowed on the grounds that under the 1951 Local Government Ordinance the concurrence of the local council to the sale should have been, but was not, obtained.

56

REPORTS OF SETTLEMENT COMMISSIONERS

collect anything. If the farm is for a local man he pays no tribute, but should the stool incur debt he with others helps to pay.'

Statistical Tables based on Figures extracted from the Reports of the Reserve Settlement Commissioners

The average area acquired by 46 companies was nearly 1,000 acres as table I shows. The largest acreage acquired was 4,374—nearly 7 square miles; the smallest acquisition was 96 acres. The 6 companies which acquired 2,000 acres or more accounted for about a third of the whole acreage.

I: Acreage acquired by Company

Acreage acquired by company	No. of companies	Total acreage
2,000 and over	6	15,359
1,000 to 1,999	10	14,439
500 to 999	12	10,049
250 to 499	9	3,539
Under 250	9	1,453
Total	46	44,819

It is interesting to see from table II that in two-thirds of all cases the total cost of the land was between £200 and £800 and that the figures in the two columns show a similar distribution, despite differences in dates and locality. (But no claims are made regarding the representativeness of the statistics.)

II: Total Cost of Company Land

	No. of companies	
	Reserve Settlement Commissioners' cases	Other[1]
£1,000 and over	6	5
£800 to £999	8	5
£600 to £799	13 ⎫	4
£400 to £599	25 ⎬ 54	13
£200 to £399	16 ⎭	16
Under £200	5	8
	73	51

[1] Figures extracted from a collection of 'customary conveyances' relating to sales of Akim Abuakwa land to stranger cocoa-farmers at various dates from 1897 until recently. (In many cases the date on the conveyance is considerably later than the date at which the sale occurred.) The highest price paid was £1,568 to the Odikro of Pramkese in 1950 (or before), the lowest £35 in 1907 (or before) to the chief of Tafo. The earliest recorded sale was one in 1897 (receipt dated 1933) for which £200 was paid to the Odikro of Osiem by five Krobo.

Strong evidence that land is cheaper, per unit of area, the larger the area that is bought, is provided by tables III and IV.

APPENDIX II. 1

III: Relationship between Size of Land bought by a Company and the Cost per Acre

Size of company land (acres)	Total acreage	Total cost (£)	Average cost in shillings per acre
2,000 and over	15,359	4,336	6
1,000 to 1,999	14,439	7,217	10
500 to 999	10,049	6,365	13
250 to 499	3,539	4,326	24
Under 250	1,453	2,265	32
Total	44,819	24,509	11

IV: Relationship between Cost per Acre and Average Acreage of Company Lands

Price/acre	No. of company lands[1]	Average acreage of company lands
Under 10s.	19 (13)	1,605
10s. and under £1	13 (2)	665
£1 and over	14 (1)	405
Total	46	974

[1] The number of lands of 1,000 acres or over is shown in brackets.

V: Dates of Purchase of Land[1]

Reserves other than in Volta Region[2]

Year of purchase of land by company[3]	Number of companies[3]	Price of cocoa[4] to the producer £ per ton
1921	1	20
1925	5	33
1926	5	29
1927	8 ⎫	43
1928	10 ⎬ 24	48
1929	6 ⎭	35
1930	3	32
1931	2	15
1932	2	17
1933	1	16
1934	–	10
1935	2	14
1936	3	15
1937	1	38
	49	

See footnotes to table VI.

REPORTS OF SETTLEMENT COMMISSIONERS

VI. Dates of Purchase of Land[1]

Asuokoko River and Chai River Reserves
(Volta Region)[2]

Year of purchase of land by company[3]	Number of companies[3]	Price of cocoa[4] to the producer £ per ton
1925	1	33
1926	1	29
1927	2	43
1929	1	35
1933	1	16
1934	2	10
1935	1	14
1936	3	15
1937	8	38
1938	1	12
	21	

[1] Only those cases in which dates were ascertained with reasonable certainty are included in tables v and vi, and the tables exclude all cases in which claims for compensation were disallowed, either because the land had been bought after notice of the creation of the Reserve, or for other reasons. The Commissioners were well aware of the distinction between the date of purchase of the land and the date of payment for it—the latter often being indeterminate, owing to payment in instalments.

[2] To eliminate the possibility that the impending creation of a Reserve brought about a rush to buy land, figures for the Worobong, Southern Scarp and Kwekaru Reserves are omitted—see the list below: in no other case is this consideration likely to have had any influence. The decline in the rate of purchase after 1928 is not to be explained by the creation of Reserves (and the consequent ban on purchase of land within them) as only two of the Reserves were created before 1933.

[3] Most, though not quite all, of the purchasing groups were companies.

[4] From *Cacao*, F.A.O., Bulletin no. 27, November 1955, table vi, p. 93. Although the reliability of the figures is somewhat suspect, and prices in many of the remote areas in question would have been much lower than these averages, the general trend indicated is probably reliable enough for our purposes.

List of Forest Reserves in which Alienations included in Tables V and VI were Situated, showing Dates of Alienations

Auro River. In Akim Kotoku, north of Akokoaso. Notice of creation of Reserve served 1934. Three cases: 1927, 1929, 1931.

Dede. In Akim Abuakwa, between Begoro and the Afram river. Notice of creation of Reserve served 1937. Sixteen cases—some dates approximate: 1925 (1), 1926 (2), 1927 (1), 1928 (4), 1929 (1), 1930 (3), 1931 (1), 1932 (1), 1936 (2).

Abisu. In Kwahu, due east of Asakraka. Notice of creation of Reserve served 1939. Three cases: 1925 and 1927 (2 cases).

Worobon. The Kwahu portion of the Reserve—there were no alienations in the Akim portion. Notice served 1928. One case, 1928, excluded from tables v and vi.

Atewa Range Extension. In Akim Abuakwa. Notice of creation of Reserve served 1938. Six cases: 1925, 1928 (2), 1935 (2), 1937.

APPENDIX II. 1

Southern Scarp. Kwahu portion. Created under by-laws 1927. Three cases: 1925, 1926 (2), excluded from tables v and vi.

Northern Scarp. Kwahu. Notice of creation of Reserve served 1934. One case: 1927.

Esen-Epam. In Akim Bosome and Akim Kotoku, between Akroso and Oda. Notice of creation of Reserve served 1936. Five cases: 1921, 1925, 1926, 1929 (2).

Kwekaru. In Akim Kotoku, south of Pra, north of Asuom. Notice of creation of Reserve served before 1931, when the Reserve Settlement Commissioner conducted his inquiry. Two cases, both 1928, excluded from tables v and vi.

Mamang. West of Abirem, mainly in Akim Kotoku, partly in Akim Abuakwa. Notice of creation of Reserve served 1933. Five cases: 1928 (2), 1929, 1932, 1933.

Birim Extension. Mainly, or entirely, in Akim Abuakwa. Two cases: 1925, 1927.

Pra-Birim. In the area of the confluence of the Pra and Birim rivers, Akim Abuakwa. Notice of creation of Reserve served 1939. Six cases: 1926 (2), 1927 (2), 1928 (2).

Asuokoko River. West of Ahamanso, Volta Region; partly in Buem, partly in Krakye. Notice of creation of Reserve served 1939. Twenty cases: 1925 (1), 1926 (1), 1927 (2), 1929 (1), 1933 (1), 1934 (2), 1935 (1), 1936 (3), 1937 (7), 1938 (1).

Chai River. North of Asuokoko Reserve. Notice of creation of Reserve served 1954. One case: 1937.

Neung. South of Tarkwa, Wasa Fiaso state. Notice of creation of Reserve served 1935. Two cases: 1928, 1929.

APPENDIX II. 2

THE KWESI KOMFO AREA

The Kwesi Komfo Area, which lies about five miles west of Suhum, is entirely road-less; it takes its name from an Akim village which can be seen on the northern boundary on map 3. With an area of some ten square miles, it is bounded by a number of streams, including the Mame, the Kua and the Saforosua; and other streams flow through the area. Much of the land to the west is very hilly (hence the long thin strips, crossing the contours and running from north to south, which originally belonged to individual Amanokrom and Larteh farmers) and the mountainous Atewa Range forest Reserve lies to the north-west. As the map shows, the Area boundary cuts across some of the company lands—including the large Mamfe/Saforosua company, to the north-east (see Appendix II. 8, p. 70).

Although the plan is based on an analysis of Ministry of Agriculture records relating to the present-day ownership of all the thousands of cocoa-farms within the Kwesi Komfo Area, the intention is to indicate the original pattern of land-ownership soon after the land was first disposed of by the chief of Apapam. Thus, subsequent sales have, as far as possible, been ignored, unless they occurred on a substantial scale in the early days. While there are some uncertainties (it is not clear, for instance, whether the individual Tutu farmers owning land in the middle of the area were associated with each other when the land was first acquired), the more important of which are indicated by the broken lines on the map, the map probably gives a fairly reliable impression of the situation in about 1920, by which time most of the company lands had been divided, even if the farmers had not all started planting cocoa.

The date at which land sales started in the locality cannot, unfortunately, be stated precisely. Only one date was ascertained with reasonable certainty, this being 1912, the year the Abonse (Kyerepon) company bought its land to the south-west of the area—this company is identical with the Kyerepon company near Nobeso, see

THE KWESI KOMFO AREA

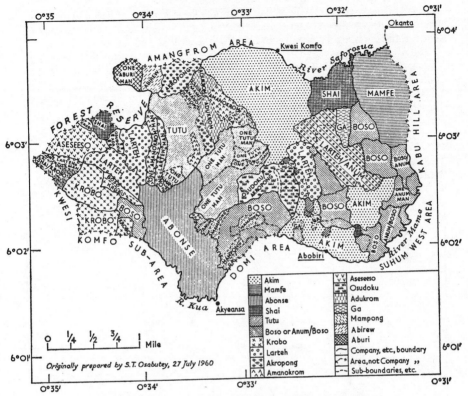

3 Holdings of cocoa-land in the Kwesi Komfo area.

Appendix II. 4 (p. 62). The first-comers, who may have been Mamfe or Anum/Boso farmers, are unlikely to have arrived much earlier. Many farmers report that their farms were in bearing by 1918 (at the time of the 'influenza'); most of the land sales presumably occurred before 1914.

Such was the extent of land sales in southern Akim Abuakwa that there are many Ministry of Agriculture Areas where there have never been any native Akim cocoa-farmers. This particular Area lies on the old route between Nsawam and Apapam (which is only six miles farther north) and this may be why many Apapam farmers established cocoa-farms there—though whether before or after the arrival of the strangers could not be ascertained. Their farms, which are mostly about one to three acres in area, can be recognized at a glance on the block plans, forming a mosaic such as is usually found only in the immediate neighbourhood of the older Akim towns. There are altogether hundreds of Apapam farms and they form two blocks, one of which is centred on the Akim village Kwesi Komfo, the other on Abobiri, to the south.

The great variety of stranger-farmers here is astonishing, there being perhaps no other locality where nearly all the principal migrant peoples are so well represented. (Aburi farmers are, however, ill represented—the Aburi family lands proper all lie considerably farther south.) The district lay near the limit of the western migration by foot and by 1910, or so, when the strangers first got there, all the principal migrant farmers of southern Ghana, including those who had been slow off the mark, were

61

APPENDIX II. 2

engaged in the scramble for land. An unusually large number of individual farmers from patrilineal societies was attracted there, some of whom, among them Mampong and Ga, having bought 'second-hand land' in the early days.

The Abonse company land has an area of 439 acres. The map shows that many company lands are much smaller than this and it follows that many of the farms owned by individual migrants are quite small—comparable in size with Akim farms. This is especially true of Anum, Boso and Osudoku farms, many of the farmers having been former cocoa-labourers who had little money available for land-purchase.

APPENDIX II. 3

COMPANY LANDS IN THE NANKESE AREA

Nearly all the land in this Ministry of Agriculture Area (which is one of several based on the town of Nankese) was sold to a small number of companies of strangers over a

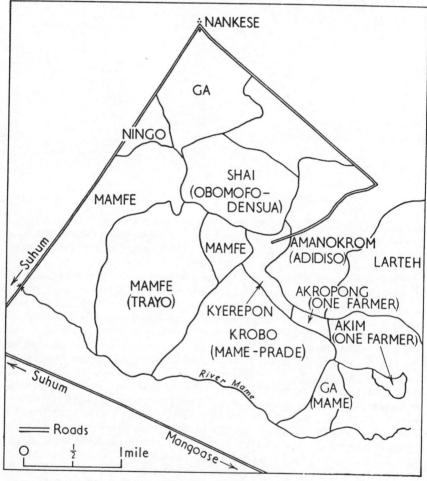

4 Company lands in the Nankese area.

THE KYEREPON COMPANY NEAR NOBESO

short period, in about 1906, by the chiefs of Asafo and Maase—see a reference to the boundary disputes between these chiefs on p. 140n. The simplicity of the resultant pattern of land-holding contrasts with that in the Kwesi Komfo Area (Appendix II. 2, p. 60) which is of comparable size. In the whole of this Area there is believed to be only one native Akim farm-owner—whose farm is shown on map 4.

The Area boundary cuts across company boundaries (except in the south, where both correspond with the river Mame), so that, for the sake of clarity, it has been omitted.

The Obomofo-Densua and Mamfe/Trayo companies (see Appendices II. 7, p. 69, and II. 5, p. 65) are in this Area. The large Mame/Prade company consists of Krobo from Somanya; there is a flourishing 'town' situated on this company land near its eastern boundary which, when it was visited in 1957, included a primary school with 4 teachers and 125 pupils. The curiously shaped Kyerepon land, north of the Mame/Prade land, seems to have been a residual area, left over from earlier sales.

The large Amanokrom land, which has an area of about 730 acres, was bought by 11 farmers, 9 from Amanokrom, 1 from Akropong and 1 from Larteh. Although the Amanokrom people are matrilineal the group was a company proper and the land was neatly divided into strips.

The Ga company land which lies to the south-west of Nankese (on which part of the town area now lies), was said to have been bought by 7 Ga farmers, 6 from Teshi and 1 from Nungua. Before buying this land some of the members had been growing maize at Danfa, south of Aburi, just beneath the ridge, where, it was said, they had bought their land *in company*.

The leader of the Ga/Mame company was said to have been a chief of Adenkrebi, in Akwapim, whence the Ga farmers had migrated for the purposes of growing food and the oil-palm. Of about 13 original members of the company, about 9 were Ga, the remainder coming from Berekuso (Akwapim), which lies about 2 miles from Adenkrebi. The area of this land is 165 acres. The land was not rectangular and as farming proceeded the farmers twice had occasion to remeasure some (or all) of their strips in accordance with the procedure described in Appendix II. 6 (p. 67).

APPENDIX II. 4

THE KYEREPON COMPANY NEAR NOBESO

Location and area. This company land lies about nine miles west of Suhum in the Kwesi Komfo Area—see Appendix II. 2 (p. 60). It extends between two streams, the Kua and Kuawa, which unite at its southern tip. The area of the land, as surveyed today, is about 439 acres.

Date of acquisition and cost. The land was bought, for about £500, from the chief of Apapam in 1912; it was divided in about 1913. Some of the farmers delayed planting until after the war.

The company members. The company leader was Yaw Ofori, who later became the chief of Abonse (Akwapim). The number of original company members was about 19, of whom perhaps 12 came from Abonse, 5 from the neighbouring (and closely connected) Aseseeso and 1 each from two other Kyerepon towns, Abiriw and Awukugua. A few of the members were relatives (mainly brothers), most of them were friends; many of them had been members of an earlier company, also headed by Yaw Ofori, which had acquired land at Amanase, south of Suhum, in about 1905.

The original division of the land. The company secretary, who was also a company

APPENDIX II. 4

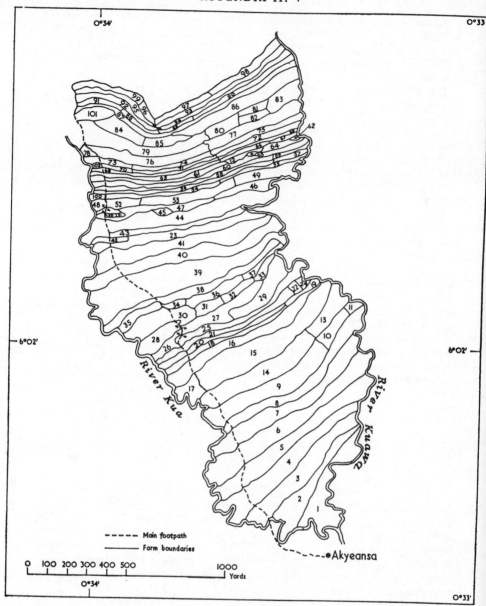

5   The Kyerepon company land near Nobeso.

member, now lives in Abonse—being a 'scholar' he assisted his fellow-farmers with the record-keeping. He has a list showing the number of ropes of land, at £5 a rope, which each member is supposed to have bought; the total, according to this list, is about 100 ropes, which, at 12 fathoms a rope, is roughly the length of the main path, to the west of the land, from which farming started. Yaw Ofori, the leader, acquired the

THE KYEREPON COMPANY NEAR NOBESO

largest portion of land, an area of 106 acres which now consists of farms 1 to 8. His brother acquired the next largest portion, now farms 39 and 40, of about 40 acres. Including the leader and his brother, 11 original members acquired areas of over 15 acres.

The subsequent division of the land. Eighty-six people are recorded as farm-owners today, 33 of them being women. Some of these farmers, especially those owning small acreages, may be 'notional farmers'—i.e. relatives in whose names the true owners have, for one reason or another, chosen to register part of their land—and this may be why as many as 37 farmers appear to own no more than $2\frac{1}{2}$ acres. A superficial glance at the map of this company land might suggest that it was a Krobo or Shai company; but the extent to which strips have been divided transversely shows that this is un-likely for (unless land is resold to outsiders and Krobo and Shai farmers seldom do this on any scale) these farmers always divide their strips longitudinally. Here there were few sales to outsiders and the extent of transverse division is associated with the fact that many relatives, other than sons, have inherited, or have been given portions. Nor has there been much longitudinal division of strips, such as results from division between sons, for in only 4 cases has more than one son inherited. Farms 16 and 60 have passed from the original farmer to a son without division and farm 44 has passed intact to a grandson. Farms 40 and 39 belong, respectively, to an original farmer and his son. Some fathers give farms to their sons during their lifetimes, some do not; Yaw Ofori is said to have retained the whole of his area until his death, when it was divided into 8 strips (farms 1 to 8), 4 going to sons, 1 to a daughter, 1 to a paternal grandson, 1 to a paternal great-grandson and 1 to a son of his brother's daughter. As much as two-fifths of the whole area (43 per cent) is today owned by 12 farmers with farms of 10 acres or more; 1 of these farmers is an original, while 8 are sons, 2 are daughters and 1 is a grandson of an original.

APPENDIX II. 5

THE MAMFE/TRAYO COMPANY

Location and area. The land is situated south of Nankese (see map 4), its southern boundary being the river Mame. It is said that Trayo was the name of an Akim hunter who was resident in the area when Mamfe cocoa-farmers first arrived there. The area of the land is about 990 acres.

Date of acquisition and cost. Papers dated 1907 and 1911 record the receipt, by the Chief of Asafo, of two sums of £350 in payment for this land; the actual date of pur-chase was probably a year or two before 1907. Many of the farmers waited a very long time before they started farming on any scale: it is said that the purchaser of share IV, for instance, never farmed his land and that it was not until about 1930 that his relatives went there.

The company members. The 8 company members were all from Mamfe (Akwapim); 2 of them, one being the leader, were brothers, the remainder were said to have been friends. Two of the members, or their successors, sold all their land; in one case the property was first mortgaged, in 1919, to a firm of merchant-produce shippers with a London address, who presumably foreclosed as much of it was subsequently bought at an auction by a very wealthy Akropong farmer-creditor, the owner of many other cocoa-lands.

The sequence of migration. At the time of the purchase of this land the leader (the purchaser of share VI) is said to have been a cocoa-farmer at Abrodiem, west of Pakro, and he did not start planting at Trayo until after the war; although when the swollen shoot became serious, at the end of the nineteen-thirties, he had still not completed

APPENDIX II. 5

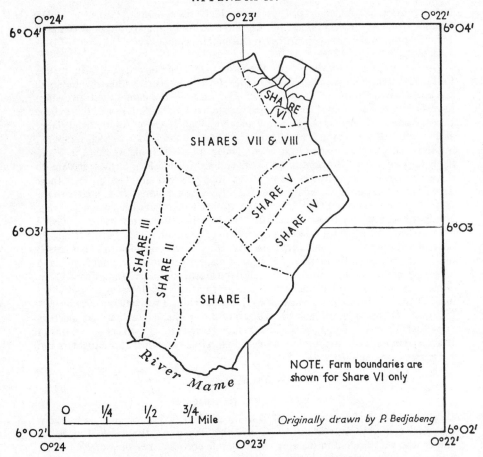

6 The Mamfe/Trayo company land, near Nankese.

planting his area, he (or his sons) had by then acquired three further lands, only one of which is said ever to have been planted. The owner of share I had first grown cocoa near Adawso; he started farming at Trayo about 1917; he subsequently acquired a large land in the Adakwa area (north-east of Suhum), reselling much of it to other farmers, and he also bought land in three other districts. The owner of share II is said to have come to Trayo direct from Mamfe. The owner of share III had been, like the leader, at Abrodiem. The owner of share IV had been a cocoa-farmer at Asuoya. A document records that the owner of share VIII had planted 19 acres by the time the property was mortgaged in 1919.

The original division of the land. Map 6 shows the original division of the land into 7 not 8 portions, for it proved impossible to distinguish shares VII and VIII, each of which was entirely sold. Farm boundaries are shown for share VI only. All the original members are now dead and no one now knows why the land was not divided into strips running from a base-line. Although informants insisted that the shares had been measured, the actual acreages, as surveyed today, bear no relationship to the number of ropes each original member is said to have bought—memories, presum-

THE MAMFE/TRAYO COMPANY

ably, being at fault. Shares I to VI have areas of 274, 115, 67, 127, 66 and 79 acres respectively, and shares VII and VIII together make up 261 acres.

The subsequent division of the land. All the original farmers, except the owners of shares III and VI, resold some or all of their land, the total resold being 442 acres; some of the purchasers were individuals (mainly not Mamfe people), some sub-companies. On the deaths of the original farmers most of their property passed to their sons, though with shares II and IV the 'mother's side', represented by the deceased farmers' sisters (or their descendants), also benefited—see p. 134. The leader's share (share VI) passed to a son. Practically the whole of share I passed to a son—an absentee farmer, a teacher, Share II was divided among the original farmer's sister (who got about a half) and his son and daughter (each with about a quarter). Share III was divided between 4 sons. Share IV, which had lain unplanted until about 1930, was ultimately divided into strips between 4 sons, 2 daughters and 3 descendants of the original farmer's sisters, 2 of whom are women. Share V was first divided between 2 sons and later passed to their sons.

APPENDIX II. 6

THE SHAI/NANKESE COMPANY

Location and area. This company land, which has an area of about 596 acres, lies astride the road from Nankese to Akwadum; the town of Nankese has now spread over part of the land.

Date of acquisition and cost. The land was bought from the chief of Asafo, in about 1906, for about £700.

The company members. The original company membership numbered about 34, of whom 28 were Shai (both friends and relatives); the remainder were from Ada (4 members) and from Prampram and Ningo (1 each). The leader of the company was Shai and was succeeded by his son, the present owner of farm 1.

The original division of the land. The base-line of the land, from which farming started, was the long northern boundary, which followed the Asuboni stream for part of its length; this was the line along which the strips, in ropes of about 12 fathoms, were measured originally, and it has a total length of about 120 ropes. The individual farmers were allocated strips varying in width from 1 to 8 ropes, the price being about £5 12s. a rope. [A group of original farmers was questioned as to the number of ropes bought by each original member; the relationship between their figures and present-day farm acreages was, in most cases, so close as to suggest that the farmers' memories were unusually reliable.] As only about four of the original farms have been longitudinally divided, the original layout can be clearly seen on map 7. The explanation of the transverse 'split' and the 'shifting' of the strips as indicated by the arrows (which means that many farmers have to cross other strips in order to reach the continuations of their own) lay in the need to remeasure the strips consequent upon the tapering of the land. The farmers remeasured all the strips along the new base-line (the transverse split), using a shorter rope than the original one—a rope which should have borne the same ratio to 12 fathoms as the length of the transverse split did to the original base-line.

The subsequent division of the land. The map and other records relate to a date, over ten years ago, when the Ministry of Agriculture first started to treat this area for swollen shoot, and at that time perhaps 20 of the original 34 farmers were still alive. Of the remainder, 2 had sold all their land, 6 had been inherited by a single son, 1 by a daughter, 4 by 2 or more sons and 1 by a son and a grandson. In each of the 5 latter cases (in which more than one farmer had inherited) the strips had been divided

APPENDIX II. 6

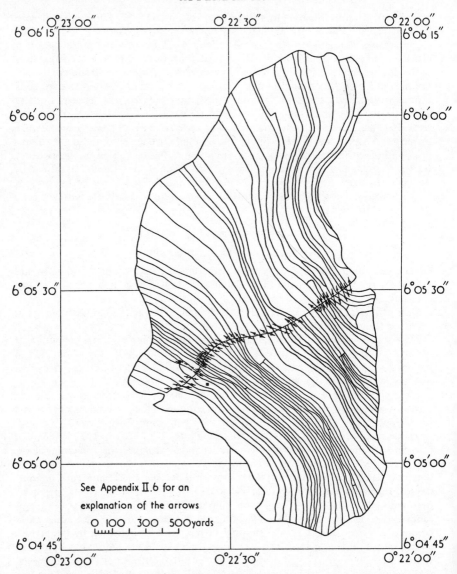

7   The Shai/Nankese company land, showing farm boundaries.

longitudinally—thus the three strips north of the most southerly strip are owned by three brothers whose father's strip had been divided among them. Such transverse division as can be seen on the map was always the consequence of sales of land to outsiders—there are 18 outside farmers and they own about 60 acres. The total number of original farmers plus inheritors of original farmers who are recorded as owners of farms shown on the map is 41—only 9 more than the corresponding number of original members, if the 2 members who sold all their land are omitted. The 20 sur-

THE SHAI COMPANY AT OBOMOFO-DENSUA

viving original farmers are recorded as owning 279 acres, sons and daughters (of whom there are only 2) 220 acres and other relatives 37 acres.

APPENDIX II. 7

THE SHAI COMPANY AT OBOMOFO-DENSUA

Location and area. This company land, which approximates to the ideal 'matchbox' shape (see map 8, inbetween pages 71/72), lies about three miles south of Nankese. Its area is about 560 acres.

Date of acquisition and cost. The land was bought from the chief of Asafo about 1906. The price was perhaps about £600.

The company members. Present-day farmers (none of whom are original farmers) say that the original membership of about a dozen Shai farmers consisted of 3 sub-groups, the first consisting of the leader alone, the second of about 5 or 6 friends from Kodiabe (near Ayikuma) and the third of about 4 brothers. The acreages acquired by the three sub-groups were, respectively, 174, 162 and 223. Three, or possibly four, of the original members (or their inheritors) sold land to outsiders, the total so disposed of being 105 acres.

The original division of the land. The strip-farms were measured along the eastern boundary which was the base-line. The main path on which most of the villages, or cottages, are situated lies to the west of the base-line. The leader of the company was allotted the area now consisting of farms 65 to 78; the second sub-group's area was farms 43 to 64; the third group acquired the remainder.

The subsequent division of the land. The company leader retained farm 78 (84 acres) for himself and although at the time inquiries were made he had been dead for over fifteen years his farm had still not been divided among his children—all the cocoa had, of course, died of swollen shoot and there had been little replanting. During his lifetime the leader gave away farm 71 to the sole child of his senior wife and an approximately equal area, consisting of farms 72 to 75, to the 3 children of his junior wife—who received respectively $8 \cdot 8$, $8 \cdot 2$ and $17 \cdot 8$ acres. Farms 72 and 73 are now owned by a grandson and granddaughter of the original farmer, their father having died. Farm 74 is owned by a woman; she explained that it would be her brothers' sons, not her own sons, who would inherit this farm on her death. The remainder of the area acquired by the leader was sold to Kyerepon and Ningo farmers. There are 15 inheritors of the members of the second sub-group, these being 10 sons, 3 daughters, 1 step-son and 1 grandson. Not all the original farms have been longitudinally subdivided—farms 43, 44 and 55, for instance, have their original boundaries. The strip made up of farms 55 and 64 was bought by a man with 6 sons; one of the sons went away and the father gave a strip each to the remaining sons, keeping none for himself; later on the absent son returned and was given farm 59 by three of his brothers. The 12 inheritors of the four or more brothers who composed the third sub-group are 3 sons, 7 daughters and 2 grandsons. A total of 80 acres (out of 223 acres) was sold by members of this group to outsiders; thus the owner of the most northerly strip sold all his land, except farm 14 which is now owned by his daughter. Longitudinal division of a strip is nearly always associated with inheritance, but the strip that originally consisted of farms 25 to 32 was longitudinally subdivided so that it might be resold, farms 26 and 28 being retained and now being owned by a son and a daughter of the original farmer. According to the Ministry of Agriculture records, the total number of farm-owners today is about 61, of whom 32 are inheritors of original farmers; as many as 11 of these inheritors are daughters of original farmers (and one is a granddaughter) but

APPENDIX II. 7

it is probable that some of them are acting for their brothers and are not the real owners; 14 of the inheritors are sons. Four of the 32 inheritors own farms of 20 acres or more; 9 between 10 and 20 acres; 14 between 5 and 10 acres; 4 between 1 and 5 acres; and only 1 under 1 acre. The measurement of the farms appears to have been remarkably accurate and acreages, as surveyed by the Ministry of Agriculture, accord well with the farmers' statements of 'area' in terms of ropes. The farmers appear to stop short at dividing '1-rope farms', a rope being 12 fathoms.

APPENDIX II. 8

THE MAMFE/SAFOROSUA COMPANY

Location and area. The Saforosua stream, which provides the northern boundary of this company land (see map 9), is a small tributary of the Densu. The land lies about two miles south of Kibi-Odumase and is partly in the Kwesi Komfo Area (Appendix II. 2) and partly in the adjoining Kabu Hill Area. Its area, including portions sold to outsiders, is about 759 acres.

Date of acquisition and cost. The land was bought from the chief of Apapam, presumably a few years before 1914—the precise date could not be ascertained. Present-day informants had no idea of its price.

The company members. Six farmers, 5 from Mamfe (Akwapim) and 1 from Akropong, were associated in the purchase of the land which was 'bought especially for the children'. The leader (who is said to have died in 1952, aged eighty-two) was associated with his full brother, his wife's brother (from Akropong), his mother's brother and two distant paternal relatives; the leader acquired the most easterly strip, strip I, the other farmers strips II to VI in that order. Probably only 1 of the 5 Mamfe farmers retained any substantial portion of land for his own use, the others giving nearly all their land away, mainly to their sons; the Akropong farmer retained about 40 acres. Four of the original farmers resold substantial acreages to outsiders; to simplify the map the boundaries of the many farms owned by these outsiders have been omitted.

The original division of the land. The base-line for measurement was the Saforosua stream. A son of the purchaser of strip VI purported to recollect the number of ropes (of 24 *abasam*) which each original member had bought. Although the correspondence between these figures and acreages as surveyed today was found to be poor, the informant's figures were not necessarily incorrect as the plan shows that the eastern boundary of the land is much longer than the western boundary so that a close relationship between strip-width and area was not to be expected. This informant was unusual in being able to volunteer figures for the lengths of the east and west boundaries; these were of the right order of magnitude, though they understated the discrepancy. The acreages of each of the strips I to VI as surveyed today are: 224, 166, 152, 42, 33 and 142.

The subsequent division of the land. The company leader gave most of strip I (other than the portions he resold) to 2 of his sons who now own farms 57 + 64 and 63 + 61, respectively 59 and 98 acres. (Farm 61 happens to be registered in the name of the son of the owner of farm 63.) The leader's brother, who is said to have died in 1959, retained the area of farm 55 for his own use, giving away most of the remainder of strip II to 4 sons. The Akropong farmer retained 44 acres from strip III, giving away 15 acres to a son and 18 acres to a daughter; his inheritor is his nephew, who is also the leader's son and is the owner of 98 acres in strip I. The owner of strip IV gave most of his land away to 2 sons and 1 daughter and the owner of strip V gave most of his land to 4 sons. Strip VI was divided longitudinally, as the map shows, the owners of farms 3

70

THE MAMFE/SAFOROSUA COMPANY

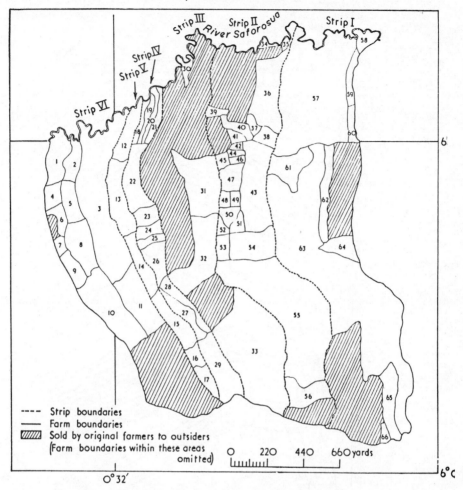

9   The Mamfe/Saforosua company land.

and 11 being the children of one of the original farmer's wives, those of farms 8, 9, 10, etc. the children of another wife; this original farmer retained no land for himself. Of the total company area (net of sales to outsiders) of 561 acres, 385 acres are at present owned by 17 sons of original farmers; 51 acres are owned by 7 daughters of original farmers; 52 acres have not yet been divided between sons following the deaths of original owners; 44 acres are owned by the maternal nephew who inherited the Akropong farmer; and 29 acres are owned by 9 other relatives.

Other points. Of the 17 sons of original farmers who own land here, none is resident in a newer cocoa-farming area; 10 of them live on the land, 1 in nearby Odumase, 1 in Suhum and 1 (only) in Mamfe. The owner of farm 3 said that he would take over farm 11 from his sister on her death and that, the property not being self-acquired, his younger brother, not his son, would be the next inheritor; he said that practice varied —'some people allow farms to be registered in the names of grandsons, some do not'.

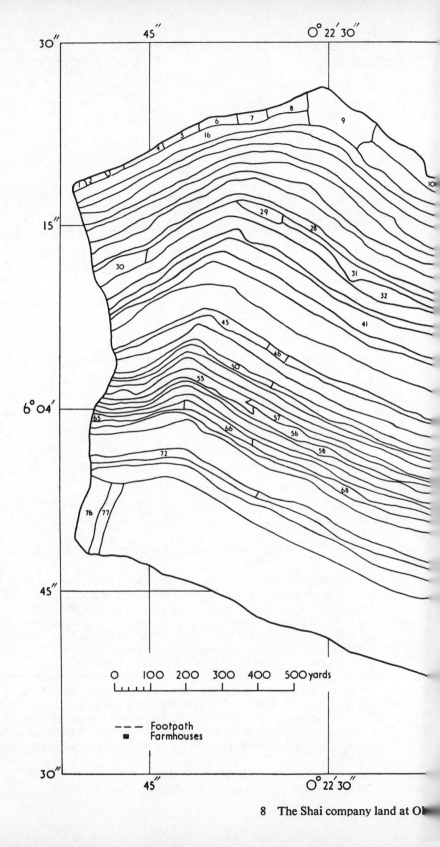

8 The Shai company land at Ob

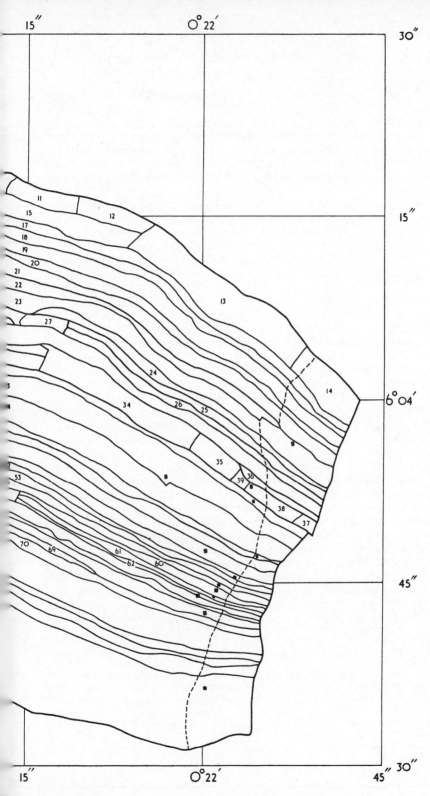

a, showing farm boundaries.

APPENDIX II. 9

THE 'HUZA' SYSTEM

The Akwapim cocoa-company system which developed soon after 1900 was modelled on the Krobo—or *huza*—system of group land-purchase which had come into existence some half a century earlier, and is probably unique in Africa. The outlines of this Krobo system have for long been familiar[1] and the main concern here is with regarding it as a prototype. Nor is it proposed to dwell on the remarkable energy and creativeness of the Krobo, a people who remain as deeply dedicated as ever to the agricultural way of life and who have greatly impressed all those who have had occasion to study them.

The Akwapim company system is regarded in this book as a modification, rather than a copy, of the *huza* system for two main reasons. The Akwapim company may be regarded as a group, or club, formed for the purpose of achieving a limited purpose—namely the purchase of land; once this purpose has been achieved the club lapses (ceases to exist), although the members and their successors, who are on the land together, do not of course disperse. The Krobo *huza*, on the other hand, is a group with social functions which continue indefinitely—it is a form of political organization, an organism. Each *huza* has its *huzatse* (or 'father'), as well as other officials, but with Akwapim companies, as has been emphasized, the office of leader lapses once the limited purpose for which the group was formed has been achieved.

The other important distinction between the two systems is that the Krobo had territorial ambitions, while the Akwapim had not—this is true despite the Akwapim/ Akim Abuakwa dispute over jurisdiction, which is the subject of Appendix v. 3 (p. 154). The Krobo system was centrally organized (managed and controlled) by the paramount chiefs themselves, but the Akwapim company system was based entirely on individual initiative, there being no co-ordination whatsoever of the activities of different companies. The two Krobo states, Yilo and Manya Krobo, knew well what they were doing—they knew that their *huza* were marching like armies over the mountain country, buying *all* the land;[2] the Akwapim company farmers, on the other hand, competed with each other in buying land from the Akim and there was no one even in a position to describe their general progress—let alone to influence or control them.

It was a commercial crop, the oil-palm,[3] which provided the Krobo with much of their incentive to move into the uninhabited forest land, mainly owned by the Akim, but also by the Akwapim, which lay north of their homeland on the plain between Akwapim and the Volta river; and their expulsion from the Krobo mountain in 1892, by the Gold Coast government, hastened their search for good agricultural land. Although Krobo-Odumase was the seat of early cocoa-growing experiments, it is

[1] Apart from Dr M. J. Field's article, which is referred to below, there are various sources of information on the *huza* system, the most important of which are unpublished: the latter include *Award in the Akim Abuakwa/Manya Krobo Boundary Dispute*, by the arbitrator, H. S. Newlands (1922), and *Aweso: A Manya Krobo Huza*, by S. La Anyane, Ghana Ministry of Agriculture, based on research undertaken in 1956. See also Nene Azu Mate Kole, 'The Historical Background of Krobo Customs', *Transactions of the Gold Coast and Togoland Historical Society*, vol. I, part IV (1955), and 'Afrikanische Waldhufen- und Waldstreifenfluren', by Walther Manshard, in *Die Erde*, Berlin, Heft 4, 1961.

[2] So that land acquisition was both orderly and, as some have put it, 'progressive'; as, in addition, many of the tracts that were acquired were very large, the pattern of land-holding in Krobo country is simplicity itself compared with that in the historic cocoa-growing area of southern Akim Abuakwa.

[3] The Krobo are always supposed to have been much the most important producers of palm produce for export in the pre-cocoa days, but statistics of area production are lacking.

THE 'HUZA' SYSTEM

probable that it was the Akwapim example which was mainly responsible for impressing the Krobo with the possibilities of the new commercial crop. This had two results: firstly that many of the existing *huza* in Krobo country proper were partially and gradually turned over to cocoa-growing and secondly that the Krobo farmers, in particular the Yilo Krobo, started imitating the Akwapim directly by buying land in Akim Abuakwa on 'island sites' (i.e. not contiguous tracts as in Krobo country) for the express purpose of cocoa-growing, some of it situated in areas, for instance within the arc of the river Densu, where it was clear that no territorial ambitions were involved. It is for the scientists to say whether it was as a result of the 'over-clearing' of the forest that the Krobo area between Koforidua and the river Volta, which once seemed so promising for cocoa-growing, has now largely reverted to food-growing and oil-palm cultivation—so that most of the cocoa-farms owned by Krobo farmers are now situated outside Krobo country.[1]

By 1861, or thereabouts, the Krobo were purchasing land on both sides of the Pawmpawm river, perhaps up to about fifteen miles from home, from the chiefs of Begoro and Tafo and also from the Apirede (Akwapim) people. The purchasing group was always the *huza* (the word applies both to the group and to the tract they purchase) and it is to be presumed that the land-selling chiefs, who always welcomed the strangers, made no attempt at fixing the boundaries of the tracts that they sold but simply permitted the farmers to align themselves on a suitable natural boundary, usually a stream, from which they farmed forward, thus creating strip-farms. In 1882 the Begoro and Jakiti people, whose claims to sell land to the Krobo conflicted, submitted their differences to the arbitration of Konor Sakite, Paramount Chief of Manya Krobo; following this arbitration the Gold Coast government in 1893 proclaimed that the lands from the Pawmpawm stream to Bisa were the property of the Krobo, who had thus extended their lands some twenty-four miles north of their homeland in the plain. Their progress continued and by 1922, when H. S. Newlands was appointed as arbitrator to settle a dispute between the Akim Abuakwa and Manya Krobo stools, nearly three hundred square miles of land had been purchased by the Manya Krobo *huza* alone.

A description of the *huza* system was provided by Dr M. J. Field,[2] who surveyed and studied a large *huza* land in Krobo country and discussed the migratory process. Dr Field laid much emphasis on the fact that 'no farmer is content with land on one *huza* alone'—that 'the typical farmer has responsibilities on two, three or even four separate *huzas*'. She noted the incredible thriftiness of the Krobo farmers—'who regard land as virtually the only thing on which money ought to be spent'. She pointed out that although the Krobo farmer is passionately attached to his purchased land, yet his village, or farmstead, is his mere working-place, his town on the plain being 'home'.

Dr Field described the parcelling of land among *huza* members, each of whom bought the number of 'ropes' of land he could afford—all of this being in accordance with the description given in chapter II of the procedure adopted by the Akwapim companies. She also described the practice of building all the farmhouses on the land in 'ribbon' fashion along a main path, which ran close and parallel to the base-line. This main path has remained, to this day, characteristic of Krobo (and Shai) farmers, its existence reflecting the social cohesion of the group. Akwapim farmers, by con-

---

[1] The northern boundary between Manya Krobo and Akim Abuakwa has remained indeterminate to this day.

[2] M. J. Field, 'The Agricultural System of the Manya-Krobo of the Gold Coast, *Africa*, April 1943.

APPENDIX II. 9

trast, are individualists, each man building his 'village' at the point on his portion of the company land which seems most convenient, without regard to his neighbours' intentions.

Dr Field describes the *huza* group as composed of people who were 'often, but not necessarily, kinsmen' and it seems certain that social factors have always been apt to have more influence on the composition of the group than with Akwapim companies, which are typically (though not invariably) groups of friends. Nene Mate Kole, Paramount Chief of Manya Krobo, told the present writer in March 1959 that while most members of a *huza* usually (though not necessarily) belong to the same clan, the clans to which the farmers' wives belong might also be represented. He said that when the members of the *huza* had been farming for some time, they started contributing towards the purchase of land on another *huza*—though groups seldom reproduce themselves exactly.

As noted in chapter II, the lands owned by Krobo (as well as Shai) farmers are characterized by very neatly drawn strips. In comparison with the groping amateur approach of the Akwapim, the Krobo seem like 'professional surveyors'—by the admission of the Akwapim themselves who, nowadays, increasingly resort to the employment of paid surveyors. This meticulous drawing of the strips (this aptitude for accurate measurement) presumably partly reflects the fact that the Krobo attach even more importance to land, *as such*, than the Akwapim. The Akwapim are far more commercial in their attitude than the Krobo—far more given to reselling land among themselves. While both Krobo and Akwapim farmers developed the practice of *automatically* investing a large part of the proceeds from one land in the purchase of another, certain Akwapim were also interested in investing funds in cocoa-buying and transport businesses. The Krobo are so concerned with fair division of land among themselves (and between sons on the death of their father) that this sometimes leads to absurd results—as with a large Krobo company near Asikasu (in Akim country) where many of the strip-farms are even too narrow to be plantable. The Krobo farmers are evidently 'instinctive geometers': Nene Mate Kole said that they had, for long, been familiar with the practice, see p. 45, of remeasuring strips with a shorter or longer 'rope' when, as farming proceeded, it was found that the land tapered or broadened.

So old and remarkable is the *huza* system, so striking are the Krobo strips on maps and air photographs—see Manshard, *op. cit.*, that the widespread belief that strip-farms are *necessarily* associated with the Krobo is not hard to understand. In 1913 the Secretary for Native Affairs, F. G. Crowther, spoke[1] of 'a very rich cocoa district between Begoro and the Volta river' where the Krobo had acquired a great deal of land. 'The tribes purchase the land in what they call strings, that is, so many measures of rope, in large squares from the village communities of Begoro, Tafo or Kukurantumi. The people who have taken the land have planted it with cocoa...' It is as true today as it was in 1913 that 'the Krobos do not live in large villages. Every quarter- or half-mile you will meet a single family consisting of a man, wife or wives and children, living on a farm.'[2] There are still few towns of any size in the mountain country and even Asesewa, one of the largest and most renowned of all the rural food markets in Ghana, is best regarded as a market rather than a residential town.

[1] West African Lands Committee, *Minutes of Evidence*, p. 354.   [2] *Ibid.* p. 355.

CHAPTER III

THE FAMILY LAND

In the last chapter it was emphasized that a company of cocoa-farmers is essentially a group of non-kinsmen associated together for the sole and commercial purpose of buying land for cocoa-growing from a vendor chief. Because, in their dealings with one another, the company members are untrammelled by considerations of kin, they attach great importance to the fair division of land, in accordance with the sum subscribed by each farmer. This division is effected by means of drawing strips from a base-line, the whole land being shared between the members before farming starts. Not only is the original division into strips, but if subsequent division between sons of the original farmer is necessary, further longitudinal subdivision is always entailed. It is very unusual for portions of strip-farms to be made available during the lifetime of the original farmer to kinsfolk other than sons, and although the individual property acquired by the original farmer should always be considered as in process of conversion to lineage property, the relevant lineage (or segment) stems from the original farmer himself,[1] not from his forebears.

The company system, in its application to cocoa-farming, came into existence shortly after 1900, in connection with the migration across the river Densu, and it is an observed fact that the farmers who adopted it belonged to patrilineal societies.[2] Certain matrilineal Akwapim migrants, the farmers from Aburi and associated towns[3] and those from Akropong, organized their trans-Densu land-purchase quite differently, adopting what is termed in this book the 'family land'[4] system. The family group which buys the family land is nearly always readily distinguishable, in practice, from the company, though not necessarily linguistically.[5] Such groups are small, are usually dominated (both in the short and in the long runs) by leaders or heads and consist, as will be seen, of relatives and affines only—if the land is small the leader may have no associates. As

[1] Where this is apparently not so, the usual explanation is that it was the father who put up the money to buy the land.   [2] See Appendix vii. 2 (p. 199).

[3] In this and the following chapter the place-name 'Aburi' in general includes the associated towns Nsakye and Ahwerease—see Appendix i. 4.

[4] As there is no mention whatever of 'family lands' in the literature, it has been necessary to decide which of several possible terms to adopt. The farmers themselves employ the term 'family land' in many connections and there are clearly objections to defining it here in this special sense; but the same objections apply to the alternative terms 'lineage land' and 'abusua land', which have been rejected as too linguistically cumbersome. To avoid confusion, the general class of property usually called 'family land' by lawyers and others is as far as possible denoted as 'lineage land'. See chapter iv.

[5] Akropong farmers, in particular, are apt to apply the English word 'company' to closely-knit family groups, such as Boah—Appendix iii. 8 (p. 100).

75

THE FAMILY LAND

with the company lands, the boundaries of the family land as a whole are determined at the time of purchase from the vendor chief. Each member of the family group farms independently on his own portion (or portions) of the family land. In the earliest days individual rights, within the land, were established by the traditional method of clearing and planting, no measurement, allocation or formal division being involved. Later on, as the farm maps suggest, many of the farmers either divided the whole, or part, of their land in advance of farming or farmed forward from roughly measured base-lines. Although rudimentary strips are often apparent on the maps, it does not follow that any attempt was made to relate the area of the strip to the sum contributed by the farmer. These roughly drawn strips do not resemble the strips of the company farmers for, as will be seen, a mosaic pattern of farm-ownership soon develops within them and further longitudinal sub-division never occurs.

As the years go by, company and family lands become increasingly easy to distinguish on the maps. In accordance with the customary rules of inheritance of the patrilineal farmers,[1] strip-farms are apt to be divided longitudinally between sons and the narrower the strips the more striking they are on the maps. With the (Akan) matrilineal inheritance system, on the other hand, there is a single successor, and no division of farms follows death. As time goes by a mosaic, or cellular, pattern[2] of farm-ownership, or occupation, develops within the family lands as a consequence of the willingness of original farmers to allot portions of land (most of which are small) to members of their *abusua* and others. As will become apparent in chapter IV[3] the family land system plays the part of a social security

---

[1] See chapter IV.

[2] There is a superficial resemblance between this mosaic pattern (see e.g. the map of Akotuakrom, Appendix III. 3, p. 91) and the pattern of land-holding around towns such as Akokoaso or Asafo, where all the farmers are native Akim, although there is always at least one farm on each family land which is much larger than the general run of farms. For this reason and also because most native, as distinct from migrant, cocoa-farmers are matrilineal (Ashanti, Akim, Fanti, etc.), it might be thought that the family land was *the* typical form of organization, although actually there is no evidence of its adoption except by matrilineal Akwapim migrants. The pattern of farm-holding of the native farmers of Akokoaso, etc. was established at a time when land was plentiful, each citizen acquiring, in the course of time, some three to six separate small plots which were usually somewhat dispersed, as farming spread outward from the town where all the farmers lived. Although in *Akokoaso* Beckett states (*op. cit.*, p. 56) that there is 'a natural tendency for families of the same clan to become neighbouring farmers' and that the 'farms of one clan tend to be grouped in particular localities', at the same time (p. 57), 'it is the exception rather than the rule to find a farmer with all his farms in the same locality'; a diagram at the end of the book shows that representatives of several clans are to be found in most parts of the Akokoaso farming area, so that in that locality the concept of a clan farming area is of very limited application.

[3] Although the distinction between individual and lineage property is apt to become blurred, even during the lifetime of original farmers, it has, nonetheless, been found convenient to consider the 'evolution' of family groups (occupying family lands) as an aspect of the operation of the customary rules of inheritance—see chapter IV. This chapter, therefore, resembles chapter II in being static and descriptive, but there is much unavoidable overlapping with the subject matter of chapter IV.

THE FAMILY LAND

system, according rights over small portions of land to members of the *abusua* who require them—and hence the mosaic pattern.

In the early eighteen-nineties, when the Akwapim cocoa- (and coffee-) migration began, most of the migratory groups, whether composed of matrilineal or of patrilineal peoples, consisted of small sets of relatives, such as brothers, brothers and paternal cousins, a father and his sons, an uncle and his maternal nephews. At that time most of the lands were relatively small, many of them being situated in a strip of land east of the river Densu, between Adawso and Koforidua, where a land shortage soon developed. When it became apparent that further expansion westward over the river Densu was an urgent necessity, the Aburi people found their natural gateway at Nsawam (which is an Aburi town) wide open—and for some reason, which is as yet unclear, most of the largest and oldest tracts of land acquired by the matrilineal Akropong also lie in the extreme south.[1] The chief of Apapam, and to some extent also the chief of Asamankese, was only too willing to sell large areas in the extreme south at prices which seemed relatively low, even at that time, so that there was no necessity for the Aburi farmers to combine together with their friends, on a commercial basis, to raise the cash required, even had they been so inclined. But in the area farther north, around Nankese for example,[2] where for geographical reasons the Larteh, Mamfe, etc. farmers sought to buy land, the land-sellers, the chiefs of Asafo, Maase and other towns, owned far less land and would, perhaps, have expected higher prices than the chief of Apapam, even had the demand for land not been enhanced by the ability of the Larteh, Mamfe, etc. farmers to organize themselves in land-purchasing companies. While cause and effect are hard to disentangle, it is thus possible that geographical as well as sociological considerations are relevant to the question of why the Aburi people did not form or join companies but continued on the old lines—thus creating, as it were by accident, a new form of organization, the family land.

Fieldwork on the historic family lands[3] has been much hampered by lack of farm maps. Nearly all the Aburi family lands lie in the former Abandoned Area.[4] Fortunately, the Aburi (Nsakye) family land known as Akotuakrom was mapped in 1959 by Dr J. M. Hunter, of the University of Ghana—see Appendix III. 3 (p. 91);[5] this land was bought in about 1905, earlier than any of the other lands for which farm maps are avail-

---

[1] See chapter VIII. The Akropong were very short of land in Akwapim and felt hemmed in by their neighbours, the patrilineal Guan and Kyerepon. See map 16, at end.

[2] See chapter II, p. 50.

[3] Situated in the historic cocoa-growing area, see map 1. For family lands situated outside this area, there are no reliable farm maps.

[4] See Appendix I. 2 (p. 24).

[5] The present writer is very grateful to Dr Hunter for making his findings and maps available at this stage.

77

THE FAMILY LAND

able. Both Sakyikrom (Appendix III. 1, p. 86) and Ahwerease-Akim (Appendix III. 6, p. 97) are lands which were acquired last century and Appendices on them are included although it is realized that the quality of the information provided does not compare with that on the mapped lands.* The following table summarizes certain of the information given in the eleven Appendices to this chapter:

Family Lands[1]

	Name of land	Origin of farmers	Leader or nuclear group	Area (acres)	Area retained by leader etc.	Approx. date of purchase
	(1)	(2)	(3)	(4)	(5)	(6)
(i)	Sakyikrom	Nsakye & Aburi	Nana Sakyi	2	n.a.[3]	(1896)
(ii)	Land near Krabokese	Nsakye	4 brothers	4	n.a.	1909
(iii)	Akotuakrom	Nsakye	Sampson Akotua	357	n.a.	1905
(iv)	Kofi Pare	Aburi	Kofi Pare	1,152[5]	372	1912
(v)	Kwame Tawiah	Aburi	Kwame Tawiah	n.a.[6]	n.a.	1916
(vi)	Ahwerease-Akim	Ahwerease (Aburi)	Agyiri Kwasi	7	n.a.	1899
(vii)	Omenako	Akropong	Omenako	486	206	1907
(viii)	Boah	Akropong	4 matrilineal cousins (2 pairs of brothers)	163	113	1908
(ix)	Akropong/ Bepoase	Akropong	2 brothers & a matrilineal cousin	380	380	n.a.
(x)	Dome/ Amanokrom	Amanokrom	The leader	294	294	n.a.
(xi)	Dome/Aburi	Aburi	The leader	62	62	n.a.

[1] For further particulars see Appendices to chapter III. All these lands are situated in the historic cocoa-growing area of Akim Abuakwa.
[2] Over 3 miles long.   [3] = not available.
[4] Perhaps of the order of 400–500 acres.
[5] Exclusive of small unsurveyed portion, see map 11, p. 93.
[6] A private surveyor's plan exists covering 156 acres—but this is possibly not the whole area.
[7] About a mile long.

Notes on Table

Col. (1)   Most of these lands will be readily identifiable by those who know the localities in question, though the names are not, in all cases, those by which they are known to farmers. For reasons which will be obvious to readers of Appendix

* Brief particulars relating to two other unmapped Aburi lands are also included—the land near Krabokese (Appendix III. 2, p. 89) and Kwame Tawiah (Appendix III. 5, p. 96).

78

THE FAMILY LAND

III. 8 (p. 100), it has been thought desirable to conceal the identity of land (viii) under a false name.

Col. (3)   Further particulars are given in the summary list below.

Col. (4)   In comparing areas of family lands, it should be remembered that such lands are in no sense 'farms', but rather areas within which farming occurs. The areas shown are retained acreages after any resales to outsiders. Dr Hunter has estimated that between a half and three-quarters of the area of Akotuakrom may have been under cocoa before swollen shoot.

Col. (5)   The acreages shown are those originally allocated to, or appropriated by, the leader or nuclear group shown in col. (3). All the leaders and members of nuclear groups made land within their holdings available to others. As with col. (4), areas sold to outsiders are excluded. The figures are estimates.

Col. (6)   The dates of purchase of lands (i), (v) and (vii) are particularly uncertain: land (i) was possibly bought much earlier than 1896.

List of Original Members of each Family Group[1]

(i)   *Sakyikrom*

There is much difference of opinion in Sakyikrom as to who were the original associates of Nana Sakyi, but the list certainly included Afum Yaw (a classificatory maternal uncle of Nana Sakyi) and Moses Adjei (a son of a male member of the *abusua* to which Nana Sakyi belonged).

(ii)   *Land near Krabokese*

Four brothers of whom the eldest was the leader.

(iii)   *Akotuakrom*

Sampson Akotua and his younger brother Philip Afwireng.

(iv)   *Kofi Pare*

Kofi Pare probably had 6 associates who were: 3 members of the *abusua* (sons of 3 sisters of Kofi Pare's mother); 2 grandsons (one maternal the other paternal) of Kofi Pare's maternal grandfather; the husband of a woman member of the *abusua*.

(v)   *Kwame Tawiah*

Kwame Tawiah is said to have been accompanied by 2 brothers, 2 sisters (together with their 2 sons) and 2 sons of his mother's sister, but it is not known whether each of these people became a farmer in his own right; it was said that Kwame Tawiah's mother and a brother (who was too elderly to accompany him) each also subscribed for land.

(vi)   *Ahwerease-Akim*

The head of the group, Agyiri Kwasi, was said to have been accompanied by 8 maternal nephews—5 sons of one of his sisters and 3 of another, and also by one of his brothers who 'hived off' on to an adjoining piece of land, now considered 'separate'.

(vii)   *Omenako*

Omenako had at least 5 associates including: a maternal nephew, the husband of one of his sisters, the wife of one of his sons, one of his sons and a distant member of the *abusua* who was married to one of his sisters.

(viii)   *Boah*

The nucleus of the original group of 9 people consisted of 2 pairs of brothers whose mothers were sisters. The other 5 original members were: a son of a maternal cousin of the afore-mentioned cousins and two of his former slaves (who had been adopted

[1] For further particulars see Appendices to this chapter.

79

THE FAMILY LAND

by the *abusua*), a son of one of the afore-mentioned cousins and a member of the *abusua*—a son of a maternal grand-daughter of the eldest sister of the cousins' mothers.

(ix) *Akropong/Bepoase*
Two brothers and their mother's sister's son.

(x) *Dome/Amanokrom*
The leader alone.

(xi) *Dome/Aburi*
Probably the leader alone.

Family groups always[1] have leaders, or heads, and very often, especially if the area be large,[2] the family land ultimately becomes known by the leader's name—a name by which it continues to be known after his death.[3] Such is the importance of personal initiative in the establishment of the land that it is not surprising that family lands never bear the names of men who did not actually settle there.[4] Where (nowadays at any rate) there is no obvious leader (as in 2 of the 11 cases in the above table), this is probably usually because the land was bought by one man for the use of his kin. Thus the Boah land (Appendix III. 8, p. 100) may have been bought by an uncle for his matrilineal nephews and it is to be presumed that one man was concerned with the purchase of the Akropong/Bepoase land (Appendix III. 9, p. 104) for the use of his patrilineal as well as his matrilineal kin.[5] When a number of brothers buy land, one of them is bound to emerge as the leader, if only because land-vendors are accustomed to dealing with individuals; this leader is likely to be the eldest of the brothers, unless he is primarily engaged in other work.

In the early stages, leaders are very often, though not always, associated with others, as the above table shows, and this is especially likely if the land be large. Such associate farmers may, or may not, be concerned with the actual purchase of the land—given the dominance of the leader this is not a matter of much importance; they are defined as farmers to whom substantial portions of land, over which the leader relinquishes control, are allotted originally. Such associates must not be confused with ordinary *abusua* members to whom small portions of land, over which they have usufructuary rights, are granted as a matter of course, so long as any

---

[1] Even if the leader is merely the spokesman for a small group of kinsmen there is still a sense in which he exists; usually he is far more than this.

[2] Most of the family lands included in the table are certainly larger than the average for the historic cocoa-growing area and it is for this reason that land (xi) is included as a reminder that small lands are quite common.

[3] Sometimes, indeed, the land may not be known by his name until after his death. All that is certain is that the change from an original name, based perhaps on that of a hunter's shelter or natural feature, to the leader's name, often occurs very gradually.

[4] They certainly never bear the name of the woman from whom members of the matrilineage count their descent.

[5] It is noteworthy that neither of these lands is known by the purchaser's name, for he did not reside there.

80

THE FAMILY LAND

unplanted land remains.[1] Very often, though perhaps not invariably,[2] each original associate, unlike the ordinary members of the *abusua*, is responsible for meeting part of the cost of buying the land, but as already noted, there is no reason to think that the sum subscribed by an individual necessarily bears (or is even intended to bear) any close relation to the area allocated[3] to him. It is the general rule, as column (5) of the above table shows, that the leader acquires a larger share than anyone else. Thus, Omenako (the leader of family group (vii)), acquired (and retained) 206 acres out of 486 acres and the share of Kofi Pare (group (iv)) was 372 out of 1,152 acres, leaving 780 acres for his 6 associates.

In discussing this question of associates further, it is necessary to distinguish between Aburi and Akropong lands and the former will be considered first. If the land is a large one, some of the leader's associates are likely to be non-members of his *abusua*. But this does not mean[4] that they are mere friends—reliable people with whom the leader happens to be associated, as though in a company. If a man is associated with his sister's husband, this will be because he has been able to persuade the father of his maternal nephews that it is only right and proper for him to assist in buying a land which will ultimately benefit his sons. If he is associated with his wife's brother, this will ensure that part of the land ultimately passes to his own sons. That latent or potential conflicts between the matrilineal and patrilineal principles have sometimes been resolved in this way is a historical fact. But there is no reason to believe that the need to resort to such 'solutions' has tended to increase as time has gone by—that the sense of conflict is any more pronounced today than it was sixty years ago. At that time an investigator might well have forecast the imminent collapse, as a result of the development of commercial cocoa-farming, of the Aburi 'matrilineal system', partly on general grounds and partly because prominent Christian farmers, ministers, catechists and others who were, of course, concerned to provide for their sons,[5] were so much in evidence as purchasers of trans-Densu lands. Today no such prognostication can be ventured, it having meanwhile become apparent that the family land

---

[1] This is the way farmers explain the system of granting usufructuary rights—and it is necessary to rely on what they say about the old days. But they are clearly over-simplifying, for original farmers (leaders and their associates) take their time over planting the portions they have earmarked for their individual use and do not allow their relatives to crowd them out. See chapter IV.

[2] At this late date it has naturally proved very difficult to collect information on this point.

[3] In the earliest days, as already noted, there was no formal allocation, 'appropriation by cutlass' being the rule, as at Ahwerease-Akim, Appendix III. 6 (p. 97).

[4] See chapter IV.

[5] These early Christian farmers were probably more inclined than any Aburi farmers at any time since to buy lands which at the start were divided between their sons and their *abusua*. Such a procedure tended to lead to the establishment of two family lands, providing respectively for the sons' *abusua* and that of their father, so that it represented an evasion of conflict rather than a solution.

THE FAMILY LAND

system is a form of matrilineal organization which has not merely survived intact but has also proved its strength.

Nor did this strength result from the fact that the Aburi family land system permitted the reconciliation of the matrilineal and patrilineal principles—indeed this can be regarded as almost incidental. The system grew from strength to strength because it accorded the individual enterprising farmer sufficient scope to operate as a commercially viable entity, while at the same time enabling him to benefit from the continued general support of his matrilineage. The less fortunate or less enterprising members of the matrilineage appreciated the need to allow their leaders to go on investing money, which might not strictly be regarded as their individual property,[1] in the purchase of a succession of lands[2] over which, at the outset at any rate, they had complete individual control, because they trusted in the strength of the matrilineal principle and knew that their own security would thus, in the long run, be enhanced.

Because the head of an Aburi family land usually retains a considerable area for his own use and because some (if not all) of his principal associates are usually members of his *abusua*,[3] a high proportion of the whole area of the land is normally farmed by *abusua* members. Thus at Kofi Pare the total area taken over by Kofi Pare himself and by those of his associates who were members of his *abusua* was 741 acres, out of a total (surveyed) area of 1,152 acres. While, as time goes by (see chapter IV), some of this land is likely to come under the (possibly temporary) control of non-members of the *abusua*, such as sons of original farmers, there may also be a contrary tendency for some of the land originally allocated to non-members of the *abusua* to come under the control of members, as when the leader was associated with his sister's husband, whose sons, to whom he may grant land, are members of his *abusua*. Reliable factual information on the composition of original family groups is sadly deficient at present, for it cannot be obtained from present-day farmers unless inquiries are related to farm maps, which, as already noted, seldom exist for these old Aburi family lands. However, on the basis of the information which has been collected so far, it seems permissible to risk the assertion that Aburi family groups are always composed entirely of people who are related to the leader either by blood (matrilineally) or through the male line, or by marriage, and that the matter of their choice is closely bound up with the practice of cross-cousin marriage—see chapter IV.

Although, as has already been noted, Aburi fathers sometimes buy

---

[1] See chapter IV.   [2] See chapter VII.

[3] It is usually appropriate, for present practical purposes, to regard the leader's *abusua* (or matrilineage) as stemming from his maternal grandmother, this being a segment of the lineage through which descent is traced. To avoid circumlocution the *abusua* to which the leader belongs is referred to as 'the leader's *abusua*', although *abusua* heads are always women and the procreative role of males is non-existent in relation to 'their' *abusua*, unless they happen to be married to their cross-cousins—see chapter IV, p. 124.

82

THE FAMILY LAND

lands for their sons,[1] it seems unlikely that they are 'associated' with their sons in the purchase of a land, the father having one portion, the son another. The list of Kofi Pare's associates includes no sons, even though the finance for purchasing the Kofi Pare land was derived from a land at Pakro which had originally been acquired by Kofi Pare's father.[2] As when companies are formed, the leader of a new group may choose his associates, as did Kofi Pare, from among those who happened to have been working on an earlier-acquired land.

On all the larger Aburi family lands there are immense *abusua*-villages,[3] such as Kofi Pare (1,626 pop., 170 houses), Sakyikrom (1,085 pop., 74 houses), Ahwerease-Akim (365 pop., 25 houses), Akotuakrom (230 pop., 17 houses). The process of growth of these settlements has scarcely been studied—social geographers and others tend to confine their attention to towns on the main roads. Perhaps it is usual for each of the original farmers to start by building one or more cottages, compounds, or farmhouses always known to the farmers as 'villages', on his own portion of land, to accommodate his labourers as well as himself. The members of his *abusua* to whom small portions of land are granted will also live in these villages when they first arrive, intending later to build houses of their own near-by. As time goes by there is a tendency for the farmers to build new and somewhat superior[4] houses near the leader's house on the leader's land; the cottages on their own land may then be abandoned, maintained for use as temporary shelters (or as cocoa-drying stations) during the harvesting season, or turned over to labourers,[5] who sometimes prefer to live with their families in solitude rather than in the residential centre. Very gradually, it is often surprising how gradually, other amenities, such as schools, markets, churches, may develop, and specialist craftsmen such as weavers, of whom there was a group in Kofi Pare in

[1] 'Sometimes, but uncommonly', said the chief of Aburi, the Adontenhene of Akwapim, 'a father will buy a land for several sons and divide it between them.'

[2] This is an exceptionally well-documented case, see Appendix III. 4 (p. 92) etc.

[3] The figures shown in brackets are derived from the 1948 Census and show first the recorded population and second the number of compounds or houses. The population of associated villages may well be included, especially in the case of Kofi Pare. Despite the destruction of most of the cocoa by swollen shoot, large numbers of people continued to reside in the *abusua*-villages, depending mainly on food-farming; owing to the natural increase of population, and the brake on migration resulting from poverty, the larger settlements, such as Kofi Pare, may have suffered no decline in size, but at the time of writing the 1960 Census figures are unpublished.

[4] In most villages there is no close relationship between the wealth of the farmer and the size or dignity of his house, this being in marked contrast to the situation in the home town. But in some of the oldest and largest villages, including Sakyikrom, Ahwerease-Akim, the land near Krabokese (ii) and Akotuakrom, the standard of housing compares with that in Akwapim, though only in Sakyikrom (which is a law unto itself) are enormous Italianate mansions to be found.

[5] Few farm labourers were employed in the very early days (see chapter VII), but many of the largest lands ultimately supported many more or less permanent labourers who, together with their families, made up a large proportion of the resident population; nearly all these labourers departed as a result of swollen shoot.

THE FAMILY LAND

1959, may be attracted as immigrants;[1] though most of the blacksmiths, carpenters and other craftsmen are cocoa-farming members of the original *abusua*.[2]

So far as is known, the really large *abusua*-villages are always of Aburi origin. From accounts given in Akropong it had been supposed that there might be an Aburi-scale *abusua*-village on the large, old, Akropong land (near Adeiso) called 'Mfojoboating' on the one-inch map;[3] but a visit there showed that the nuclear settlement consisted of several cottages only. Apart from *abusua*-villages proper, in the southern portion of the historic cocoa-growing area there are many other large villages off the main roads, some with populations of several hundred people, and these often have very mixed populations. Thus at Asarekrom, about six miles north of Adeiso, which was said to have been founded by Mampong people, the following 18 farmers happened to turn up at a meeting one day in 1959: Mampong (6), Berekuso (3), Adukrom (2), Aburi (2), Larteh, Akropong, Tutu, Accra (1 each) and 1 former labourer from Togo.

Many of the Akropong family lands, as distinct from the nuclear residential settlements, are impressively large, especially the very oldest in the deep south. Although it is true that the Aburi own far more large lands than the Akropong, the basic distinction between Aburi and Akropong lands is not a matter of size, but of the composition of the family group and its long-term cohesion. Many more members of an Aburi than of an Akropong *abusua* have been apt to flock to a land of a given size in the historic cocoa-growing area—and there are many possible explanations for this. Certainly the lesser degree of corporate matrilineal feeling among the Akropong is reflected in the fact that the individual farmers usually show little inclination to remove from the villages on their own farms[4] to a central point.

Highly relevant also is the fact that some Akropong farmers pay so much regard to the rights of sons that it would seem almost appropriate to

[1] Farmers working on other lands, as well as employees of the Ministry of Agriculture, and others, may come to reside in *abusua*-villages with amenities, such as schools and markets to offer. Thus, Dr Hunter found that about 40 per cent of those resident in Akotuakrom were neither members of the family nor farmers (or labourers) on Akotuakrom land.

[2] Between the wars little was done to improve the accessibility of these *abusua*-villages; recently, despite the swollen shoot, there has been more road-building (sometimes, as at Akotuakrom, paid for by the farmers themselves, and sometimes 'self-help'), but there are still many large settlements in southern Akim Abuakwa which cannot be reached by lorry. In the rainy season of 1959 the road to Kofi Pare was very bad; but the inhabitants were proud of their one-way street system.

[3] See p. 224.

[4] There are some districts where a great many Akropong farmers appear to have bought land either independently, or in informal association, and it is not certain that the relationship between the original farmers was such as to justify the use of the term 'family land': an example is a part of the Kabu Hill Ministry of Agriculture Area, west of Omenako, where it proved impossible, in the time available, to unravel the complex pattern of farm-ownership presented by the maps.

84

THE FAMILY LAND

regard them as subject to a dual inheritance system.[1] The position is at present obscure, but the evidence, as far as it goes, seems to suggest that most Akropong farmers (unlike their Aburi counterparts) pay at least some regard to the patrilineal principle, as did Omenako, one of whose 'original associates', to whom a considerable area of land was granted, was a son. But it would, at the same time, be hard to imagine a more ideal specimen of a group to which matrilineal principles apply than the Boah group—apart from the inclusion of one son (farmer (H), see Appendix III. 8, p. 100) in the list of those to whom land was granted originally.

With Akropong (as with Aburi) farmers, it is the general rule that family groups should consist of relatives and selected affines only. The latter may effectively provide a useful addition to the finance available to members of the *abusua* for land-purchase: in the case of the Omenako land (vii), two of Omenako's five associates were husbands of his sisters, whose children were thus also members of his (Omenako's) *abusua*.

The structure of the Boah family group is fascinating. The nucleus of the group was two pairs of brothers whose mothers were sisters. As a result of much discussion with an elderly educated member of the *abusua* who has inherited farms there, and who remembers childhood visits to the land at the time of its purchase, the impression was formed that there was a sense in which one of the original associates (he perhaps the principal source of finance) had been a certain matrilineal cousin of the 'nuclear cousins' (called 'the slave trader' in Appendix III. 8, p. 100) who had died more than ten years before the land had been bought. His 'participation' was recognized by treating as original associates both one of his sons and also two of his former slaves, who had been adopted into the matrilineage.

The Akropong family land at Bepoase (Appendix III. 9, p. 104) is another ideal specimen, illustrating one manner of reconciling the matrilineal and patrilineal principles. The land was divided among two brothers and their mother's sister's son, their respective shares being 128, 126 and 128 acres.[2] One of the brothers is said to have died soon after farming started and the whole of his land was divided, in neatly drawn strips, among his own and his brothers' sons and daughters—i.e. among the patrilineal descendants of the deceased's father. When, later on, the other brother died, the whole of his farm passed to his matrilineal successor—his sons having already been provided for on the first brother's land. With the third farm, that owned by the matrilineal cousin of the brothers, both matrilineal and patrilineal principles were recognized in its subdivision,

---

[1] See chapter IV.

[2] Whether such a remarkable degree of equality was achieved by chance, or with the help of a surveyor, is not known.

THE FAMILY LAND

either during the lifetime of the original farmer or after his death, and his sons and daughters now happen to be in charge of a greater proportion of the acreage than his matrilineal kin.

So much has been written about the matrilineage as a corporation[1] that the use of the expression 'family land' may, quite wrongly, suggest that farming is, in some sense, corporate. It is therefore, necessary to insist that individuals never farm *jointly* (though a resident farmer may help an absentee, or a son may work on his father's land) and that they seldom even share labourers.

A family land, then, is an area within which individual members of an *abusua* farm portions of land. The next chapter is concerned with the evolution of the land-holding group over time and with the factors which determine the tenure position of individual farmers. Here it need only be added that the Ministry of Agriculture is right to ignore all these complications when registering the names of farmers: for all practical purposes the 'owner' is the person who, for the time being, has the right to farm the portion of land in question and, except in the interim following a previous owner's death, it is usually possible to establish his identity without too much difficulty.

APPENDIX III. 1

SAKYIKROM

Sakyikrom, which lies across the river Densu just west of Nsawam, might well be supposed to be the oldest, the largest and the most remarkable of all the 'family lands' in Akim country. The splendid town of that name (see plate 14), which had a recorded population of 1,085 in 1948, and 74 houses, is situated, like Nsawam, in the state of Akwapim and, during the earlier years of the migration, was the seat of the Omanhene of Akwapim when he crossed the river for 'political' purposes. The land was bought from the chief of Apapam, at a date which was certainly no later than 1896, by Nana Sakyi (hence Sakyikrom) and his associates, most of them from Nsakye, some from Aburi; it is at least three miles long from east to west and partially encloses, though it does not include, the mountain Nyanao. The estate was a 'launching pad' for scores of famous Aburi and Nsakye farmers: any sociological exploration of the ramifications of Aburi land-ownership in southern Akim country would have to start at Sakyikrom. But Sakyikrom itself is a 'freak', not a prototype—that the people refer to themselves as Akwamu, not Akwapim, and that their chief is, by virtue of his office, a member of the Akwamu *oman*, are facts sufficient to set it apart.

Especially as nothing of the history of Sakyikrom has, as yet, been recorded in print, the present author was placed in a dilemma. The more inquiries that were made, the more perplexing, fascinating and at the same time irrelevant (to present purposes)

---

[1] 'The family was a corporation; action and even thought were corporate affairs. It is not easy to grasp what must have been the effect on West African psychology of untold generations of acting and thinking, not in terms of oneself, but in relation to one's group. . .' Rattray, *Ashanti Law and Constitution*, p. 62.

did this history appear. It seems unlikely that the acquisition of the land had any connexion with cocoa-farming—and much of it has probably always been marginal for cocoa. The economic factors which generally motivated the migrant farmers were here replaced by others, for there seems no reason to doubt the oral tradition that it was because of land disputes at Nsakye that Nana Sakyi and his associates were advised, by the Rev. Edward Samson, to provide themselves with a permanent home on the other side of the river. The residents of Sakyikrom town are almost unique[1] in being neither migrants (as defined in this book) nor native Akim.

But as so many of the Aburi family lands (proper) proliferated from Sakyikrom, and as the Sakyikrom people themselves are so keenly interested in their history, it seems appropriate to record the following notes based upon information so eagerly provided[2] in June and July 1960, partly in the hope that others may be stimulated to pursue the history further.

The early history. Most perplexing was the insistence of all present-day residents that the founders of Sakyikrom had arrived in Nsakye, from Akwamu, *shortly* (i.e. ten years or so) before their removal across the river. This insistence would have been more comprehensible had it not conflicted with the genealogical material provided in Sakyikrom, according to which Nana Sakyi was of the fifth descendant generation in the line stemming from Aba Tawia, the *abusua* head. This information seems entirely plausible to Mr Ivor Wilks[3] who thinks that Aba Tawia, who married Ohene Osae of Aburi, probably arrived in Akwapim between about 1730 and 1760. If, as seems likely, it was her son Akotua who founded (or re-founded) Nsakye, perhaps around 1800, then the connexion with Nsakye had endured for some ninety years when the removal to Sakyikrom occurred.

The date of purchase of the Sakyikrom land. The general presumption is in favour of a date around 1890 to 1896—certainly no later, for it is an undoubted fact that the Sakyikrom people were 'the first to arrive in the area' and bought their land before the Ahwerease-Akim (see Appendix III. 6, p. 97). Mr Samuel Krow, aged about eighty, a son of Nana Sakyi, said that he was a youth at the time of the purchase and that he was living on the land at the time of the Samori war of 1896.

Nana Sakyi and his associates. While each elderly resident was inclined to compile his own personal list of Sakyikrom's founders, all were agreed in including Moses Adjei and Afum Yaw, as well as Nana Sakyi. Although Moses Adjei is sometimes referred to as a member of the Aba Tawia *abusua*, he was probably rather a son of a male member; he may have been born about 1809 and according to his tombstone in Sakyikrom graveyard was baptized in 1862. Although Afum Yaw is always referred to as a nephew (*wɔfase*) of Nana Sakyi, the genealogy (which may, in this respect, be incorrect) shows him as a classificatory maternal uncle. Nana Sakyi is said to have died in 1914 and may have been born about 1840. He was the first chief of the town and was succeeded by Afum Yaw—who died a few weeks later. The third chief was Kwame Osae, a maternal nephew of Nana Sakyi; the fourth chief was Kwame Obuba (alias Yaw Krow), who belonged to another *abusua*—the 'second *abusua*'; the fifth, W. F. Adarkwa, was a member of yet another *abusua*—the 'third *abusua*'. Nowadays

---

[1] The neighbouring Daaman, (1) in the list below, may be somewhat comparable.

[2] The list of those who kindly gave information is too long to cite, but includes Mr Branu Addo (stool secretary, whose welcoming attitude made the inquiry possible), Mr Sampson Yao Krow (who, in 1952, compiled an unpublished *Handbook of Sakyikrom*) and Mr Opoku Darko (who, with the help of the older generation, had laboriously collected genealogical material, extending over nine generations and including over one hundred and fifty people).

[3] Of the Institute of African Studies, University of Ghana.

APPENDIX III. 1

the chiefs of Sakyikrom are drawn from each of these three *abusua* in strict rotation. (Members of the first *abusua* were said to own 55 houses in Sakyikrom, of the second *abusua* 5 and of the third only 1.)

The extent of the land and its early development. The land (which is as yet unmapped by the Ministry of Agriculture) extends westwards from Sakyikrom town to Anoff on the present main road, four miles west of Nsawam. It includes Noka (or Nuka), a village between Nyanao and the main road, which is said to have been founded by Atweri Kwasi (a maternal nephew of Nana Sakyi). The width of the land was not ascertained, but it was said that the village called Asante Kwaku is on land that was resold by the Sakyikrom people. All were insistent that there had originally been no division of land among the founders, but that each had farmed 'according to his strength'. Gradually the founders had been joined by their matrilineal kin and others, although some of the young men were described as 'reluctant'. Although there is no evidence that the farmers were particularly keen on cocoa-growing in the early days, the carrying of cocoa-seedlings from Nsakye to Sakyikrom is well remembered. It was said that much later on, around 1920, many Agona, Ga and other men had come to work on the land 'for nothing', so that they might take cocoa-pods away with them to plant elsewhere.

List of Aburi (and Nsakye) Family Lands 'associated' with Sakyikrom

(Those place-names marked with an asterisk are all family lands which are shown on the one-inch Ghana Survey, the spelling on that map being followed in most cases.)

The following Aburi (or Nsakye) family lands in southern Akim Abuakwa were many of them listed in *Handbook of Sakyikrom*; informants considered them to be 'associated' with Sakyikrom because the founder was believed either to have lived there before moving farther north or west, or to have been a member of one of the three Sakyikrom *abusua*. The list is certainly very incomplete and informants could not vouch for its entire accuracy.

1 *Daaman.** This land, which was bought from Asamankese, runs from the 'town' called Daaman (situated on the old main road to Adeiso) to the Asuaba stream (near Obuobisa village) and is certainly one and a half miles long; to the south it extends as far as Anoff (said to be the name of one of Daaman's 'brothers'). Daaman resembles Sakyikrom in being a 'town' with many splendid houses, still in good repair, and it does not occur in all the lists of lands associated with Sakyikrom for the reason, as one informant put it, that 'they established a real stool there'. The farmer Daaman was said to have been the son of a 'brother' of Nana Sakyi and may have lived for a time at Sakyikrom. Some 500 people live at Daaman today.

2 *Maamedede.** This land was one of the first direct offshoots of Sakyikrom, whether or not it was bought by Nana Sakyi himself. It lies directly west of the Akropong land Obuobisa, which in turn is west of Daaman. (Its name is said to derive from a woman—Mammy Dede—who ran a 'chop bar' at the place.) The land is said to be very large and parts of it were resold to others, including Kwasi Nyarko (a well-known Larteh farmer), Adu Kwadjo from Akropong and some Ningo farmers. Kwaku Atopah, a leading member of the third *abusua*, is said to have lived at Maamedede.

3 *Meretuam** (Obenyao).** Situated about two miles north of Adeiso, this land is said to have been bought by Obeng Yaw whose successor, Opanyin Samuel Krow (son of Nana Sakyi), said that Obeng Yaw's mother was his mother's twin sister.

SAKYIKROM

4 *Aworoso* (near Kraboa-Coaltar), founded by Kwabena Amarko, who was a son of Adubea, a sister of Afum Yaw. He is commemorated by a very big house in Sakyikrom, with a high wall.

5 A land near *Otoase* (on the road to Coaltar), founded by Kwasi Darko, a member of the third *abusua*.

6 *Sukyerema** (possibly adjoining (3)), founded by Opare Kwabena, who was a son of a male member of the first *abusua*.

7 Four lands at *Adiembra*, south of Kraboa-Coaltar, were bought by Afum Yaw.

8 *Okomso** (or Ampofokrom),* about six miles north of Adeiso, was founded by Ampofo, said to have been a servant of the Rev. Edward Samson.

9 *Kuaho** (one and a half miles north of Coaltar), founded by Yaw Krow, the fourth chief of Sakyikrom, and a member of the second *abusua*.

10 *Takorase*, about a mile south of (6), founded by Tio Kwasi, Afum Yaw's son.

11 *Sakyikrom-Afaben* (near Adeiso), founded by Kofi Pare II (not Kofi Pare I, see (13)), son of a daughter of a sister of Nana Sakyi.

12 *Asuaba*, near Adeiso, founded by Kwadjo Donkor, a member of the second *abusua*.

13 *Kofi Pare.** This land, founded by Kofi Pare I, who was a member of the second *abusua*, is the subject of Appendix III. 4 (p. 92).

14 *Amfaho* (Amfahum on the map), on the Amfa stream between Krabokese and Coaltar, was founded by Kwadjo Agyare, who had been a servant of Awuku Kwame, a maternal nephew of Afum Yaw.

15 *Ahwerease*, near Adeiso, founded by two brothers, Atta and Obuom, who were members of the second *abusua*.

16 *Krabokese*. The founder of the town of Krabokese, near Coaltar, was Kwakwa Ababio, a paternal nephew of Nana Sakyi.

17 *Onyamkyere,** slightly north of (3), founded by Simeon Ayeh, son of Moses Adjei.

18 *Asudom,** about a mile north of (17), was founded by Akotua Kwaku, a member of the second *abusua*.

19 *Kuaho-Afaben*, described as between Coaltar and Dokrokyewa (possibly Duedukrowa* on the map), founded by Kofi Dei, son of Nana Sakyi.

APPENDIX III. 2

AN ABURI (NSAKYE) FAMILY LAND NEAR KRABOKESE

Situated slightly north of Krabokese to the west of the road to Coaltar, this well-known family land, which includes an uncultivated mountain of over a thousand feet, was bought from the chief of Apapam in about 1909 by four brothers from Nsakye, near Aburi. When the land was visited in July 1958 the elder surviving brother was found to be inhabiting an immense 'village', a group of nearly twenty compound houses, many of them very large. Despite the death of all the cocoa from swollen shoot, about 200 people, descendants and other relatives, were living in the village, dependent on food-farming.

The elder surviving brother, Mr 'X', a venerable figure, had in his possession a receipt for the land issued in October 1915, some six years after the land had been bought. This had been signed by Kwame Mane, the chief of Apapam, and by his linguist Yao Bosompem and recorded that the land, the boundaries of which were

APPENDIX III. 2

defined by reference to the names of neighbouring farmers, had originally been sold to an elder brother who had died in 1913 and that a younger brother had now taken charge: 'Therefore I have this day given a receipt to this said ['X'] that if anyone wants to trouble him about this land, I shall evidence him that I was the party who sold this land to him. The amount with which he bought the land was £100.'

The brothers were said to have come straight to the land from Nsakye, where their father had for long grown a little cocoa; Mr 'X' thought that the money for buying the land had come from palm-oil. They were said to have started farming soon after they had bought the land. Mr 'X' and other informants insisted that the land had not been measured at the time of its purchase ('it was not sold by the rope') and that there had been no formal division between relatives, each of whom had farmed in a convenient place. The first formal division, he insisted, would occur in connexion with replanting, presumably after the Ministry of Agriculture treats the area (which in 1958 lay within the Abandoned Area) for swollen shoot—but exactly what he meant was unclear.

The four brothers were soon joined by a small number of other relatives (as well as by their own wives and children), all of whom were said to have been members of their *abusua*. After 'the influenza' (1918), six sons of their mother's sisters came and were granted land. When the eldest brother died in 1913, Mr 'X', who succeeded him, gave each of his brothers' sons a portion of land. First of all Mr 'X' said that each of the brothers, and others to whom land had been granted, had always farmed independently, meaning that each had owned his portion of land and that they had not shared labourers. Then he added that 'every day you work together', meaning that there had been a system of working together on each other's land in rotation, until they had started to employ annual and other labourers in, he thought, 1916. Later, Mr 'X' employed up to nine annual labourers on his own farm.

The number of independent farmers soon became large. No women were given land, but any member of the *abusua* resident in the area was entitled to a share at the age of about fifteen and sons, also, received portions. (There were found to be many adult sons and grandsons resident in the village in 1959.)

Mr 'X' said that he had had more than a thousand loads of cocoa from his own portion (or portions) of land before the swollen shoot—an estimate which seemed entirely reasonable to the assembled company which included a well-informed local cocoa-buyer. (One of Mr 'X's' maternal nephews put the figure, on another occasion, at 3,000 loads.) No one knew how large the land was and it was naturally impossible to form any idea of the extent to which it had formerly been devoted to cocoa- and food-growing respectively—it was just vaguely insisted that the whole area, apart from the sides of the mountain, had been farmed at one time or another. The country is rather hilly and after one had walked rather slowly westwards from the village for some twenty minutes one's companions said that more than half of the land lay ahead —from which it was judged that an estimated total area of 400 to 500 acres was reasonably modest.

The brothers bought, or acquired, various other cocoa-lands, some of which were never planted. These included a large area near Sefwi-Bekwai, acquired in 1949, portions of which were rented to other farmers. But the land near Krabokese remains the home from home—a place to which people from the declining home town, Nsakye, come to celebrate some of their festivals.

APPENDIX III. 3
AKOTUAKROM

The present writer is greatly indebted to Dr J. M. Hunter, of the Geography Department of the University of Ghana, for making the results of his study of this family land available prior to publication. As no farm maps were available (Akotuakrom being situated in the former Abandoned Area), Dr Hunter was obliged to survey the land himself—in 1959. Perhaps the most important of his findings relate to the bush fallow system, but this and many other aspects of his work are not touched on here. (See Hunter, J. M., 'Akotuakrom'—Bibliography, p. 254.)

Location and area. Akotuakrom is situated about eight miles north-west of Nsawam and is approached *via* Mafukrom, which lies slightly west of the road to Coaltar. The area of the land, as surveyed by Dr Hunter, is 357 acres; as map 10 shows it has the shape of a right-angled triangle, the Koran stream forming the southern base and its tributary the Kitiwa running part of the way along the hypotenuse. Where the boundary does not coincide with a stream it is marked with boundary plants.

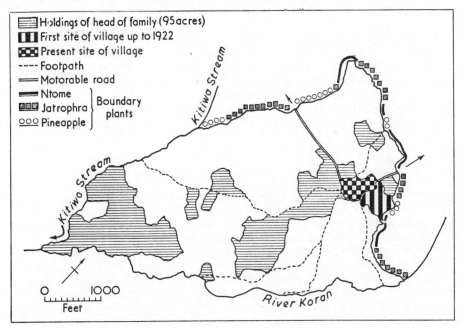

10 The Akotuakrom family land.

Date of acquisition and cost. The land was bought in about 1905 from the chief of Asamankese. A paper dated 1913 records the payment of £20, but whether this was a post-dated receipt for the whole amount, or merely an instalment, is not known.

The original members of the family group. Two brothers, Sampson Akotua and Philip Afwireng, bought the land. They were said to have travelled directly from their home town Nsakye, near Aburi. Akotua died in about 1937 and was succeeded by his

APPENDIX III. 3

younger brother Afwireng; Afwireng died in 1957 and was succeeded, in 1961, by a son of his eldest sister. (When the land was surveyed in 1959 the eldest sister herself was the temporary successor.) How much land the brothers originally reserved for their own use it is now impossible to say, though it was, presumably, a large proportion of the whole; the remainder was granted, as time went by, to members of their *abusua*, to their sons and also to one outsider.

Present-day holdings. Practically all the cocoa on the land died of swollen shoot and when the area was surveyed in 1959 it was found that 20 farmers were in a position to exercise rights as food-farmers. These farmers were 4 sisters of the original brothers, 6 maternal nephews, 3 other maternal relatives, 6 sons of Afwireng and 1 other farmer who had inherited rights originally granted to his father—an Ashanti man, a friend of the brothers, who had originally been granted land on *abusa* terms. The then successor (a sister of the brothers) held 95 acres (see map), the next largest areas being held by another sister (34 acres), a maternal cousin (23 acres) and a third sister (23 acres); Afwireng's 6 sons held usufructuary rights over 54 acres. The 20 farmers owned altogether 67 holdings. Only 4 of the farmers, all of them with small holdings, were failing, through their absence, to exercise their food-farming rights. The temporary nature of the rights held by sons is illustrated by the fact that all Akotua's sons, as well as his wives, left the land, possibly from their own free choice, following his death.

Other points. One of the most striking findings was that in 1959 the 4 biggest food-farmers were all women. Omitting the then successor, it was found that 3 women, with 21 per cent of the total area of the land, had 36 per cent of the total area under food. Dr Hunter estimated that, before swollen shoot, more than half of all the cocoa was grown by Afwireng who owned about a quarter of all the land and employed about 20 labourers. In about 1921 Afwireng had bought a land of over a square mile in area near Asikasu, much of which he had given to his sons; other (smaller) lands had been acquired elsewhere by other members of the family group.

APPENDIX III. 4

THE KOFI PARE FAMILY LAND

Location and area. The Kofi Pare family land is situated in a locality formerly known as Wansanbirampa, about ten miles west of Coaltar. The area of the surveyed portion of the land is about 1,152 acres; this acreage excludes an unsurveyed portion (the outline of which is shown on map 11) and areas to the north which were resold, probably long ago. The Ayensu stream and its tributary the Suwurum mark the southern and western boundaries. In 1948 the recorded population of Kofi Pare 'town', together presumably with associated villages, was 1,626.

Date of acquisition and cost. It is known that Kofi Pare, an Aburi farmer, first approached the chief of Akantin, a small Akim town about ten miles north of Asamankese, with a view to buying this land in about 1911, the purchase being concluded about a year later. The price of the whole land according to a document (the sum being independently confirmed by informants) was £400—plus boundary cutting, etc. expenses of about £100. Kofi Pare had previously been farming at Pakro where his father, Mensah Akoanankran, had bought land—see p. 222. It is said that there was little cocoa-farming on this new land until after 1918.

The original members of the family group and the division of the land. Kofi Pare had 6 original associates, of whom 3 were members of his *abusua*, each of whom was the head of a sub-group:

THE KOFI PARE FAMILY LAND

No. of sub-group	Acreage of surveyed portion	Original farmer and (if deceased) his successor (K.P. = Kofi Pare)[1]
1	372·2	K.P. himself; he was succeeded by a maternal nephew who is now the *odikro* of the town of K.P.
2[2]	169·1	A son of a daughter of K.P.'s maternal grandfather. He was succeeded by his younger brother who lives in Aburi.
3	201·4	A maternal cousin of K.P., still resident in K.P.
4[2]	87·6	A son of a son of one of K.P.'s grandfathers. It was said that most of the land was later 'given away' by K.P. himself to one of his wife's relatives.
5	126·4	A son of a younger sister of K.P.'s mother; still resident in K.P.
6[2]	153·5	A paternal relative of K.P. who married a member of the *abusua*; he was succeeded by his maternal nephew.
7	41·9	A son of an elder sister of K.P.'s mother; he was succeeded by a maternal nephew.
	1152·1	

[1] While most of the relationships were checked with older people, members of the younger generation of K.P. residents were found to be surprisingly ignorant of their precise relationship to people whom they had known all their lives and as they were inclined to guess some errors may have crept in.

[2] Non-members of K.P.'s *abusua*.

Considerable persistence in deleting artificial farm boundaries on the Ministry of Agriculture's block plans (boundaries which had been added for administrative convenience), combined with the expert help of one of K.P.'s youngest sons, finally revealed the existence of a rough strip-system running in a north-westerly direction from the rivers Suwurum and Ayensu, each strip having been owned by one of the 7 original farmers; some of these strips, e.g. those owned by sub-groups 5, 6 and 7, which touch the river Suwurum near its confluence with the Ayensu, are of a fairly uniform width, having presumably been measured. It was found that each of the sub-groups was the owner of one main strip (5 of which were based on the rivers) and that each of them, except one, also owned other portions.

The subsequent division of the land. In 1959 there were 137 farmers registered as owning land within the surveyed area. The heads of sub-groups 3 and 5 were still alive and they, together with the 5 successors of the heads of other sub-groups, owned about 466 acres—or about 40 per cent of the whole area. Of the remaining farmers, at least 55 were maternally related to the head of their sub-group and they were the registered owners of 362 acres, or 30 per cent of the whole. There were at least 19 sons and daughters who had been granted land and they owned altogether 97 acres, or 8 per cent of the whole; in some cases, though not in all, their land had been granted to them for use during their lifetimes only. Heads of sub-groups had apparently been free to allocate land to their relatives and others as they thought fit, without reference to Kofi Pare (or his successor), but much of the land included in sub-group 4 was said to have been 'given away' by Kofi Pare himself.

APPENDIX III. 4

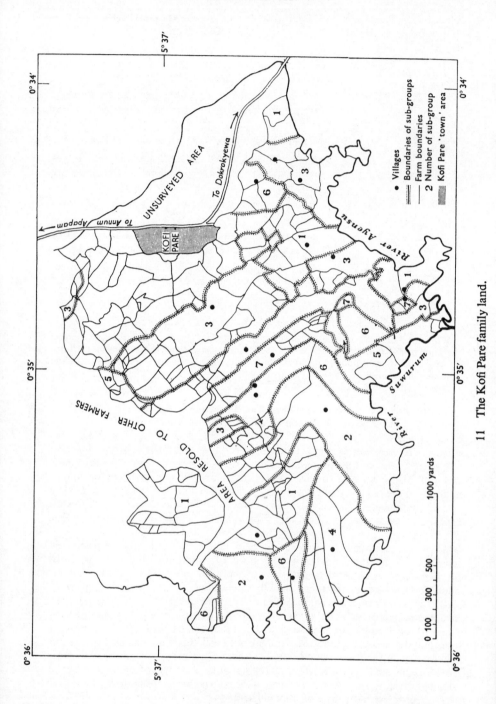

11 The Kofi Pare family land.

THE KOFI PARE FAMILY LAND

	Number of sub-group							
	1	2	3	4	5	6	7	Total
Head of sub-group or his successor:								
Acreage	84·0	138·2	75·9	34·8	62·1	50·7	20·0	465·7
No. of farmers	(1)	(1)	(1)	(1)	(1)	(1)	(1)	(7)
Maternal relatives of head of sub-group:								
Acreage	139·8	18·3	85·9	48·9	35·1	13·1	20·9	362·0
No. of farmers	(18)	(9)	(11)	(4)	(3)	(6)	(4)	(55)
Sons and Daughters of head of sub-group or his successor:								
Acreage	66·9	—	19·0	3·9	6·1	—	1·0	96·9
No. of farmers	(7)	—	(7)	(1)	(3)	—	(1)	(19)
Other:								
Acreage	81·5	12·6	20·6	—	23·1	89·7	—	227·5
No. of farmers	(23)	(1)	(11)	—	(12)	(14)	—	(61)
Grand Total[1]								
Acreage	372·2	169·1	201·4	87·6	126·4	153·5	41·9	1152·1
No. of farmers	(49)	(11)	(30)	(6)	(19)	(21)	(6)	(142)[2]

[1] Many of the farmers own more than one farm. If all the portions within any strip held by one individual are regarded as one 'farm', then the total number of farms owned by the 137 farmers is about 200; the number of such farms owned by heads of sub-groups or their successors were, for sub-groups 1 to 7 respectively, 7, 3, 5, 2, 4 and 1.

[2] This total is greater than the total number of farmers as several farmers own farms in more than one sub-group.

Owing to the original relationships between sub-groups and the operation of cross-cousin marriage as time has gone by, the kinship classification of land-ownership is fraught with difficulty if the land is regarded as a whole. Some of the 'sons and daughters' of one sub-group may be members of the *abusua* of another sub-group.

The larger farmers. Apart from the 7 heads of sub-groups or their successors, there are only 6 farmers with holdings of 20 acres or more, these being:

Sub-group	Relationship to original head of sub-group	Acreage
1	Son of daughter	20·9
2	Maternal niece	20·5
3	Female maternal relative	29·4
4	Brother of successor	28·9
5	Maternal nephew	23·3
6	Unknown affine	21·6

Sub-division in the lifetime of an original farmer. The extent and nature of the sub-division that is apt to occur during the lifetime of an original farmer is shown by the following table relating to sub-group 3, the head of which is still living in Kofi Pare:

95

APPENDIX III. 4

Relationship to original farmer	Acreage of holding		No. of farmers
Original farmer himself	75·9	75·9	1
Brothers	4·6 11·5 1·4	17·5	3
Sister	2·5	2·5	1
Maternal nephews	8·3 11·8	20·1	2
Maternal niece	2·3	2·3	1
Other maternal relatives	6·7 1·9 5·5 29·4	43·5	4
Sons and daughters	1·5 0·9 1·7 4·2 7·3 2·0 1·4	19·0	7
Wife	2·8	2·8	1
Others		17·8	10
Total		201·4	30

Residence. In 1959, by which time nearly all the cocoa had died of swollen shoot, 55 of the registered farm-owners were resident (or normally resident) on the Kofi Pare land and they were the owners of 647 acres. A further 39 farmers were resident in Akwapim, in older farming areas (such as Nsawam or Adeiso) or (a small number only) in Accra; most of these farmers were in a position to pay regular visits to Kofi Pare or to reside there to the extent that might be required for farming purposes; the total acreage in their charge was 319, including 138 acres owned by the present head of sub-group 2 who lives in Aburi. Of the remaining 43 farm-owners, only 18 were definitely reported to be living in other cocoa-growing areas (mostly in Akim country), but the whereabouts of some of the remainder was unknown to informants—this whole group owned 187 acres.

APPENDIX III. 5

KWAME TAWIAH

Kwame Tawiah was an Aburi farmer who bought a land near Odumkyere, about six miles north of Adeiso, in about 1916 from the chief of Asamankese. This land, which now has an area of at least 156 acres, was the subject of an article, entitled 'The Farm at Odumkyere—Kwame Tawiahkrom', in *The Ghana Farmer* (vol. II, no. 4, pp. 148–9) by Kwame Tawiah's maternal nephew, Mr Ofosu Appiah of Nsawam—this being the only published account by a cocoa-farmer of the replanting, following devastation by swollen shoot, of an Aburi family land.

On the occasion of a visit to the family land in February 1959, Mr Ofosu Appiah (see plates 4 and 9) said that Kwame Tawiah's first cocoa-lands had been at Ankyiase

KWAME TAWIAH

and Deigo, in the hinterland west of Aburi; he said that when Kwame Tawiah installed himself on the land at Odumkyere he had been accompanied by 2 brothers, 2 sisters (together with their 2 sons) and 2 sons of his mother's sister, and that another of his brothers, who had been too old to accompany him, as well as his mother, had assisted in the purchase of the land. They had started cultivating about four years after the land had been bought—perhaps in 1920. From the earliest times they had employed contract labourers, who had lived in one large village.

APPENDIX III. 6

AHWEREASE/AKIM

The Ahwerease/Akim family land, which is of the order of a mile long and which lies about three miles west of Nsawam, north of the mountain Nyanao, was bought from the chief of Apapam in about 1898[1] by an Ahwerease (Akwapim) man who was said to have been accompanied by 8 maternal nephews—5 sons of one sister and 3 of another. (He was also accompanied by a brother—but he at once hived off on to the northern portion of the land, which has since always been considered 'separate'.) In the course of time each of these 8 nephews built a large house in the village now named Ahwerease (which lies just north of the present main road from Nsawam to Adeiso and had a recorded population of 365 in 1948)—houses which are always referred to by their founders' names. When the family group first came to the land each nephew 'farmed as he liked', there having been no division of land in advance of farming. As the land had originally been 'bought for the nephews', and was not given to them at a later stage, each of them was free to deal as he liked with the area he had appropriated and apart from maternal kin many sons and 'grandsons' (some of whom, owing to cross-cousin marriage, may also have been matrilineally related) were living on the land when it was visited in 1960.

APPENDIX III. 7

THE OMENAKO FAMILY LAND

Location and area. Situated about two miles north of Suhum, west of the main road to Kibi, the Omenako family land takes its name from an Akropong farmer, Kwabena Omenako, who was the leader of a group which acquired the land. The area of the land, as surveyed by the Ministry of Agriculture, is 486 acres (including 6 small farms of a total area of 15 acres which lie within the land and were sold to outsiders): the original area was considerably larger as much land at the periphery was sold to outsiders.

Date of acquisition. The date of purchase of the land from the chief of Apapam is tentatively put at 1907. It was said that farming first started about two years later.

The original farmers (see map 12). Omenako had at least 5 associates and the land was distributed between them as the following list shows. (The acreages given are net of subsequent resales.)

[1] The author is indebted to Nana Kwame Kwakye, the sole survivor of the eight nephews, for the information he gave in 1960. He was certain that he had been living at Twereboanda (as the area was then called) for about two years before accompanying Capt. Benson on his journey to Ashanti, and it therefore seems reasonable to suggest that the land was bought in about 1898. Nana Kwame Kwakye said that they had bought the land at about the same time as the land at Ayi Bonte had been bought by the Rev. William Obeng of Aburi and his brother and that they had arrived 'long before' Daaman (see p. 88) and Akotua (see Appendix III. 3, p. 91). In fact he was sure that their only predecessors in the neighbourhood had been the farmers at Sakyikrom.

97

APPENDIX III. 7

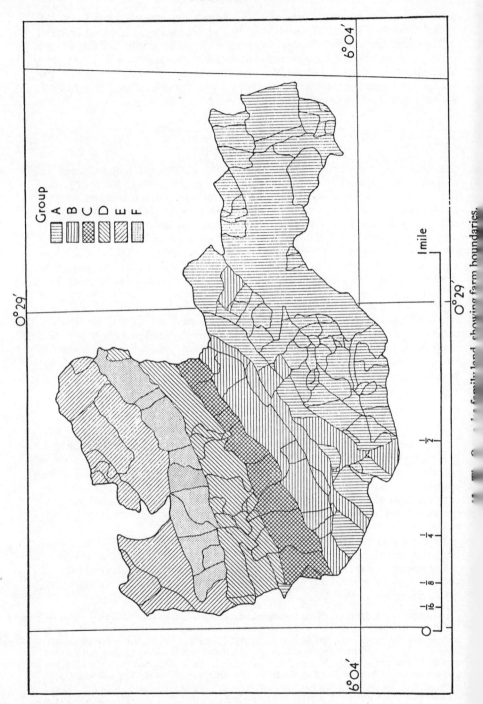

THE OMENAKO FAMILY LAND

(A)	Omenako	206·6 acres
(B)	A maternal nephew of Omenako	65·9 acres
(C)	The husband of one of Omenako's sisters	38·4 acres
(D)	The wife of one of Omenako's sons	48·0 acres
(E)	A son of Omenako	73·9 acres
(F)	The husband of one of Omenako's sisters	38·7 acres

The subsequent division of the land. Omenako himself is said to have given away much land to his relatives during his lifetime and presumably most of his associates did likewise. None of the original farmers survives today and such land as they had retained for their own use passed to their successors on their deaths.

About three-quarters of the whole acreage is owned by farmers who are members either of Omenako's *abusua* or of the *abusua* of the head of their sub-group (if this is a different one). It is possible that (D) was a member of Omenako's *abusua* and if (E), also, were married to a cross-cousin, then there has been more consolidation of ownership in Omenako's *abusua* than appears from these figures. In 1959 there were 92 farm-owners registered by the Ministry of Agriculture, of whom at least 15 were deceased, either because the relatives had not yet troubled to re-register the farm, or because it had originally been registered in the name of a deceased farmer.

Distribution of Acreage among Farmers
(Numbers of farmers are shown in brackets)

Group	Members of Omenako's abusua	Members of abusua of head of group	Sons of head of group	Daughters of head of group	Sons of daughters of head of group	Other relatives	Affines	Others (inc. 'unknown')	Total
	(1)	(2)	(3)	(4)	(5)	(6)	(7)	(8)	(9)
(A)	125·7	—	20·7	3·0	26·2	18·3	7·2	5·5	206·6
	(17)		(3)	(3)	(4)	(9)	(3)	(6)	(45)
(B)	44·9	—	8·2	3·7	—	9·1	—	—	65·9
	(6)		(1)	(2)		(2)			(11)
(C)	33·5[1]	—	—	—	—	—	4·2	0·7	38·4
	(2)						(1)	(1)	(4)
(D)	—	48·0[2]	—[2]	—[2]	—[2]	—[2]	—	—	48·0
		(10)							(10)
(E)	—	64·8	—	0·5	7·7	—	0·9	—	73·9
		(4)		(1)	(2)		(1)		(8)
(F)	36·0[3]	2·7	—[3]	—	—[3]	—[3]	—	—	38·7
	(7)	(1)							(8)
Sold to outsiders	—	—	—	—	—	—	—	14·7	14·7
								(6)	(6)
Total	240·1	115·5	28·9	7·2	33·9	27·4	12·3	20·9	486·2
	(32)	(15)	(4)	(6)	(6)	(11)	(5)	(13)	(92)[4]

[1] Two matrilineal grandsons of (C), who are members of Omenako's *abusua*, as (C) was married to Omenako's sister.

[2] The 2 sons, 3 daughters and other relatives of (D) are all members of her *abusua*.

[3] The total of 7 farmers shown as members of Omenako's *abusua* includes 1 son and 5 maternal grandsons of (F)—whose wife was a member of the *abusua*.

[4] Seven farms notionally registered in the names of the real owner's relatives (mainly his daughters) are here regarded as part of the real owner's property; their inclusion would have raised the total number of present-day farmers from 92 to 99.

APPENDIX III. 7

Notes on Table

Col. (1) All known members of Omenako's *abusua* are included, whether or not the original head of the group was a member of this *abusua*.

Col. (2) This column applies only in those cases where the original head of the group is not known to have been a member of Omenako's *abusua*.

Col. (5) While most of the farmers included here are thought to be 'real grandsons' (in the female line) of the original farmer, some of them may be grandsons of the original farmer's sisters—and thus members of the original farmer's *abusua*.

Col. (8) Cases where the identity of the farmer is unknown, or where land was sold to outsiders, are included in this column.

Twelve of the 92 farmers own 10 acres or more and they own altogether 253 acres; 10 of these farmers are *abusua* members, one is a son of Omenako and one is a son of Omenako's daughter. Much the largest acreage is the 64 acres owned by one of Omenako's maternal nephews. Excluding these 12 farmers and also the 6 outsiders shown in the table, 74 farmers remain, of whom 47 are men (who own an average of $3 \cdot 6$ acres) and 27 are women (average acreage $1 \cdot 8$). Women are often given very small portions: 10 of the 27 women owned less than an acre, compared with only 7 of the 47 men.

APPENDIX III. 8

THE BOAH FAMILY LAND

Location and area. The Boah family land (a name which conceals the identity of the family group) is situated about two miles from Nankese just north of the Nankese to Akwadum road. Farming started from the eastern boundary which is jagged owing to a hill and outcrops of rocks (see map 13). The total area of the land is 163 acres.

Date of acquisition and cost. The land was bought from the chief of Maase in about 1908 for about £200 plus expenses. (There had been a dispute about a land that had been bought previously and this land was substituted for it.)

The original buyers of the land. The nucleus of the family group (see fig. 3) was two pairs of brothers from Akropong, (A) & (B) and (C) & (D), whose mothers were sisters. (A), the elder son of the younger sister, is said to have been the leader. Before acquiring this land the cousins were said to have been living in a village near Akropong where they were dependent on food-growing and the oil-palm. Although each cousin was notionally allocated 4 ropes of land, there was no division between brothers, (A) & (B) taking the areas now represented by farms 26 to 34 (together 63 acres) and (C) & (D) the area of farms 8 to 13 and 16 to 25 (50 acres). Strips notionally regarded as 2 ropes wide went to (E), who was the son of a certain maternal cousin of the 4 cousins and is here referred to as 'the slave trader' (he is said to have met his end 'some time before 1895' while trading on the Volta) and to (F) a former slave of the slave trader; these two strips now consist of farms 3 to 5 and farms 6, 7, 14 and 15 and have acreages of $16 \cdot 4$ and $14 \cdot 4$. A few years after the original division had been made, land to the west of the area was granted to 3 more farmers, these being (G), a descendant in the female line of the eldest daughter of the lineage head (this lineage head being the maternal grandmother of the 4 cousins); (J), another ex-slave of the slave trader; and (H), a son of (C). (G) and (J) together owned the area now consisting of farm 1 and (H) owned farm 2.

100

THE BOAH FAMILY LAND

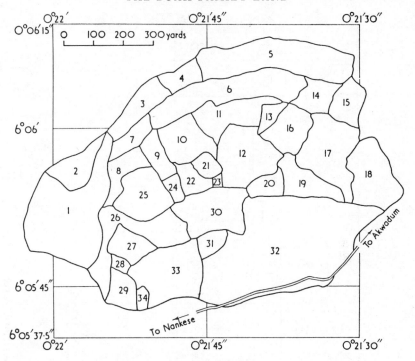

13   The Boah family land, showing farm boundaries.

The subsequent division of the land

Land originally owned by (A) and (B). When (B) died in about 1921 he was temporarily succeeded by his elder brother (A) until the real successor, who was (K), came of age. When, later on, (A) died his farm went to the same successor (K). (K) succeeded to 40·6 acres altogether. Other farms, or land, in the strip were distributed as follows:

Farm no.	Acreage	Present owner
26, 32	6·9, 33·7	The successor, (K).
27, 34	2·7, 0·6	(A)'s son. He was given one farm and bought another.
28	0·6	A gift to (A)'s step-daughter.
29, 30	2·5, 6·9	These farms were sold to (L), who is married to his 'cross-cousin' (M).
31	1·3	Given to (M), a maternal niece of (K).
33	7·6	Sold to a brother-in-law of (A), who was succeeded by his maternal nephew.

Land originally owned by (C) and (D). When (C) died in about 1921 he was succeeded by (D). When (D) died in about 1927 he was succeeded by (K). But the total area now in the possession of this successor, (K), is only 11·5 acres, out of the total

APPENDIX III. 8

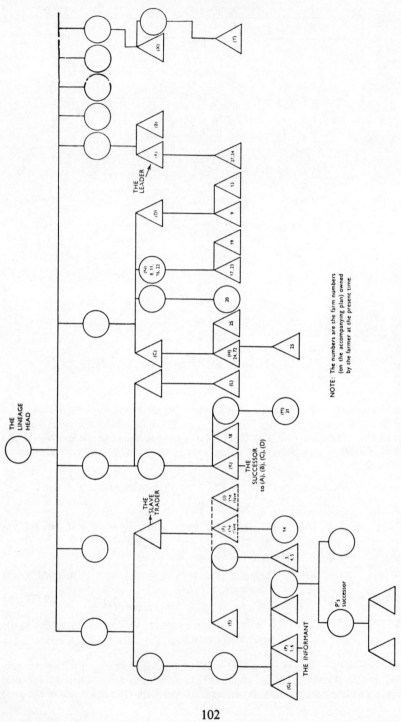

Fig. 3 The Boah matrilineage.

THE BOAH FAMILY LAND

area of the strip of 50·0 acres. Other farms, or land, in the strip were given away as follows:

Farm no.	Acreage	Present owner
10, 12	5·2, 6·3	The successor, (K).
8, 11, 16 22	3·3, 1·1, 3·6, 2·0	(N), the sister of (C) and (D).[1]
9	1·8	Given to (D)'s son.[2]
13, 21	1·0, 1·2	Given to another son of (D).
17, 23	7·1, 0·2	Maternal nephew of (C) and (D) and son of (N).
18	6·0	Brother of (K).
19	3·0	Another son of (N).
20	1·7	Maternal niece of (C) and (D).
24	0·9	Given to (H), son of (C).
25	5·6	Bought, 'or at least in the eyes of the family', from his father (C).

[1] The farms were reportedly given to her after the deaths of her brothers.
[2] It was said that as the farm had been given to the son by the father, it would pass in turn to the paternal grandson.

Land originally owned by (E). (E), a son of the slave trader, died in about 1955. His successor, a maternal nephew, lives away from the area and although he is the real owner of farms 3, 4 and 5, they are registered as follows:

Farm no.	Acreage	Registered owner
3	3·6	Resident maternal nephew of (F)—not the successor.
4	2·3	(L)—the owner of farms 29 and 30.
5	10·5	Registered as owned by (E), but looked after by the registered owner of farm 3.

Land originally owned by (F). As (F) had been a slave he had no maternal relatives and on his death his farm passed to the slave trader's successor (P).

Farm no.	Acreage	Registered owner
6	10·0	The ex-slave's 'successor', (P).
7	1·9	Sold to (H), son of (C).
14	1·4	(F) gave this farm to his daughter.
15	1·1	(F) gave this farm to a 'slave-woman's son' whose children were members of the *abusua* as he married (C)'s sister.

Land originally owned by (G) and (J). The ex-slave (J) was similarly placed to (F) and on his death his farm also passed to (P). On (G)'s death his farm passed to his younger brother (P). These two farms are together farm 1, which has an area of 15·0 acres.

Land originally owned by (H). Although this farm of 4·7 acres is still owned by (H), who is alive, it is registered in the name of a resident brother.

103

APPENDIX III. 8

Summary of present farm ownership

Relationship[1] to original farmer	Number of farmers	Total acreage	Owners of acreages of 10 or more (acres)
Successors[2]	4	100·1	52·1 (K)
			25·0 (P)
			16·4 (E)[3]
Other members of original farmer's *abusua*:			
Maternal nephews	3	16·3	
Maternal nieces	2	3·0	
Sister	1	10·0	10·0 (M)
	6	29·3	
Farmer (L)[4]	1	9·4	
Sons	4	12·9	
Daughters	1	1·4	
Other relatives[5]	3	10·2	
Total	19	163·3	103·5

[1] The table shows the relationship of the present farm-owner to the farmer, whether (A), (B), (C), etc., who originally owned the land.

[2] Including the original farmer (H), who is still alive and owns farms 7 and 24 as well as 2.

[3] The owner of this acreage is in fact (E)'s successor—although various other farmers are listed as owners by the Ministry of Agriculture.

[4] Although (see above) this farmer is not a member of the *abusua*, he is married to such a member.

[5] A son of a brother-in-law, a step-daughter and a sister's husband.

Resident farmers. Four of the farmers resident on the land, or in neighbouring Nankese, are responsible for most of the farming. They are: (P); (L), who is in charge of (K)'s property, as (K) is in Akropong; (D)'s son, who is the owner of farm 9; and (E)'s maternal nephew (not his successor), the registered owner of farms 3 and 5.

APPENDIX III. 9

AN AKROPONG FAMILY LAND NEAR BEPOASE

Location and area. The land (which was possibly originally part of a larger area bought by a wider group of Akropong farmers) lies about three miles west of Coaltar and about six miles north of Adeiso. It has an area of about 380 acres.

Date of acquisition and cost. The land was bought from the stool of Apapam not long before 1914—but the exact date could not be ascertained. Present-day farmers do not know the price that was paid. There was a long delay, of perhaps ten years or more, before planting started.

The members of the family group. The 3 original members of the group were 2 Akropong brothers and their mother's sister's son (whose father came from Mampong). The father of the two brothers, who may have helped them to buy the land, had been a cocoa-farmer near Tinkong and Teacher Mante. The elder of the two brothers is here called Kwabena Owusu for convenience.

AN AKROPONG FAMILY LAND

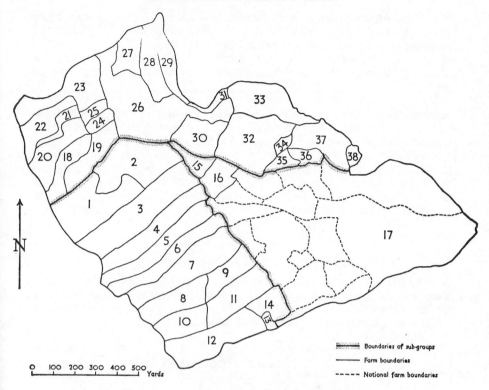

14 The Akropong family land, near Bepoase.

The original and subsequent division of the land (see map 14). The land was originally divided into 3 almost precisely equal portions. Kwabena Owusu took the area now represented by farms 1 to 14 (128 acres), his brother the area of farms 15, 16 and 17 (126 acres), and his maternal cousin the area of farms 18 to 38 (128 acres). It is said that Kwabena Owusu died soon after he had started to plant his land and, as the plan shows, his area was divided into strips, each of which was allotted to a paternal grandchild of his father. Thus, farms 1 to 4 (12, 14, 18 and 10 acres) went to 4 sons of Kwabena Owusu, who was his father's eldest son; farms 5 and 6 (9 and 8 acres) went to sons of a younger brother of Kwabena Owusu; farm 7 (14 acres) went to a son of yet another younger brother; and farms 8 to 14 (8, 6, 6, 7, 12, 1 and 4 acres) went to 4 daughters and 3 sons of the brother who had been associated with Kwabena Owusu from the start—i.e. the original owner of farms 15 to 17.

Turning to the area allocated to this younger brother, it is possible that farms 15 and 16 should have been included with Kwabena Owusu's area as they, also, were given to Kwabena Owusu's father's grandchildren—farm 15 to Kwabena Owusu's daughter and farm 16 to a former wife, a cross-cousin, of the owner of farm 1, i.e. a daughter of one of Kwabena Owusu's sisters. The remainder of the area, now consisting of farm 17, has remained undivided to the present day. The original owner, Kwabena Owusu's brother, 'died long ago' and was succeeded first by one and then by another younger brother. The family has considered it wise to divide the whole area of this farm (which is 120 acres) into smaller areas for the purposes of registration with the

APPENDIX III. 9

Ministry of Agriculture, and, as the plan shows, it has been arbitrarily chopped up into 15 separate 'farms', each of which is registered in the name of a member of Kwabena Owusu's father's *abusua*, one of whom is the long-deceased original owner of the land whom his relatives 'want to remember'. (This division appears, for the time being, to be entirely notional, having no effect, for instance, on who replants the land.)

The land owned by the third original farmer (Kwabena Owusu's mother's sister's son) was divided into some 20 farms following the original farmer's death. These farms are owned by 13 farmers who are: 3 sons and 3 daughters of the original farmer, who own the sub-area consisting of farms 26 to 31 together with farms 35 to 38 (the sons own 49 acres, the daughters 15 acres); 5 members of the original farmer's *abusua* (this being identical with Kwabena Owusu's *abusua*), respectively 2 sisters, 2 maternal nieces and a maternal nephew, who own farms 19 to 25 and also 33, making a total area of 5 acres; and 2 maternal grandsons of the original farmer who own farms 32 and 34, which are together 13 acres.

APPENDIX III. 10
AN AMANOKROM FAMILY LAND NEAR DOME (SUHUM)

Location and area. Situated about five miles to the south-west of Suhum this family land was a portion of a larger area parts of which were resold to Aburi and other farmers. The area of the family land today is 293·8 acres, including one farm detached from the main area, and not shown on the map.

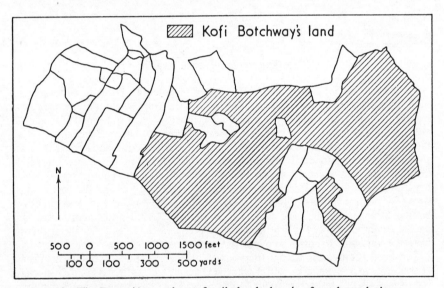

15 The Dome/Amanokrom family land, showing farm boundaries.

Date of acquisition. The date of purchase of the land from the chief of Apapam is tentatively put at 1914, it being probable that farming did not start until about 1920.

The head of the group. The land was bought by an Amanokrom (Akwapim) man, here called Kofi Botchway. Kofi Botchway's maternal uncle was said to have been the

AN AMANOKROM FAMILY LAND

owner of a 'mighty land' at Kwame Boso, which is near mile-post 36 on the road between Mamfe and Adawso and it may be that it was he who bought the Dome land for his nephew: Kofi Botchway's father was an Aburi man and before moving to the Dome land he had been farming on his father's land near Ahamahama (between Aburi and Nsawam). Kofi Botchway lives in Amanokrom in a house built from the proceeds of the land and when he was visited there in 1959 it was said that neither he, nor any other member of his family, was taking any interest in the replanting of his portion of the family land, amounting to 153 acres, though at least three of his nephews and numerous other relatives were resident on the land.

The division of the land. The area of 153 acres retained by Kofi Botchway is shown on map 17. Kofi Botchway gave away nearly a third of the whole acreage of the family land to 13 members of his *abusua*, of whom 8 were maternal nephews and 3 were sisters. Most of the remaining acreage is at present in the possession of 5 of Kofi Botchway's sons who have been granted usufructural rights. Such strips as can be seen on the map are not, in this case, associated with division between sons.

Farm-owner (showing relationship to Kofi Botchway)	Acreage	No. of farmers
Kofi Botchway himself	153·6	1
Maternal nephews	54·9	8
Sisters	32·0	3
Other members of the *abusua*	5·3	2
Total for members of *abusua*	245·8	14
Sons	38·1	5
Descendants of maternal nephews	5·9	4
Paternal grandchildren	4·0	2
Grand Total	293·8	25

Five of the 25 farmers own acreages of 10 or over: these are Kofi Botchway himself (153·6 acres), 2 of his maternal nephews (14·6 and 10·8 acres), a sister (15·4 acres) and a son (12·1 acres). Eight of the remaining 20 farmers own farms of between 5 and 10 acres (total acreage 55·9), another 8 between 2 and 5 acres (total acreage 27·5) and a further 8 under 2 acres (total 3·9 acres).

APPENDIX III. 11

A SMALL ABURI FAMILY LAND NEAR DOME (SUHUM)

Location and area. This land adjoins Kofi Botchway's land (see Appendix III. 10, p. 106), and was either bought directly from the chief of Apapam or from Kofi Botchway. It has an area of 62·5 acres. It is possible that part of the area acquired originally was resold to other Aburi farmers.

The head of the group. The purchaser of the land, an Aburi farmer, was said to have bought four other cocoa-lands before this one. His maternal nephew, the present 'chief' of the village on the land, said that his uncle had divided his whole land between his maternal nephews and nieces during his lifetime.

Present-day ownership. Of the total area of 62·5 acres, 51·8 acres is owned by members of the original farmer's *abusua*. Three maternal nephews own 10·5, 10·8

107

APPENDIX III. 11

and 9·6 acres and another owns a small farm of only 1·0 acres. Six maternal nieces together own 8·1 acres and 2 sisters own 7·0 acres and 4·8 acres. Several of the larger farmers own several farms. The 10·7 acres owned by non-members of the *abusua* is mainly in the possession of sons of maternal nephews (of original farmers). Despite the death of the cocoa from swollen shoot, and the small size of the land, as many as 8 of the total of 19 farm-owners were resident on the land in 1959, in apparently poverty-stricken conditions, and a further 6 were resident in Aburi.

CHAPTER IV

THE OPERATION OF THE CUSTOMARY RULES OF INHERITANCE[1]

I: COMPANY LANDS[2]

Customary law, in many parts of Ghana, has for long recognized, or tolerated, the practice of the outright sale[3] of land. The sellers are chiefs, who act on behalf of the community as a whole. The buyers are individual cocoa-farmers who, whether or not they are associated with other buyers in land-purchasing companies, act for themselves alone. Although these individual buyers usually have many motives, not the least of which may be the desire to provide their sons or grandsons with a 'new land', the act of purchasing a land is essentially similar to that of purchasing a piece of cloth or a lorry—the land at the time of its acquisition being the individual (or private) property of the purchaser. Lawyers usually denote such land as 'self-acquired property', in contra-distinction to the other main class of property—'family property'. Family property (here denoted as lineage property) is not owned by an individual, though individuals may exercise rights in relation to it, but by a lineage, or corporate group.

In the eyes of the law the presumption is in favour of family property:[4]

If land be free today in the hands of its acquirer, it will tomorrow resume its fetters in the hands of his heirs.[5]

No owner impresses on the land any permanent form of tenure.[6]

[1] In *Nigerian Land Law and Custom*, Mr T. Olawale Elias states (p. 215) two principles which should be borne in mind in discussing the customary rules of inheritance, and these apply equally well to Ghana, where little cocoa-land is willed under Ghana common law. These principles are: (1) that 'the inheritance of property is governed by traditional canons of descent and not by *wills*, unless, of course, a person has expressly made a will or married according to English law, when other considerations will apply. . . There is accordingly no need to divide the customary rules of inheritance into testate and intestate. . .'; (2) 'That, because of the pluralistic tendency of social norms and concepts, especially in the matter of land usage, there is a constant interplay between tenure and inheritance. In such a situation, therefore, there is bound to be a measure of overlapping in stating the principles of either.'

[2] The first section of this chapter relates in particular to Akwapim and Shai patrilineal inheritance systems and it also serves, to some extent, as a general introduction to the second section on matrilineal systems.

[3] As this chapter is written by a legal layman for legal laymen, legal terminology is not employed. The term 'outright sale' is meant to convey (see chapter v) that the land vendor cannot, in any circumstances, reclaim the land once the sale has been concluded so that, for example, the vendee is free to resell it to anyone else. The question of the jurisdictional interest of the stool is a different one—see chapter v.

[4] See an Editorial Note on the case of *Makata v. Ahorli* in *The West African Law Reports*, vol. 1 (1956).

[5] J. M. Sarbah, *Fanti Customary Laws* (1897), p. 78.

[6] This remark of Sir William Brandford Griffith, one time Chief Justice of the Gold Coast is quoted on p. 180 of *Land Law and Custom in the Colonies* by C. K. Meek.

109

RULES OF INHERITANCE

With regard to the timing of the process it is usually considered that:

personally acquired property which is not disposed of by testamentary disposition becomes family property on the death of its owner;

though it is added that:

the family group for this purpose may be a smaller unit than the family group which has power of disposal over property that always has been family property.[1]

In general the authorities are impressed with the present-day vitality of lineages as land-holders:

It must not be supposed . . . that the lineage organisation and lineage ownership of land is everywhere breaking down in Africa. . . There is, indeed, good evidence that in many areas of Africa lineages are now becoming alive to the value of their holdings and entrenching their position as landed proprietors.[2]

. . . there is plenty of evidence to show that even in the progressive Colony of Lagos family ownership continues to be an integral feature of the social life. . .[3]

But although 'the great bulk of property is held subject to family interests', 'those interests—so uncertain is the law—are no more capable of exact definition than are those held by individuals'.[4]

The lawyers are compelled by circumstances to take the existence of the great dichotomy for granted—there is individual property on the one hand and family property on the other. But the actual process of conversion of the one into the other has not been a social problem, so that it has received much less attention from lawyers than might have been expected.[5] It is furthermore true that in Ghana, as in Nigeria,[6] local court material only is reliable for certain research purposes, some of the decisions reported from the higher courts embodying serious misconceptions of the particular customary law involved.[7] One of the present purposes is to suggest that a study of the process by which, during the last

[1] See an Editorial Note on the case of *Makata v. Ahorli* in *The West African Law Reports*, vol. 1 (1956).

[2] C. K. Meek, 'Some Social Aspects of Land Tenure in Africa' from 'Land Tenure', a special supplement to the *Journal of African Administration*, October 1952, p. 17.

[3] C. K. Meek, *Land Law and Custom in the Colonies*, p. 297. Mr Meek was concerned to dispute the view of several Nigerian judges that family ownership of land was 'a dying institution'. He added that 'The whole history of land legislation and litigation in the Colony of Nigeria during the last eighty-five years provides a signal example of the necessity of a sociological rather than a purely legal approach to problems of tenure in African communities'.

[4] A. J. Loveridge, 'Wills and the Customary Law in the Gold Coast', *Journal of African Administration*, October 1950, p. 27.

[5] But see Appendix IV. 1 (p. 131).

[6] It is because so little attention has been paid by lawyers to the patrilineal Akwapim that references are made to authorities on comparable Nigerian patrilineal societies.

[7] See the doubts cast on material taken from Supreme and High Court judgments by P. C. Lloyd in 'Some Notes on the Yoruba Rules of Succession and on "Family Property"', *Journal of African Law*, vol. 3 (1959). (It is very unfortunate that Dr P. C. Lloyd's masterly and authoritative *Yoruba Land Law* appeared too late—1962—to be of use here. The same applies to *Principles of Customary Land Law in Ghana*, 1962, by Mr Justice N. A. Ollennu.)

sixty years, the farms and lands owned by the migrant farmers have passed from one generation of owners to another, provides an opportunity of studying the practical working of the rules[1] of inheritance—an opportunity such as has occurred in few other parts of Africa, considering the relatively long history of cocoa-growing in Ghana, the nature of the migration and the existence of the farm maps.

The first point that must be clarified in connexion with this practical inquiry is whether the legal dichotomy is at all appropriate for present purposes. Do the migrant cocoa-farmers themselves see a clear-cut distinction between individual and lineage property? Certainly the question must be asked in such a way as to avoid many of the unavoidable difficulties encountered by anthropologists. This practical examination is not concerned with all the possible rights in, or uses of, the land but only with rights in relation to cocoa-growing. This is one reason why the notion of a 'cluster of rights'[2] is too sophisticated for present purposes and why the 'undying fallacy of anthropological work'[3]—the problem of individual versus communal land-tenure—is disregarded.

When considering a cocoa-farmer's relationship to a land or farm it is necessary to pay regard to the extent of his individual right to:

(a)   sell the property outright to whomever he wishes and to use the proceeds freely;

(b)   pledge the property on whatever terms he is able to negotiate;

(c)   give the property away or to grant usufructuary rights to whomever he wishes;

(d)   bequeath the property to whomever he wishes.

If the farmer possesses an entire freedom in regard to (a) to (d) then *for the time being* the land or farm may be considered to be his complete (100 per cent) individual property.

Imagine at the other extreme a farmer who possesses usufructuary rights only—his rights in regard to (a) to (d) being entirely non-existent. (The word 'usufructuary' as normally used in this book implies that the farmer lacks rights over the land as such, but has been granted permission to pluck and sell the cocoa from it during his lifetime or for a shorter period: the legal sense of the word is entirely different.) Such a farmer totally lacks individual control over the farm as such.[4] He is, as it were, at

---

[1] Some anthropologists have urged the present writer to avoid the use of the word 'rule' altogether, there being so much flexibility in the practical operation of inheritance systems; others have suggested that the emphasis on this flexibility has been overdone. The use of the word 'rule' does not signify agreement with either of these viewpoints.

[2] See *Tiv Farm and Settlements* by Paul Bohannan, Colonial Research Studies, no. 15 (1954), p. 31, where it is pointed out that so many people may have rights in a piece of land that it is often better to refer to 'a cluster of rights'.

[3] See Bohannan, *op. cit.*, p. 34, the 'undying fallacy' being Malinowski's expression.

[4] The extent to which he can depend on the continued existence of his usufructuary rights during his lifetime is a separate question—in some cases such rights may be terminated following the death of the farmer who granted them.

RULES OF INHERITANCE

the opposite end of the spectrum to the farmer whose control over the farm is complete.

In between these two extremes lie numerous possibilities and it is here that the fact of obligations as well as rights may be introduced. A man who has inherited a land or farm may be obliged by custom (though not by law) to grant usufructuary rights over portions of it to certain lineage members, and with the aid of its net proceeds to render financial help to others. But at the same time the degree of his individual control and the extent to which it operates to his personal interest must not be underestimated, this being especially true of the company farmers who never grant formal usufructuary rights (such as would result in the grantee being registered as the farm-owner by the Ministry of Agriculture) to indigent, or other, kinsmen, as is the way of matrilineal farmers.

So it is the contention here that if an individual migrant cocoa-farmer's relationship to his land (or farm) be regarded in this practical spirit in terms of the degree of individual control which he exercises, it then ceases to be appropriate to ask whether it is his individual property or not, but that it is the degree of individual control which must be considered.

Turning now to the separate question of whether a land (or farm), or portions thereof, should be considered to be lineage property, here again practical circumstances make it appropriate to regard this as a matter of degree—in contra-distinction to a situation (which is not a matter of degree) where every member of a clan has a right to a portion of ancestral land for food-farming purposes. The question may be considered from the point of view of a potential farmer—a member of the lineage: the greater his chances of being allotted usufructuary rights over a portion of the property and the greater the potential extent of those rights, the more inclined he will be to regard the property as 'lineage property'. From the point of view of the farmer who created the property, the extent to which he considers it to be lineage property will first of all be reflected in his willingness to grant farming rights to his kin—and once these rights have been granted his attitude will be coloured by the objections to withdrawing them.

It is hoped that this chapter will throw a little light on the processes which result over the years in (a) the loss of individual control and (b) the creation of corporate (lineage) control. The analogy of the two spectra—relating respectively to the degree of individual and of lineage control—is in a way absurd, for it is, of course, impossible to denote points on them in arithmetical terms, so that it is necessary to use such cumbersome expressions as 'full individual control', 'partial individual control' and 'modified lineage property'.

An immense difficulty has to be faced. This is that while on the one hand the rules of inheritance are 'part and parcel of the social structure',[1] on the other hand the social structures of the various patrilineal Akwapim societies have never been described even in outline. It is certainly impossible not to appear to be over-emphasizing the importance of these rules—and to be ignoring 'the constant inter-play between tenure and inheritance'.

This point is well brought out in any attempt to discuss the association, which, as is constantly emphasized, is an *observed fact*,[2] between patrilineal societies and the company system and matrilineal societies and the family land system. It may be that the patrilineal societies have some common characteristic, other than their inheritance system, which should be used as an 'explanation' of their ready adoption of the company system. But in the absence of evidence to the contrary it is difficult not to over-simplify the relationship between the company system and the rules of inheritance.

There is some evidence[3] that the introduction of migratory cocoa-farming brought about modifications in the traditional inheritance system of certain of the patrilineal Akwapim in accordance with which a man's property was controlled or administered after his death by a lineage successor who might (depending on which society is being considered) be a son of the younger brother of the deceased. Such traditional successors were apt to take advantage of the new situation, regarding the valuable cocoa-farms, with which they were quite probably unfamiliar, as personal to themselves and failing to pay due regard to the needs of the sons (and widows) of the deceased. The change to a system whereby a man's self-acquired cocoa-farms in practice passed directly to his sons was possibly associated, in some of the societies at any rate, with the introduction, soon after 1900, of the company system. This company (or strip) system permitted the equitable division of property among a man's sons on his death. With the matrilineal migrants there is no need for division of property after death, for there is a single inheritor only, and it is very interesting to note that the maps show that even among predominantly matrilineal people, division by means of neatly drawn strips is always associated with the transfer, by gift or inheritance, of property to sons.[4]

If it is necessary, as it may not be if the deceased owned several lands, for a farm to be divided between the sons of several wives of the deceased, then the most usual system,[5] among both patrilineal Akwapim and

---

[1] Meek, *Land Law and Custom in the Colonies*, p. 193. And the rules 'cannot be altered without altering also the social system of which they are an expression'. He adds that 'much more knowledge is required of the native rules of inheritance'.
[2] See Appendix VII, 2, p. 199.   [3] See Appendix IV. 3 (p. 133).
[4] See, for instance, Appendix III. 9 (p. 104).
[5] Dr M. J. Field comments: 'None of the "usual systems" is rigid. A step-son, an adopted son, a son-in-law, a wife, etc. who has worked well with the deceased, may be given

RULES OF INHERITANCE

Adangme peoples, is that which is often conveniently denoted as 'division between wives'[1] (i.e. division between 'houses')—the sons of each wife *taken together* receiving approximately equal shares, no regard being paid to the number of children of each wife. (The commonsense assumption involved in these rules is that sons will honour their obligations to look after their widowed mothers.) When it comes to the partition of the portion which has been allotted, as it were, to each wife (or house), there seems to be no rule as to whether each son, who requires a share, should receive an equal portion: perhaps this is usually the general idea,[2] though in some cases the senior son may get more than his brothers. The fact that Akwapim farmers object, for agricultural reasons, to the further sub-division of 'one-rope farms' is of practical importance. But even if more than one son is interested in claiming rights over a strip which is wide enough to be sub-divisible, it does not follow that such formal sub-division will necessarily occur, especially among some peoples, notably Larterians; it may be that each resident farmer will farm forward from a position on the base-line, taking care not to encroach on his brother. If only one of the brothers is resident in the area and there has been no formal division, then that brother may regard the whole area as a modified form of individual property—recognizing that his absent brothers may assert their rights later on.[3] This brother will, as it were, suffer from several 'disabilities' in relation to the property: if he plants the whole area he cannot be sure that in future he will be entitled to the whole usufruct, for his brothers may return and claim a portion of the planted area; and then there is the separate point that as it was his father, not he himself, who originally 'created' the property, all his father's grandsons (not only his own sons) will in principle (though not necessarily in practice, when the time comes) be entitled to a share on his death. But before considering this process further, the various devices by which the individual seeks to impose his will on future generations must be further considered.

a bigger share than those who have "customary rights" if it is believed that he, or she, will "look after the property well for those who come after". The welfare of the unborn and immature is always kept in mind in the allocation of property and responsibility.'

[1] Pogucki in *Report on Land Tenure in Adangme Customary Law*, p. 41, states that property is occasionally apportioned in equal parts to all the sons of the deceased, irrespective of their mothers, in which case the senior son may, or may not, obtain a larger share. There is no corresponding information for any of the patrilineal Akwapim, but for farmers with large numbers of wives it happens that the point is seldom of practical importance as much-married men tend to own large numbers of lands none of which need to be divided between wives.

[2] The maps show that sons seldom receive precisely equal shares, but this may be due rather to the exigencies of the situation (unrectangular lands, the situation of cottages and so forth) than to intentions.

[3] In general the company system is much less accommodating to relatives who change their minds and come back to the land than is the family land system, this being because the principle of longitudinal division of strips always involves the resident brother in relinquishing some of his planted area to his returning brother; very few instances of transverse division of strips by brothers have been noticed, but there was one at Obomofo-Densua—Appendix II. 7 (p. 69).

RULES OF INHERITANCE

Fathers are sometimes so successful in identifying themselves with their sons, in economic terms, that there is really no means of telling whether a father or a son is the owner of a land or farm.[1] As a Tutu (Akwapim) farmer said, the process may even benefit the grandchildren during the lifetime of the grandfather:

The practice is that a man gives some of his land to his children during his lifetime. In the old days the grandfather would give his son a portion so that the son might make money and buy another land. He, the son, gives a portion of this new land to the grandchildren.

In giving land to their sons during their lifetimes,[2] fathers may follow the rules which would have operated on their deaths.[3] Such sons may suffer from some disabilities in relation to the property (they may not, for instance, be as free to sell[4] it as they would have been if they had bought it themselves, though pledging is usually a practicable alternative), but their control is likely to be greater than that exerted by sons who inherited their father's property on his death—e.g. there is likely to be no question but that their sons only (not also their brothers' sons) will inherit on their deaths, just as though they had themselves been the original farmers. As though admitting that the creation of lineage property has been postponed the father (who made gifts to his sons) may keep a portion for his own use in the knowledge that this will at once be transformed into lineage property on his death, being regarded as a 'reserve' for use in emergency which is not 'owned' by whatever person is put in charge of it.

Chapter VII is concerned with economic aspects of the migratory process and much stress is laid there on the expansionary nature of the farmers' involvement in a process which is in many respects essentially capitalistic. But in buying sequences of lands the farmers are, of course, impelled by many other motives, one of which may be regarded as a resistance to the drift towards lineage property. (Of course corresponding to this resistance is the urge to submit to the ties of kinship, the events of history being seen as the outcome of the conflict.) One of the measures of a farmer's success in resisting the drift may be the extent to which subdivision of strip-farms is avoided and our maps show that there is often less subdivision than the application of the 'principles' of inheritance would suggest.[5]

[1] P. C. Lloyd, *op. cit.*, p. 14, refers to 'the gradual manner by which sons succeed a father'.
[2] As, for example, the Mamfe farmers did at Saforosua—see Appendix II. 8 (p. 70). See also Appendix IV. 2 (p. 132).
[3] There are examples of the operation of the rule of 'division between wives' in relation to gifts both at Saforosua and at Obomofo-Densua.
[4] Most sales of land, as distinct from farms, occur in the early days before there has been much planting of the strip and, especially if his father has meanwhile died, a son may be free to resell.
[5] Of course there are many reasons, apart from the ownership of a large number of lands, why strip-farms may not be subdivided. A farmer may have few sons, or most of his sons may be uninterested in cocoa-farming.

115

RULES OF INHERITANCE

If farmers are questioned regarding the process of loss of individual rights over land they very often fail to understand what is meant—and it is highly significant that there are no satisfactory unambiguous Twi equivalents (such as are bound to be employed in ordinary conversation) for individual and lineage property.[1] But sometimes it is clear that in principle they regard this process of loss as complete when the last of the sons of the original farmer has died and the grandsons have come into occupation.[2] In presuming thus, they may be regarding the rules of inheritance with an unnecessary awe—assuming them to operate more quickly and ruthlessly than is in fact the case. What do the farm maps show?

These maps are, unfortunately, not as helpful in this connexion as might be expected, for although most of the companies in the mapped area of southern Akim Abuakwa bought their land half a century or more ago, only a small proportion of the land is, as yet, in the possession of grandsons (of original farmers)—see table I, p. 119. (The surprising fact that most of the land is held by sons is, presumably, to be explained by the youthfulness of the so-called 'original farmers' who, for one reason or another, including the delays that were apt to occur before serious planting began, were often, in fact, the sons of those who first put up the money.) But the maps do show that 'division among grandsons' occurs, although some farmers say that as such property is lineage property it 'ought not to'. Inquiries show that farms are seldom registered in the names of grandsons who are not sons of the deceased owner of that particular portion of land. While resident grandsons may have to make way for grandsons hitherto non-resident, they will certainly continue to exert usufructuary rights over a part of the land for as long as they wish. Indeed, this being a point which is often overlooked, residence in an area is a 'dimension' of almost comparable importance to kinship in determining the continuity of rights. It is worth noting, in this connexion, that sons show much more sympathy towards their sisters on the grounds that their children cannot inherit than they would if there were not a large element of individual control exerted by inheritors.

As for the position of women farmers, it is certainly clear that many of them suffer from many disabilities in the extent of their individual control.[3] It is unusual for a woman to be a company member in her own right,[4] and it is usually only those fathers who have no sons who contem-

---

[1] Thus a word such as *agyapade*, which originally (and by derivation) related to inherited property, is often nowadays also applied to individual property. However, *abusua asase* is a satisfactory rendering of 'lineage land'.

[2] Adding that if there are a great many sons of the original farmer it may be completed earlier. But on the other hand some grandsons insist that they exert a large degree of individual control.

[3] This is in great contrast to the position of native Akim women cocoa-farmers who usually stand in the same relationship to their farms as their male counterparts and who in some areas, such as Akokoaso, comprise about half the cocoa-farming population.

[4] Occasionally women invest their trading profits in the purchase of land through com-

RULES OF INHERITANCE

plate buying land for their daughters. A woman who possesses the status of an original farmer (because, say, her father bought the land for her), has as much control over her property as a man would have, and her children may inherit. But (as at Obomofo-Densua: see table I) a great proportion of the women farmers in whose names company farms have been registered by the Ministry of Agriculture are daughters who are representing their non-resident brothers (or who, being widowed or divorced, have been treated compassionately by them on their return to the land, which may have been their birthplace), or wives who have been granted usufructuary rights by their husbands—the farms reverting to their husbands' sons on their deaths. Occasionally daughters as well as sons inherit on the death of their father, but it seems that (unless the farms are very small) such daughters are nearly always unmarried—possibly usually the mothers of children whom their fathers have adopted as their own. And with Mamfe and Mampong farmers (see Appendix IV. 3, p. 133), there is the curious recognition of the 'mother's side', which means that portions of farms sometimes pass to one of the sisters of the deceased or her daughters (or sons). The difficulty over generalization is not only that practices vary, but also that beliefs about practices vary. Thus, one Mamfe farmer insisted that 'daughters inherit equally with sons'—whether they are married or not.

But with some Akwapim farmers, it seems to be usual for all resident daughters to be given the use of small portions of land—perhaps rather kitchen gardens than cocoa-farms. In the case of the Kyerepon company at Nobeso 14 daughters hold land (compared with 21 sons), but if the 2 largest farms are omitted it is found that the total area owned by the 12 daughters is only 22 acres.

Although, in general, the control exercised by women in their individual capacities is slight, and although they suffer from the (associated) disability of knowing that farms which they have inherited from their father will pass to their brothers or their brothers' children, yet as the effective (though not the legal) custodians either of their husbands' or of lineage property they are apt to exert much power—much of the cocoa-farming at Obomofo-Densua, for instance, being the responsibility of women. Many husbands leave their farms in the full charge of their wives, while travelling about managing the work on their various lands.

Among all the many practical difficulties encountered by the investi-

---

panies, but they usually do this through the agency of men. While most wives live with their cocoa-farming husbands in the farming areas, they are often prevented by the need to care for infants from being the first to settle in the forest before food-farms have been established. In West Africa it is generally true that men are more often formally associated, for economic purposes, with groups of their friends than are women (in officially sponsored co-operatives, as well as more spontaneously), though small trading partnerships are very common with women. Commercial though the behaviour of women is in many ways, they lack a commercial attitude to land.

RULES OF INHERITANCE

gator in the field, the studied vagueness of many farmers is perhaps the most puzzling. Many farmers prefer not to clarify their relationship to a farm over which they have assumed effective charge—presuming that any requests for clarification which they might put to their relatives would raise questions which had better lie latent. Much of this indeterminateness has resulted from the chaos following swollen-shoot disease. Many resident farmers seem indifferent to the fact that the farm they are in charge of is registered in the name of (say) an absent brother. They may replant the devastated farm without any firm thoughts for the future— this fact standing in extraordinary contrast to the general anxieties about the *inexorable* rules of inheritance which the farmers feel, express and act on at other times. Time and time again, inquiries about how farmers stand in relation to their absent owner-brothers have been received with the indifference which polite informants use as their defence against ignorant questioners: time and time again, it has become clear that nothing has been agreed between them, little has been discussed and that there is no long-term plan.[1] The more sophisticated farmer may try and justify the fact that it is he who is replanting the farm by referring to his obligations to his brother, while those who are not trying to rationalize their behaviour will casually convey the casualness of the situation. Here, again, is an indication of the importance of 'residence'.[2]

As for the future, it remains to be seen whether we are not just beginning to witness the dawn of another revolution. Perhaps some of those who replant portions of old lineage land which have been devastated by swollen shoot, will find themselves in the possession of full individual rights—corresponding to the rights traditionally accorded to those who clear plots for themselves in their native area?

The following tables throw light on some practical aspects of the operation of the customary rules of patrilineal inheritance during the last half-century or so. Had the companies in question happened to have been smaller ones (and many company lands *are* much smaller), average farm size would probably have been smaller also. While no representativeness is claimed for these companies in terms of size, there is no reason to think that as Kyerepon, Mamfe or Shai companies they are particularly unrepresentative, so far as concerns the practical operation of the rules of inheritance.

[1] It does not follow that 'inefficiency' will result. In the event of a dispute later on, there will always be some kinsman prepared to advise or take decisions.

[2] Such is the mobility of some (though not all) of the farm-owners that residence is a matter of degree. A farmer who usually lives on another land, or in his homeland, may be considered as effectively resident if he turns up sufficiently at crucial times of the year—and many elderly farmers who might be thought to be in full retirement in Akwapim in fact do this. A fully non-resident farmer is one who never turns up from one year's end to the next.

RULES OF INHERITANCE

I: Present Ownership of Retained Acreage

Relationship of present to original farmer	Kyerepon/ Nobeso		Mamfe/ Trayo		Shai/ Nankese		Obomofo- Densua (Shai)		Mamfe/ Saforosua	
	(A)		(B)		(C)		(D)		(E)	
	ACRES									
		%		%		%		%		%
Original farmers	29	7	—	—	280	52	—	—	96[3]	17
Sons	187	46	405	74	210	39	272	60	385	69
Daughters	58	14	53	10	10	2	131[2]	29	51	9
Grandchildren	69	17	20	4	18	3	43	9	—[4]	—
Sisters[1]	3	1	60	11	—	—	—	—	6	1
Other relatives	58	14	10	2	18	3	9	2	23	4
	404	100	548	100	536	100	455	100	561	100

II: Numbers of Present-day Farmers

Relationship of present to original farmer	Kyerepon/ Nobeso	Mamfe/ Trayo	Shai/ Nankese	Obomofo- Densua (Shai)	Mamfe/ Saforosua
	(A)	(B)	(C)	(D)	(E)
	NUMBER OF FARMERS (excluding outsiders)				
Original farmers	4	—	20	—	2[3]
Sons	21	12	17	15	17
Daughters	14	3	2	11[2]	7
Grandchildren	21	1	2	5	—[4]
Sisters[1]	1	4	—	—	3
Other relatives	18	1	2	1	6
	79	21	43	32	35
Number of farmers originally[5]	19	6[6]	34	12	6

[1] Including sisters' descendants.

[2] Most of these are probably 'nominal owners', see p. 117.

[3] These two original farmers were actually dead at the time inquiries were made, see note (*c*) and comment (i) on p. 121.

[4] Although some surviving sons appeared to have given land to their sons, these gifts are here disregarded as they represented future intentions only.

[5] The figures are those shown in the table on p. 53.

[6] Excluding two farmers who sold all their land.

RULES OF INHERITANCE

III: Present-day Farm Areas

		Kyerepon/ Nobeso	Mamfe/ Trayo	Shai/ Nankese	Obomofo- Densua (Shai)	Mamfe/ Saforosua
		(A)	(B)	(C)	(D)	(E)
(1)	Total retained acreage	404·0	548·0	535·8	454·7	561·0
(2)	Number of farmers today	79	21	43	32	35
(3)	Average acreage —total	5·1	26·1	12·5	14·2	16·6
(4)	Average acreage —sons' farms	8·9	33·7	12·4	18·1	22·6
(5)	Largest farm acreage	26·2	180·2	36·4	114·5	98·2[4]
(6)	Next largest farm acreage	20·3[1]	78·7	33·5	31·7	58·8
(7)	(5)+(6) as a % of (1)	12%	47%	13%	32%	28%[5]
(8)	Average acreage —exclud. (5) & (6)	4·6	15·2	11·3	10·3	12·2[6]
(9)	Average acreage —sons' farms exclud. (5) & (6)	8·0	14·6	9·4	9·6	15·2[7]
(10)	Average acreage —daughters' farms	2·9[2]	17·8[3]	4·8[3]	1·2	7·3
(11)	No. of sons' farms —over 10 acres	8	11	10	6	13
(12)	ditto —under 10 acres	13	1	7	9	4
(13)	ditto —under 5 acres	7	—	3	4	—
(14)	ditto —between 5 & 20 acres	13	9	11	8	13
(15)	No. of farmers with farms over 10 acres	12	16	23	12	17
(16)	% of total acreage owned by (15)	43%	93%	76%	70%	86%

[1] Owned by a daughter.
[2] Excluding (6).
[3] Average based on very small numbers.
[4] The owner of this farm has also, in fact, inherited to a further 43·9 acres, which is still registered as owned by the deceased original farmer.
[5] The percentage is 36 if the 43·9 acres (see foregoing footnote) is included.
[6] The average acreage is 11·3 if the 43·9 acres is excluded.
[7] The average acreage is exclusive of (5) and (6) although (5) is owned by an Akropong nephew, who succeeded his uncle, not by a son. The acreage is 12·3 if the 43·9 acres is excluded.

RULES OF INHERITANCE

Notes on Tables I to III

(a) For further particulars see Appendices to Chapter ii.
(b) See notes on Table 'The Original Size of Strip-farms', chapter ii, p. 53, relating to definitions of 'retained acreage' etc.
(c) The figures are derived from the records of the Ministry of Agriculture and in general relate to the date at which the area was first surveyed. The area in which (C) is situated was surveyed soon after 1948 and a number of the original farmers have died since then—and even at that time some of the farms may have been registered in the names of deceased original farmers. (A) and (E) were not surveyed until about ten years later and (B) and (D) in the mid-fifties.

Comments on Tables I to III

General Note: The calamity of swollen shoot has brought about a measure of redistribution of ownership that would not otherwise have occurred and some of the farmers have been alive to the possibilities of using the Ministry of Agriculture as a kind of firm of unpaid surveyors prepared to assist in the drawing of new boundaries. This may mean that, for example, more farms are registered in the names of infants, schoolchildren, etc., than had the Ministry merely recorded existing boundaries.

(i) For a variety of reasons, including the partial identification of fathers with sons, the practice (partly accidental, partly deliberate) of continuing to register farms in the names of farmers long since deceased, the out-of-dateness of the Shai/Nankese figures, etc., little reliability should be attached to the separate figures for original farmers and sons; nor, in the case of Obomofo-Densua, are all the daughters the real owners of the farms registered in their names. If the acreages owned by original farmers and their sons and daughters are added, it is found that this total represents between 67 per cent of the total retained area (Kyerepon/Nobeso) and 95 per cent (Mamfe/Saforosua).

(ii) With the exception of Obomofo-Densua, the proportion of the acreage registered in the names of daughters is small.

(iii) As noted above (p. 116) the proportion of the acreage in the hands of grandchildren (mostly grandsons) is low, except in the case of Kyerepon/Nobeso; moreover, some of the grandsons' fathers are still alive and resident in the area, in which case the grandson is usually a notional farm-owner.

(iv) The number of present-day farm-owners (always excluding outsiders to whom land was sold by company members) is in all cases (save Shai/Nankese, for which the figures are particularly out of date) at least three times the number of original farmers.

(v) Present-day average farm size varies between $5 \cdot 1$ acres (Kyerepon/Nobeso) and $26 \cdot 1$ acres (Mamfe/Trayo), but there is so much dispersion that these figures have little significance.

(vi) There are still some very large farms, the largest being 180 acres (Mamfe/Trayo). Taking the two largest farms for each company, it is found that eight out of ten of them are owned by sons of original farmers, one (Kyerepon/Nobeso) by a daughter and one by the maternal nephew (the successor) of an Akropong farmer who was a member of the Mamfe/Saforosua company. The two largest farms in each company account for between 12 per cent and 47 per cent of the total retained acreage of the company.

(vii) If these ten largest farms are omitted, as being exceptional, there is found to be some uniformity in the average size of farms owned by sons—the average varying only between 8 acres (Kyerepon/Nobeso) and 15 acres (Mamfe/Saforosua). Daughters' farms are significantly smaller. It would appear to be no accident, see p. 51, that the

121

RULES OF INHERITANCE

Mamfe farms are larger than the others. Taking all the companies together, only 14 out of 82 of the sons' farms are under 5 acres and 54 of them are between 5 and 20 acres.

(viii) Eighty farmers, out of a total of 210, own farms of 10 acres or more and with all the companies, save Kyerepon Nobeso, such farmers own at least 70 per cent of the total acreage.

II: FAMILY LANDS

The family land presents such an extraordinary contrast to the company that it is seldom possible to speak of them in the same breath. However, it is true that both types of organization owe their existence to individual farmers who are concerned to express their individuality in this creative manner. In both cases these individuals tend to lose their power of individual control as time goes by, there being a corresponding tendency (though not precisely corresponding) for the corporate control by the lineage to increase.

Before considering whether the 'great dichotomy' of the lawyers applies, in practice, to family lands, a few introductory notes on the nature of the matrilineal system[1] must be provided for the sake of those readers who are not generally familiar with it. Fortunately there have been so many distinguished investigators of Akan matrilineal societies from the time of Rattray onwards,[2] that there is no lack of literature to which the reader may be referred.[3]

'Every person of free matrilineal descent . . . is by birth a member of his mother's lineage (*abusua*). . .'[4] (The same term *abusua* is used for the clan as for the lineage.)

. . . The right of inheritance is confined to the matrilineage and men take precedence over women in the inheritance of a man's property. Brothers should take precedence over sisters' sons and the latter come before sisters. Formerly a mother's sister's son . . . inherited in preference to own sister's son. Nowadays this is not so and if no male heir descended from the deceased's mother is eligible, his own sister will demand acknowledgement as heir rather than permit the mother's sister's son to inherit. In inter-personal relations the trend is to stress lineal connexions in successive generations in preference to collateral connexions of higher genealogical status.[5]

As noted in chapter III the classical family land is the Aburi land. The Aburi people are basically Akwamu (see Appendix I. 4, p. 28) and there

---

[1] It is, of course, realized that the inheritance system is but one aspect of the social structure—and that the attempt to isolate it necessarily does damage to one's thinking.

[2] And before: 'Indeed the outlines of the Akan system were known to scholars long before Rattray first described it.' (Fortes, *African Systems of Kinship and Marriage*, p. 253.)

[3] Much the most useful work for the general reader is '*African Systems of Kinship and Marriage*', edited by A. R. Radcliffe-Brown and Daryll Forde, both for its (85-page long) introduction to African kinship systems by A. R. Radcliffe-Brown and for the chapter by Professor M. Fortes on 'Kinship and marriage among the Ashanti'. Apart from Rattray's three works, the list of books on Ghanaian matrilineal systems includes *Akan Laws and Customs* by J. B. Danquah and *Akim-Kotoku* by M. J. Field.

[4] Fortes, *op. cit.*, p. 254.   [5] Fortes, *op. cit.*, pp. 261–2.

122

RULES OF INHERITANCE

seems no reason to doubt the general applicability to them of Professor Fortes's findings in Ashanti. Again, with the Akropong people, who are basically of Akim origin, the matrilineal rules of inheritance operate in a familiar manner, although patrilineal principles sometimes receive some recognition.

With both Aburi and Akropong farmers it is unusual for a man's farm to pass on his death to an *elder* brother; inheritance by the next younger (uterine) brother is usual and it is not uncommon for property to pass through the hands of several younger brothers in succession before coming under the control of a *wɔfase*, i.e. a son of one of the deceased's sisters —the man who is often popularly supposed to be the first inheritor. Although, other things equal, a son[1] of the deceased's *eldest* sister is the preferred inheritor, he may be passed over in favour of the son of another sister if he is evidently unsuitable.[2] Residence on the land is seldom a factor of much importance in the choice of an inheritor, for however many lands a farmer may have 'created' he will only have one inheritor—in contrast to the patrilineal farmer who may have as many inheritors as he has sons. (But resident nephews who are not inheritors often represent their absent inheritor-brothers, taking upon themselves, in so doing, a large measure of individual control.)

There is evidence (see Appendix IV. 4, p. 135) that the development of commercial cocoa-growing has brought about a 'streamlining' of the inheritance system such that it is nowadays very unusual for farms to pass to anyone other than a younger brother (or sister) or a 'direct *wɔfase*' of the deceased—this being in accordance with the trend stressed (see quotation on p. 135) by Professor Fortes.[3] But while the system has been streamlined in response to the new economic pulls and pressures, it has in no wise been 'whittled-down'.[4] On the contrary (as noted in chapter III)

[1] The presumption in favour of the eldest son of the eldest sister is perhaps not nearly so strong as that in favour of a son of the eldest sister.

[2] '. . . as the heir has in every case to be approved by the lineage head and his elders, the claim of an incompetent or spendthrift man can be set aside in favour of a junior nephew of better character.' (Fortes, *op. cit.*, p. 271.)

[3] In the case *Enin v. Prah*, High Court (Lands Division), 31 January 1959, it was held that under customary law a deceased's 'immediate family' consists of 'all who were descended matrilineally from the same womb as himself—his surviving brothers (if any), his surviving sisters (if any) and the surviving children of his sisters, dead or alive'; it was further held that 'it is the family so defined (or, in the absence of any such, the matrilineal descendants of the mother's mother) who alone are entitled to the beneficial use and enjoyment of the self-acquired properties left by a deceased.' (From *The Ghana Law Reports*, 1959, part I, p. 44.)

[4] This fact stands in extraordinary contrast to the general belief. Thus Mr C. K. Meek, an impeccable authority, states: 'Among the matrilineal peoples of the Gold Coast there is a distinct tendency nowadays for all forms of self-acquired property, including cocoa estates, to be devised to sons, rather than to sisters' sons.' (*Land Tenure and Land Administration in Nigeria and the Cameroons*, Colonial Research Studies, no. 22, 1957, footnote, p. 179.) In *The Gold Coast, 1931*, A. W. Cardinall states, p. 84, that 'the tendency for the maker of a cocoa plantation to leave his property to his son rather than his sister's son has almost brought a change from matrilineal to patrilineal descent'.

123

it has proved its strength, and whereas in the old days the whole of a man's house property in Aburi might have passed to a man's children on his death, nowadays, according to the Adontenhene of Akwapim, the claims of the matrilineage have been strengthened in recognition of the fact that houses are built from the proceeds of family lands.[1]

Most writers on matrilineal systems emphasize the existence of 'tensions and strains' resulting from a 'father's' conflicting obligations towards his sons and maternal nephews and from a 'son's' conflicting loyalties towards his father and maternal uncle.[2] (In Ghana the existence of a great volume of unresolved conflict has been so taken for granted that there have been few to point out that this has not been reflected in the work of the courts.) But, as pointed out by Radcliffe-Brown, 'tensions and strains and possibilities of conflict exist in any system of rights and duties'.[3] ('There is no reason why a system of mother-right should present more difficulties for individual adjustment than a system of father-right.'[4]) The family land system may be regarded as an extremely efficient device for overcoming the inherent possibilities of contradiction within the matrilineal system.[5]

If, following Dr Audrey Richards, the central difficulty is regarded as that of 'combining recognition of descent through the woman with the rule of exogamous marriage',[6] then it would appear that the large family group, in which, as our examples have shown, the leader's associates are apt to include several affines, solves this 'matrilineal puzzle'[7] very neatly—for it is often possible for both man and wife to continue residing on the family land where each was living before marriage and where each of them may have been born.

Although the fundamental importance of cross-cousin marriage,[8] i.e. marriage between the children of a brother and a sister, at all stages in the evolution of a large family land is now only too apparent to the present writer, it must be admitted that this was not properly appreciated when the fieldwork was undertaken and certain opportunities of collecting

[1] Many Aburi farmers build two or more houses in Aburi, one for the matrilineage and the others for the wives and children; but whether, in so doing, they pay any regard to the origins of the finance is not clear—presumably not.

[2] This is of course a greatly oversimplified way of looking at the matter.

[3] *Op. cit.*, p. 80.   [4] *Ibid.*

[5] Most of the criticism of the matrilineal system results from the difficulty of understanding it.

[6] Chapter on 'Some types of family structure amongst the Central Bantu' in *African Systems of Kinship and Marriage*', p. 246. 'Descent is reckoned through the mother, but by the rule of exogamy a woman who has to produce children for her patrikin must marry a man from another group. If she leaves her own group to join that of her husband her matrikin have to contrive in some way or other to keep control of the children, who are legally identified with them.' Dr Richards regards the husband's 'right to determine the residence of the bride' as crucial (p. 208).

[7] *Ibid.*

[8] All the authorities already cited pay much attention to the matter of cross-cousin marriage.

RULES OF INHERITANCE

facts on the subject were neglected.[1] When purchasing the land, leaders are sometimes associated, as the all-too-scanty data suggest, with their sisters' husbands—whose sons will be members of their *abusua*. (Occasionally men are associated with their sisters themselves, and indeed there are a few family lands which bear the names of women leaders, but it is true with family lands, as with companies, that the original farmers are nearly always men.) Then leaders may be married to a cross-cousin: it is very likely, for instance, that one of Kofi Pare's many wives was a daughter of one of his father's sisters—for this would have meant that the children were members of Kofi Pare's father's lineage, and Kofi Pare (see Appendix III. 4, p. 92) had always been closely associated with his father's cocoa-farming activities. As time goes by the members of the older generation who are settled on the land will have the opportunity of promoting marriages between their daughters and their sisters' sons, thus ensuring that their inheritor is also the father of their maternal grandchildren.[2] The kinship structure of the group resident on a large land is likely to become extremely complex. The population will not be static: there will be some sons who depart for other lands and some daughters who marry elsewhere; there will be others who seek to return to the land. 'But always when someone is trying to go away someone else is trying to come back.'[3]

In order to emphasize that the inheritor takes over obligations and duties towards his kinsmen, as well as rights in relation to the property (that he is permitted to exercise his rights *so* that he may fulfil his obligations), he is often denoted as a 'trustee', 'custodian' or 'manager'. One of the points to be considered is whether, in practice, inheritors usually lack individual control to the extent implied by this terminology.

Turning now to the practical questions involved, Aburi and Akropong family lands must be distinguished. If it is appropriate to apply the ideas involved in the legal dichotomy to the Aburi land, does the 'moment of change', at which the conversion from individual to family (or lineage) property is supposed to occur, correspond with the date of the death of the original creator of the property—the leader or his associate? If the question is put like this, it is at once apparent that the answer is 'no—not necessarily'.[4] Especially if a land is large it is usual for a considerable number of farmers, most of them members of the matrilineage, to be granted usufructuary rights during the lifetime of the original farmer,

[1] But these opportunities, in relation to the historic family lands, are necessarily limited: 'large farmers', unless they be prominent Christians, usually have several wives and it is often, in fact, impossible to get reliable information about marriages contracted fifty years ago.

[2] This is the type of cross-cousin marriage which Professor Fortes regards as preferred in Ashanti, *op. cit.*, p. 279.

[3] M. J. Field, *op. cit.*, p. 111. On this page of Dr Field's book there is an excellent diagram illustrating cross-cousin marriage for those who like to think in such terms.

[4] See Appendix IV. 1 (p. 131).

RULES OF INHERITANCE

rights such that they cannot be withdrawn. To the extent that such rights have been granted, lineage control may already be said to have established itself. Some of those who exercise these rights will have been encouraged to go to the land to assist the original farmer, perhaps on the tacit understanding that they will benefit; others will have sought permission to join him because they were in need. The data show that while the areas allotted to individual farmers for either or both of these reasons are always small, relative to the area retained by the original farmer (be he leader or associate), their total may be a significant proportion of the whole and this without regard to whether the original farmer still survives. Thus in the case of Kofi Pare (Appendix III. 4, p. 92), although the heads of sub-groups 3 and 5 were still alive at the time inquiries were made, neither of them was the registered owner of more than half the area he had originally acquired, the remainder being occupied by relatives.

So, if many members of the matrilineage are already congregated on the land, the death of the original farmer may not bring about a significant redistribution of usufructuary rights.[1] Certainly the matrilineage, in its corporate capacity, will have been responsible for the choice of inheritor (or for endorsing the deceased's expressed wishes), but once that inheritor has been appointed things may carry on much as before, and there may, in practice, be no distinction whatever between the original farmer and his younger brother who has inherited his property. The process of conversion to lineage property had reached a certain stage when the original farmer died—and his death had no influence in hastening the process.

That this is so may be seen very clearly in relation to lands which were unplanted at the time of their purchaser's death and which had not been formally given away by him during his lifetime: the inheritor's relationship to such a land may be in no wise different from the original purchaser's, so that he considers it as (for the time being) his individual property.

It would seem that, as with the company farmers, two separate processes may be postulated—the one involving the growth of lineage control, the other involving a decline in individual control. In chapter VII it is argued that the enterprising migrant farmer corresponds, in capitalist terms, to a manager—and it may, perhaps, be added that members of the matrilineage correspond, after a fashion, to shareholders. Expanding this notion somewhat, such a farmer may be regarded as exerting two separate, though overlapping, functions: firstly that of managing the property on behalf of the matrilineage (in the way in which the head of a family firm in Britain manages the business on behalf of his family) and secondly that of promoting his own individual interests. And the point, in this con-

---

[1] Although the deceased's wives may prefer to depart, they are unlikely to hold much land. The sons, too, may depart, though there appears to be no general rule on this. The point is that matrilineal kin will not be disturbed in the exercise of their rights.

nection, is that an inheritor continues to exercise both these functions when he takes over from the original farmer.[1]

So far as the large family lands are concerned, the conclusion is, therefore, that the process of conversion from individual to lineage property is in the early stages more rapid and in the later stages more gradual than is commonly supposed.[2] The leader of a family group may lose much of his individual control during his lifetime. An inheritor may continue to exert the same degree of individual control as was exerted by the original farmer. If the original farmer retained half of the original area for his own use, the inheritor may continue to farm that portion, as though it were virtually his individual property—such disabilities as he suffers from, e.g. his inability to sell the land, having been suffered also by his predecessor. The inheritor's function as trustee and custodian will be exercised in relation to the other half of the property: thus if a relative exercising usufructuary rights dies, or moves away, it will be he who will be expected to take decisions, in consultation with others, about the future use to which the land or farm should be put.[3]

It is contended that the members of the matrilineage are aware of the compromise reflected in the dual functions of the inheritor. On the one hand they are glad to leave him free to exert more individual control than he would traditionally have been entitled to *because they recognize the importance of the role of the individual in expanding property*; on the other hand they do more than lean heavily on their traditional rights, in demanding that portions of unplanted land should be allocated to them as though the property were clan land. If the area of cocoa-farming land (purchased and available) increases as rapidly as the number of cocoa-farming members of the appropriate matrilineage,[4] then there may be no reason why a conflict should ever develop.

Whether more and more kinsmen have tended to crowd on to the large old Aburi lands as time has gone by it would have been impossible to say—even had it not been for the dislocations resulting from swollen shoot. (Even if the number of separate farms shows no tendency to increase as a result of further sub-division following the deaths of those to whom usufructuary rights were granted in the first instance, populations might increase, each farmer having more dependants.) But whether this is so or not, it is important to note that owing to the operation of the rules

[1] If the inheritor is a brother who owns adjoining land he will literally annex his elder brother's property (making no practical distinction between the two areas).

[2] This is a general statement which disregards the fact that different people stand in different relationships to different portions of the land—which can seldom be regarded as a whole.

[3] See the note on the position of the *abusua panyin* in Appendix iv. 4, p. 136.

[4] So many members of some Aburi matrilineages have bought lands for themselves as individuals, that the notion of lineage land has become too complex to be handled conveniently in practice—and many inheritors, it is safe to say, have no idea of the extent of what they have inherited. See Appendix iii. 1 (p. 86) on Sakyikrom.

RULES OF INHERITANCE

of inheritance there is a powerful tendency within many of the larger lands for more and more land to be consolidated in the 'ownership' of a few inheritors, especially where (as at Akotuakrom[1]) two or more brothers were among the original associates, the whole of their property passing to one inheritor on the death of the last survivor. As the number of separate lands owned by members of the matrilineage is nearly always on the increase, and as one inheritor succeeds to all the lands of the deceased, ever-increasing areas are apt to fall under the control of individual inheritors.

The death of virtually all the cocoa on the oldest family lands has made it impossible to study whether, as a result of these consolidating and expansionary tendencies, too much responsibility (or potential responsibility) rests with too few people. Certainly it would be easy to conclude that this would turn out to be one of the great socio-economic problems of the future, were it not evident that many maternal nephews, who do not happen to be inheritors, regard themselves (and are regarded by others) as to all intents and purposes the inheritors of the land on which they happen to reside.[2]

The extent of the disturbance in the natural working through of this process resulting from swollen shoot cannot as yet be assessed. It may be, as suggested above, that individuals will assert new (though modified) individual rights over areas previously farmed on a usufructural basis—so that the process will be, as it were, 'rejuvenated'. But if this does not happen, perhaps after three or four generations, 'when the memory of the original acquisition has faded', the land will come to be regarded as 'ordinary kin group land'.[3]

It has been insisted elsewhere (p. 81) that the capacity of the Aburi family land system to provide for sons is incidental, not part of its basic strength. It is no part of the function of fathers to encourage the economic enterprise of their sons, though fathers may wish to 'thank' their sons (for their services) with the offer of a piece of land, or to provide them with a minimum of security if their (mother's) matrilineage fails them. The reasonableness of this has always been recognized by the father's matrilineage. Unless an original farmer has already granted usufructuary rights over the whole of his land to members of his matrilineage (and it is doubtful if this ever occurs), he is, presumably, usually[4] free to grant such

---

[1] At Akotuakrom the consolidating tendency may have been cancelled out by gifts to sons.

[2] They may or may not owe their position to the fact that the inheritor has been chosen without regard for his interest in cocoa-farming.

[3] See *The Native Economies of Nigeria*, vol. I, part I: 'The Rural Economies,' by Daryll Forde, section on the Ozuitem Ibo of Bende, p. 65, for an analysis of the growth of communal control over land acquired by individuals in this patrilineal food-exporting society.

[4] The members of the *abusua* may be so grasping that it is by no means certain that a man is *always* free to give away portions of his self-acquired property irrevocably to his sons—though he would always be able to do this in the early stages of the existence of a land.

RULES OF INHERITANCE

rights to his sons within the portion of land he has retained for his own use and such is the degree of individual control exerted by inheritors that they may be in like position. At Akotuakrom (Appendix III. 3, p. 91), Afwireng is believed to have installed his sons on the land at the time that he succeeded his brother Akotua, but it may be that these sons took over the portion which had been his from the start.

Sometimes (see Appendix IV. 4, p. 135), Aburi fathers give portions of land or farms away to their sons 'irrevocably'—i.e. the farms do not revert to the father's *abusua* on the son's death. Such gifts involve the performance of the *aseda* ceremony. It is here tentatively suggested that the notion of 'patrilineal property' does not exist in Aburi in relation to cocoa-farming land. So when a father gives land away 'irrevocably' to his son it means in effect that one matrilineage (the father's) gives land away to another (the son's).

The figures given in the Appendices to chapter III, together with other information, suggest that unless there are special circumstances, arising for instance from cross-cousin marriage, portions given to sons are usually fairly small. Thus at Kofi Pare 9 out of 15 of the 'son's farms' were under 5 acres, compared with only 13 out of 36 of the farms owned by male members of the *abusua*.[1]

Turning to the Akropong family lands, there are, as has been seen, two distinct types—the basically matrilineal type (as represented by Boah) and the (possibly much rarer) mixed patrilineal-matrilineal type (as represented by the land at Bepoase). Much that has been concluded about the Aburi family land applies, also, to the former type. Thus on the Boah land, farmer (P) who has inherited twenty-five acres (partly from his elder brother and partly directly from one of the ex-slaves) exerts a high degree of individual control. His matrilineage does not expect him to grant usufructuary rights over any portion of this twenty-five acres to any member of the *abusua* and he appears to be free to devote the proceeds of the land to the purchase of other lands. (In 1953 he bought a large land west of Kankan of which he proposes—there is no evidence of this decision having been imposed on him—to give half to his sons and half to his *abusua*.) Certainly (P) is not in a position to sell his Boah land—not that he would wish to do so; though he could doubtless pledge it if he wished. It is as unlikely that his *abusua* would give him permission to grant portions of this land to his sons as it is that he would apply for such permission—the remedy for this is in his own hands, namely the purchase of another land. Certainly he has certain moral (not legal) obligations, from which he would not wish to escape, to assist members of his *abusua*

[1] The Amanokrom farmer who bought the land near Dome (Appendix III. 10, p. 107) allocated 92 acres to 13 of his matrilineal kin and 38 acres to 5 of his sons (for use during their lifetimes only)—the average in each case being about 7 acres; this farmer retained 153 acres for his own use.

129

RULES OF INHERITANCE

financially—but such is his status in life, apart from his work as a farmer, that these would exist in any case. So far as his income from cocoa-farming is concerned it should be borne in mind that his affairs are private—members of the *abusua* do not know how many loads of cocoa he produces on his various lands, or what expenses have to be deducted before arriving at the net proceeds.

The tendency towards consolidation of ownership as a consequence of inheritance has operated strongly with the Boah group, and at the present time a greater proportion of the whole area is controlled by one farmer than ever before—he being the successor, (K), of the two original pairs of brothers, who is registered as owning about half the whole area (fifty-two acres). It happens that in his case his power of individual control is slight, for being a cripple who lives in Akropong he has handed over much of his responsibility to resident farmers, of whom the most important is (L), whose wife (a cross-cousin) is an *abusua* member; as he also owns much land elsewhere it may suit him to relinquish control here altogether —allowing others the use of the usufruct. The practical importance of 'residence' is again evident.

At Omenako (Appendix III. 7, p. 97), on the other hand, the tendency towards consolidation happened not to operate strongly, partly because many of the farmers, including Omenako himself, gave away much land to many people during their lifetimes and partly owing to the kin-structure of the original group of associates. Here there is only one really large holding (64 acres), which is owned by one of Omenako's maternal nephews. But on the other hand, there has been a tendency, as time has gone by, for the ownership of certain farms to revert to Omenako's *abusua*. There are many small farms of a few acres at Omenako, most of the smallest of which are owned by women—perhaps being primarily food-farms, allocated to those resident on the land or in nearby Suhum.

Turning to Akropong/Bepoase (see p. 85 and Appendix III. 9) the 'grandchildren' in whose names farms 1 to 14 are registered are well aware of the limitations on their individual control. Only three of them, all grandsons, are resident on the land and the keenest of them, the owner of farm 1, in a sense regarded all fourteen farms as the property of his patrilineage. But he yet remained unaware of the implications of this, insisting (though others in Akropong differed from him) that his sons would be unable to 'inherit' his farms directly from him after his death. However, his enthusiasm over replanting his own, his brothers' and even his cousins' strips suggested that he was motivated by an unconscious assumption that the vigorous would ultimately inherit the earth.

From the example of this same land, Akropong/Bepoase, it can be seen that large farms (such as farm no. 17, 120 acres) sometimes remain intact over the generations, though only if the matrilineage (in general) is other-

RULES OF INHERITANCE

wise provided for, as they were in this case. Although this particular farm has been notionally divided between members of the *abusua* (one of whom is the long-deceased original owner) the whole area is actually owned by the youngest brother of the original farmer—the extent of whose individual control is slight as he does not live in the area.

APPENDIX IV. 1

A BRIEF NOTE ON THE LEGAL CONCEPTS[1] OF SELF-ACQUIRED AND FAMILY PROPERTY

The legal presumption in favour of family property (see p. 109) partly reflects ideas about the inevitability of the conversion of self-acquired property into family property and is partly an historical relic from the days when it was considered that few individuals had the opportunity of creating individual property. The layman studying published court judgments is bound to be struck by the extent to which certain authorities are quoted and re-quoted over the decades. One of these is H. W. Hayes Redwar and the following statement is hallowed:

'. . . The mere fact of land being acquired by purchase does not prevent it from becoming impressed with the character of Family Property, as it often happens that the Head of a Family Community employs the funds of the Community in such a purchase, and that circumstance at once makes it Family Property. Moreover, any assistance from members of a Family, whether in money or otherwise, may make that Family Property which at first sight appears to be Individual Property.'[2]

There are, then, circumstances in which individual property 'at once' becomes family property and this has been re-emphasized very recently:

'By custom, where one member of a family acquires land for himself with his money as his individual property, and other members of the family developed that land with their own money or labour by building on it or farming it, the property immediately acquires the character of family property and ceases to be the individual or exclusive property of the member who purchased the land with his own money. Because the land in its developed state is the result of the combined contribution of members of the family, it cannot in its entirety be the product or achievement of any single one of the members of the family who contributed to make it what it is. The purchaser and each of those who developed it has a life interest in it. The purchaser of the land, together with all who developed it, can dispose of the whole estate in it without reference to the head and other members of the family. But upon the death of the member who bought the land or upon the death of any one of the members who had so developed it, the property becomes full family property with all the incidents of family property.'[3]

But as time has gone by, there has been in general less and less emphasis on the possibility of 'instantaneous conversion' (see below) and more and more insistence on the probability that the change will occur at the death (intestate) of the first owner. The probability is sometimes so great as to merge into a presumption, a presumption

---

[1] Ghana Common Law.

[2] H. W. Hayes Redwar, *Comments on some Ordinances of the Gold Coast Colony* (1909), p. 80.

[3] From an unreported judgment of the Land Court delivered in Accra on 17 February 1958, in the case of *Boafo v. Staudt*.

131

APPENDIX IV. 1

that 'can only be displaced by satisfactory evidence that during his [an individual's] lifetime he parted with the property by giving it to another'.[1]

The new circumstances resulting from the purchase of land on a vast scale by individual migrant cocoa-farmers more than half a century ago have received little examination, for the very good reason that few disputes involving farmers each of whom owns a farm within a particular company or family land have reached the courts. Pronouncements have been general ones, such as the following from the Chief Justice of Nigeria, in reference to Redwar (see above):

'The cocoa boom led to large numbers of individuals amassing wealth by their own efforts and purchasing property for themselves with the proceeds; so that the presumption in favour of all property being family property is not nearly so strong today as it was thirty years ago.'[2]

There is increasing recognition of the fact that the individual is free to do what he wishes with money which has been given him by the family for his personal use or advancement. In 1959 it was pronounced as follows by the Court of Appeal in *Larbi v. Cato*:

[Financial support is] 'by way of gift for the advancement of the younger generation, and while it places upon them certain recognised moral obligations towards the family it does not stamp everything that they afterwards acquired by their own maiden efforts, either as lawyers, doctors, merchants or by activity in other fields with the mark of family. If the contrary were the correct view, there is hardly a person of distinction in the country who could claim to possess anything that he could call his own and much of the volume of customary law on the disposal of an inheritance of self-acquired property would be cast away, which is the *reductio ad absurdum* of the whole argument.'[3]

The process of conversion is, of course, a one-way process, from which there is no escape—'once family property, always family property':

'. . . the fact that the members of a class entitled for the time being to the enjoyment of family property are reduced to one does not cause the property to lose its character as family property and become the absolute property of that person.'[4]

And the mere possession of family land by an individual, over a long period such as twenty-five years, cannot mean that such ownership has 'ripened into full ownership of the land'.[5]

In 1917 the West African Lands Committee commented in its report that it

'was one of the principal difficulties in ascertaining the present state of the law that there is nothing approaching to a complete or accessible record of the decisions of the Supreme Court'[6]

and the present writer must admit to having found herself similarly hampered.

APPENDIX IV. 2

GIFTS AND 'SAMANSEW'

The legal presumption that property held by an individual becomes family property on his death intestate 'can only be displaced by satisfactory evidence that

---

[1] From vol. I of *Selected Judgments of the West African Court of Appeal*, p. 329, *Larkai v. Amorkor*, per Deane, C. J. (Ghana).

[2] From *Selected Judgments of the West African Court of Appeal*, vol. II, p. 378.

[3] *Ghana Law Reports (G.L.R.)*, 35.

[4] See *Mills v. Addy* (1958), *West African Law Reports (W.A.L.R.)*, vol. III, p. 357, per Ollennu, J.   [5] *Ibid.*   [6] *Draft Report*, p. 37.

GIFTS AND 'SAMANSEW'

during his lifetime he parted with the property by giving it to another';[1] and 'Native law requires to establish such a gift a public affirmation by the donor of the gift in the presence of the other members of his family and an acknowledgment by the donee of the gift by the slaughter of a sheep or by thanking the donor with a bottle of rum.'[2]

Later on it is necessary for the donee to make further gifts to the donor, through relatives or friends: the donor and his relatives and friends assemble in a formal way to receive the donee's representatives.

When a gift has thus been made *inter vivos*, there is no possibility of the reversal of the transaction. The interest which the donor had in the land has passed irrevocably to the donee and on the donee's death it will, in the natural course, be his successor who will benefit. Many farmers appear to 'give away' farms to their sons and other relatives (who are then registered as the owners by the Ministry of Agriculture), when in fact they are merely allowing them to make use of the farms during their lifetimes. The farmers always explain that in such cases the *aseda* (or thanks-giving) ceremony has not been performed. On the son's death the farm will revert to his father or his father's successor, unless, as sometimes happens, the son's successor is invited, as a matter of grace, to perform the *aseda* ceremony—which is then regarded as having had retrospective effect.

From time immemorial it has been possible for a prominent man who is seriously ill to dispose of his self-acquired property by a 'deathbed declaration', *samansew* (*saman*, a departed spirit; *nsew*, a declaration, to make intentions clear)—a noncupative will in legal terminology. Such a declaration is not binding on the family, though it is always treated with respect, and it may nowadays be evidenced by a written record. As alienation by *samansew* is a species of gift *inter vivos*, it is made with as much publicity as possible and the beneficiary must provide drink, *aseda*, to signify his acceptance. As ownership does not pass until the death of the donor, there is no inspection of the land, the beneficiary is not placed in possession and there are no further 'drinks'.

APPENDIX IV. 3

NOTES ON THE LARTEH, MAMFE AND MAMPONG INHERITANCE SYSTEMS

As little has ever been recorded about the inheritance systems of the patrilineal peoples of Akwapim (the Guan and the Kyerepon), the following brief notes relating to the three Guan towns (Larteh, Mamfe and Mampong) are presented in the hope that it will be realized that they represent no more than incidental findings in the course of the present work. Thorough sociological investigations[3] will be necessary before the outlines of the various systems can be described. These notes relate to the inheritance of cocoa-land and farms only, particular reference being paid to modifications resulting from the migration.

Larteh

From the practical point of view one important fact is quite clear: namely that a man's self-acquired property normally passes on his death to his sons (and to no one else), the sons (taken together) of each wife receiving (in principle, if not in practice) approximately equal portions.[4] The sons are then expected to 'look after' their

---

[1] *Selected Judgments* (West African Courts of Appeal), vol. i, p. 329.　　[2] *Ibid.*

[3] Such as are now being made in Larteh by Mr D. Brokensha of the University of Ghana, to whom the present writer is grateful for information.

[4] See p. 114.

133

APPENDIX IV. 3

widowed mothers with the aid of the deceased's property; and they have, in practice, entire control over this property.

But although this is how things work out in practice (so that, from the point of view of the Ministry of Agriculture the deceased's farms become registrable in the names of his sons) and although a man's resident son will *automatically* assume responsibility for his farm on his death, strictly speaking it is the deceased's 'inheritor' (*odiadefo* in Twi) who authorizes the sons to exert their rights. This 'inheritor' (who is better regarded as a 'manager of the estate', or a 'trustee' or 'executor') has various duties, including those of 'burying' the deceased, disposing of his property to those entitled to benefit from it and arranging for his debts to be paid.

Ideally the inheritor should be a son of the deceased's father's younger brother, but there are many practical reasons why some other member of the patrilineage may be chosen when the *abusua panyin*, the most senior member of the patrilineage, calls the people together for the purpose of making the appointment. The inheritor is, of course, never a son of the deceased: traditionally it was his duty to marry the deceased's widow and to care for her children until they came of age.

Apart from the inheritor there is the 'deputy-inheritor' who, ideally, is the junior brother (having the same mother as well as the same father) of the deceased: he is described as 'the messenger—the one who is sent to buy rum'.

According to Mr Eugene Ohene Walker of Larteh, the migration across the river Densu brought about an important change in the inheritance system. In the old days the inheritor had himself been entitled 'to use' the proceeds of the deceased's property for the benefit of the widows (whom he may have married) and the children. But the existence of the rich trans-Densu lands led to his abusing his position, sometimes passing the proceeds to his own sons. Besides, inheritors (unlike sons) were often unfamiliar with the newly acquired lands. Therefore it came about as a result of the 'cocoa-business' that inheritors lost much of their power of control over lands which had been acquired by the deceased—though not, it should be noted, over local lands.

Opinions differ in Larteh on the question of the speed of conversion of individual (self-acquired) property into lineage (*abusua*) property—the Twi word *abusua* (matrilineage) is, rather curiously, applied to the Guan patrilineage—and on this, as on many other matters, there is certainly no standard practice. Much depends on the number of patrilineal (cocoa-farming) descendants of the original farmer, in relation to the number and size of the cocoa lands he acquired. As the third generation of migrant cocoa-farmers is only just emerging, much remains to be formulated in the light of experience and the studied vagueness of the usual authorities, the elderly, reflects much uncertainty.

Mamfe

While the Mamfe inheritance system is basically similar to the Larteh system and presumably suffered similar modifications as a consequence of the migration across the Densu, it has an additional special feature—a feature which is so entirely lacking in Larteh that any suggestion there as to its existence in any of the other Guan towns is greeted with incredulousness.

This special feature is the recognition, for inheritance purposes, of what in common parlance is always called 'the mother's side'—and which, in practice, as the farm maps and other information show, invariably involves the deceased's sister (or possibly her daughter, if she be dead). If a man has not 'helped' his sister by giving her some of his self-acquired land in his lifetime, then it is usually considered that his sister is entitled to one-third of his property on his death—an obligation which is sufficiently

LARTEH, MAMFE AND MAMPONG SYSTEMS

fulfilled by giving her a portion (a notional one-third) of *one* of his self-acquired properties.

Despite the proximity of Mamfe to her two matrilineal neighbours, Amanokrom and Akropong, this practice certainly does not represent a 'sop' to the matrilineal principle—though it is sometimes rationalized as such. Mamfe people always explain it in terms such as —'we look after our sisters very well'. Dr Esther Goody points out[1] that the practice of recognizing 'the mother's side' appears to have something in common with usages among the Guan-speaking Gonja of Northern Ghana.[2]

The practice of giving away much land to sons *inter vivos* is particularly common in Mamfe (see, for example, Saforosua, Appendix II. 8, p. 70) and it is said that any small portion of land that a man had retained as his own, after giving the rest away, is sometimes regarded as a 'reserve' on his death—being 'looked after', on behalf of the patrilineage, by his eldest son.

Mampong

In Mampong also (a nominal) one-third of self-acquired property sometimes passes to a successor other than the sons of the deceased. This successor is certainly always a male member of the patrilineage (for instance a son of the deceased's younger brother) and clearly the practice has nothing in common with the recognition of the 'mother's side' in Mamfe—though Mampong and Mamfe people themselves do not always understand this. One rationalization of the practice which was given in Mampong was that it represents recognition of the financial assistance rendered by the patrilineage at the time the land was acquired by the deceased.

APPENDIX IV. 4

NOTES ON THE ABURI AND AKROPONG INHERITANCE SYSTEMS[3]

As has been emphasized in chapter IV, the matrilineal inheritance systems of the Aburi and Akropong farmers were in no wise 'undermined' by the migration—there were, indeed, senses in which they grew and developed. But some changes have occurred. Thus in both Aburi[4] and Akropong (as well as in Anum[5]) there is no doubt that the migration speeded up the process by which 'the distant cousin system fell into disuse'—by which is meant that the tendency has become marked, as Professor Fortes found it had in Ashanti, for 'the line of inheritance to be limited to the matrilineal issue of the man's own mother and her sisters'[6]—or, in the case of self-acquired property, to the issue of the man's own sisters.

A specific instance from Akropong will illustrate this transition. On the death of a farmer, Sieku, his cocoa-farms were claimed by Ansaku, whose maternal grandmother had been one of the elder sisters of Sieku's mother; but Fianko the 'direct *wɔfase*', Sieku's sister's son, put in a counterclaim. Litigation resulted and this ulti-

---

[1] In conversation.

[2] Local Court material would doubtless throw much light on this practice and Mr D. Brokensha draws attention to evidence given on 24 June 1957 in the course of a lengthy case (117/1956) heard in Akropong Local Court.

[3] These brief notes relate only to cocoa-lands and farms and not, for instance, to house property.

[4] The present writer is indebted to the chief of Aburi, the Adontenhene of Akwapim, for much information.

[5] According to Nana Danso Ntow V, Krontihene of Anum, to whom the present writer is much indebted for written and oral information.

[6] M. Fortes, 'The Ashanti Social Survey: A Preliminary Report', *The Rhodes-Livingstone Journal*, no. 6 (1948), p. 14.

APPENDIX IV. 4

mately reached the High Court in Accra in about 1940, where judgment was given for Fianko. It was said that other more recent cases had led to the same result and that the new system 'had taken root so that everyone accepts it'—though the old-style successor, Ansaku, might sometimes be granted a portion of land. 'Even women', said the male informant, 'nowadays feel encouraged to claim estates if they are in the direct line and they have no brothers.'

Today Ansaku is the *abusua panyin* of the *abusua* stemming from Abayera, his maternal great-grandmother. What have been the changes in the role of the *abusua panyin* as a result of the migration? (The *abusua panyin* may be defined in practical terms as the oldest and wisest member of the *abusua*—ideally a senior son of a senior sister.) His principal function is that of presiding over the group which appoints a man's successor on his death. But the extent to which the *abusua panyin* may act as an adviser, administrator or 'manager' on other occasions is very variable—this partly reflecting the generation depth of the *abusua* over which he 'presides'. While in relation to decisions necessitated by day-to-day farming operations, the *abusua panyin* is by no means necessarily 'defunct' (some are very active, especially where the successor happens to be a woman), it is often difficult for him to keep in touch with events on the distant lands. Individual initiative has increased:

'True it is that he had his masters back at home, yet here in the jungle, he was his own *abusua-panyin*.'[1]

The position of Sons in Aburi
(exclusive of Berekuso)

As inquiries have been much hampered by the lack of farm maps, the following conclusions are rather tentative:

(a) The farmers do not themselves see any developing conflict between the matrilineal system and their wish to provide for their sons—see p. 124 on the practice of cross-cousin marriage.

(b) As most *abusua* now own much cocoa-land, there is less reason today than there was, say, in 1900, for an enterprising father to feel obliged for reasons of economic necessity to provide a land for his son.

(c) It is quite common for fathers to grant lifetime usufructuary rights over portions of land to such sons as happen to reside on a family land—such portions of land are always small relative to the area owned by the father himself.

(d) Some farmers make a practice of giving land (or farms) away irrevocably to their sons, this involving the performance of the *aseda* ceremony—see Appendix IV. 2 (p. 132). As with (c) the areas are usually small. No idea of the usualness of the practice was formed. On the son's death the property passes to his *abusua*—for instance to his sister's son. Effectively, therefore, one *abusua* has given land away to another.

(e) If, as occasionally happens, a father buys a land *for* his sons, such property may remain outside the matrilineal system indefinitely—i.e. be handed down the male line: although this general statement of principle was made in Aburi, no certain instances of such 'patrilineal property' were in fact encountered. (The concept of 'rights' passing down the male line indefinitely is said to exist in relation to local land planted with yams or oil-palm.)

The position of Sons in Akropong

Cross-cousin marriages are important among the Akropong as among the Aburi, and most Akropong farmers find no necessity to provide *directly* for their sons by buying

---

[1] Quoted from 'Across the Prah', by A. A. Opoku, see Appendix I. 5.

ABURI AND AKROPONG SYSTEMS

them a land for their exclusive use. But two distinctions between the Akropong and Aburi systems seem clear:

(a) Akropong farmers are more inclined than Aburi farmers to buy lands expressly for their sons (or for division between their sons and members of their *abusua*) and are also (unlike Aburi farmers) sometimes 'associated' with their sons in the early stages of developing a family land—see p. 85.

(b) Cocoa-land sometimes passes through the male line indefinitely—and not only in cases where land was originally bought expressly for sons. (Such cases are indicated by the existence of neatly-drawn strip-farms on the maps.) Although it is puzzling that so many Akropong farmers should be ignorant of this practice, it yet appears that it is nothing new—not necessarily a 'modification' which sprang from cocoa-growing.

CHAPTER V

AKIM ABUAKWA LAND SALES IN RELATION TO CUSTOMARY LAW

Although lawyers and social anthropologists have long been agreed that there is nothing newfangled about rural land sales in southern Ghana, writers on cocoa-farming, if they have noted the occurrence of such sales at all, have shown a remarkable lack of sophistication in their approach. Taken aback by their findings, they have usually sought (see Appendix I. 1, p. 18) to explain their former ignorance in terms of the modernity of the practice and have therefore assumed that it was the commercial success of cocoa-growing over the decades which *ultimately* led to the toleration by traditional authorities of such 'uncustomary' dealings. Whether the date be 1910 or 1960, land sales are always supposed to be 'increasing' (in response, say, to swollen shoot)—to be a new factor in the situation. One of the chief reasons for this[1] is that economists and others untrained in law or social anthropology often have the utmost difficulty in grasping the broad outlines of that awe-inspiring subject 'land-tenure'. This chapter, which is addressed by a legal[2] layman to others similarly situated, represents an attempt to draw together source material bearing on the matter of land sales to stranger cocoa-farmers under Akim Abuakwa customary law. Unlike most of the other chapters in this book, it relies scarcely at all on the findings of oral interview.

It is hardly necessary, for our purposes, to inquire when rural land sales first began in earnest—whether after (if not before) the nominal abolition of the slave trade in 1807, or towards the middle of the nineteenth century when the development of commercial agriculture,[3] combined with the growth in population, resulted in land scarcity in some areas. But it must be accepted as a historical fact[4] that the notion, if not the practice, of selling land to strangers has been familiar to many Akim Abuakwa chiefs

[1] See also pp. 12 ff. for a broader discussion.

[2] See footnote 3, p. 109; here again, legal terminology is not employed.

[3] It is not even necessary to assume an association between the growth of commercial agriculture and land sales for, as pointed out by Elias (*op. cit.*, p. 173), 'even within the context of a purely subsistence economy of land usage' there are apt to be forces which temper the rigour of the traditional system against the principle of alienation.

[4] See Appendix v. 1 (p. 149) and also Appendix I. 1 (p. 18)—especially the quotations from Sir William Brandford Griffith; on p. 496 of *West African Lands Committee* (W.A.L.C.) *Minutes of Evidence*, the following is quoted from a note by Griffith: 'From my judicial experience in land cases I should have no hesitation in saying that in ancient times land could be sold... The idea of sale of land as between natives was so very definite and was so taken for granted that I have never had occasion to consider the question.' See, also, Appendix VIII. 2 (p. 240) for evidence of extensive sales of land in the Densu valley by the chiefs of Asafo and Maase in the eighteen-sixties.

138

for at least a century. Perhaps the earliest transactions involving Krobo farmers were more in the nature of 'transfers between chiefs' than purchases involving individual sellers, but by 1861, or thereabouts, the Krobo were purchasing land on both sides of the Pawmpawm river from the occupants of the Begoro and Tafo stools and the *huza*[1] system of land-purchase may by then have been fully developed, with cowries as the usual medium of exchange. Mr Pogucki has suggested[2] that dealings in land probably evolved independently among different tribal groups and there is no need to suppose that chiefs elsewhere were influenced by happenings in the areas subsequently incorporated in the states of Yilo and Manya Krobo. Outside the Krobo area, wholesale alienation by Akim Abuakwa chiefs seldom occurred until the eighteen-nineties, by which time the practice of out-and-out sale had been well fortified by established usage, being part of (not alien to) customary law.

The sellers of the land were not the Omanhene himself,[3] but various sub-chiefs, the successors of those who had been settled on the land for several centuries. These chiefs[4] were free, in consultation with their councillors, to sell unoccupied portions of land in order to pay debts incurred by their stools—a condition which, as time went by, was more honoured in the breach than the observance.[5] The greatest practical obstacle encountered by these chiefs was not squeamishness about the propriety of selling land of which they were the mere custodians, for if their people became restive about the extent of the sales, they were always easily pacified with a proportion of the proceeds,[6] but uncertainty about boundaries. The boundaries between them were literally indeterminate, in the sense that no line could be drawn such that the settlers on one side of it adhered to one stool and those on the other to another. The proprietary rights of the various stools had been casually determined by their people, by itinerant farmers, food-gatherers and (in particular) hunters, who had

---

[1] See Appendix II. 9 (p. 72). The means by which land was acquired in the area which subsequently became Krobo country is a matter outside the scope of this chapter.

[2] See Pogucki, *op. cit.*, vol. II, p. 32, footnote.

[3] See M. J. Field, *Akim Kotoku*, p. 10: 'It is often said by Akim people "An *omanhene* has no land". This is not strictly true, but it is very nearly so. . .'

[4] Individuals, as distinct from chiefs, have been prohibited from selling uncultivated forest land. See J. B. Danquah, *Cases in Akan Law*, p. xxxi; however, the rule has sometimes been broken—see Case A. 24.

[5] But as emphasized by Dr J. B. Danquah (*An Epistle to the Educated Youngman*, p. 31), indebtedness was often a specious reason: 'Our chiefs are very fond of selling lands, especially when they can find a specious reason for it, e.g. to pay for the costs of a Stool land litigation in the Supreme Court, to pay off an old standing Stool debt, or to perform the funeral custom of a deceased Chief.' But as some degree of indebtedness is a natural or normal condition, there was little need for the exercise of ingenuity in inventing excuses for land sales.

[6] To which, as they very well knew, they had no entitlement. Although there was no hard-and-fast rule as to the proportions allotted to the stool, the chief (personally) and the elders, it is certain that the people, *qua* individuals, were never supposed to benefit. (See *The Belfield Report*, Cmd. 6278.)

established huts or small settlements in the forest away from home at a time when 'land had no value'; there was naturally much overlapping and intermingling and much land also which, lacking hunters' footpaths, was virtually unexplored. The thicker the forest and the more remote the land from the seat of the chief, the greater the degree of doubt that was apt to prevail, so that it is not surprising that one of the most troublesome areas of indecision lay in the deep south, nearly thirty miles away from Apapam,[1] the seat of the principal land-selling chief—and this, as it happened, was one of the areas where trans-Densu cocoa-growing first began. Reading the papers relating to the Apedwa/Apapam land dispute of the eighteen-nineties,[2] it is difficult not to feel that the Travelling Commissioner, H. M. Hull, was a little hard on Apedwa when he protested that their 'boundary was quite impossible; nobody could understand or follow it, not even the Apedwas themselves' and that he was, at the same time, rather over-welcoming to the 'extreme simplicity' of the claim made by the clever Apapams.

This uncertainty about boundaries has been one of the principal causes of litigation between vendees as well as vendors, having often led to the inadvertent or deliberate selling of the same land by different chiefs to different purchasers.[3] The local courts have sometimes recognized the situation quite bluntly.[4] While there may be something in the idea that gained currency in the latter years of last century, that every square inch of land is owned by 'someone', there may be no agreement as to who this 'someone' is.[5]

[1] The recorded populations of Apapam and Apedwa in 1891 were only 530 and 1020—figures which, judging from later Censuses, may have been of the right order of magnitude.

[2] See Appendix v. 2 (p. 151).

[3] According to Danquah (*Akan Laws and Customs*, p. 218), if 'there is an adverse claim by another stool, the onus of proof of the vendee's right and title to the property rests with the vendor's stool. He is the principal witness of the vendee.'

[4] Dealing with the boundary between Apapam and Asamankese lands the Omanhene's court at Kibi observed that 'there existed no definite boundary between the two Stool lands from time immemorial'. (Case A.24, *Cases in Akan Law*.) According to Case A.32, there was no defined boundary, each party exercising his rights 'with regard to cottages and villages owned or settled by the people of either town'. In September 1914 (Kibi State Council Letter Book, letter no. 427), the Omanhene noted, in a letter to the Benkumhene of Larteh, that 'the long dispute which arose between the Chief of Apedwa and Chief of Asafo in connection with the boundary between their stool lands remains quite unsettled. . .' This uncertainty is, of course, a general characteristic of state as well as internal boundaries: 'The evidence establishes in the clearest manner that no one stool knew with certainty the territorial limits of its lands and in even less degree did the States of Akim Abuakwa and Akwapim know theirs.' (From the Finding in the Matter of the Stool Lands Boundaries Settlement Ordinance (Akwapim State), *Ghana Gazette*, no. 14, 18 February 1959.)

[5] The following extract shows how intermingled were the ideas of land-ownership and cottage-ownership: 'I am *odikro* at Asafo. About 3 years ago Maase *odikro* Bompa went and sold land extending from Asubiresu to Obomofodensu [*sic*] thence to Amanase. All Asafo people met and said that it was not right that cottages belonging to Asafo people had been sold and so they should go and seize same by hanging palm leaves thereon. Bosompem came and asked me why. Myself and my people replied that it was not right that since there was no stool debt the Asafo's cottages should be sold, and that if there was any debt

AKIM ABUAKWA LAND SALES

Despite all that has been said to the contrary during the last fifty years, and all the fruitless action that has resulted from an endeavour on the part of the paramount to catch up with events, out-and-out sale, or absolute sale, with no conditions whatsoever attached,[1] was the traditional practice in Akim Abuakwa, as in Akwapim and certain other areas.[2] The form of the *guaha* ceremony, the customary act of conveyance which is necessary for the validation of sales, makes this perfectly plain. One of the purposes of the ceremony is to placate the spirits who are obliged to move away owing to the transfer of ownership; another is to inform the permanent spirits of the place—streams, hills, big rocks and big trees—and to ask them to prosper the newcomer. There are many published descriptions of this ceremony,[3] among them the following, which is reasonably up to date and was intended to be read by those familiar with tradition:

> The sale of land, as indulged in by the Gold Coast people, is absolute sale when executed under the guaha custom. . . In ancient times guaha custom was also executed in connection with the sale of slaves and it was common to see a number of cowries under one's seat to indicate the various slaves bought. . . The intended purchaser applies to the one who owns it and intimates him of the intended purchase. Customary presentation of rum is generally made to the vendor, the desired length will be cut and the area properly demarcated. Then the price is rated, and, after due deliberation, the rate is reduced. The man who sells the land will then pour a libation to his gods, who are supposed to be living on the said land in spirit form, and also to his ancestral spirits (i.e. of the departed ones). In this ceremony prayer is offered to the effect that the land in question is being given away to the purchaser 'outright', and therefore they should remove from the place and settle elsewhere, for the purchaser will come to settle in the locality with his own spirits. After this part of the purchasing money is paid. If all is not paid, then a time specific to both parties will be fixed for the settlement of the balance. . .[4]

Another purpose of the ceremony is to provide 'evidence for future

at Maase, the Maase cottages should be sold and not Asafos. Bosompem swore upon me and took me to Asiakwa [to the Divisional chief]. Asiakwahene and his people arranged that the land should not be sold. Accordingly myself and Maase Odikro paid £10 each. About a year and a half, Asafo people got some debt and so they went and sold the land in question. Afterwards Bosompem also got debt in consequence of a case at Accra. He came back and asked for help from Asafos . . . and I said I shall pay the debt with my people.' (From Civil Record Book, Omanhene's Office, Kibi. Kwame Akuffo of Akropong claimed that land had been sold to him by *odikro* Bosompem of Maase; the defendant was Kofi Twum, the chief of Asafo. The case was heard on 1 February 1907.)

[1] The absolute freedom of land-purchasers to resell to others is a practical indication of this. The actual sellers, the sub-chiefs, were not concerned with the question of jurisdiction—which is a separate matter, see below.

[2] See Pogucki, *op. cit.*, vol. III, p. 32, footnote.

[3] Including the following, from J. G. Christaller (*op. cit.*). The 1881 edition is cited, as the later edition omits the italicized words (italicized by Christaller himself): '*Guaha*: a halm, straw, or stalk of grass, with some cowries strung on or added to it, *serving to conclude the sale of* a person or thing by tearing it asunder and putting the parts into the hands of witnesses, at the same time distributing to them the small amount of money (perh. 25 strings) given by the buyer besides the actual price. . .'

[4] From *The Sunlight Reference Almanac of the Gold Coast Colony and its Dependencies*, by Oheneba Sakyi Djan (1936), p. 98.

AKIM ABUAKWA LAND SALES

reference', this being made clear by Mr A. A. Opoku (Appendix I. 4, p. 35) in his account of an occasion when children as well as adult witnesses were employed, as they could be expected to live longer. Although the use of documents, evidencing the sale of land, may now be regarded as part of the customary law of Ghana (see Appendix v. 6, p. 160), the performance of *guaha* is still obligatory.

Neither of these descriptions makes any reference to the reversible nature of the transaction, such as is contained in a statement of the 'strict law of Akwapim'[1] made in an Accra court in 1904 by Thomas Martin Adade, chief councillor to the Omanhene of Akwapim:

Each of the sureties holds three of the stringed cowries whilst the 'linguist' makes an oath that if the vendor wilfully comes back and takes his land he will have to pay double the purchase-money and that if the purchaser refuses to complete the purchase any money already paid will be repaid to him, but without interest or expenses.[2]

But whatever the variations from place to place and from time to time in the forms of the ceremony, it is quite certain[3] that Akim chiefs have never been in the habit of reclaiming land which has been sold with proper ceremony to stranger cocoa-farmers. And when a sale is found invalid, because the land had previously been sold to someone else, it is usual for the seller to replace the original land with another, both parties preferring this, the buyer being conscious of the ever-increasing scarcity of good land.[4]

The *guaha* ceremony is a necessary part, but only a part, of a whole procedure which is much less standardized than many writers suggest. Publicity is the most important requirement and this is tied up with the matter of identifying the land. According to some authorities, the contract of sale becomes complete when the parties agree on the purchase price and the purchaser seals it with the offer of 'drink'. The subsequent completion of the sale, including the performance of *guaha*, requires further publicity and members of adjoining lands may be invited to be present to avoid future disputes. Those who demarcate or cut the boundaries should be remunerated by the purchaser, although their leader is appointed by the seller.

Much emphasis is laid in this book on the fact that land is very often

---

[1] The Akwapim form of the ceremony is essentially similar to the Akim form.

[2] From the case of *Akiempong (sic) v. Kojoko and others*, quoted in 'The Journal of the Society of Comparative Legislation', vol. VII (part I), 1906, p. 275.

[3] This conclusion had been arrived at before noting Sir William Brandford Griffith's comment on the rule that the vendor must pay double for the return of the land: 'I should not say there ever was a case where the vendor came back and wanted the land again when he has sold it out and out.' (W.A.L.C., *Minutes of Evidence*, p. 489.)

[4] In 1906 a farmer who had been offered the refund of his purchase money replied that he 'was more in need of land than money' and that he had 'come down purposely to buy the land on account of starvation'. (From the same case as that referred to in footnote 5, p. 140. Sellers often pacified buyers by hastily giving them another land before the case reached the court.)

paid for in instalments and there is evidence that this has been so since the earliest days of the migration.[1] While some money has to pass at the time of the performance of *guaha*, this sum may be small.[2] Land-sellers are as insistent as land-purchasers on the fact that actual ownership passes at the time of the performance of *guaha* and perhaps they have sometimes regarded themselves as entitled, in the very early stages, to reclaim the land without paying double the purchase price, if the buyers are obviously unlikely to start paying the instalments.[3] Although exact information is very hard to come by, the impression has been gained that buyers often pay a good deal less for their land than the sum originally agreed, whether orally or in writing, and that they tend to get away with this unless their inability (or reluctance) to pay becomes all too apparent in the early years. As noted elsewhere,[4] it often takes farmers several decades to complete payment, by means of irregular and unplanned instalments, which are sometimes almost forcibly extracted from them by the vendor chief (or his successor) who may come and reside in Akwapim for the purpose; and as time has gone by it has become increasingly common for the instalments to be met from the proceeds of growing cocoa on a previously acquired land—not from the unpaid-for land.

The conclusion that, traditionally, land-vendors have imposed no conditions of sale on those to whom they have sold their land, ignores the possible interests of a third party—the Omanhene or paramount chief. The reckless and unconditional sellers, those who took advantage of the opportunities provided by the flexible traditional system, which tolerated occurrences on a scale which had never been envisaged, were the sub-chiefs in whom the real power resided; there was no disputing that they possessed the right to relieve 'public indebtedness' by selling public lands. Although, as related below, the Omanhene has usually considered himself entitled to a proportion, which varied from time to time, of the actual

---

[1] *Report upon the Customs Relating to the Tenure of Land in the Gold Coast* (1895), contains (p. 35) a description of the *guaha* ceremony by H. M. Hull in which it is made clear that if the vendee 'fails to pay up at the appointment' the vendor 'has no power to sell the land to anyone else but must wait for his money'. Dr Danquah states the matter thus: 'If part-payment is made [at the time of the performance of *guaha*], time may be given for settlement of the balance purchase money.' (*Akan Laws and Customs*, p. 217.) In a judgment given in the Omanhene's court in 1914 it was observed that 'in most cases the land purchasers do not pay the purchase money for a long time after they had bought the land'. (*Cases in Akan Law*, p. 33.) The Akwapim and other strangers who resold land have, also, often been willing to take instalments.

[2] 'Quite a small sum must have been used for the purpose of cutting "guaha" in the olden times. . .' (*Akan Laws and Customs*, p. 217.)

[3] Certainly there is something of a conflict here between traditional and commercial practices, and this partly explains the reluctance of buyers and sellers alike to discuss the delicate issues involved. Generally, once *guaha* has been performed the seller is a trespasser if he ventures on the land without permission, and the only right that remains to him is that of demanding payment of the balance outstanding; he seldom sues the buyer, who knows how to stave off litigation by paying off small sums from time to time.

[4] See Appendix II. 1 (p. 55), etc.

143

AKIM ABUAKWA LAND SALES

sale proceeds, this, in fact, he has very seldom received. Nor have the other conditions which he sought to impose from about 1913 onwards been observed by vendors. It was as true in 1929[1] as in about 1907, that the sub-chiefs acted independently and 'quite knew what they were doing'.[2]

Indeed this was so as early as 1897 when the Gold Coast government intervened in the Apedwa/Apapam land dispute[3] and the painstaking work of H. M. Hull, the Travelling Commissioner, throws much light on contemporary attitudes. Despite the reported decision of the Supreme Court in 1893,[4] both judiciary and administration were entirely practical in their attitude to land sales, the former even encouraging them by the threat of compulsory auctions to pay legal expenses. No one mentioned conditions of sale. The Omanhene must have been aware of the dispute which, according to the chief of Apapam, had first been heard at his court in 1894—when the chief of Apedwa had 'bolted away' and taken action at Accra; but he was in no way involved and was not present when the Governor imparted his decision to the two sub-chiefs. H. M. Hull, it will be noted, took the sale of 'surplus land' for granted—the Apedwa people, he commented, already had all the land they needed 'and a great deal besides to sell if the people wished'. His concern was to prevent the people of Apedwa and Apapam 'becoming hopelessly ruined' by the expenses of litigation[5]—he had little regard for the piecemeal decisions of the courts and in the end he complained that he had been badly let down by the Governor.[6] The most cynical comment came from the Chief Justice, Sir William Brandford Griffith, who remarked that the people would have to

---

[1] '... you are well aware that the Okyeman State Council have passed several laws in an honest attempt to put a stop to the sale of lands in Abuakwaland, *and you are aware that none of these enactments has really been effective.*' (J. B. Danquah, *An Epistle to the Educated Youngman...*, p. 31—the present writer's italics.) 'These lands are gone for ever and Akim Abuakwa territory is ... gradually being cut off slice by slice, like bread on a breakfast table... There is no reason why we should not stop the habit of absolutely alienating (*sic*) our interests in land, just for the boose of a day's funeral custom.'

[2] As noted by F. G. Crowther, see Appendix I. 1 (p. 21). Crowther rightly considered (W.A.L.C., *Minutes of Evidence*, p. 362) 'that the community alienating its land' did not trouble much 'about theory or principle', but was simply concerned to raise money.

[3] See Appendix v. 2 (p. 151).

[4] See W. M. Macmillan, *op. cit.*, p. 86. 'When therefore in course of time, well-established and valuable cocoa-trees had given rise, in spite of the edict of 1893, to effective claims of land-ownership, the Supreme Court could only as it were throw up its hands and pronounce at last in 1918: "all the courts can do, and what they should do, is to accept accomplished facts!" '

[5] According to Sir Keith Hancock, it was no accident that the opposition to the abortive 1894 and 1897 Lands Bills was led by lawyers who stood to benefit from the prevailing disorders. (W. K. Hancock, *Survey of British Commonwealth Affairs*, vol. II, part II, p. 182.) See Appendix v. 1 (p. 149).

[6] In a letter of 2 February 1901 (ADM 11/1265) H. M. Hull said that he was 'very sick' at the result of the Apedwa/Apapam dispute: 'I got to the bottom of the whole subject and when the people were summoned, the Governor's decision should have been given and no attention paid to any questions raised other than those mentioned in my report.'

work hard producing more palm-oil and rubber in order to meet their legal expenses and that this would help to 'swell the revenue'. Had Hull's efforts been successful and provided a precedent, perhaps the chief of Apapam would not subsequently have been in such a hurry to dispose of his southern lands so cheaply and in such vast parcels. Uncertainty about boundaries may encourage sales: the fact that a chief has sold land in an area may even, later on, be regarded as evidence of the existence of proprietary rights there and, in any case, chiefs are anxious to lay their hands on any immediate cash before their right to do so is challenged. Greater certainty might have been detrimental to the developing cocoa-industry.[1]

The sellers of the land, the sub-chiefs, exercised no judicial powers in relation to the strangers to whom they had sold land, so they were not concerned with the question of whether such sales involved, or might involve, a transfer of jurisdiction. Nor, despite the Krobo example farther east, did any serious apprehension appear to have been felt in Kibi until soon after the enstoolment, in November 1912, of Nana Ofori Atta, who was quick to appreciate the implicit dangers in the situation as well as the overt territorial ambitions of the Omanhene of Akwapim. The political consciousness of 'stranger-towns', such as Asuboi, Yaw Koko and Amanase, was developing fast at this time, as was only to be expected considering that the great exodus from Akwapim had begun nearly ten years earlier, that the cocoa was flourishing beyond belief, that the majority of the settlers in this area were Akwapim and that nuclear settlements were gradually forming themselves on the main road south of Suhum,[2] these being partly inhabited by farmers who had removed from cottages on their own lands and partly by labourers, craftsmen, traders and others who had followed in their wake. Had the strangers been troublesome people, with any inclination to pick quarrels either with individual Akim (of whom there were very few resident in the area) or as between themselves (on tribal lines), more official cognizance would perforce have been taken of their existence. But the farmers felt constrained to be on their very best

---

[1] The purchasers were so keen to acquire their land that they were little deterred by the uncertainty about boundaries. Nor was this the only uncertainty: especially when buying Apapam land, they were often faced with the question of whether to trust the party who purported to have the right to sell. Not only did chiefs depute linguists with complete authority to act on their behalf, but there were also sub-chiefs of Apapam who appeared to be able to sell land independently. (See Case A.51, *Cases in Akan Law*, in which Kwasi Komfo, who was said to be a non-native of Apapam, claimed that he had been authorized to sell land on behalf of the chief of Apapam. In about 1901, Omanhene Kwasi Akuffo of Akropong bought land through one Kwaku Sono, who purported to act for the chief of Apapam (Kibi, Civil Record Book, 10 August 1906); the chief of Apapam subsequently repudiated this action and judgment was given in his favour at the Omanhene's Tribunal— see also the connected Case A.30, *op. cit.*)

[2] Referring, in 1906, to the Akwapim migration, F. G. Crowther, then District Commissioner of Kwahu and Eastern Akim, had reflected that he did not think it would be many years before a big cocoa-industry had developed on the road north of Nsawam. ('Notes on a District of the Gold Coast', p. 178.)

145

behaviour; they delighted in causing no trouble and in preserving, as they have done over the years, some of the inscrutability of the perpetual stranger. All the strangers, irrespective of their origin, were agreed on this and the resultant sense of common purpose was valuable in reducing tension in such an ethnically heterogeneous society.

Documentation is poor and the date of establishment of the first Akwapim tribunals in these towns has not been ascertained. They were under the authority of headmen, or *adikro*, who professed to derive their authority from the Omanhene of Akwapim. It had, presumably, never been the intention of Nana Ofori Atta to appoint Akim chiefs of these stranger-towns, but from 1913 onwards he made it clear that it was he, not his Akwapim counterpart, who should confirm the elected Akwapim chiefs in office, a view with which the District Commissioner concurred. He also hit back directly at the Omanhene of Akwapim by introducing conditions of sale,[1] based on by-laws which, in fact, never received the necessary approval of the Governor. To act thus was to shut the stable door after the horse had escaped—though unwittingly, Nana Ofori Atta having no idea, either then, or later, of the extent to which his people's lands had been 'sold away'.[2]

Certain documents relating to this famous dispute over jurisdiction, which was never administratively resolved and which ultimately lapsed, are summarized in Appendix v. 3 (p. 154). So inherently unpolitical are the stranger-farmers, so intent have they always been on their economic purpose, that this dispute has meant little to the ordinary individual, who never spontaneously refers to it when reminiscing on cocoa-farming matters. Had it not been for the territorial designs of the then Omanhene of Akwapim, which were later fanned by the award made by H. S. Newlands in 1922,[3] and for the consequential anxiety of Nana Ofori Atta,[4] the dispute over the tribunals might have died down as quickly as it had flared up.

Reference has already been made to the traditional relationship of the Omanhene to the land-vendors. The history of the modifications in this relationship which resulted from the widespread sales of land will now be related—constantly bearing in mind that the extent of the control exerted

[1] See p. 148. The Omanhene of Akwapim always held that these conditions of sale were 'not common to native customary law'.

[2] This opinion is partly based on scrutiny of papers in the Omanhene's office at Kibi.

[3] See p. 73. This was so despite the fact that Newlands explicitly stated that the acquisition of land by the Akwapim in Akim Abuakwa was 'not communal' so that no transfer of jurisdiction could have been held to have occurred.

[4] Nana Ofori Atta was greatly upset by the indignity of having to attend the 1915 meeting at Nsawam and official papers in the Omanhene's office at Kibi well reflect these anxieties. In *The Akim Abuakwa Handbook* Dr J. B. Danquah records (p. 116) that 'according to usage and wont, the Omanhene was not supposed to travel with his stool across the Densu and the Birim except during war time, but the State Council saw the urgency of the matter and gave a due permission to the Omanhene to travel to Nsawam'.

by the Omanhene always fell far short of what he himself supposed[1] it to be, especially in financial terms.[2]

According to the 'arrangement or custom' existing in the old state of Akim Abuakwa before 1883, one-third of 'whatever came out of the land' went to the Omanhene.[3] This somewhat notional *abusa* (or one-third) share was of universal application—with treasure trove, gold nuggets, snails, tapped rubber, palm-oil, elephant and other game etc., the finder, gatherer or extractor could retain no more than one-third, or two-thirds, for his own use, the remainder having to be handed over to the traditional authority.[4] Whether the latter in turn handed over a proportion to the Omanhene depended on personal and political considerations, grown largely from history. That, traditionally, the stool of Asamankese did not render such 'tribute' seems clear;[5] equally well, other stools may have been in the habit of doing so. Probably, though, there was always something rather haphazard about the operation of the rule: as though it applied only to that which *happened* to come from the land,[6] to chance rather than to planned occurrences. Certainly when the large-scale alienations to cocoa-farmers began to be made in the eighteen-nineties, it does not seem to have occurred to anyone that the Omanhene might be entitled to a share of the proceeds. 'Nowadays', lamented the Omanhene in 1901, 'the people are unwilling to do as it is customary to be done.'[7]

'In or about the year 1902'[8] the so-called 'Quarter meeting' occurred, at which the paramount's share 'on the alienation of Stool lands in the State' was fixed at 'one-quarter of the purchase price, consideration money, rents[9] or profits, instead of one-third thereof, as had hitherto been customary'. (Much later on, probably in 1920, though the date is unclear,

---

[1] There was, throughout, a large element of wishful thinking in the Omanhene's attitude. As a number of paramount chiefs made clear to Belfield in 1912 (see Cmd 6278), they had no right to expect a proportion of the income from concessions. The Secretary for Native Affairs, F. G. Crowther, noted (p. 55, Cmd 6278) that the land attached to the stool of the paramount was often 'limited to the precincts of his house'.

[2] Occasionally the Omanhene showed a realistic appreciation of his helplessness. Thus in October 1914 (according to Akim Abuakwa State Papers) he went so far as to suggest that all 'oaths' relating to land alienations should be taken before the D.C., so that he in turn might consult the Omanhene, who would thus become aware for the first time of what was going on.

[3] From the Asamankese Arbitration Award, see Appendix v. 4 (p. 157).

[4] 'The forest between Gygyeti [Jejeti] stream and the Okwao [Kwahu] mountain is rich in edible snails of fine proportions and the original granting Chief reserved to himself a royalty upon these delicacies which still exists. Four-footed beasts, bush cows, elephants and deer are commonly either wholly or in part reserved as Royalties.' (*Report upon the Customs Relating to the Tenure of Land on the Gold Coast*, 1895, p. 29.)

[5] See Appendix v. 4 (p. 157).

[6] In principle the rule applied to receipts, as such, from whatever source. Thus if a town collected £30 by holding a dance, in principle £10 should have gone to the Omanhene. Equally, the Omanhene was, in principle, supposed to give two-thirds of his receipts to his Oman members.

[7] From a letter to the Colonial Secretary (SNA.ADM 11/1096).

[8] According to the *Asamankese Arbitration Award*.   [9] See Appendix v. 5 (p. 158).

the proportion was raised again to one-third.) At the same meeting it was laid down that the *previous* consent of the paramount should be obtained before stool lands were sold—a rule which, it is safe to say, was invariably broken.

On 24 December 1913, a year after Nana Ofori Atta's accession, new by-laws were passed,[1] both with the intention of curbing the rate of sale and to make the Omanhene's interest clear; it being 'expedient to prevent the vulgar and undue alienation of Eastern Akim stool lands hitherto conserved', the consent of the Omanhene was to be obtained if land were leased, sold or disposed of by any chief, the fine for non-conformity being £5 and two sheep for each 'rope'. This was followed up by the issue for the first time in 1914 of printed forms, headed 'Conditions of Sale of Lands in Eastern Akim',[2] which were intended for use whenever land was sold; there is no need to list these conditions in detail, for they never operated effectively and were soon amended. But the intention was clear: by reserving unto himself mining and timber rights, treasure trove and minerals (including gold), the Omanhene was asserting his right of jurisdiction over the lands—a point which was emphasized by the first stipulation to the effect that the purchaser and his heirs would be subservient to him.

The task of tracing all the changes in the relevant by-laws since 1913 has proved impossible—but it is rendered unnecessary by the facts that the government often failed to endorse the changes and that the sub-chiefs were both defiant and ignorant. In 1922 when H. S. Newlands was appointed as arbitrator in the Akim Abuakwa/Krobo land dispute[3] it was claimed that thirteen conditions of sale were detailed to purchasers before the performance of *guaha*: but this was a pious expression of principle rather than a realistic statement of actual practice. A full declaration of customary law relating to land in Akim Abuakwa was later formulated, being published in the *Gold Coast Gazette*.[4] It was asserted that the ownership of all stool land was vested jointly in the paramount and subordinate stools; that it was necessary for the stool to grant permission to strangers to cultivate forest land, an amount not exceeding one-third of the value of the crop being payable to the stool, together with the customary drink; and that the paramount was entitled to a one-third share of the proceeds from the sale of all stool land. According to a recent statement by the Omanhene's linguist,[5] it had been necessary since 1926 (*sic*)

---

[1] Which, as had already been noted, were not endorsed by the government.

[2] Later on the word 'sale' was sometimes, hopefully, struck out and replaced by 'grant'.

[3] His report has, unfortunately, never been published. (The award was set aside by the Supreme Court in 1923 on technical grounds.)

[4] 9 April 1932.

[5] See the (unpublished) report on alienations in the Atewa Range Extension forest reserve by Mr C. H. Cooke, Reserve Settlement Commissioner, 1955, these reports being referred to in Appendix II. 2 (p. 55).

AKIM ABUAKWA LAND SALES

for land-selling chiefs to obtain the advance sanction of the Omanhene. The implication of the linguist's insistence that two-thirds of the mineral and timber proceeds should go to the state was that it was only the 'right to farm' and not the land itself which had been sold. He said that the paramount stool was entitled to 10 per cent of the purchase price for the benefit of state funds and that, in addition, one-third of the balance went to the paramount and his elders.

This linguist referred to the existence of an official at Kibi called the Lands Secretary who, he said, had collected records relating to sales of land that had occurred both before and since the opening of his office some fourteen years previously. In 1957 this official kindly permitted scrutiny of his records relating to land sales, from which it was clear enough that very few indeed of the stranger-farmers had cared to go to the trouble and expense of registering their acquisitions, at that late date, as they had been urged to do. The pathetic scrappiness of the lists at that time is the best proof that can be offered of the utter helplessness of the Omanhene to impose his will (except as has been seen occasionally[1]) on his sub-chiefs during the sixty years that had elapsed since the large-scale selling of land had begun.

APPENDIX V. 1

THE WEST AFRICAN LANDS COMMITTEE
(WITH A NOTE ON THE 1897 LANDS BILL)

The purpose of the West African Lands Committee (W.A.L.C.), which was appointed in June 1912 (the chairman being Sir Kenelm E. Digby) was:
'to consider the laws in force in the West African Colonies and Protectorates (other than Northern Nigeria) regulating the conditions under which rights over land or the produce thereof may be transferred and to report whether any, and, if so, what, amendment of the laws is required, either on the lines of the Northern Nigeria Land Proclamation or otherwise.'

The *Draft Report*[2] was completed in the course of 1915 and published, for official circulation only, in April 1917—it was not until the nineteen-fifties that it was taken off the secret list by the Colonial Office. *Minutes of Evidence etc.*[3] and *Correspondence and Papers Laid Before the Committee* had been published earlier.

References are made to[4] W.A.L.C. in Appendix I. 1 (p. 20) and elsewhere in this book and Meek (*op. cit.*) contains a Note on the Committee's work, pp. 177–86. Here it is only proposed to note the very cautious nature of the Committee's approach and their bias in favour of what they regarded as 'native custom':
'There is, however, some evidence that in the Gold Coast the development of the

---

[1] It should be added that it was the Omanhene's insistence that he was entitled to a one-third share of all rents and profits derived from alienated lands which led the stools of Asamankese and Akwatia to try to sever their connection with him. (See Appendix v. 4, p. 157). During the nineteen-twenties a number of other sub-chiefs, including Tafo, Abomosu and Apinaman, were destooled for the unlawful selling of land.

[2] African (West), no. 1046.   [3] African (West), no. 1047, April 1916.
[4] African (West), no. 1048, June 1916.

APPENDIX V. 1

cocoa industry has been instrumental in encouraging the sale and mortgaging of native lands in a manner inconsistent with native customs.' (*Draft Report*, p. 99.)
In the country districts. . . 'legislation should have as its aim the checking of the progress of individual tenure and the strengthening of native custom.' (*Draft Report*, p. 103.)
On p. 111 of the Draft Report it was recommended that chiefs and heads of families should be restricted to the issue of leases or 'customary transfers for occupation and cultivation . . . a proviso being added that no such transfer shall operate to deprive the community or family of the land itself'. It was also recommended that individuals should not be entitled to sell or mortgage the land they occupy, all of which could be presumed to be family or community land.

The 1897 Lands Bill

(See Meek, *op. cit.*, p. 170, for particulars of the 1894 and 1897 Gold Coast Lands Bills.)

Included in W.A.L.C. *Correspondence and Papers*, p. 274, is an extract from a speech by the Governor, Sir W. Maxwell, in the Legislative Council, 29 June 1897, in which he stated that on arrival in the Gold Coast two years before he had found 'that there was no authoritative exposition in any published work on the subject of land tenure in the Colony . . .' and that he had, therefore, called for reports which were published in *Report upon the Customs relating to the Tenure of Land on the Gold Coast*, 1895 (*op. cit.*). 'I have not been able to find', he said, 'that any consistent theory on the subject of tenure is deducible from such judicial decisions as are available.' The 1897 Lands Bill represented the Governor's attempt to control 'concession-hunters' and others who, as he considered, were persuading chiefs to 'deal uncontrolled with private rights . . . in a manner wholly unknown to the native tenure of West African tribes.' (From a message to the Legislative Council on 10 March 1897, quoted on p. 41 of W.A.L.C., *Draft Report*.) The concession-hunters (according, again, to p. 41 of the report) were flocking to the Gold Coast and entering into negotiations with native chiefs owing to 'a speculative movement on the London Stock Exchange which soon attained considerable proportions'. In comparison with this the purchases of land by migrant cocoa-farmers were insignificant (large-scale purchasing of Akim Abuakwa land had only just begun) and they received no mention.

As is well known the 1897 Lands Bill was abandoned as a result of a deputation to Joseph Chamberlain in August 1898 which represented (according to W.A.L.C., *Correspondence and Papers*, p. 274) the 'Kings and Chiefs of the Western Province', and the idea of vesting unoccupied land in the Governor as public land was abandoned.

According to a Memorandum by Sir Walter Napiers included in W.A.L.C. *Draft Report*, the Bill had sought:

(i) To deal with a number of concessions *already* granted;
(ii) To regulate the granting of future concessions;
(iii) To define the rights of the Governor and of the chiefs with respect to 'public land'—viz. land not subject to individual rights;
(iv) To transmute tribal and family holdings into individual ownership.

With regard to (iii):
'A native chief or head of a family was to be precluded from creating, except with the consent of the Governor, any private right in any land under his control, except as follows: He might authorise a native to occupy land as a site for a habitation or for agricultural, industrial or trading purposes, or he might allot land for shifting cultivation.'
Purpose (iv) was to be promoted by conferring:

150

THE WEST AFRICAN LANDS COMMITTEE

'a "settler's right" upon any native in possession by native tenure, at the commencement of the Ordinance, of land which he used as the site of a habitation or for non-shifting cultivation and also upon any native who after the commencement of the Ordinance occupied public land under the authority of his chief for 3 successive years.' (This settler's right was to be permanent and heritable.)

The burden of the representations against the Bill was that all land was owned by natives ('tribally, communally, by families or by individuals') and that the proposed powers over public land would be a violation of native rights.

Had the Bill been passed it would probably have been a dead letter so far as concerned the sale of land to stranger-farmers in Akim Abuakwa: but had this not been so, its existence would surely (owing to the resultant 'red tape') have greatly impeded the development of cocoa-growing in southern Ghana.

Sir Keith Hancock's view of the 1894 Lands Bill (*op. cit.*, p. 184) was that it was understandable that 'literate Africans and British humanitarians' should have raised a shrill outcry against it, that some of the former and all the latter 'honestly mistook the shadow of law for the substance of policy' and that the colonial government, which had 'no designs of taking land for the benefit of settlers or planters', was 'honestly attempting to serve the interests of the community'. His view that before the end of the nineteenth century the chiefs had shown, in their response to the concession-seekers, that they were 'incapable of protecting the people's land', was far truer than it was possible for him to realize—given that Akokoaso (see p. 19) was represented to him as a 'modal' cocoa-village (p. 275), being thus, presumably, typical of those areas where (*op. cit.*, p. 284) 'commercial individualism has really gone full speed ahead'.

APPENDIX V. 2

THE APEDWA/APAPAM LAND DISPUTE OF THE 1890's[1]

The principal object of a lawsuit in Accra in December 1894 was to settle whether Apedwa or Apapam had the right to own the land from which a ferry was operated over the river Densu at Nsawam. The plaintiff, the chief of Apedwa, alleged that his predecessor had given permission to one, Adoagyiri, to settle on the land, which lay within the area controlled by his stool and that he had started and worked the ferry for him, later giving him 'canoes in payment for the permission given to him to live on the land'. The defendant, the chief of Apapam, alleged that the land lay within the area controlled by him and that it was his predecessor who had granted Adoagyiri permission to live on the land. Adoagyiri himself, whose occupation only went back some eight years, denied that permission had been given by the chief of Apapam, but admitted that when he first went on the land his right to be there had been challenged by the Apapam people. Judgment was given for the chief of Apapam.

In about March 1897 the chief of Apedwa claimed damages from the chief of Apapam for trespass on land situated by Yaw Koko's village.[2] Yaw Koko stated that he had obtained permission, some four or five years previously, to build his village from the chief of Apedwa's predecessor to whom he had paid tribute. Judgment was given for the chief of Apedwa.

In October 1897 it was reported to H. M. Hull, the Travelling Commissioner, that a breach of the peace was likely to occur: 'The people of Apapam accused the Apedwas of selling some land [at Akwamu Amanfosu or Akrofosu] which by a recent decision

---

[1] Ghana Government Archives, SNA.ADM 11/1265.
[2] This village is nowadays a well-known place-name on the Nsawam to Suhum road.

151

APPENDIX V. 2

. . . had been judged to belong to Apapam and that, in consequence . . . the Apapams were going to fight the Apedwas.' On 4 November Hull met the two chiefs at Kibi and induced them to let matters rest until he could investigate further. At this meeting the chief of Apapam stated that he had lost the case against Apedwa in 1897 because he had admitted to paying for food he had taken while living at Yaw Koko's village; the Chief Justice had, therefore, concluded that the land could not have belonged to him, as if it had 'I would have taken what I wanted without payment'. He lost the case and was expected to pay expenses of £87 15s. 6d. 'I went to my town and soon after was notified that if I did not pay that money, all the lands known to belong to me, Densu, Akwamu Akrofosu, Abiberi, Okunam, Krabo and Akuntam would be sold by public auction. I paid the money.' He went on to add that he had subsequently 'heard that the chief of Apedwa had sold Akwamu Akrofosu . . . I went to Dome to see the land. At Dome I sent to see if the land had really been sold and they came and reported it had: new boundaries had been cut and boundary-trees planted. . .'

In his report on the meeting H. M. Hull said that the sheriff's notice served on the chief of Apapam had stated that unless the decree of court were satisfied, the stool and certain lands 'known as the property of the chief of Apapam will be sold by public auction on 31st May. Amongst these lands is listed "Akwamu Amanfisu".' The fact that Akwamu Amanfosu was so specified appeared to him to be 'somewhat of a recognition on the part of the court of Apapam's claim to this piece of land, for supposing . . . the land had been sold by auction, the court would have sold land which Apedwa claims and a part of which he has just actually sold'. The courts, it appeared, were 'disinclined to give a sweeping judgment by which the ownership of the whole of this land might be decided once for all'. He, therefore, submitted that 'if the ownership of this large piece of territory to the west of the Nsawam to Apedwa road is to be settled by test actions . . . there seems an excellent likelihood of both Apedwa and Apapam becoming hopelessly ruined'.

He went on 'to raise a word of protest against the method . . . generally employed by the court in settling these land disputes', the results of which were seldom commensurate with the expense to which litigants were put. He had been informed that the Apedwa people had already incurred expenses exceeding £2,000. 'The cost incurred by the Asamans of Akim Abuakwa in their long standing land dispute with the Accras amount to £1,600 and when I was returning from Sefwhi in May, the people of Denkera Mampong told me their chief had involved them in debt to the extent of £1,900 in a dispute as to the ownership of a ferry across the river Pra.' It seemed to him that 'steps should be taken to obviate this ruinous expenditure' and he suggested that a competent officer should be sent in such cases to map the land, to collect evidence and to submit this to the court for further inquiry (if necessary) and final decision.

This advice was taken and it was H. M. Hull himself who, in December 1898, made a compass survey of part of the boundary[1] and who collected evidence from the parties so that the Governor himself might take a decision. It being clear that the courts of law 'were unable to obtain any satisfactory evidence as to the ownership of these lands', he decided 'not to confuse matters by any prolonged cross-examination of principals or their witnesses, but to lead both sides to state their respective boundaries'.

Hull was impressed by the simplicity of the Apapam claim to all the land west of the old Bunkua road 'from Apedwa Densusu to Nkuntanumi on the Densu near

[1] In the archives there is an 1897 map of the Nsawam to Apedwa road, showing villages, which was drawn by a surveyor.

152

THE APEDWA/APAPAM LAND DISPUTE

Nsawam'. (The Senior Presbyter at Kibi, then aged about fifty, had been informed of this boundary when a boy.) The chief of Apedwa 'was not equally well prepared with his boundary', and his witnesses contradicted each other. The points he specified on the boundary, which was some twenty miles long, were 'almost unknown and disconnected'. ('A tree in the midst of a primaeval forest with no tracks leading to and fro can hardly be called a distinguishing mark.') The 'worthlessness of the evidence given by his witnesses' could be contrasted with the 'impression of truth' given by the Senior Presbyter at Kibi, whilst the chief of Adadientem, near Apapam, 'a man of about 70, spoke more as though he were recounting some youthful reminiscence than as if he were giving evidence in the heated and partial way in which natives are wont to speak on behalf of the party they support'. In any case the nature of the terrain was such that the only practicable boundaries were the Apapam to Densu or Apedwa to Densu roads—a conclusion which was strengthened by the Apedwas' recognition of the Apapam claim to Akwamu Akrofosu—the legendary 'and deserted site of the old town of Akwamu'.

Having helped to settle the boundaries of New Juaben, Hull 'knew something of the extent of the Apedwa land'. He said that Apedwa *already had as much land as was needed for its inhabitants and a great deal besides to sell if the people wished* [our italics]. He, therefore, concluded that the existing main road (the Apedwa to Densu road in its new alignment) should form the boundary; this would involve both parties in conceding narrow strips of land to the other.

In presenting this conclusion to the Colonial Secretary he pointed out that although 'the land in dispute is but little' it yet derived 'considerable value from the reason that it abuts on the main road'. '*It has never formed part of the ancient stool property of either place, but has been annexed in the continued absence of its real and former owners*' [our italics]. He said that whatever decision was taken on the main issue, two well-known men in the service of the Basel Mission who had bought land at Yaw Koko should be justly treated: they were Okanta (who had presented title deeds relating to land he had purchased from Apedwa) and a teacher who had purchased his land from Apapam.

The Colonial Secretary accepted this decision in outline, but in the light of the judgment in favour of Apedwa that had been given by the court he considered that the boundary should pass to the west of the main road in two areas, including that of Yaw Koko's farm and village; he also thought that it should be ascertained whether the Apapams had any objection to certain hunters' shelters, which had been made by the Apedwas on their side of the boundary, remaining there.

On 14 February 1899 the governor duly saw the two chiefs to convey this decision to them. 'H. E. saw the chiefs of Apedwa and Apapam ... but as the matter was one of great complication and neither side was willing to give way in any degree in order that a settlement might be arrived at, H. E. decided to leave matters in *status quo* and the two parties to their remedy in the Courts of Law.' Reporting a couple of years later, Hull said that the failure to agree had been due to the chief of Apedwa who, at the last moment, 'did not hold loyally to the arrangement made and got Mr Hutton Mills to represent him'. When the Acting Colonial Secretary commented that it had been a pity that the parties could not have been prevailed on to agree 'as the very object for which Mr Hull went up to settle the boundary has been frustrated, namely the ending of further litigation and consequent expense', the Chief Justice, Sir William Brandford Griffith, replied (2 March 1899): 'Mr Hull's work will not have been in vain. His map will be of the greatest use to the Court in arriving at a proper conclusion. The decision of the Court will cost the parties some hundreds of pounds—to get which they

APPENDIX V. 2

must produce more palm oil and rubber—and I can conceive other ways in which their litigation will help to swell the revenue. The two contending parties will be the only sufferers.'

So far as is known the two chiefs did not subsequently raise the matter with the government. The governor met both of them in February 1901, but neither referred to it, although they had ample opportunity of doing so. He thought there would undoubtedly be further trouble as the Nsawam to Apedwa road was being replaced by a new road under construction by the Gold Fields of Eastern Akim Ltd, the alignment of which deviated considerably from that of the old road, 'as it goes in one straight line from Apedwa to Amanase'.

APPENDIX V. 3

THE AKWAPIM/AKIM ABUAKWA DISPUTE OVER JURISDICTION

In 1908 it was laid down by the Governor (Sir John Rodger) that 'natives who settle on land within the Division of a Chief, whether in the Colony or Ashanti, must obey the lawful orders and regulations and conform to any approved Bye-Laws issued by that Chief'.[1] This definite statement was made because there appeared to be some 'misapprehension' on the 'subject of the personal and territorial rights of Chiefs, and the corresponding obligations of natives owning personal allegiance to one Chief, and residing on land which is within the division of another'. On the 'general question of migration from one division to another' the Governor laid it down that strangers of several years' standing 'should not be interfered with in any way, provided they create no disturbance and obey the lawful orders of the Chief within whose division they are residing'; 'but their withdrawal from the authority of their tribal chief or settlement on land within the jurisdiction of another Chief should, in the first instance, be strongly discouraged, unless such withdrawal or new settlement be for some valid reason or with the consent of both the Chiefs concerned'. 'Every case of withdrawal or new settlement' it was concluded 'must be considered and decided on its own merits'. (Earlier, in 1907, the Governor had ruled, in relation to Juaben towns in Akim, that a distinction should be made between purchase of stool land by individuals and communities, the former, but not the latter, becoming subject to the local chief.)

In 1913, according to Nana Ofori Atta,[2] Omanhene of Eastern Akim,[3] a number of Akwapim headmen, from towns such as Suhum and Asuboi, came to him voluntarily, asking to be confirmed in their appointments as *adikro*. In June 1913 the Omanhene reported these appointments to the District Commissioner. In December 1913, see p. 148 above, new by-laws were passed at Kibi one of the purposes of which was to assert the Omanhene's continued right of jurisdiction over the purchased lands. In April 1914 the *odikro* of Asuboi resigned and the Omanhene himself made a temporary appointment until the subsequent election of Ohene Kwadjo; when he confirmed this latter election he was aggravated to learn that the Omanhene of Akwapim had done likewise. On 5 June he had 'heard of the second invasion', learning that 'the linguist with many followers had come to Asuboi to annex the land up to the Densu at Apedwa'. In September, if not before, he had protested to the government about the fact that the Omanhene of Akwapim was claiming jurisdiction over the stranger-farmers resident in the southern part of his state.

[1] Ghana Government Archives, S.N.A. 571.
[2] In his evidence at the meeting in March 1915, see below. (From papers preserved in the Omanhene's office at Kibi.)
[3] The state of Akim Abuakwa was at that time styled 'Eastern Akim'.

THE DISPUTE OVER JURISDICTION

In a letter of 24 September 1914 to Oheneba Amoanyami of Asuboi[1] the Omanhene said that he had no intention of interfering with the rights of the people of Asuboi 'to their private properties acquired by them individually', but that they should 'clearly understand that so long as they remain at Asuboi . . . they are entirely under my jurisdiction'. The D.C. at Kibi ordered the odikro of Asuboi to come to Kibi, but this he refused to do.

Worried by the possibility of disturbances and uncertain of its attitude to the Akwapim Tribunals at Asuboi and elsewhere (which professed to derive their authority from the Omanhene of Akwapim), the government sought to arrange a meeting between the two paramount chiefs. On 23 January 1915[2] the Omanhene at Kibi wrote to the Commissioner, Eastern Province, saying that ill-health prevented his going to Nsawam for this purpose; later on he decided that it was his duty to go there—having first consulted his legal advisers Casely Hayford and T. Hutton Mills—and the meeting took place on 16 March.

No decision was taken at this meeting, which was presided over by F. G. Crowther, Secretary for Native Affairs. The Omanhene of Eastern Akim argued that it was because the Akwapim farmers had bought the land as individuals that there had been no transfer of jurisdiction. The Omanhene of Akwapim claimed that towns such as Abantin, Mangoase, Asuboi and Suhum were 'owned by' the Akwapim residents in their own right—they being subject only to the rule of their fathers and elders who gave them the money to enable them to purchase that land'. He said that it had been the influence of the government which had induced the Omanhene of Eastern Akim to claim jurisdiction over Asuboi. 'As soon as a collection of people make themselves into a community, form a council and establish a *kuro* they are entitled to elect from among themselves their own headmen subject to the jurisdiction of the original head chief.'

The Omanhene of Akwapim followed up his statement at the meeting with a letter of 18 March 1915,[3] bearing the address 'Sakyikromme, near Nsawam, Akwapim', which was headed 'Akwapim/Abuakwa Boundary Question'. This very interesting but not wholly accurate letter had several purposes, one of which was to prove that the Akwapim outnumbered other cocoa-farming settlers, such as the Shai and the Ga. He was concerned to show that the lands had been bought outright and that no conditions—other than the vendor's right to resume possession on payment of double the purchase money—had been imposed at the time of purchase. Mindful of the Krobo example, he emphasized that the Akim lands acquired by his people were contiguous with 'the old Akwapim boundary'. He ingeniously argued that the land had been bought indirectly by Akwapim chiefs: 'This is custom in Akwapim whereby a chief has to divide his stool land among his subjects and his subjects also divided their shares to their sons who cultivate and earn money wherewith Abuakwa lands are purchased and their fathers almost invariably finance them for that purpose also, so that according to native law the purchases are made indirectly by and for the stools of Akwapim.' Nearly every chief in Akwapim, he insisted, had acquired land in Abuakwa 'and the greater majority of Akwapims have already crossed the Densu and settled on the area in dispute. It is also clearly manifest that most of the remaining subjects will continue shifting of cultivation to that forest.' He cleverly concluded by noting that a late Omanhene of Eastern Akim, Amoako Atta II, had himself sold land at Suhum, to the family of the Mankrado of Amanokrom, the ownership of which had been disputed between Apapam and Apedwa.

[1] Kibi State Council, Letter Book.   [2] *Ibid.*
[3] Ghana Government Archives, S.N.A. 60/19/5.

APPENDIX V. 3

He had promised to follow this letter up with another showing 'how each of the towns came to be founded', but when he came to look into the matter further he realized (letter of 9 April 1915[1]) that the situation was far more complicated than he had supposed[2] and that to write up the evidence 'would cost a whole year of hard work'. But he yet managed to sustain the erroneous impression that in many cases Akwapim stools had somehow been indirectly involved *as such*: 'I find that in a few cases individuals bought for their families, in some cases small stool owners purchased for their families and in other cases chiefs of importance purchased for their stools as in the cases of New Ahwerease (near Nsawam) and New Nsakye.' He concluded that as the Akwapim were 'fully settled on all the lands south of a straight line drawn westward from the Kukurantumi-Juaben boundary to the source of the Densu River near Suhum and continuing through the Atewa Range to Mfranta and along the Ayensu River'—so the Ayensu River should be his western boundary, subject to any rights possessed by the chief of Asamankese: 'In fixing a boundary of this nature a native would just mention the border towns belonging to the one jurisdiction and those belonging to the other jurisdiction and leave the question of actual territorial boundary to the border towns: e.g. Suhum people must know of the extent of their lands, and so Kokoso and Adawsu people will also know where they meet with the Abuakwas.'

The chiefs of Yaw Koko, of Lower and Upper Amanase, of Suhum and of Otoase, all of them natives of Akwapim, combined together to address a petition, dated 22 August 1915, to the Secretary for Native Affairs.[3] They claimed that they had 'found it necessary to elect and install chiefs to try cases among us according to the laws of our country', but that they had lately received a letter from their Omanhene informing them that the S.N.A. had suspended the powers of their tribunals 'to prevent riots which might occur between ourselves and the people of Eastern Akim' so that 'we must send all our criminal cases to the D.C.'.

'... there are no Akims among us in our village which we founded in forest in which no man lived and the Akims do not claim our lands round here. We are all Akwapims living here with our labourers and tenants and there is no probability of friction between ourselves and the Akims or people of any other division; although we have a few Accras who bought building plots from us and built thereon after the foundation of the towns and they are subject to our jurisdiction.'

'These villages and the surrounding cottages contain nearly as many Akwapims as there are in our native towns in Akwapim and we need some local native protection from day to day.'

As far as can be ascertained, although the government soon formed the view that jurisdiction should be exerted by the state of Akim Abuakwa alone, no action was taken and the dispute continued to cause much concern for many years. In 1926[4] it was reported that 'Far and away the most important question of administration which remains to be decided in this Province is that of the right of jurisdiction over the "foreigners"—mainly Akwapims but with a considerable number of Shais, Gas Ningos and Pramprams interspersed among them—who have purchased land and founded villages in the South Eastern portion of the Birim District.' The Omanhene of Akwapim, the Manche of Shai and others, had been encouraged by the award in the

---

[1] Ghana Government Archives, S.N.A. 60/19/5.

[2] There could be no better evidence of the politically unplanned nature of the migration—of its dependence on individuals.

[3] S.N.A. 60/19/5. A similar petition was sent, 24 August, by the chief of Asuboi.

[4] *Report on the Eastern Province for 1925–6.*

156

THE DISPUTE OVER JURISDICTION

Manya Krobo/Akim Abuakwa Arbitration of 1922 (the arbitrator being H. S. Newlands) and had argued that jurisdiction had passed to them as Newlands had found it had to the Krobo—and this despite Newlands' own insistence that this conclusion should not be drawn, see p. 146, footnote 3. 'It would appear', argued the Report on the Eastern Province, 'that their claims to jurisdiction have arisen through a failure to distinguish between the terms "purchase by a company" and "purchase by a community" which are in no way synonymous and to realize that a foreigner does not, by obeying the local laws of the Division in which he lives, sever his allegiance to the stool of which he is a subject by birth.'

APPENDIX V. 4

THE ASAMANKESE ARBITRATION

The Award in the Asamankese Arbitration of 1929 (which is included in *Selected Judgments of the Divisional Courts of the Gold Coast Colony*) is a most valuable source of historical material relating to the relationship between the stools of Asamankese (and Akwatia) and the paramount chief at Kibi. As Appendix v. 5 (p. 158) makes clear, land-tenure conditions in the Asamankese area are very different from those prevailing elsewhere in southern Akim Abuakwa and for this and other associated reasons the findings in this case are not of general application. This brief note deals only with the 1929 Award and makes no mention of the subsequent appeals, by Asamankese, to the Divisional Court at Accra, to the West African Court of Appeal and to the Privy Council. (See, also, Appendix v. 5, p. 158, and p. 147 above.)

The Arbitrator concluded (clause 5) that it was not necessary for the paramount chief to assent to the sale of land by the stools of Asamankese and Akwatia, but that, despite this, the paramount was entitled to a one-third share of all rents and profits of lands alienated by these stools (clause 6). It was further reiterated, in clause 14, that the paramount was entitled to a one-third share of 'whatever comes out of' the land. 'I am confident', said Mr Justice R. E. Hall in his summing up, 'that the claim that the Omanhene is the owner of all lands in Akim Abuakwa has been grossly exaggerated'.

In October 1921 the stools of Asamankese and Akwatia had sought permission from the Governor to sever their connexion with the paramount, arguing that the power exercised by the Omanhene had by immemorial custom and usage been limited to mere paramountcy and not to ownership involving any interest or share of any toll or tribute derivable from the stool lands. The petition referred to the Omanhene's insistence on his right to a quarter of the tolls levied on strangers: 'This new practice has been rigorously enforced to the damage and inconvenience of . . . numerous tenants, who are Gas, Fantees, Aquamus, Ashantees or Juabengs, Yorubas, Wangeras, Hausas and other tribes of West African nationality.'

From the evidence produced, much of which is given in detail in the report, it is clear that the Asamankese stool had been following a very inconsistent policy for many years with regard to alienations of land, sometimes regarding it as expedient to inform the paramount of what was going on—though usually regarding it as none of his business. Their general argument was that as they were Akwamu who had taken no part in the war with the Akim in 1730 and had thus remained in uninterrupted occupation of their lands (never having withdrawn beyond the river Volta), these lands could be owned and enjoyed by them 'without interruption from any other stool'.

157

APPENDIX V. 5

APPENDIX V. 5

THE 'RENTING' OF LAND TO STRANGERS IN THE ASAMANKESE AREA[1]

The chief of Asamankese, whose people owned a vast, though very ill-defined, area of land which extended as far east as the mountain Nyanao, to the west of Nsawam, was more cautious than his neighbour, the chief of Apapam, in selling land outright to immigrant cocoa-farmers and most of the large areas so alienated before about 1914 were situated far away from Asamankese town, towards the southern boundary of the area. In certain parts of the area it had long been the custom to collect 'tolls' from Ga strangers who came to grow food there, so that when, later on, Ga, Awutu, Akwapim and other farmers sought permission to grow cocoa the same practice was apt to be followed, although the crop was a permanent one. It was a practice which appealed to the subjects of the stool, or to certain of them, as the 'tolls' or 'rents' were collected by so-called 'caretakers' (to give them the name by which they have been known for several decades) who were entitled to retain a portion, at least, of the revenue.

A little information on the origin of this system is contained in 'The Award in the Asamankese Akim-Abuakwa Arbitration', 1929, see Appendix v. 4 (p. 157); there is reference to a law case of 1895 between Kwaku Amoah (of Asamankese) and Manche Ababio and others, in which the court gave power to continue the collection of annual tolls—and 'in which the boundary was fixed one mile from the river Densu'. A letter of 30 January 1916 from Kwaku Amoah to the Omanhene at Kibi stated that it had been his predecessor as chief of Asamankese (whom he had succeeded in 1893), 'who began to grant permission to farmers to work on the land on condition that they should pay to him an annual rent of their income', and that 'it was being done long years gone by when even cowries were then used'. From about 1901, according to the same source, the stool of Akwatia had also 'granted leases of lands to several persons'. It was said that it was not until about 1916, as a result of a dispute over collection, that 'the fact of the collection of tolls' came to the notice of the Omanhene.

The cocoa-farmers who hold their land under this system of tenancy today invariably and confusingly refer to it as 'abusa' (one-third) and can usually offer no explanation for this. They pay an annual cash rent, based in principle on the area and yield of their farm (or farms) to an Akim 'caretaker', who represents the chief (being appointed by him) and who is entitled to retain one-third of the rent as his remuneration—the remainder being divided between the local and traditional authorities. Despite the designation 'abusa', it is by no means certain that the system, as it first applied to cocoa-farmers, involved the division of the cocoa into thirds—present-day opinion differs on this point. Perhaps practice varied. One of the oldest inhabitants of Mepom, an Awutu man who arrived in the district with his uncle well before 1910, insisted that the Mankrado of Asamankese, from whom they had obtained permission to 'farm as they like' (no boundaries being fixed in advance), was first paid a 'drink' of £12 (with two sheep and two bottles of Schnapps) and later claimed one of every three planted farms as his property, always choosing the best farm. This they regarded as 'cheating' and 'wondering what to do, they suggested the payment of rent as an alternative'. The original farmer was joined by many of his relatives and they proceeded to make many widely dispersed farms, on land of their choice. He claimed that the rent was finally fixed at £180 annually for all these farms and that it had not been reduced as a result of swollen shoot.

Other informants insisted that there had been a time when individual farmers had

[1] This account is based on the position in 1958 when inquiries were made.

158

THE 'RENTING' OF LAND

been presented with the choice of whether to pay an annual rent or to relinquish a third of the planted farm area. There were some who considered that the latter alternative was preferable in affording the stranger all the security that would go with an outright sale and others whose view was that cash-renting tenants had full security of tenure (themselves and their successors), though rents might be varied. Inquiries show that in some, at any rate, of the areas where 'renting' is common,[1] local Akim farmers own only a small proportion of the land, so it was presumably usual for the caretaker, or the chief, to resell the 'one-third of the farm area' returned as payment by the stranger.

Others again, among them one particularly well-informed official, insisted that one-third of the farm area would be 'seized' if the caretaker failed to collect the rent that was due; first he said that the stranger would then be the 'owner' of the residual two-thirds, but later he corrected himself, saying that he would still have been a 'tenant'.

It is significant that present-day caretakers are usually members of the Akim *abusua* which had been responsible, originally, for allocating the land to the stranger. (The system appears to be of widest application in relatively accessible areas, on the main road, such as Asuokaw, Mepom and Asikasu, to which it is convenient for the 'caretaker' to travel if, as is usually the case, he does not live near-by.) One informant said that 'in the old days each Akim man took possession of a large area'. Whether or not there is any truth in this, it is clear that under this system individual Akim (presumably family heads or their representatives) were apt to be closely associated, at all stages, with the allocation of land to strangers.

This was presumably why, in 1915, 'the Ohene ordered a general annual rent collection to be made', appointing six collectors, the *asafo* appointing another six, whose duty it was to go round with the caretakers, visiting all his villages and collecting the rent. (Information from an interesting memorandum, in the D.C.'s Office at Kibi, on the Asamankese 'native tenure system of leasing land to strangers', which reported the result of a survey of farm rents which began in 1940 and which was never, apparently, completed.) In about 1920, according to the same source, difficulties arose over the collection of rents from Ga tenants:

'A case was taken before the James Town Manche and settled in favour of Asamankese. Following this an arrangement was made by which the *abusa* was commuted for a fixed money payment of £6 per man. [It is not clear what form it had previously taken.] A nominee of the James Town Manche was appointed the collector. . . Similar arrangements have been made with other tenants. . . Often these rents are purely nominal. . . They are frequently reduced when the cocoa crop or the price is poor. . .'
Here again it is stated that the practice of seizing a third of the land applied when the tenant defaulted on his rent.

In some cases there was a general commutation of '*abusa* and individual rents' for a communal payment. This happened, for instance, at Krodua, where a company of seventeen Fanti farmers agreed to pay, through their headman, an annual total rent of £110. Because of the existence of these communal, group or family rents, it was impossible to form any idea, from the rent-rolls kept by the local authority, of the average sort of level of rent which might be paid by an individual.

---

[1] In most districts where 'renting' is common there were also sales of land to individuals and companies (most of the selling probably occurring later than the 'renting') and a very complex land-holding system has resulted, as shown by farm maps in the Asikasu and Mepom Areas.

159

APPENDIX V. 6

DOCUMENTATION OF LAND SALES

In the early days of land sales to cocoa-farmers it was unusual, though not unknown, for a document, or record, to be drawn up at the time of sale. Conveyances formed 'no part of a sale by native law and custom' (A. Allott, *Essays in African Law*, 1960, p. 252), such sales depending for their validity (see p. 141 above) on the proper performance of the *guaha* ceremony. But even in the early days, before 1914, it was not unusual for a document to be drawn up at some later stage, perhaps many years later when the purchaser's interest was menaced by a third party, and this has now become so common that the practice is 'part of the modern customary land law of Ghana' (Allott, *op. cit.*, p. 252), though the performance of *guaha* is still necessary.

While these conveyances are 'no more than evidentiary' (Allott, *op. cit.*, p. 252), much money is wasted on 'private surveys which are usually merely ground plans unrelated to the triangulation of the Colony' (Meek, *Land Law and Custom in the Colonies*, p. 171). In the areas unmapped by the Ministry of Agriculture, the research worker in search of reliable documentation finds it difficult not to take these surveys too seriously—though many of them are quite worthless. 'The worthless surveys are often regarded by their possessors as title deeds, and unscrupulous claimants to land use them to overawe less sophisticated occupiers whom they wish to dispossess.' (Meek, *op. cit.*, p. 171.)

Mr C. H. Cooke, lately a Reserve Settlement Commissioner (see Appendix II. 1, p. 55), has commented, in a private communication, that many of the so-called 'legal documents' drawn up by letter-writers in connexion with sales of land are valueless: 'In fact, in most cases the parties agreed, after the documents which they so proudly produced had been translated and explained to them, that the contents did not represent at all what they had verbally agreed at the time. Generally, therefore, one discarded such documents and relied mainly on oral evidence, supported where possible by money receipts for payments made towards the sale price.'

'Although many attempts have been made in the Gold Coast courts... to argue that lands which have been dealt with by written documents between natives are no longer under native tenure' (Meek, *op. cit.*, footnote, p. 180), yet 'the mere fact of using an English form of conveyance does not create an English form of tenure'. (See also Meek, pp. 296–7.)

160

CHAPTER VI

THE BACKGROUND ECONOMIC CONDITIONS

What were the background economic conditions in the early eighteen-nineties when the migration of Akwapim cocoa-farmers began to get under way? This chapter is a summary attempt to consider those conditions and serves as a preface to chapter VII on the 'migratory process'.[1] Scarcity of source-material prevents proper examination of many topics. The first section of the chapter is more general and goes farther back in time than the (somewhat overlapping) second section in which an attempt is made to list the main economic factors which need to be taken into account in considering how it came about that the migration was launched at that particular moment in time.

The Akwapim are an agricultural people whose social and political organization is based on towns, all of them centuries old.[2] All the principal Akwapim towns, from Aburi in the south, to Akropong, Adukrom and Larteh in the north, lie on top of the main Akwapim ridge,[3] some of them, such as Akropong and Abiriw,[4] being so close together that the visitor cannot tell where one ends and the other begins. Much of the food required for local consumption has always been grown on the hills and slopes leading up to the ridge, within easy walking distance of the towns.[5]

Perhaps it was not until the last few decades of the nineteenth century that the farmers began to move off the ridge westwards towards the river Densu and northwards towards the Adawso area, in search of good farming land, building huts or 'permanent camps' in which they could live when farm work was pressing, or for longer periods. Some of these farmers concentrated on growing food for their own consumption or for sale (or exchange) locally; others established what may be termed 'oil-palm plantations'—that is, they introduced the oil-palm in areas where it was not already growing wild. The chiefs of the Akwapim towns are not the custodians of their people's land (though it is said that of late some stool land has come into existence) so land sales have traditionally involved families or clans,[6] not chiefs. The inhabitants of some Akwapim

[1] See also chapter VIII on the geography of the migration.
[2] See Appendix I. 4 (p. 27).
[3] Which bifurcates in the middle, Larteh lying on the south-easterly spur.
[4] The one matrilineal, the other patrilineal—as are Amanokrom and Mamfe, which are also very close together.
[5] Little is, as yet, known about Akwapim land-tenure, which requires studying town by town.
[6] Owing to the heterogeneity of the Akwapim population and to lack of basic facts relating to land-tenure, terms such as 'family' and 'clan' are here used very loosely.

161

BACKGROUND ECONOMIC CONDITIONS

towns, such as Aburi, were in a position to exercise rights over more land than they required: they seldom bought land. Others, such as Larteh and Akropong people, found it necessary to buy land from inhabitants of other towns, in order to expand their agricultural work. Present-day tradition affirms that many of the original sellers of land away from the ridge were hunters attached to one or other of the towns, such as Tutu, Mampong or Mamfe.

As pointed out by Christaller,[1] the Akwapim (as well as the Krobo and the Ga) are to be contrasted with the Akim, who never establish food-growing villages:

> The Akems [*sic*], having sufficient cultivable land in the neighbourhood of their dwelling-places, do not build villages or hamlets at greater distances to live there part of the year for agricultural purposes, as the Akuapems, Akras, Krobos, &c, do; in Akem we may, therefore, speak only of towns, though some of them be very small in size.

Each Akwapim village in the hinterland was established by an individual and each was, in that sense, attached to that individual's home town—or 'mother town' to use Christaller's term. (Christaller lists seventeen home towns, or nineteen if Larteh be regarded as two, Ahenease and Kubease, and if Abonse be considered as independent of Awukugua.) Some of the villages, such as Konko or Awbum (in relation to Akropong), grew into agricultural out-stations of some size, others remained very small. Christaller provided a list of the number of villages attached to each home town, the date presumably being the eighteen-seventies. Akropong was recorded as having more villages (twenty-seven to thirty) than any other town and it is interesting that Mamfe[2] should have been recorded as having as many as nineteen. But Christaller realized the arbitrariness of these figures, noting:

> Of some of these towns many more villages might be counted, the same name being often applied to a number of separate villages, distinguished by the names of their founders or owners added to the common name.[3]

An official report of 1883 expressed the matter similarly:

---

[1] It is perhaps not well known that the 1881 edition of Christaller's *Dictionary* includes, as Appendix C, a Geography of the Gold Coast and Inland Countries, this being described as a 'framework for a future Geography'.

[2] The relative wealthiness of the Mamfe farmers during the early phases of the cocoa-migration is possibly partly to be explained by their keenness in establishing oil-palm plantations to which these villages were attached.

[3] This problem has always tended to baffle the Census-takers. Among over two hundred Aburi villages listed in the 1931 Census report many bear the same name and are completely indistinguishable: thus there are 3 villages called Opare Kwaku (with 4, 2 and 2 compounds) and so forth. Most of the villages have always, presumably, been very small. Thus in 1931 the number of one-compound Aburi villages was 90, the corresponding numbers of 2, 3 and 4 compound villages being 82, 42 and 20. Of over 400 villages listed as adhering to Akropong in 1931, as many as about two-thirds were one-compound.

162

BACKGROUND ECONOMIC CONDITIONS

Most of the principal towns lie along the top of the main ridge. The King named Quamin Fori lives at Akropong, which is in about the centre of them, on either slope and on and over the ridges to the east and west are numerous villages, many of these are grouped being very small and bear a name common to all, which is generally the name of the founder of the village or else of the man who owns the most land about that part.[1]

This same report put the population of Akwapim, as estimated by the German missionaries, at 30,000 to 40,000. (Christaller himself (*op. cit.*), p. 642, put the figure at 40,000—compared with an estimate of 50,000 for Akim Abuakwa.) According to the first Census of population in 1891, which was probably not at all accurate, the population of Akwapim was 57,583, of whom as many as 53,970 were recorded as living in eighteen of the largest towns on the ridge.[2]

The palm-oil and kernels produced in Akwapim were exported through a number of ports, including Prampram, Akuse and Accra and as oil-palm produce from Krobo country and elsewhere also went through these ports, it is impossible, the statistics being based on exports by ports, to form any idea of the quantity which originated in Akwapim. (In 1890, see Appendix vi. 2 (p. 176), the Gold Coast's exports of palm-oil were £144,788, of palm kernels £78,433, the two products together making up about a third of the total value of all exports.) Nor, of course, can the quantity of Akwapim palm produce produced for local consumption be estimated. But it is clear enough that the cash economy of Akwapim was based on the oil-palm,[3] on trading as well as production:

Though not carried on perhaps to the extent that it is in Croboe [*sic*], the production of palm oil is the chief industry of Aquapim [*sic*]; there are large districts devoted to this to north-eastward where the plantations join those of Akim and Croboe, also at the foot of the mountains to the westward and in the valleys between the ranges.[4]

It is one of the weaknesses of the 1889 *Report of the Commission on Economic Agriculture*[5] that there is little discussion of the position and possibilities in different regions of the Gold Coast. In 1893 the Governor, Sir William Brandford Griffith, caused inquiries to be made by District Commissioners on whether oil-palm plantations were being established.[6] Most of the D.C.'s reported that such plantations had never existed, but the reply from the D.C. at Akuse stated that:

... even prior to the year 1886 the Krobos and Akwapims have taken largely to forming plantations of palm trees ... and even up to date the people ... are still cutting down fresh forests in several other places for new palm tree plantations.

---

[1] *Further Correspondence regarding Affairs of the Gold Coast* (1883), Cmd 3687, p. 26.
[2] See Appendix viii. 4 (p. 248). Those living in the villages may not have been counted.
[3] See also dispatch relating to the dullness of trade, Appendix vi. 1 (p. 174).
[4] Cmd 3687, *op. cit.*, p. 27.
[5] See references to this report in Appendix vi. 1 (p. 175), unpublished report, AD.195/335.
[6] Dispatch dated 12 June 1893 (ADM.1/494, no. 171). (This and similar catalogue references in this chapter relate to Ghana Government Archives.)

BACKGROUND ECONOMIC CONDITIONS

Of the organization and scale of production in Akwapim, little is known beyond the fact that the cultivation of the oil-palm has always been men's, not women's, work. This is a matter of great significance in a society where all the food crops, except yams and maize, are largely cultivated and harvested as well as sold by women. Only the oil-palm put significant sums into the pockets of the men, which they could use for the purchase of land, for although women assisted in the preparation of oil, it was not 'theirs to sell',[1] as with the other crops.

In 1890 there was an extraordinary increase in the value of rubber exports,[2] brought about by an increase in both the quantity exported and price. With a total value of £231,000, compared with only £55,000 in 1889, the value of rubber exports actually exceeded the value of exports of palm-oil and kernels together. In 1893 Ghana ranked third among the rubber-producing countries of the world and the level of exports was well maintained until 1914. Little is known about how the collection and trade were organized,[3] but it is known that wild-vine rubber was being collected in the eighties in Akim, Akwapim, Wasa, Ashanti (both south and north of Kumasi), Krobo country and east of the Volta river—there was little cultivated rubber until much later. So the area of production was much wider than that for palm produce, the costs of transport from inland areas not being so prohibitively high. Although in the eighteen-nineties and earlier a little rubber was collected in the forests of northern and western Akwapim, the Akwapim people primarily benefited as rubber traders. As early as 1883 many Akropong men were engaged in the trade, if the following account, which is doubtless exaggerated, has some truth in it:

Some Christians also from this town [Akropong] who find no means here to provide for themselves and family have left to the Volta district and elsewhere to seek for employment. Owing to the trade in gum or India Rubber which is very strong and very much demanded by the merchants, nowadays most of our Christian (men) as well as nearly all the male inhabitants of Akropong have gone to Akem and Okwawu [Kwahu] for its purchase.[4]

In 1958–60 many elderly inhabitants of Akwapim spontaneously recollected, in conversations with the present writer, the participation of their

---

[1] Although women may sometimes market oil from their husbands' plantations, they are then always acting on their behalf—as they are also when they sell their husbands' maize.

[2] The writer is greatly indebted to Mr H. J. Bevin, lately of the University College of Ghana, for drawing her attention to the importance of rubber exports and for much other unpublished historical material on this and other subjects. See H. J. Bevin, 'The Gold Coast Economy about 1880', *Transactions of the Gold Coast and Togoland Historical Society*, vol. II, part II, 1956.

[3] As late as 1906 Crowther (*op. cit.* p. 180) noted that 'it is difficult to write of rubber with any degree of accuracy'. He considered that owing to improper tapping its collection was then confined 'to the more remote parts'.

[4] From Basel Mission records in Basel extracted by Mr H. J. Bevin (B. M. AFRICA (1883), vol. II, no. 54).

164

BACKGROUND ECONOMIC CONDITIONS

forebears in this trade in rubber in the eighteen-nineties, regarding it as a source of capital for land-purchase for cocoa-growing.

The work of the petty trader was described by Sir William Brandford Griffith in 1893:

There is further in this Colony a vast and almost inexhaustible field for what is known as the petty trader, semi-educated men[1] who purchasing small quantities of dry goods and other articles saleable to the natives of the interior carry them to the inland towns and villages and either sell them or barter them for rubber, palm kernels, monkey skins, or other marketable exports and so turn over their money twice, to great advantage, as a rule, to themselves.[2]

Associated with a general expansion of trade and of rubber exports in particular was the fact that British silver coin was fast coming into circulation at the beginning of the eighteen-nineties, although the first bank, the Accra branch of the Bank of British West Africa, was not opened until 1897. In 1889 gold dust and nuggets had been officially demonetized[3] and by 1893 it was reported that nearly all the coin in circulation was sterling and that cowries were in use among Africans for petty transactions only.[4] Much of the coin that was minted in the U.K. for circulation in West Africa in the early eighteen-nineties probably reached the Gold Coast.[5]

It may be that the increased demand for coin was partly due to the fact that the merchants were yielding to the sellers' insistence that they should be paid for produce in cash rather than in kind.[6] In February 1888 the

---

[1] Because of the work of the Basel Mission educational opportunities were much greater in Akwapim than in most parts of the Gold Coast.

[2] Dispatch dated 6 March 1893 (ADM 1/492, no. 67).

[3] Exports of gold dust had fallen almost entirely into the hands of the mercantile community who were using it as an article of trade and remittance rather than as legal tender. See ADM 1/489, 7 May 1889.

[4] See Robert Chalmers, *A History of Currency in the British Colonies*, H.M.S.O., 1893, p. 215. Christaller, *op. cit.*, 1881 edition, had recorded that 'the Akems use gold-dust, the Akuapems cowries for their currency'.

[5] The older coin was probably becoming very scarce. The Demonetization Ordinance of 1880 had restricted the currency to: gold and silver British sterling, Spanish and South American doubloons (which had practically ceased to circulate), American Double Eagles and Eagles, French 20-franc pieces and gold dust and nuggets at £3 12s. an ounce. In Chalmers, *op. cit.*, the circulating stock of coin in the Gold Coast was roughly estimated at £100,000 in 1891. According to A. McPhee, *Economic Revolution in British West Africa*, p. 236, the average value of British sterling silver issued for circulation in West Africa in 1891–5 was £116,323. Recorded imports of 'specie' into the Gold Coast in 1890 and 1891 were £119,415 and £86,479, but Mr H. J. Bevin has pointed out that much of this was subsequently re-exported.

[6] The gap in commercial records of this period is astonishing (especially bearing in mind the excellent documentation that exists for earlier times) and scarcely any information is available on this important subject. As late as 1903 Lugard complained that the Niger Company's trade was still based on barter—see A. H. M. Kirk-Greene, 'The Major Currencies in Nigerian History', *Journal of the Historical Society of Nigeria*, vol. II, no. 1, December 1960. See also G. L. Baker, 'Research Notes on the Royal Niger Company—its Predecessors and Successors', in the same issue of the aforementioned journal: 'The most regrettable gap in the more recent history of Nigeria is the period between 1870 and 1900 when commercial firms were opening up the Interior' (p. 151).

BACKGROUND ECONOMIC CONDITIONS

Omanhene of Akwapim asked Governor Sir William Brandford Griffith if he could 'instruct the merchants of Adda to pay in cash instead of in gin for palm-oil', to which the Governor replied that 'the matter was one between the buyer and the seller and that they had the remedy in their own hands'[1]—surely as broad a hint as was needed that the government would not disapprove of pressure being brought to bear on the merchants, perhaps by the threat of a boycott. In 1893 Governor Griffith noted[2] that money was 'in very great request by the trading community in order to enable shippers to extend their purchases of rubber, palm oil and palm kernels, which are being brought down to the Coast in considerable quantities and for which together with timber, there is considerable demand and competition'. He added that British silver was 'being carried to Ashanti in considerable sums in order to pay for large quantities of rubber which are brought down from that country'.

When, in 1958 to 1960, elderly Akwapim residents were questioned as to the origins of the finance which had enabled their forebears to buy land for cocoa-farming in the earliest days, most of the emphasis was on the oil-palm, on trade as well as production. They also mentioned: general trading, trading in salt, rubber, parrots, skins, blankets from the north, ivory, cloth, imported rum, etc. Among the most prominent of all Akwapim migrant cocoa-farmers were some who before 1900 had travelled as traders to Nigeria and elsewhere in West Africa, and craftsmen, such as carpenters and blacksmiths, who had sought jobs abroad.[3]

Various circumstances relevant to the launching of the migration of cocoa-farmers in about 1892 and its continuance throughout the nineties are now listed[4]—in arbitrary catalogue fashion so as to emphasize the difficulty of determining their inter-connections and relative importance, though obviously some of them, such as (1), were *necessary* conditions and others were not.

(1) Greatly increased supplies of seeds and planting material for the orchard crops cocoa and coffee, with which the Akwapim people had for long been somewhat familiar, were beginning to become available, especially at Aburi Gardens. This important matter is dealt with at some length in Appendix vi. 1 (p. 170) and the facts speak for themselves. Coffee had preceded cocoa as an export crop,[5] see Appendix vi. 2 (p. 176),

---

[1] ADM 1/488. Mr Bevin states that there is much evidence that spirits regularly passed through many hands, without being consumed, thus acting as a 'store of value'.

[2] ADM 1/492, 18 March 1893.

[3] According to the *Report* on the 1891 Census the exodus of skilled craftsmen was causing concern at that time and it was urged (p. 24, para. 96) that accurate records should be kept of 'mechanics and artisans generally leaving the colony for other parts of the Continent'. On p. 8 of the *Report* it was noted that the greatest attraction was exerted by the labour market of the Congo Free State.

[4] This is partly a recapitulation of the first section of this chapter.

[5] According to Mr H. J. Bevin, Akwapim was certainly the best known coffee-growing area and probably the most productive.

BACKGROUND ECONOMIC CONDITIONS

and Sir William Brandford Griffith considered it much the more promising of the two.[1] The value of coffee-exports exceeded that of cocoa-exports until 1897: thereafter coffee-growing declined rapidly, mainly owing to destruction by insect borers. The uprooting of coffee-trees on the purchased lands and the subsequent planting of cocoa is well remembered in Akwapim today and the early stages of the migration of farmers should be regarded as a coffee-cum-cocoa migration.

(2) The export prices of palm produce (both oil and kernels) had fallen considerably after 1885[2] and did not recover again for another twenty years. In 1886 the Omanhene of Akwapim informed the Governor that 'his people had almost ceased carrying palm-oil and kernels to the coast as, after defraying the charges for transport, there was a loss upon the business'.[3] So it may have been that after 1885 the Akwapim farmers ceased to set so much store by the long-term prospects of an export crop on which they had so much depended. That the oil-palm provided the principal source of finance for buying land for cocoa-growing has already been noted: whatever the importance of rubber trading, it is certain that more farmers had *some* income from the oil-palm than from any other source. Akwapim farmers and traders were well situated geographically to participate in the general trade in palm produce, through the ports of Akuse, Prampram, Accra, etc., and Dodowa, three miles from Mampong on the plain south-east of the ridge, was one of the important early trading centres. (As Appendix vi. 2, p. 176, shows, the volume of exports of palm produce showed no immediate fall as a result of the development of cocoa-growing, oil exports being maintained up to about 1910, kernel exports for a few years longer: but production for export by Akwapim farmers may have fallen earlier.)

(3) The importance of the 1890 boom in rubber exports, as a source of capital then and later for the purchase of land, has already been mentioned. (It is interesting to note that, later on, the Akwapim rubber traders were themselves responsible for spreading cocoa-seeds far and wide.[4]) Presumably much of the initiative for the development of trade in this product, which required processing at the port before export,[5] came

---

[1] See Appendix vi. 1 (p. 174).

[2] Figures extracted from annual *Blue Books* (official sources of statistical and other information) by Mr Bevin show that the export prices of palm-oil in £ per thousand gallons were: 1884 = 84, 1885 = 75, 1886 = 49, 1887 = 47, ... 1897 = 53 ... 1902 = 56 ... 1907 = 64 ... 1910 = 79. The figures for 1884 and 1885 include Lagos (which is why the table in Appendix vi. 2 (p. 176) starts with 1886) and are, therefore, not entirely comparable with subsequent figures; but although Lagos oil is always said to have fetched a higher price than Gold Coast oil, this fact is unlikely to have accounted for most of the drop between 1885 and 1886.

[3] ADM 1/485, 6 April 1886.

[4] Mr Ivor Wilks has told the present writer that Ashanti farmers planted cocoa as far north as Akumadan, just south of Takyiman, before 1900, the seed having been brought there by Akwapim who were engaged in the rubber trade with the Nkoranza area, Akumadan being a collecting point.

[5] '... rubber, before it is shipped to European ports, is cut in small pieces, cleaned,

167

BACKGROUND ECONOMIC CONDITIONS

from expatriate trading firms, many of whom were German, though rubber exports went mainly to Britain.

(4) The increased circulation of British silver coin in the early eighteen-nineties, which has already been noted, may have a special significance. It may be that such coin was far more acceptable to the chiefs of Apedwa and Apapam than older coin or cowries, so that its existence played a part in promoting the sale of land, for general farming purposes, in southern Akim Abuakwa, before the possibilities of cocoa-production had been appreciated by the Akwapim farmers.[1] (On the other hand it may be that all the initiative lay with the Akwapim land-buyers—who simply found themselves with money on hand to invest.)

(5) The population of Akwapim, one of the healthiest districts of Ghana, was presumably increasing—though population statistics are no guide. While there was, in general, no shortage of agricultural land, the inhabitants of some towns found it necessary to go farther and farther afield (see p. 161 above) and future land scarcity could have been foreseen.[2] As already noted, the male population did not, in general, consider food-farming a sufficient or worthy occupation, most of the planting, weeding and harvesting being done by women, though the idea of export agriculture, on an expanding scale not limited to the home market, appealed to their creative spirit.

(6) Many Akwapim men already had highly expansible sets of wants, being aware, through education,[3] travel[4] and contact with others, of conditions in other parts of the world. Apart from the Akwapim traders and craftsmen (see above), many of whom had originally (themselves or their forebears) been trained by the Basel Mission, there were labourers and carriers who sought jobs in connexion with the Ashanti wars, on the building from 1898 of the Sekondi railway, or in the expanding coastal towns. Ministers of religion, catechists, teachers, and prominent Christians generally, were among those most sensitive to the possibilities of the

washed and pressed, and qualities thus treated realize better prices than others. . . Enterprising traders have found it profitable to buy the dirty Cape Coast rubber and export it to Accra, there to be cleaned before it is shipped to Europe. . .' (*Report* on 1891 Census, p. 23, para. 88.)

[1] It is impossible to imagine that the large-scale selling of Akim land which developed after 1900 could have occurred in the absence of a proper medium of exchange. It is true that the Krobo had earlier used cowries when buying their *huza* land (see Appendix II. 9, p. 72), but although the total area of land that they had acquired had been large, the number of separate transactions, and the sums involved, had been tiny in comparison with transactions in southern Akim Abuakwa, and no proper market in land developed, if only because purchases had been 'progressive'.

[2] Certain towns, such as Larteh, would presumably soon have suffered from a shortage of good agricultural land, had the bulk of the population not removed across the Densu, see Appendix VIII. 4 (p. 248)—though had the migration not occurred the population would have increased less rapidly.

[3] In 1891 (see *Report* on 1891 Census, p. 141) the average attendance of pupils at Basel Mission Schools in the eight Akwapim towns where these schools existed was 620, consisting of 423 boys and 197 girls.   [4] See, e.g., p. 205, Larteh, No. 10.

BACKGROUND ECONOMIC CONDITIONS

new crops and if the 'scholar-farmer' was sometimes derided, though usually only in public, his influence and example were profound.

(7) The Akwapim had for long bought and sold agricultural land within their own state; oil-palm plantations had been established on land acquired for the purpose away from the immediate vicinity of home towns. Perhaps resembling the Yoruba of western Nigeria,[1] the Akwapim had what may be termed a 'mobile agricultural outlook'; they were accustomed, unlike the Akim, to erecting temporary habitations as farming outposts of the home town, in which they might sometimes happen to reside for long stretches of time.

(8) So the idea of buying land on the Akim side of the river Densu was originally merely an extension of Akwapim agricultural practice. Early pioneers such as Omanhene Kwasi Akuffo, see Appendix VIII. 2 (pp. 240–1), pointed out the way, not only to the farmers of Akwapim but also to certain Akim chiefs, notably Apapam and Apedwa, who soon realized the possibilities of gain from selling land which had hitherto been 'valueless'. African lawyers, also, were gaining strength and their attitude did much to encourage the sale of land.[2]

(9) As noted by Christaller (see p. 162 above), the Akim are a sedentary, non-migrant, agricultural people, a fact which cannot be understood entirely in terms of a plentiful supply of fertile land. However, in the eighteen-nineties, there was no reason at all for the Akim to be interested in cultivating the uninhabited forests of the south, considering that there was so much equally fruitful land nearer home. That these southern forests were uninhabited, save by wandering hunters, is well known, and a remarkable map of the Gold Coast published in 1885 by the Basel Missionaries[3] shows the words 'Dense Forest and Swamps' running across the whole of the Akim area enclosed within the arc of the river Densu.[4] The Akim population was too far removed from the ports for transport of palm-oil for export to be a commercial possibility on any scale and the two main exports, gold and rubber, were 'collected', sometimes by non-Akim people, rather than produced. That a people with no tradition of

---

[1] It has been estimated that nearly three-quarters of the adult male inhabitants of Ibadan, with its population of over half a million, are farmers whose land lies up to 20 miles away from the centre of the city. Owing to the Yoruba habit of building huts for temporary residence in farming areas, these town-dwelling farmers may provide an exception to the suggested rule that in West African conditions the rapid expansion of cocoa-growing always involves migration. The agricultural population may already have been sufficiently mobile by about 1910 when, judging from the export figures, the rate of planting of cocoa first started to increase rapidly in western Nigeria, and this may be why *Nigerian Cocoa Farmers*, by R. Galletti and others, scarcely mentions migration.

[2] See chapter V.

[3] Of which there is a copy in the Library of the Ghana Survey Department, Accra.

[4] In 1876 it was noted that 'in the larger level district of the south-east [of Akim] are only two small towns, viz. Osanease and Asamang, the remainder of that portion, with the exception of a few sparsely scattered hunters' huts, being totally uninhabited'. (Capt. J. S. Hay, 'On the District of Akem, in West Africa', *Journal of the Royal Geographical Society*, 1876.)

BACKGROUND ECONOMIC CONDITIONS

economic agriculture should have been responsible for creating the Ghana cocoa-growing industry was beyond the bounds of possibility. And, as has been seen in chapter v, the Akim chiefs were not prevented by custom or convention from selling the uninhabited lands, of which they were the custodians, to strangers who were in a position to purchase and utilize them.

(10) It was, of course, a necessary condition for the development of cocoa-growing that European produce-buying firms should already have been established on the coast and that they should have been willing to handle the new crops.[1] But the role of these merchants was much more passive than is commonly supposed, their organization, so far as cocoa was concerned, being based solely on the ports.[2] As they were out of touch with producers, there was little they could do to bring about improvements in the quality of the bean[3]—an urgent task which the government soon had to recognize as its own.[4] In the earliest days before the emergence of a class of middlemen, the farmers had to make their own transport arrangements to get the cocoa to port, hiring carriers (of whom, fortunately, there was a more than adequate supply) when family labour was insufficient. In the eighteen-nineties the farmers were entirely independent of improved internal transport facilities, which followed, but did not precede, the development of cocoa-growing.

APPENDIX VI. 1

THE INTRODUCTION OF COCOA INTO THE GOLD COAST

The Basel Mission

'In 1843 the Basel Mission began their second invasion of the country and carried on their work under the aegis of the Danish Government. They were thus brought into the closest contact with the early efforts of that power to introduce agriculture of an

---

[1] Most of the cocoa was probably handled by German firms in the earliest days, certainly much more cocoa was shipped to Germany than to Britain. Astonishingly little is known of the late nineteenth-century history of the British merchants on the Gold Coast—most historians are interested in earlier periods. Considering the longer run, it is important to note that the world demand for cocoa increased *pari passu* with the greatly increased world supply, so that world prices were well maintained until 1921, at a much higher level in *real* terms than today (1961). Annual world cocoa-production (in thousand metric tons, with the Ghana quantity shown in brackets) rose as follows: 1893–94=75 (neg); 1901–02=127 (2); 1910–11=251 (40); 1920–21=372 (118) (Statistics from F.A.O., *Cacao*, Table I.)

[2] See chapter VII, p. 179. As late as 1906 a Basel Missionary, Mohr, noted that 'the individual producer seldom comes into touch with the European merchants'. (From records extracted in Basel by Mr H. J. Bevin, file D.102,I,9.)

[3] The processing of the crop, the fermenting and drying, has always been the responsibility of the farmers themselves, but in the earliest days most of the cocoa was sold 'wet'.

[4] For years the quality of Gold Coast cocoa was as low as any in the world, and for years it was the chief task of the Department of Agriculture to bring about improvements in this quality—problems of 'production' being consequently neglected.

THE INTRODUCTION OF COCOA

exporting character and were so to speak the natural inheritors of the plantation started by the Danes at the foothills in the neighbourhood of Dodowa.'[1]

The Basel Mission made systematic efforts to raise the standard of agriculture and continually experimented with new crops, of which one was cocoa. As pointed out by Wanner,[2] no one individual missionary was responsible for the introduction of cocoa, which resulted from a fortunate combination of circumstances. Cardinall notes that in 1856 'the Mission were farming an agricultural station at Akropong growing chiefly coffee and fruits as well as experimenting with grasses for thatching'. According to Wanner, Johannes Haas was the first missionary appointed as 'agricultural officer' there and in the autumn of 1857 he received some cocoa-seeds[3] from Surinam, the seedlings from which died in 1858. Johan Jakob Lang took over the agricultural experiments from Haas in 1858 and obtained more cocoa-seeds from another Basel missionary, Auer, who had brought them from Cap Palmas. In November 1861 Lang reported that he had then got ten little cocoa-trees, which were very delicate. In January 1863 it was reported that all but two of these carefully nurtured trees had been destroyed by beetles or worms, and by August only one remained. This last tree survived to bring forth blossom and fruit. In 1865–6 Lang sent cocoa-seed to Basel Mission stations at Aburi, Mampong and Krobo-Odumase. In 1867 the tree at Akropong produced twenty pods, of which ten ripened—one being stolen. Small coffee- and cocoa-nurseries were established at Akropong; some cocoa was replanted— there were ninety slips, of which twenty-five survived. In 1868 Lang departed, stressing the potential importance of cocoa and requesting the Mission to do all in its power to expand this industry.

Lang's successor was Henri Marchand, whose first report said that many seedlings had died or been eaten by insects, that some had been stolen and that the survivors were barely alive. To prevent theft he built a fence with a gate, but both seedlings and gate disappeared. In 1870 after a dry season and further ravages by worms, the last cocoa at the Akropong agricultural station died, the station being handed over to the local people: but the trees at Odumase and elsewhere survived and further cocoa- growing experiments were made at Aburi in the eighteen-seventies, the Rev. Schrenk being one of those concerned.

At about this time, or earlier, Akwapim farmers began to establish their own cocoa- and coffee-farms. Then there was the Rev. C. C. Reindorf who in 1862 went into temporary retirement on a land near Aburi which he had named 'Hebron', where he made a coffee-plantation.[4]

The Basel Mission also introduced cocoa directly into Akim Abuakwa. In 1890 Mohr,[5] who was then stationed at Begoro, 'introduced from Kamerun through Bro. Bohner two sacks of cocoa pods, for distribution among the Akim Christians'. He added that:

[1] A. W. Cardinall, *The Gold Coast*, 1931 p. 82. *Report of the Commission on Economic Agriculture*, 1889, stated that coffee had been introduced by the Basel Mission, from the West Indies, in 1843 and that the early plantations which had been destroyed by the Ashanti in 1869 had been, at least in part, re-established. The Basel Missionaries were not the first to introduce cocoa (or coffee) into the Gold Coast—see Cardinall, *op. cit.*, p. 82, and also references to coffee-growing in 1807 and 1841 in *Report from the Select Committee on the West Coast of Africa*, part I, Appendix, 1842, p. 14.

[2] Gustaf Adolf Wanner, *Die Basler Handels-Gesellschaft A.G., 1859–1959*, from which much of the material in this Appendix is drawn.

[3] Cardinall, *op. cit.*, erroneously states they were seedlings.

[4] See Carl Christian Reindorf, *The History of the Gold Coast and Asante* (1895). (Reindorf was not an Akwapim.)

[5] See footnote 2, p. 170. (From a report made by Mohr in 1906, Mr Bevin's translation.)

APPENDIX VI. 1

'One had some years before, here and there, heard of an Akwapim man in Mampong,[1] who possessed a tree... Of course most of the pods which I obtained at that time were already spoilt and comparatively few capable of germination. But very soon young trees were successfully obtained at our station in Akim and by that means cocoa was introduced into Akim and its cultivation has in a few years completely driven out that of coffee... Within a few months large coffee plantations became completely overgrown and reverted to bush.'

According to Wanner (*op. cit.*), Mohr sold pods at 2s. 6d. each, in opposition to either Tetteh Quashie or Peter Botchway of Mampong (the writer did not know which) whose price was £1.

Tetteh Quashie

It is now generally believed that the famous Tetteh Quashie,[2] who was a Ga blacksmith from Christiansborg, established a cocoa-nursery in Mampong (Akwapim) with pods which he had brought back in 1879 from Fernando Po, where he had been working as a labourer. How far is it possible to verify these facts today?

In the Gold Coast *Annual Report* for 1902, Tetteh Quashie was named and the date of the introduction of the pods given as 1879. But in 1909 the Director of Agriculture[3] put the date at 1882 and the place of origin of the pods as 'the Cameroons'.[4] The West African Lands Committee reported[5] in 1917 that the industry had been introduced 'in the early eighties by a native of Accra upon his return from employment upon a cocoa plantation in the Island of Fernando Po'. In 1927 Governor Guggisberg wrote[6] that one pod had been brought to Mampong in 1876 and that the first transplantation had occurred in 1881—a photograph in his book, p. 41, is captioned 'First Cocoa Farm in the Gold Coast, belonging to J. W. Hammond, nephew of Tetteh Quashie, planted 1881'. Since 1928, when £250 was voted to Tetteh Quashie's family by the Gold Coast government in recognition of his having been the first person to plant cocoa in the Gold Coast, 1879 seems to have been the generally accepted date of Tetteh Quashie's return and Fernando Po the agreed place of origin of the pods.[7]

The present writer has no comment to offer on these facts, except to record that in 1960 a number of elderly farmers in Mampong independently volunteered the opinion that it had not been Tetteh Quashie himself who had gone to Fernando Po, but a maternal relative and/or apprentice, sometimes called Agya, who had presented pods to his uncle or master on returning from the island where he had been working as a labourer. If only because it seems unlikely that a skilled blacksmith would have gone to Fernando Po to work as a labourer, these statements seem plausible, though in themselves they do nothing to detract from the significance of Tetteh Quashie, whose

[1] Perhaps Tetteh Quashie, though he was a Ga.

[2] The 'Tetteh Quashie Memorial Hospital' at Mampong has recently been opened; paid for from Cocoa Marketing Board funds, it cost about £500,000 and has over 100 beds. A complete wall of Tetteh Quashie's small house on the main road in Mampong has been adorned with a colourful representation of the history.

[3] W. S. D. Tudhope, 'The Development of the Cocoa Industry in the Gold Coast and Ashanti', *Journal of the Royal African Society*, vol. IX, October 1909. (There is no reason to think that Tudhope was a reliable authority on matters of this kind.)

[4] In M. A. Chevalier, *Le Cacaoyer dans l'Ouest Africain*, 1908, p. 188, the Cameroons was stated to be the most likely place of origin.

[5] W.A.L.C., *Draft Report*, p. 96.

[6] F. G. Guggisberg, *The Gold Coast* (A Review of the Events of 1920–6 and the Prospects of 1927–8), dated 3 March 1927.

[7] Although there is no doubt about the identity of the man himself, the Nowell Report wrongly stated (para. 46) that he was a 'Fanti labourer'—one 'who was evidently destined to be a national hero'.

172

THE INTRODUCTION OF COCOA

contribution was that of establishing a small cocoa-nursery[1] in Mampong from which he sold, or distributed, pods or seedlings to Akwapim farmers.[2]

Governor Sir William Brandford Griffith

Sir William Brandford Griffith was Governor of the Gold Coast from January 1886 (when the Gold Coast and Lagos were separated) until April 1895. Brought up in Barbados, whence his great-grandfather had emigrated from Wales, his first job had been a clerkship in the Colonial Bank at Antigua. According to his son[3] it had been because later on, as Auditor-General of Barbados, he had espoused 'the cause of the Government in the matter of confederating several Islands' and had thus incurred 'great unpopularity with the planter class', that he had gone to England in 1878 to ask for an appointment elsewhere and had eventually been posted to Lagos as Lieutenant-Governor in 1880. With his West Indian background, he soon began to take a great practical interest in promoting the cultivation of new economic crops in West Africa; as early as 1882 he had introduced into Lagos 'some cocoa, coffee, vanilla and nutmeg plants and other West Indian fruits and vegetables from Trinidad and Barbados which flourished well'.[4]

If the Governor's own recollections were not at fault,[5] it may have been in 1885 that he first introduced cocoa into the Gold Coast: reporting on a 'palaver' that he had attended in Akropong in 1888,[6] he remarked that the Omanhene had informed him that 'the cocoa plants which I had sent up to him after my visit to the place in the year 1885 had failed'. It may have been in 1886, as tentatively suggested by his son,[7] that he persuaded a superintendent of the Cable Company[8] who had recently been transferred from Accra to San Thomé to send him a consignment of cocoa-pods; but if that were the date it is puzzling that two years later, in 1888, he himself commented that he would endeavour to obtain pods from San Thomé[9]—as though for the first time. In 1886 he had noted that he intended to obtain some cocoa-pods from Trinidad (not

---

[1] Tetteh Quashie's farm has recently been surveyed by the Ministry of Agriculture and its area is reported to be 0·94 acres.

[2] Who was responsible for producing the first recorded exports of 121 lb of cocoa in 1885 (after which no more exports were recorded until 1891—80 lb) cannot be ascertained, though it is often assumed to have been Tetteh Quashie himself. One Mampong informant said that Tetteh Quashie had brought his cocoa to Peter Botchway (a well-known Mampong trader who, together with his brothers, bought a large trans-Densu cocoa land in 1897) 'because he was a rubber trader' and that Peter Botchway had sent it 'to the agents of the Basel Mission in Accra'. In 1888, according to Governor Sir William Brandford Griffith whose eyes were wide open, there was little cocoa to be seen in Akwapim.

[3] Who was also Sir (William) Brandford Griffith and who was Chief Justice of the Gold Coast from 1895 to 1911—he is referred to in Appendix I. 1 (p. 18) and elsewhere. Some of the facts in this Appendix are drawn from *The Far Horizon: Portrait of a Colonial Judge*, a discursive but interesting autobiography written by the former Chief Justice just before his death at the age of eighty in 1939.

[4] Dispatch dated 28 August 1888, ADM 1/489.

[5] There is no other evidence of his having obtained any cocoa-plants as early as 1885— or that he had gone up to Akropong that year, as well as in 1886.

[6] Dispatch dated 2 March 1888, ADM 1/488.

[7] *Op. cit.*, p. 146, where it is recorded that he had seen the pods being packed in head-loads for Aburi and that some of the seedlings were 'set out in the garden there' (this would have been before the establishment of the botanical garden proper) and that some were 'distributed amongst the neighbouring chiefs and the Basel Mission'.

[8] Submarine cable communications with England had been completed in 1886 (see Cardinall, *op. cit.*, p. 28).

[9] Dispatch dated 21 August 1888, ADM 1/489.

173

APPENDIX VI. 1

from San Thomé), in response to a request that had been made to him by the Oman-hene of Akwapim[1]:

'When on the Hills in March I paid a visit to King Quamin Fori of Akropong at his special request; and he told me that his people had almost ceased carrying Palm Oil and Kernels to the Coast as, after defraying the charges for transport, there was a loss upon the business, and he deplored this, as his country abounded in such produce. I strongly advised him not to let his people confine themselves to palm oil alone, but to encourage them to pay more attention to coffee, as it grows luxuriant in his country—I saw it growing wild by the wayside on the way from Aburi to Akropong—and also to cultivate cocoa. He said he would act on my advice and requested me to obtain some cocoa seeds for him.'

Certainly during those years, the Governor was doing all he could to persuade the people of Akwapim, as well as the Krobo, to take an interest in these crops. In Akropong, in February 1888, 'he expatiated as usual upon cotton and cocoa cultivation'.[2] And at Aburi,

'. . . which has mountain slopes of southern aspect and a fertile soil admirably suited for coffee and cocoa the former of which is already cultivated to some extent owing to the example of the members of the Basel Mission stationed there, I also emphasised the advantages of agriculture to the Africans of the place. . .'[3]

At that time coffee appeared to have much better prospects than cocoa. In August 1888 the Governor noted[4] that coffee-trees were to be found growing wild in many parts of Akwapim, but that he had only seen a few cocoa-trees 'here and there in gardens'. Later in the same month, in a dispatch[5] relating to the scheme for establishing a botanical garden at Aburi, he again noted that coffee, but not cocoa, was being cultivated to some extent 'owing to the example of the members of the Basel Mission'.

The object of establishing the Aburi gardens was made clear in this latter dispatch: 'It was mainly with the view of teaching the natives to cultivate economic plants in a systematic manner for purposes of export that I have contemplated for some time the establishment of an agricultural and botanical farm and garden where valuable plants could be raised and distributed in large numbers to the people in the neighbourhood in the first instance, and afterwards sent further into the country by pupils whom I contemplate taking from the Schools. . . By their agency when sufficiently educated for the purpose additional farms and gardens could be started and by these means the people generally would become acquainted with the fact that other products than those indigenous to the country had been introduced into it, were thriving and would be remunerative and thus observing the advantage to be gained by their propagation would be disposed to cultivate them.'

The Governor was not bound to his desk. In February 1890, ten days after his return from England on leave, he assumed personal charge of the Aburi gardens for six weeks, his primary concern being coffee.[6] He had brought with him from Monrovia, where his steamer had stopped on the return voyage, 'a dozen intelligent English-speaking Liberians who had been accustomed to the planting and treatment of coffee trees'. 'I also employed about 30 men and utilized my Hausa Escort, and in this way I had seven acres of land cleared of forest trees and of the undergrowth of smaller ones and scrub in three weeks. . .' On 23 March he handed over to Crowther,

---

[1] Dispatch relating to 'the dullness of trade', dated 6 April 1886, ADM 1/485.
[2] Dispatch dated 2 March 1888, ADM 1/488.   [3] *Ibid.*
[4] Dispatch dated 21 August 1888, ADM 1/489.   [5] 28 August 1888, ADM 1/489.
[6] Dispatch dated 28 April 1893, ADM 1/493.

THE INTRODUCTION OF COCOA

the curator, who started to clear the remaining nineteen acres. Coffee was the principal crop, but cocoa procured from Trinidad and Fernando Po was also planted. By September 1892 both coffee and cocoa were in bearing. In 1893 the unused portions of the garden were 'being gradually planted out with coffee and cocoa seedlings remaining in excess of the quantities grown for sale and unapplied for, although large quantities have been sold to the public'.[1]

But evidently some cocoa had been planted at Aburi before 1890—perhaps from the pods obtained through the Cable Superintendent. Sir Hesketh Bell in a letter to *The Times*, dated 25 February 1929,[2] quoted the following extract from his diary for 1 October 1890:

'Dined last night at the Castle and had a long talk with the Governor about Cocoa. He introduced it here about three years ago and there is an experimental patch up at Aburi. H.E. is very keen about it, as he thinks it ought to be a great thing for the Gold Coast. But the Curator has reported that the climate of this country appears to be unsuitable for cocoa and that he is checking the experiment. Sir W. B. G. knowing that I have spent several years in Grenada and was much in touch with planters there, wants me to go to Aburi and look at the little plantation and tell him what I think about it.'

Sir Hesketh Bell found that the first attempts at establishment had not been at all successful:

'As soon as I saw the patch of cocoa I was able to explain to him the chief reasons for the failure at Aburi. The plants, which though two or three years old, were little more than bare sticks, had been set out on a bleak hillside much exposed to the wind. Instead of being sheltered in their early stages, as they always are in the West Indies, by caladium and other low-growing vegetables and, later on, by bananas or plantains, they had been entirely without protection and it was a marvel that they had survived so long. The young Curator and I then selected a snug, well-sheltered little valley in another part of the grounds to which moribund cocoa plants were, by the Governor's orders, subsequently transferred. . .'

In November 1890,[3] when commenting on the *Report of the Commission on Economic Agriculture*,[4] the Governor said that he would obtain more cocoa-seed from Fernando Po. 'Nineteen hundred seeds were sent from Trinidad but the voyage appears to have been too long for them as they were dead before arrival.'

In May 1891[5] the local population was reported to be looking on at operations at Aburi with interest. The Omanhene of Western Akim had ordered one hundred cocoa plants and 'other small sales' had also been made. Later that year it was reported[6] that 'the coffee and cocoa plants look healthy—the former more especially so the soil

---

[1] Dispatch dated 28 April 1893, ADM 1/493.

[2] This letter is given in full in W. B. Griffith, *The Far Horizon*, pp. 147–8. Following the Gold Coast government's recognition of Tetteh Quashie in 1928 (see above), Sir W. Brandford Griffith wrote to *The Times*, 13 February 1929, claiming that it was from the seeds planted by his father at Aburi that the industry had sprung and Sir Hesketh Bell's letter was written in support of this.

[3] Dispatch dated 10 November 1890, ADM 1/490.

[4] *Op. cit.* The Commission considered that coffee was 'undoubtedly the first product to which intending cultivators should turn their attention'. On cocoa it commented merely: 'This is another product worthy of every attention. Attempts on a small scale have been made to introduce it into the country, but no information is available as to the results.' (In general the report makes interesting reading—thus 'All our towns are filled with young men seeking in vain a livelihood in clerical offices while vast fields of labour are left untouched.')

[5] From a dispatch on Aburi botanical garden, dated 6 May 1891, ADM 1/491.

[6] Dispatch dated 9 November 1891, ADM 1/492.

175

APPENDIX VI. 1

being apparently well adapted for coffee cultivation'. The demand for cocoa-seed lings, small as it is reported to have been, had even declined:

'At present the only demand for plants on the part of the natives is for coffee plants and there is no doubt whatever that the natives in Akwapim and Krobo are beginning to plant coffee in earnest as a means of livelihood.'

Entering the realm of living memory, a visit which the Governor paid to Akropong in July 1892[1] remains fresh in the minds of some of the oldest inhabitants of that town today. Whether he then still thought that coffee, not cocoa, was the crop of the future cannot be ascertained; but several informants independently insisted that he had urged the farmers to leave their over-crowded ridge and to cultivate 'distant forests'— an exhortation which is attached to cocoa in his hearers' minds today, though it may originally have related to coffee.

In the month of his retirement, April 1895, the Governor found himself very satisfied with the condition of the Aburi gardens.[2] Coffee especially, and also cocoa, were growing well. The local population appeared to be imitating the methods they had observed there. On the road leading up to Aburi and across the ridge to Mampong, he observed much coffee-cultivation—but no cocoa. When Sir William Brandford Griffith died of blackwater fever in Barbados in 1897, he may have been quite unaware of his achievement.

APPENDIX VI. 2

ANNUAL GOLD COAST EXPORTS, 1886–1913[3]

	Cocoa	Palm-oil	Palm kernels	Rubber	Gold	Lumber	Coffee	Total all exports
1886	—	156	48	70	75	neg.	neg.	407
1887	—	143	42	62	81	,,	,,	372
1888	—	150	69	38	87	,,	0·1	382
1889	—	137	63	55	103	,,	neg.	416
1890	—	145	78	231	92	0·5	0·2	601
1891	neg.	193	90	199	88	22	0·5	684
1892	—	179	103	167	99	36	0·3	665
1893	neg,	184	81	218	79	50	0·6	722
1894	0·5	238	112	233	77	69	1·3	850
1895	0·5	231	93	322	91	28	1·8	878
1896	2·3	127	85	314	86	52	4·1	792
1897	3·2	108	70	420	85	91	3·1	858
1898	9·6	114	66	552	64	110	2·3	993
1899	16·1	183	106	556	51	87	2·2	1,112
1900	27·3	239	97	328	38	68	1·2	885

Value, £000 (f.o.b.)

[1] The Governor was passing through Akropong *en route* to Krobo country, in order to put down customs which were objected to and to prevent access to the Krobo mountain. He subsequently found himself too hard-pressed for time to report adequately on his expedition. There is a description of the visit to Akropong in the Rev. Dennis Kemp's *Nine Years at the Gold Coast* (1898), as well as a photograph (opp. p. 164) captioned 'Palaver at Akropong, Houssa Soldiers *At Ease*', which may or may not have been taken on the same occasion.

[2] Dispatch dated 6 April 1895, ADM 1/495.

[3] Based on statistics extracted from annual *Blue Books* by Mr H. J. Bevin. Re-exports excluded.

ANNUAL EXPORTS, 1886–1913

	Cocoa	Palm-oil	Palm kernels	Rubber	Gold	Lumber	Coffee	Total all exports
1901	42·8	178	90	104	22	55	0·8	560
1902	94·9	235	132	89	97	22	0·4	774
1903	86·2	146	105	196	255	49	0·3	981
1904	200	129	87	361	346	54	neg.	1,340
1905	187	88	79	324	597	84	,,	1,646
1906	336	125	81	335	822	80	,,	1,996
1907	515	119	102	333	1,131	169	,,	2,642
1908	541	130	78	168	1,122	158	,,	2,525
1909	755	121	112	264	983	83	,,	2,656
1910	867	161	185	359	790	148	,,	2,698
1911	1,613	129	176	219	1,058	139	,,	3,792
1912	1,643	113	205	169	1,439	229	—	4,308
1913	2,489	66	159	88	1,626	366	—	4,952

Quantity

	Cocoa (000 tons)	Palm-oil (m. galls)	Palm kernels (000 tons)	Rubber (m. lb.)	Gold (000 oz.)	Lumber (m. ft)	Coffee (000 lb.)
1886	—	3·16	9·4	1·55	21	neg.	5·2
1887	—	3·08	8·0	1·31	23	,,	2·9
1888	—	3·41	13·3	0·88	24	,,	3·8
1889	—	2·90	10·9	1·24	29	,,	1·9
1890	—	2·93	12·7	3·36	25	,,	9·3
1891	80 lb.	3·89	12·9	2·95	24	1·35	13·7
1892	—	3·64	15·8	2·66	27	2·13	12·9
1893	3·46[1]	3·42	12·0	3·40	22	3·41	21·4
1894	20·3[1]	4·21	17·1	3·03	21	5·01	41·4
1895	28·9[1]	4·34	15·6	4·02	25	3·59	51·8
1896	86·8[1]	2·40	13·0	3·73	24	6·06	142
1897	157[1]	2·02	10·8	4·96	24	15·2	102
1898	414[1]	2·15	9·7	5·99	18	13·6	122
1899	715[1]	3·32	12·7	5·57	14	12·0	143
1900	0·53	4·24	12·8	3·45	11	7·44	83·2
1901	0·98	3·15	12·8	1·52	6	6·89	53·9
1902	2·40	4·23	17·0	1·60	27	2·23	23·4
1903	2·28	2·59	13·2	2·26	71	7·38	26·5
1904	5·11	2·24	11·0	4·01	94	16·0	4·9
1905	5·09	1·60	9·8	3·69	159	8·36	5·3
1906	8·97	2·14	9·4	3·65	217	7·80	2·8
1907	9·36	1·87	9·8	3·55	292	18·5	0·52
1908	13·0	2·25	9·0	1·77	289	19·0	0·46
1909	20·1	2·01	11·6	2·76	254	9·84	0·35
1910	22·6	2·05	14·2	3·22	205	14·9	0·18
1911	39·7	1·61	13·3	2·67	280	14·0	neg.
1912	38·6	1·44	14·6	1·99	378	23·6	—
1913	50·6	0·86	9·7	1·32	423	37·4	—

[1] 000 lb.

CHAPTER VII

ECONOMIC ASPECTS OF THE MIGRATORY PROCESS, 1894–1930[1]

'We travel to go and buy.'

Although the underlying purpose of this whole inquiry was that of obtaining some understanding of *present-day* economic processes and motives, the journey itself proved so interesting that the destination was almost overlooked. Nor, for the time being, can this aberration be remedied with the help of others, for it seems that what actually happened in Ghana was so much at variance with conventional notions of what 'ought' to have happened, that few of the many general works on 'problems of economic under-development' which have been published during the last fifteen years have much practical, as distinct from theoretical, relevance to the present analytical purpose.[2] Economists (other than agricultural economists) *working in the field* in Africa, and there have been few of them so far, have usually regarded trade or distribution (including transport), not production, as their proper concern and few of them have paid more than cursory attention to the rural areas; no such subject as 'the organization of production of export crops' is presumed by them to exist—it is only *after* the goods have been produced that economic organization is supposed to become interesting.

Why should this be? The twin assumptions that production is usually small-scale[3] and organizationally simple are partly responsible for this neglect. But there has, also, always been a tendency for economists to exaggerate the importance of the role of the expatriate trading firm—and this in a part of the world where trade was already well developed when

---

[1] The steadily expansionary period ended in about 1930, being succeeded firstly by a period of consolidation (in the thirties) and secondly by a vicious circle of contraction resulting from swollen shoot. This chapter in general relates to the expansionary period.

[2] In the theoretical field it may be that the ideas of Professor Gunnar Myrdal, especially as expounded in his *Economic Theory and Under-Developed Regions*, could be fruitfully applied, particularly the notion of 'circular cumulative causation'. As noted in Benjamin Higgins, *Economic Development* (p. 410), the 'chief problem in attempting a synthesis of theories of underdevelopment is still empirical'—'we do not need elaborate econometric models before we can explain the behaviour of underdeveloped economies or prescribe policies. But we do need to know what the strategic functional relations are and we need to know their general shapes'. As for the interest of anthropologists in economic aspects of West African society, they, as remarked by Sir Keith Hancock (*op. cit.*, p. 271), 'have been preoccupied with other matters'.

[3] It is, of course, the contention in this book that the statistical picture as a whole is too complex and heterogenous to be summed up as either small or large scale. As for the migrant farmers, they are apt to stand in varying relations to their various farms and lands, so that the notion of scale of production is fraught with special difficulty.

178

ECONOMIC ASPECTS

Europeans first arrived there in the fifteenth century! It has been unconsciously, or implicitly, assumed that it was the expatriate traders who 'taught the natives', if only by example, the elements of the facts of economic life—that the whole nature of the economic response of the indigene was determined by his contact with these 'agents' of colonialism. But present inquiries have shown, on the contrary, that the influence of the trader in the vital first fifteen years, or so, of commercial cocoa-growing was minimal—that he merely sat at (or near) the port receiving the produce and had no more knowledge than any other outsider as to how production was organized.[1] Nor was the Department of Agriculture (in the old days) in much better case.[2]

So as things have turned out, the initial contention that problems of internal collection of export crops are of negligible interest and importance compared with problems of production (for export),[3] has been shown to be even better justified than had been expected. And it is hoped that readers of this chapter will at least agree[4] that such problems of production are as much the province of the economist as they are of the sociologist, the anthropologist or the agronomist.

The essential nature of the migratory process

The essential nature of the migratory process is that it is forward-looking, prospective, provident, prudential—the opposite of hand-to-mouth. Had the farmers, like so many retail traders, simply been concerned to 'get rich quick' and then to go out of business, they would, to use their own terminology, have 'eaten'[5] the proceeds from their early cocoa-farms,

[1] Questioned on 13 February 1913 by the West African Lands Committee (*Minutes of Evidence*, p. 374), Mr W. A. Cadbury said that his firm carried on business in Accra only, that it had nothing to do with the collection of produce from the farmer and that he had no knowledge of tenure conditions—though his impression was that the majority of the holdings were 'very small'. As transport facilities improved, some of the merchants began to move inland: thus Chevalier, *op. cit.*, p. 195, noted that in 1905 Fischer, Swanzy, the Basel Mission and others had buying stations at Ayimensah, between Aburi and Accra. This tendency of the European merchant to confine his activities to the coast has long been recognized as a characteristic feature of the early palm-oil trade—see H. J. Bevin, *op. cit.*, pp. 78–9.

[2] Because the farmers have always been supposed, in a sense, to have been guided by 'instructions' issued to them by others, so they have always been blamed for not following these instructions sufficiently closely. The official literature emanating from the Department of Agriculture during the first quarter of a century was one long wail of complaint about the farmers' inefficiency—partly justified, no doubt, by the very poor quality of the crop.

[3] On the other hand, problems of distribution of food for local consumption may, in some areas, be more interesting and important than problems of food production; the organization of the long-distance trade in yams, plantain, *gari* (cassava meal), shallots, kola, salt, etc., is usually far more complex than the arrangements required for the relatively simple operation of collecting export produce for transport to the ports.

[4] Despite the tentative nature of the approach adopted in this chapter—which has, accordingly, been arranged as notes classified under headings.

[5] One of the manifold meanings of the Twi verb *di* is 'eat'. See Appendix VII. 6 (p. 214) for a few notes on the need to explore the vast field of 'linguistic economics'.

179

ECONOMIC ASPECTS

rather than re-investing them in other lands. Almost from the beginning, see Appendix VII. 3 (p. 200), the farmers regarded themselves as involved in an expansionary process from which they had no intention of withdrawing. Almost from the beginning, cocoa-farms established on purchased land were regarded as investments—i.e. property which existed for the purpose of giving rise to further property. The farmers found no difficulty in handling the practical notion of putting money to work—of loosing it out to multiply itself. It is quite erroneous to suppose, as some have done, that the process is merely a sophisticated variant of shifting cultivation; had this been so, the farmers would have tended to lose interest in their earlier-acquired lands—whereas there is plenty of evidence that they often remained more attached to their earlier than to their later acquisitions. Nor has there ever been any tendency for farmers to complete the planting of one land before proceeding to the cultivation of another. The pace of land acquisition was so rapid in the early days that it is perhaps reasonable to assume that, at that time, the farmers allowed themselves little scope for investment other than in land. They regarded their initial capital as a fund to be employed within the business only—this being a familiar notion to women traders and others. The Twi noun *dwetiri* is defined, by Christaller, as 'a capital or stock of money to begin trade with; a fund employed in business or any undertaking; principal'.[1]

Why so expansionary?

It is hard to disentangle the various motives. Certainly the expansionary process soon became desirable for its own sake—it was creative, adventurous and all-absorbing. It has been noted in chapter VI that many Akwapim men had highly expansible sets of wants when the process first began, being aware, through education, trade, the exercise of craftsmanship in distant places and work as labourers, of conditions elsewhere in the world. The need to secure the future was involved with the idea, so reasonable in Africa, that there is no resting-place between stagnation and growth: a business cannot be healthy unless it is expanding. On the one hand there is a desire, which took particularly strong expression with the matrilineal Aburi, to create lineage (or family) lands for the support of the lineage in general; on the other hand, much of the farmers' restlessness is to be explained as a resistance to the drift towards family property —as a desire to exert personal control over a new land.[2] Although the form of organization adopted by the patrilineal farmers was streamlined compared with the amorphous family lands of the Aburi and Akropong farmers, the results were not so different, in terms of numbers of lands

[1] *Dwetiwani* is carefully, and interestingly, defined as: 'a possessor of some little property, not exactly rich, but on the way to become so'.

[2] '... the wish to possess some object over which they might enjoy an individual and undisputed control...' (Rattray, vol. III, p. 33).

180

ECONOMIC ASPECTS

acquired and so on,[1] as might have been expected, and in this general discussion there is no need to distinguish the two types of organization.

Cocoa takes a long time, fifteen years or more, to come into full bearing and the farmers have never had any difficulty in taking an appropriately long view. The Akwapim were not as preoccupied as the Akim or the Ashanti with the glories of their past, and were thus, perhaps, more inclined to build for the future. It is because the farmers were prepared to take their time (and held as rigid a view as many old-fashioned capitalists or communists as to the wastefulness of consumption expenditure) that the pace of expansion during the first few decades was so fast and regular. The Akwapim surveys show, see Appendix VII. 1 (p. 193), that the process seldom petered out, except in a few towns such as Tutu,[2] and that most farmers (or their forebears) had purchased more than two lands. As most farmers seem to have dispensed with working capital (see p. 188 below), there was little danger (certainly insufficient to match the uninformed apprehensions of successive governments of the Gold Coast, especially around 1914 when the migration was in full flood) of the farmers finding themselves unable to maintain their older farms (their past investments) as the pace of expansion increased. These past investments were financially self-sustaining provided (as was nearly always the case except in time of war) the price received by the farmer for his cocoa exceeded costs of transport to the buying agents by a small margin.[3]

A migration which involved everybody

The expansionary process was much encouraged by the fact that, after a short initial hesitation in the eighteen-nineties, it tended to involve all the inhabitants of the main Akwapim towns. Not that it was centrally organized; it was rather a contagious enthusiasm for private enterprise. As it was everyone's aspiration to participate, so there was no question of men being motivated by a desire to free themselves from their rapacious kin[4]— in practical (not legal) terms the new lands were considered as an extension of the homeland, and there was no idea of leaving home for good. Those, like chiefs and other office-holders, who were obliged to remain at home most of the time, participated with the help of their relatives and there was never any risk of the home towns becoming totally depopu-

[1] See Appendix VII. 1 (p. 193).

[2] A town which became financially exhausted by litigation.

[3] Labourers, like farmers, are capable of waiting and of taking a long view. If as a result of a fall in the price of cocoa their remuneration per load was much reduced, they would neither run away nor stop plucking. Their interest in future cocoa-farming prospects, their work in establishing new farms and their own food-farming activities, tended to stabilize them.

[4] This common quasi-myth is better expressed the other way round: that those who migrate and make money are partly motivated by their wish to help their less enterprising or indigent kin, who therefore urge them on.

181

ECONOMIC ASPECTS

lated,[1] though they must have lost a good deal of their vitality, if not their viability, especially in the earliest days when it was not so much the practice as it is today to send the children home to school. In a town like Larteh-Ahenease it would be difficult today to find anyone (other than a stranger) whose forebears failed to participate in the migration half a century or more ago. This universal participation reflects a sort of classlessness: there are rich people and there are poor people, but none who suffer from a social inferiority preventing them from migrating. Although rich and poor alike join companies, they were primarily devices for assisting small men to migrate—farmers who could subscribe at most £5 or £10 towards the purchase of a piece of land. The fact that in the early days the richer inhabitants were often prepared to help their poorer kinsmen and neighbours to buy land through companies, by lending them money, sometimes on the security of pawns, is another aspect of the willingness to wait for a return on money—though it was even truer then than it is today that a condition of indebtedness was apt to reflect a pre-existing personal relationship between the two parties, there being no concept of large-scale philanthropy in the Akwapim towns. Then there were the rich men, like Akogyram[2] of Mamfe, who were guided by commercial (or speculative) considerations—but who yet resold land (sometimes on 'hire-purchase terms') to their fellow-townsmen only. Soon after 1900 it had become shameful, in some of the larger Akwapim towns, not to have bought a land: 'people were laughing because we were so late', said a Mampong farmer, in 1960, who had failed to buy land before about 1902. If a man 'ordered' a piece of land through a company and later found that he lacked the cash to pay for it, the company would be able to dispose of his portion to someone else—and for this and other reasons the company leader could regard his members as a group of shareholders, among whom the risks could be spread.

The land-sellers' willingness to take payment in instalments

If the capitalistic process is to develop satisfactorily, each of the various parties involved must be prepared to wait. The farmers were prepared to wait for a return on the sums they invested in land-purchase and the process of reinvestment in another land was dependent on their willingness to go on waiting. But given the farmers' poverty, this would not have been sufficient to ensure the establishment of a rapid process of expansion, involving everybody in the home towns, had it not been that the land-sellers, also, were prepared to exercise patience, so that land could, in part, be paid for from its own proceeds. Historically regarded, it is rather misleading to express the matter thus. Originally the Akim land-sellers were not so much tolerant of the fact that the eagerness of the Akwapim farmers outdid their financial capacities as they were themselves

[1] See Appendix VIII. 4 (p. 248).   [2] See p. 212.

182

ECONOMIC ASPECTS

eager to collect such windfalls as occurred, whatever the accompanying conditions. There was no competitive market for land and indeed from the land-sellers' point of view there was something to be said for a system which assured them a future income (rather than 100 per cent down-payment)—provided, of course, they could depend on the farmers to pay up. The strength of the land-sellers' position, in the early stages, was dependent on the fact that there were so few of them: the farmers were concerned to remain in friendly commercial relationship with them, against the day that they might be returning to ask for some more land. The introduction of the company system coincided with the creation of a market in land in the areas concerned, and there may have been a time, between about 1906 and 1918, when the interval between purchase and full payment was much reduced. Later on, as the farmers came to own more and more unplanted lands, as everyone tended to migrate by company and as (owing to improved transport facilities) the number of land-sellers greatly increased, the interval between purchase and payment tended to lengthen again—so that the willingness of the land-sellers to wait for payment was again an institutional factor of the greatest significance.

Land as a savings bank

Our money doesn't stay: we buy different lands with it.

Land has two main aspects: it is both a necessary factor of production and a savings bank. That it is a savings bank in a literal sense is suggested by the figures in Appendix II. 1, tables v and vi (pp. 58-9), which show that the greater prosperity of the farmers consequent upon a higher cocoa-price was *instantly reflected in increased purchases of land*. The sensitive growing-point of the economy is here displayed. It could not be supposed, given the amount of unplanted land the farmers already possessed, that they had any intention of planting these newly-acquired lands in the immediately foreseeable future. But the money was not necessarily locked up in the savings bank, for fortunately there existed (see below) a class of financier- or creditor-farmer who specialized in buying second-hand lands, or farms, from farmers who chose, or were obliged, to resell. In a part of the world where for climatic reasons most non-precious material objects developed since the stone axehead are apt to 'spoil',[1] the great merit of land is that, as farmers put it, it 'lies down'—sleeping peacefully, not wasting away.

It is true that land is often lost or mislaid (it is sometimes spoken of as 'going astray'), if it happens that the leader dies and none of his surviving associates is known to the land-vendor—or if the survivors simply do not

[1] The fatalistic connotation of this much-used, poignant word has to do with man's inability to withstand or understand the inevitable process of destruction and decay—especially, nowadays, in relation to complex objects like lorries. The nearest Twi equivalents are *see* and *hwere*, each of which also means 'spend'.

183

ECONOMIC ASPECTS

know where the land is situated. Then there are all the well-known risks of litigation. But that the farmers' reliance on the 'keeping qualities' of land is, on the whole, well founded is shown by the frequency with which it happens that land is first cultivated a quarter of a century or more after its first acquisition. Farmers who hold long strings of never-planted lands are seldom wistful about the waste of money involved, though there may be an element of injured pride which they do not care to reveal. Of course they are apt to go on hoping beyond hope that one day their financial and family circumstances will permit them to plant the forest lands; and then, sometimes, they are able to obtain some return by selling timber or other produce from land which is useless for cocoa.

Paradoxically, land-purchase is a form of 'conspicuous expenditure', as well as a form of investment, for although the land may be situated in a distant place and may never have been seen by the purchaser, nonetheless his fellow-townsmen, the people whose esteem matters most to him, will have been his associates and will be familiar with his land-purchasing activities. And if the notion of the land itself as a savings bank seems strained, then the reader may prefer to regard the company as a form of savings club—a club which invests its resources in land.

The farmers' attitude to land as a safe depository is, of course, bound up with their attitude to money.[1] While farmers are very frank about most of their farming affairs, and have no objection whatever to talking about land-purchase, their reticence over money (as such) is profound, as all social investigators in West Africa are aware. It is not sufficient to note, in this connexion, that in western society it is very improper to ask people about their monetary affairs, for in West African rural society fears on this subject run deeper, making it almost impossible to discuss such practical questions as where farmers in general (not the informant in particular) keep their money, whether in tin trunk, under mattress, in bank, etc. However questions may be phrased, they always seem to have some kind of personal connotation, usually affecting third parties; and so great is the reluctance to contemplate money, as such, that questions about where it is deposited are invariably answered in terms of the use to which it is put.[2] Much of this reticence is, presumably, bound up with fear of theft—and fear drives the farmers to invest in land. If a man has a bank account or owns a safe, he may say so (he may even untruthfully boast about the former); but most other depositories are very unsafe—farmers are much

[1] And with the rigid distinction they make between 'capital' and 'spending money', the former being invested in land. In *Ashanti Law and Constitution* Rattray describes the public accounting system of former times and mentions, p. 117, a large chest in which no sum less than a *pereguan* (about £8) was deposited, lesser sums being accumulated in another box: he actually refers to the large chest as a kind of 'capital account'.

[2] Cocoa-farmers are, of course, obliged to hold cash to finance their day-to-day purchases during the off-season.

184

ECONOMIC ASPECTS

given to padlocking the doors of their rooms, forgetting that their windows may be flimsy, their roofs vulnerable.

There are many reasons, apart from the virtual lack of banks in rural areas until quite recently, why many of the migrant farmers have an aversion to banking money. Basically, perhaps, these can be summed up by saying that they feel that there is an equivalence between banking money and handing it over to 'the government'—so generalized a concept, that the type of government needs no specification. In more practical terms, farmers may be embarrassed by the need to trust mediators, or clerks, with whom they are unfamiliar. Then, there is a belief that those who bank money are automatically obliged to pay income tax.[1] And finally, of course, the rate of interest offered on deposit accounts seems paltry.

Apart from the matter of safe custody, there are other objections to holding cash as such, one of which relates to the farmer's fear of what might happen after his death. There is the risk that some unauthorized member of the family might lay hands on the money, and the difficulty of expressing intentions clearly, when dealing in terms of a medium so slippery and elusive as notes and coin, is obvious enough. A man may say: 'half of this land is intended for the use of my sons and half for the members of my *abusua*'—and his wishes are much more likely to be put into effect than if money for the purchase of the land were found in a tin trunk after his death.

Farmers also buy land for persuasive reasons—as an encouragement to their sons and nephews to go and work there. Lacking the vigour of the younger generation, they are anxious that their money should work harder, multiply itself more rapidly, than if it remained with them. Sometimes a trustworthy son is given money to buy land for himself—'My father gave me money to come and buy.' More often the father himself buys land on behalf of his son. As a Mampong farmer put it in 1960:

It is usual when a farmer buys a piece of land somewhere and starts to till it, he thinks of his children in the future and so with the proceeds he purchases other lands. And usually he divides the unplanted land between his children while he is alive and encourages them to work there.

Finally, there are traditional values, apart from 'rational considerations', which require emphasis. Land is to the agrarian Akan what cattle are to East African pastoralists.

---

[1] The question of the farmers' liability to income tax has never been properly examined—in recent years they have been taxed so heavily through the export duty that they have been implicitly (though not explicitly) regarded as not liable to pay income tax, unless they also derive income from other sources. The problem of determining net cocoa-income, after deduction of labour and other expenses, would present almost insuperable difficulties at present.

ECONOMIC ASPECTS

The managerial function

The analogy with industrial capitalism proceeds farther. Not only is the cocoa-farm a long-term investment and the business inherently expansionary, but the farmer is a manager, one of whose functions is to oversee the work on all his various plantations, to some extent co-ordinating the activities on them. Although farmers with long 'land-sequences' spend much of their time travelling between their lands, there is no real problem of absenteeism, for whether or not labourers are employed (see below) it is usual for a relative or wife to be left in charge at each place. That the managerial work is full-time and specialized is shown by the fact that it cannot usually be satisfactorily combined with another time-absorbing occupation; the many teachers who, around 1900, abandoned their ill-paid profession for cocoa-farming did not later on return to teaching; ministers of the church were pioneer farmers, but they put their profession first and seldom bought long sequences of land; many well-to-do Aburi families include one brother who is a farm-manager and another who is a produce-buyer, and if it turns out that the latter is their uncle's successor the former will continue in effective charge of the farms.

The large Akwapim[1] creditor-farmer

Most creditor-farmers in Ghana are 'average' farmers[2] and it happens that most debtor-farmers are in like position. But some of the most famous of Ghana's migrant farmers have been large Akwapim (or Ga) creditor-farmers (or farmer-financiers), who have assisted a great many other farmers by buying, or otherwise acquiring, rights over their land or farms. Such financiers sometimes spend much of their time at home, conducting their operations from, as it were, the City of London—the Akwapim ridge; more often they play the mixed role of farm-manager and financier. As farmers they are peculiar: it is not only that they acquire many second-hand lands (see Appendix VII. 3, p. 200), but that they have a real aversion to joining companies which are too staid, cumbersome and slow-moving for their purposes. Like financiers the world over, they are volatile and ruthless and can be very helpful on occasions. They acquire

---

[1] Dr M. J. Field has pointed out that neither the Krobo nor, probably, the Ewe, farmer would ever 'juggle financially' with land in the manner here described: 'I don't think they would ever think it decent to move off the plane where farms are used for farming; they would regard it as a sort of desecration of land.' Even in southern Akim Abuakwa, Krobo cocoa-farmers seldom, if ever, resell land to non-Krobo.

[2] See *The Gold Coast Cocoa Farmer*, chapters v to vii, for a general discussion of the pledging of cocoa-farms. In general, creditor-farmers are not a class apart—and, there are nearly as many creditor-farmers as debtor-farmers (farmers who have pledged their farms). Nor are debtor-farmers a special class either, for contrary to general belief it is not so much the most poverty-stricken farmers who pledge their farms, as those whose security is reasonably good—farmers who will continue to live on their unpledged farms and thus not embarrass their creditors.

186

ECONOMIC ASPECTS

their second-hand properties in a variety of ways, by private purchase, at auctions and by pledge—they take advantage of the fact that (unknown to their families) debtors often have no intention of redeeming their pledged farms. They are even more given than other farmers to the *instantaneous* investment of cash-in-hand in farm or land.[1] During their lifetimes they sometimes appear to behave as though they had largely freed themselves from the 'family system', and this individualism, when combined with the fact that they are no more inclined than other farmers to draw up written wills, sometimes brings about financial chaos following their deaths, especially as (the social attitude to them being highly ambivalent) their debtors are apt to seize the opportunity of reclaiming their unredeemed farms, leaving the bereft female relatives in the home town to bewail their fate.[2] But if a large farmer-creditor has been sufficiently willing to delegate responsibility to his relatives on his various lands, then on his death it may turn out that he has been the founder of a great inheritance.

The employment of labourers[3]

Labour employment is *not* the crux of the matter: many capitalist farmers who, over the generations, have been accustomed to invest their surpluses in the expansion of their businesses, have never employed labourers. Many Krobo, Shai and Ga farmers,[4] in particular, continue to this day to pride themselves on their reliance on help given by their wives and kin. (Nor is the distinction between relatives and labourers necessarily hard and fast, as sons and other relatives are sometimes, for instance, employed on an *abusa* basis to pluck cocoa.) But although nearly all Akwapim farmers who own large farms, of (say) twenty acres or more, employ labourers (sometimes a great many of them) and although many quite small farmers do likewise (an element of prestige being involved), it is important to note that systematic large-scale employment of farm labourers marked the second, not the first, stage of the developing capitalistic process. Certainly the pace of expansion would have been much slower had the Akwapim not been determined to employ many labourers during this second stage, which may be regarded as starting around 1900, and had a plentiful supply of non-Akwapim labourers not been forthcoming; certainly, also, cocoa-carriers, as distinct from farm labourers, had been essential from the earliest times—they were relatives as well as non-relatives,[5] women as well as men. But the point under em-

---

[1] Like William Adjabeng Quansah Solomon—see Appendix VIII. 1 (p. 238).

[2] They are often miserably embarrassed by their inability to maintain their large house—their situation has greatly worsened as a result of swollen shoot. See plate 13.

[3] See the chapters on cocoa-labourers in *The Gold Coast Cocoa Farmer*, and also Appendix VII. 5 (p. 213).

[4] Dr J. M. Hunter points out that these are the traditional hoe-farmers—in comparison to whom the cutlass-wielding Akwapim (and Akim) seem like mere amateurs. See plate 8.

[5] Crowther, *op. cit.*, p. 177, noted that many of the cocoa-carriers were Kwahu.

ECONOMIC ASPECTS

phasis is that the launching of the migration depended mainly on the farmers' personal efforts and was not associated with the development of new, or large-scale, systems of farm-labour employment.

It is a general rule, to which there are exceptions, that migrant farmers are reluctant to 'waste their savings' on the employment of labour. This important point of principle is unrelated to the fact that in the early days the ordinary Akwapim farmer spent all that he had on the purchase of land and on unavoidable items such as seed-pods. During the first stage of the migration the farmer depended on family labour and his cash out-lay on day-to-day operations was possibly negligible. Food- and cocoa-farming have always been intimately related activities.[1] Newly planted land might first be planted with food crops and then, a little later, with cocoa. The cover crops, plantain and cocoyam, provided basic carbo-hydrates for the farmer and his dependants and sometimes, also, a sale-able surplus. As for protein, the forests were then much better stocked with game and edible snails than they are today—and, presumably, the streams with fish. The earliest-acquired lands were not far away from the homeland—where food was grown on much the same scale as formerly, the women continuing to be responsible for most of the work. Nor is there any evidence that sales of palm produce were reduced.[2] So while waiting for their first cocoa-plantings to come into bearing, the farmer and his family were presented with no unusual maintenance problems.

The second stage in the developing capitalistic process was reached when the farmer had successfully established a sufficient area of bearing cocoa *to support a labourer from its proceeds*. On his first employment the labourer might be entitled to 'use' all the cocoa he plucked from the young farm on condition that he assisted the farmer in establishing new cocoa-farms—which, later on, he would have a right to harvest. As the yield of this original farm increased, the proportion of the crop to which he was entitled fell to one-third—the traditional *abusa* share. Later on still, per-haps seven to ten years after his first employment, he might (especially if he had not been concerned with the original establishment of the farm in question) be transferred to an *nkotokuano* basis, receiving a certain sum of money for each load of cocoa he plucked, a sum always less than one-third of the value of the cocoa. The labourer who harvested the cocoa was always paid, on a piece-work basis, *from the proceeds of the farm at the time of the sale of the produce*—the farmer thus avoiding the use of work-ing capital. Although a farmer who employed labourers was free, as a consequence, to devote more time to 'management' and could more quickly develop his newly acquired lands farther west, he would not him-

[1] It is not because food-farming is thought to be 'unimportant' that it receives so little attention in this book.
[2] See p. 167.

188

ECONOMIC ASPECTS

self stop working on the land, though certain tasks, such as plucking and weeding, tended to devolve more and more on labourers as time went by.

While an active farmer with many willing relatives and enough land might have been able to pass from the first to the second stages in no more than five to seven years (for Amelonado cocoa yielded rapidly on the rich virgin soils of the old days), many farmers advanced more slowly, perhaps not attaining the second stage until a quarter of a century after they had first started buying land.

As time went by and the labour force became more settled and permanent, especially on the larger lands, a new form of family labour largely superseded the old one, this consisting of the wives and children of the labourers. With the aid of a large family a single labourer might handle up to a hundred loads of cocoa in a season. But as it cost the farmer no more to employ additional 'plucking labourers', and as supplies of labour were always plentiful, there was a tendency for more labour to be employed than was strictly necessary—except perhaps during the weeding season.

So much for these 'plucking labourers'. Annual labourers, who were never traditionally employed on plucking, but rather on work on new farms, are a different case. Unlike the *abusa* or *nkotokuano* men (who are in some ways best thought of as pseudo-farmers), they are employees proper, on the western model, whose remuneration depends on time (not effort), who work regular hours, who never bring their dependants with them, and who generally undertake all the tasks allotted to them by their master. As such labourers have to be fully maintained during their period of employment and provided with working clothes, tools and all their requirements, including money for meat and fish if meals are not prepared for them, they are not only very costly compared with other types of labourer, but are liable to involve the farmer in making cash outlays at times other than the main-crop season. It is the mark of an efficient farmer to aspire to employ such labourers, for only those with an unusual degree of progressiveness in their outlook can overcome the conventional reluctance to employ working capital in this way. But perhaps, though there is no evidence of this, the timing of the engagement of these labourers (who are sometimes employed for six months, rather than a year—but never for more than a year) is sometimes planned so that their wage (which is payable at the end of their period of employment) falls due during the main-crop season, when the farmer has cash on hand.

As for the other two types of farm labourer, the contract labourer (who is paid an agreed sum for clearing, weeding, etc. a certain area) and the daily labourer (who is paid for a day's work), it is seldom necessary for farmers to draw on their savings for their remuneration, though, again, unusually progressive farmers may overstep their reluctance and employ

189

ECONOMIC ASPECTS

gangs of daily labourers when they want to get a job done quickly. The contract labourer is free to take his time over his task and the farmer, likewise, feels free to pay for the job when it suits his convenience.

In the earliest days, up to about 1910, the ranks of labourer included many aspirant farmers—Shai, Anum/Boso, and others who lacked the finance to buy land. They were enthusiastic and their ambition to save enough money to buy a land of their own was early fulfilled. Thereafter the southern labourers were drawn from farther afield—they were mainly Ewe, not northerners. Few of these labourers have evolved into farmers (though there are some interesting exceptions)—a fact which provides yet another reason, if such be needed, for viewing the migratory process historically.

Other permitted (or enjoined) forms of investment

Apart from land, what other forms of investment have the farmers customarily permitted themselves? The present concern is with tangible forms of investment only: the chief intangible forms include expenditure on funerals and celebrations generally, on sickness and death and on other 'family calamity'.[1] The tangible forms of investment include: housebuilding in the home town; educational expenditure; the building of houses for letting in Accra, Koforidua, etc.; cocoa- and other producebuying—no longer of much importance; lorry ownership and operation. The last two of these, produce-buying and transport, were the only common forms of *economic enterprise* which sprang directly from cocoafarming: especially in the early days, trading profits were an important source of capital for cocoa-farming, but never *vice-versa*.[2]

The houses in the home town are self-made memorials, expressions of civic pride,[3] useful residences (for schoolchildren, indigent relatives, retirement, visits, etc.). Normally they are non income-yielding and unsaleable assets. Usually, though not always, they are built 'in instal-

---

[1] Traditional-style celebratory expenditure is regarded with such condescension by outsiders that the fact that it is sufficiently long-term in intention to qualify as 'investment' is overlooked. See *The Gold Coast Cocoa Farmer*, p. 78, for mention of some of the forms of family calamity (including 'inherited indebted uncle') which can only be made good by substantial outlay, analogous (if not equivalent) to investment.

[2] This observation is confirmed by Mr P. Garlick's work in other parts of Ghana. Trading is commonly regarded as a form of 'gambling'—understandably, for trading businesses are not assets like cocoa-farms, and 'goodwill' is not saleable. The Kwahu are among the best-known Ghana traders, but even with them a business seldom outlives its founder, it being each young man's ambition to set up his own concern; there is thus no counterpart to the family land. The term 'trading' in this context refers to men traders in non-foodstuffs, most of which goods are in fact imported. There is no close financial link between migrant cocoa-farming and food wholesaling as those of the food wholesalers who are not women are nearly all northerners or non-Ghanaians.

[3] 'It is the houses which show strangers a town'—a reflection of an old Akwapim resident, reported by Mr D. Brokensha. See plates 11–13.

190

ECONOMIC ASPECTS

ments', as the money for the building materials becomes available, and many of them, especially in Larteh, are never completed, a state of affairs only partially explainable in terms of swollen shoot.[1] They are memorials not only to the farmer who built (i.e. paid for) them, but also to the far-away cocoa-land which provided their economic foundation. But as such they have drawbacks. They lack that especial quality which so commends land to the farmers as a form of investment—the quality of 'lying down' and waiting: these houses require far too much maintenance, especially in times of swollen shoot.

The prestige which an Akwapim man derives from massive, sometimes ostentatious, educational expenditure is analogous to that obtained from building a colossal house. The results have been very impressive. Just as remarkable are the modest efforts of impecunious farmers to provide their sons and daughters with a good start in life. Like expatriates in West Africa, they prefer to send their children (other than the smallest) 'home' to school. A recent count made in Larteh, by Mr D. Brokensha, showed that 1,100 (out of 1,917) schoolchildren came from 'abroad' and were boarding with relatives or at school—and the number would have been much higher had it not been for the poverty resulting from swollen shoot.

Such are the rents commanded by decent residential accommodation in the main commercial centres, especially Accra, that the farmers have naturally been eager to invest their swollen-shoot 'compensation' in houses for letting. This is something 'separate' from cocoa-farming. As of old, the farmers are replanting their devastated farms with their own labour and are not looking for 'outside' funds for this purpose.

The nature of the financial interplay between migrant cocoa-farming, produce-buying and lorry ownership has not, as yet, been investigated. Profits from cocoa-farming were invested in the equipment required for these enterprises, in sheds, tarpaulins, scales, lorries—as well as in the mortgage deeds (or cash) required as security by the expatriate buying firms. But whether the profits from produce-buying and transport were often put back into land is not clear. In the nineteen-thirties nearly all the produce-buyers were effectively employees of the expatriate buying firms[2] (the slump of 1920 and the great depression having dealt mortal

---

[1] The never-to-be-completed house is a distressing and common feature of the West African urban scene—one which has never been examined in economic terms. Among its 'causes' are: over-impetuous investment in building materials as the cash becomes available (this corresponding with over-impetuous land-purchase by some farmers); theft and decay of these materials on the site; the death of the owner and lack of interest or poverty of his successors; unforeseen calamity; the failure to keep pace with dilapidation; migration; the belief that it will never be too late; dishonest contractors; superstitions about death following completion. It may be, also, that good will can be engendered by the very act of 'trying' to build a house.

[2] See The Nowell Report, Cmd 5845, 1938.

191

ECONOMIC ASPECTS

blows to most indigenous businesses); it yet remains to record, before it is too late, the history of cocoa-buying associations such as the Eastern Planters' Association (said to have been founded in 1907 by Akwapim, Krobo and Shai farmers) and the Larteh Planters' Union (founded about 1908), as well as of countless cocoa-buying firms set up by individual farmers such as Elisha Tette of Larteh and John Ayew of Mampong.

That the migration remains a migration after three generations—that the farmers are migrants not emigrants—is best illustrated by the contrast between the houses in the home towns and the farming areas. The scale of house-building in the home town—the number of separate residences, their size, quality and ornateness—is a faithful reflection of the former wealth of the farmer who built them. In the farming areas (though this is not altogether true of a town like Suhum) everyone lives in the same simple style: there is no visible means of distinguishing rich and poor—by residence, or by dress. Certainly most of the houses have galvanized iron roofs, wooden window frames[1] and sturdy (padlocked) doors and many of the compounds are, or were, cemented. They are reasonably weatherproof dwellings—which is the main intention, for no one goes indoors unless it is raining or bed-time. Certainly, also, some of the houses have many rooms: near Asikasu there is a barrack-like Krobo compound of over forty rooms, which is always called 'Police Station'. But the number of rooms merely reflects the number of people who are apt to be resident there, and this bears little relationship to the farmer's wealth. Possessions, also, apart from clothing, tin trunks and cooking pots, are cut down to an absolute minimum. And although, nowadays, the farmer may aspire to own a bed and mosquito net, the atmosphere of the camp continues to prevail.

[1] The present writer had the pleasure of conducting Professor I. I. Potekhin, of the Moscow Academy of Sciences, to the Nankese area in 1957 and of witnessing his delighted surprise over the high standard of housing enjoyed by certain Shai farmers there. He had not expected peasant farmers to have window frames—but then, as he later agreed, they are not peasants.

192

THE AKWAPIM SURVEYS

APPENDIX VII. 1

THE AKWAPIM SURVEYS: STATISTICAL RESULTS

The following tables relate to the cocoa-lands acquired during the course of the migration by present-day Akwapim farmers or their forebears. General notes on the tables follow (p. 196) and the Appendix concludes with brief interpretations of the statistical results. All the 317 farmers, with a few exceptions, were interviewed in Akwapim. The figures for Aburi and Akropong are not comparable with each other or with the rest and are of little value—see pp. 196–7.

I: Total numbers of Cocoa-Lands 'mentioned'

Town	Total number of informants	Total number of lands 'mentioned'	Average number of lands 'mentioned' per informant	% of lands acquired during lorry age[1]
Aburi[2]	111[3]	296	2·7	42
Akropong	39[4]	174	4·5	32
Larteh	64	235	3·7	41
Mamfe	20	83	4·1	46
Mampong	21	68[5]	3·2	28[6]
Obosomase	19	62	3·3	32
Tutu	20	55	2·7	22
Adukrom[7]	20	43	2·1	40
Total (6 towns)	164	546	3·3	37

[1] The lorry age began after 1918. The figures show lands acquired during the lorry age as a percentage of all lands 'mentioned'. For definition of 'lands mentioned' see p. 196.
[2] Including the associated towns, Nsabaa, Nsakye, Berekuso, Konkonuru and Ahwerease.
[3] Excluding 20 informants who were considered not to be cocoa-farmers.
[4] Excluding 3 informants who had personally acquired 10, 21 and 22 lands: had they been included the total number of lands 'mentioned' by 43 informants would have been 232, an average of 5·4. One informant who was not a cocoa-farmer is also excluded.
[5] This figure is possibly too high owing to the inclusion of a number of pre-lorry age acquisitions which should, perhaps, have been regarded as 'local lands' and excluded.
[6] Possibly too low for the reason given in the preceding note.
[7] Including 3 Aseseeso and 2 Apirede informants.

193

APPENDIX VII. 1

II: *Numbers of Cocoa-Lands 'mentioned' per Informant*[1]

Number of Informants

Total number of lands 'mentioned' by informant	Aburi		Akropong		Larteh		Mamfe		Mampong, Tutu, Obosomase	
	No.	%	No.	%	No.	%	No.	%	No.	%
1	30	27	3	7	2	3	1	5	6	10
2	39	35	9	21	15	23	1	5	14	23
3	23	21	3	7	18	28	6	30	18	30
4	9	8	5	12	15	23	5	25	15	25
5	3		9	22	4	6	2	10	5	8
6	3		4	10	5	8	3	15	2	3
7	2		2	5	—		2	10	—	—
8	1		1		1		—	—	—	—
9	—	9	1		2	8	—	—	—	—
10	—		1		2		—	—	—	—
12	—		1	17	—	—	—	—	—	—
14	1		1		—	—	—	—	—	—
22	—		1		—	—	—	—	—	—
24	—		1		—	—	—	—	—	—
Total	111	100	42	100	64	100	20	100	60	100

[1] See notes on table I.

III: *Numbers of Cocoa-Lands acquired by Informant himself*[1]

Number of Informants

Number of lands acquired by informant himself	Aburi		Akropong		Larteh		Mampong, Tutu, Obosomase	
	No.	%	No.	%	No.	%	No.	%
0	26	23	17	40	26	41	19	32
1	29	26	7	17	8	12	11	18
2	30	27	3	7	17	27	13	22
3	17	15	5	12	5	8	10	17
4	5	5	3	7	3	5	4	7
5	2	2	2	5	3	5	3	5
6	1	1	1	2	1	2	—	—
7	1	1	—	—	1	2	—	—
10	—	—	2	5	—	—	—	—
21	—	—	1	2	—	—	—	—
22	—	—	1	2	—	—	—	—
	111	100	42	100	64	100	60	100

[1] See notes on table I. The table relates to all cocoa-lands which informants said they had acquired themselves, whether through companies, family groups, or otherwise.

THE AKWAPIM SURVEYS

IV: Numbers of Cocoa-Lands acquired by Informant's Father and Grandfather

Number of lands acquired by informant's father etc.	Number of Informants			
	Lartch		Mampong, Tutu, Obosomase	
	No.	%	No.	%
0	10	16	18	30
1	14	22	17	28
2	16	25	12	20
3	13	20	9	15
4	6	9	2	3
5	3	5	1	2
6	2	3	1	2
	64	100	60	100

V: Informants who acquired No Lands during Pre-lorry Age, etc.[1]

Town	Number of Informants		
	'Mentioning' no pre-lorry-age land	'Mentioning' no lorry-age land	Total number interviewed
Akropong	—	14	42
Aburi	7[2]	31[2]	111[2]
Larteh	1[3]	20	64
Mamfe	—	1	20
Mampong	—	5	21
Obosomase	—	2	19
Tutu	—	14	20
Adukrom	4	6	20
	12	93	317

[1] See notes on table I. The table shows the numbers of informants who (themselves, or their forebears) acquired no cocoa-land during (a) the pre-lorry age; (b) the lorry age.
[2] Excluding 20 non-cocoa farmers.
[3] This informant had no pre-lorry age farm as he had started as a labourer at Asuboi.

VI: Date of Acquisition of Land by Aburi Farmers

Approximate date of acquisition	Number of lands 'mentioned'[1]
Before 1906	69
1906–19	166
1920–29	47
1930–39	67
1940–49	23
1950–59	17
Not known	15
Total	404

[1] Including lands mentioned by informants as bought by their fathers.

APPENDIX VII. 1

VII: Date of Acquisition of Land by Larteh Farmers

Approximate date of acquisition	Number of lands 'mentioned'
Before 1900	63
1900–06	21
1907–18	54
1919–22	17
1923–45	68
1946–59	12
Total	235

General Notes on Tables I to VII

The statistics presented in the above tables were a mere by-product of inquiries in the Akwapim home towns which were designed to throw light on the nature of the migratory process, and it is to be hoped that no one will be so critical of them as is the author herself. The rudimentary 'survey technique' was chiefly justified as a means of starting general conversation on many aspects of the migration, but it happened to yield some statistics relating to cocoa-lands acquired by informants and their forebears which are worth recording. Informants take a positive pleasure in listing these acquisitions—provided that a certain degree of familiarity with rural place-names is displayed by the investigator. There would, therefore, have been a case for seeking information on the location of cocoa-lands, even had the resulting material lacked intrinsic interest.

The basic statistical unit in all the tables is the 'land', this being defined as a portion, or area, acquired by an *individual* for the purposes of growing cocoa.[1] With the inquiries among patrilineal peoples the use of this unit did not present much difficulty—although, of course, it must constantly be borne in mind that 'lands' vary exceedingly in area, from hundreds of acres acquired through a company (or individually) to quite small portions perhaps bought 'second-hand'. With the matrilineal Akropong and Aburi, on the other hand, the statistical difficulties were so manifold, that the figures must be used with the utmost caution.

Most of the tables relate to lands '*mentioned*' by informants. In the patrilineal towns the procedure involved asking informants to list their fathers' and grandfathers' (as well as their own) acquisitions without regard to whether they themselves happened to have a present-day interest or stake in them.[2] Such an 'impersonal' approach was necessitated by the fluidity of the situation—by the facts that many lands have never been planted (or divided), or are lying unused as a result of swollen shoot. So lands mentioned by these informants are those in which they (or their successors or descendants) have a potential, if not a present, interest.

But with the matrilineal Aburi and Akropong farmers, on the other hand, it was

---

[1] Local lands are excluded. A 'land' may or may not have been planted, either at the time of its acquisition or later. The usages of this word correspond reasonably satisfactorily with certain of those of the nearest Twi equivalent, *asase*—which is employed in sentences such as *asase no yɛ kɛse*, meaning 'the land is big'. (The Twi word for forest is *kwae*, for farm or plantation, *afuw*.)

[2] The informant might or might not be the present 'owner' of a portion of a land bought by a forebear. Readers of chapter iv will appreciate that this statistical procedure was very unsophisticated.

196

THE AKWAPIM SURVEYS

impossible to devise any satisfactory procedure for estimating the number of lands in which the informant had a potential interest, if only because the number of lands which had been acquired by his (probably very numerous) matrilineal kinsmen (both alive and dead) might literally run into hundreds. The only practicable procedure seemed to be that of asking informants to list those *'abusua* lands' in which they had a personal stake, either as inheritor, or because they had been granted temporary usufructuary rights—although it was realized that much arbitrariness would result from the existence of the uncleared, undivided, devastated etc. lands referred to in the preceding paragraph. Lands mentioned by the Aburi farmers as acquired by their fathers could not be included in the totals (except in table VI), as no proper attempt was made to ascertain the extent to which sons derived any benefit from these lands. But as Akropong farmers more often inherit portions from their fathers than do Aburi farmers, the 14 lands which were stated to have been inherited by Akropong farmers from their fathers were included.

There would seem to be no doubt that in general the tables understate the numbers of lands acquired by the informant and his immediate forebears, mainly because of ignorance and forgetfulness. Some informants even admitted that they could not remember the full list of their own acquisitions, let alone their father's or grandfather's. Then there were doubtless some who forgot to list lands which their sons had acquired for themselves, either with money which their fathers had given them or from the proceeds of their own farming. (Informants in the patrilineal towns were not as systematically questioned as they should have been, on the present-day occupations of their sons.)

Informants were not randomly selected, although this would have been practicable on a house basis, houses being numbered for rating purposes. But as the primary purpose was not statistical and as, in the absence of the owner on cocoa-farming business, many houses are either unoccupied or are the temporary residences of kinsfolk whose ignorance of the history of land acquisition may be profound, such a procedure would have impaired the quality of the information collected and would have meant, also, that willing informants, who happened not to be included in the sample, would have been ignored.[1] The informants were, to some degree, *chosen* and most of them were old or elderly, partly by preference (they are better informed for the purpose in hand than younger people) and partly because so many of the younger men were away in the farming areas and elsewhere. Much depended on who happened to be at home and on chance encounters in the street. Although a special endeavour was made to interview certain of the best-known farmers in each of the towns, their names being listed, it does not follow that those who were interviewed were, on the whole, more successful farmers, owning longer sequences of land, than the average farmer—for many of the keenest and most dedicated farmers prefer to spend their old age away on their plantations and could not be found in the home town.[2]

Because the farmers regard the migration as a process, the acquisition of one land leading to another, they have a sound chronological sense of land-purchase, especially in regard to pre-lorry-age acquisitions—which were, in any case, usually situated farther and farther away from the home town as time went by. The patrilineal farmers were able to list their own and their fathers' acquisitions in order, almost unhesitat-

[1] Writing about methods of recording oral history, Mr J. Vansina notes that 'a sample should never be a random sample, for in history, two witnesses never have the same value and cannot therefore be considered as similar units between which one could choose at random...', *Journal of African History*, vol. I, no. 1 (1960), p. 47.

[2] But the Akropong figures were biased by the inclusion of a number of large creditor-farmers—people who are more apt to be based on the homeland than farmers in general.

APPENDIX VII. 1

ingly. Dates of acquisition were established by reference to key events, lists of which were compiled for the various towns. As the survey progressed it became less and less necessary to date pre-lorry-age acquisitions, for it had become apparent that in most localities most of the land had been acquired within a short period.

The surveys of Akwapim were carried out at various dates between October 1958 and June 1960 and supplemented the information obtained over a longer period up-country—most of which was not susceptible to this kind of statistical treatment.

Interpretation of Statistical Results

Table I. The figures for the 6 patrilineal towns are reasonably comparable, but as the number of informants in each of the towns, save Larteh, was small, detailed conclusions cannot be drawn from the figures. The average number of cocoa-lands bought by Larteh and Mamfe informants and their fathers and grandfathers was about 4; the corresponding figure for Mampong and Obosomase was about 3; and the averages for Tutu and Adukrom were somewhat lower. The percentage of all cocoa-lands which had been acquired during the past forty years (i.e. during the lorry age) varied between 46 for Mamfe and 22 for Tutu. Unless there are many Tutu cocoa-farmers who have severed their connexion with their home town, it would appear from this (and other evidence) that the pace of land acquisition by Tutu farmers has definitely slowed down.

As for Aburi and Akropong, the figures for the average number of lands mentioned by informants have little significance—as already noted. The Aburi figures exclude any lands that may have been inherited from fathers. Twelve Akropong informants claimed that they had inherited a total of 14 lands from their fathers; if these lands are omitted the Akropong average is reduced from $4 \cdot 5$ to $4 \cdot 1$.

Table II. It is here shown that table I conceals much variation, as between the towns, in the total number of cocoa-lands mentioned per informant. Despite the lack of comparability in the figures, it may be permissible to conclude that many more Aburi than other Akwapim are *dependent* on only one land—27 per cent of the Aburi farmers mentioned only one land, against 10 per cent or less in each of the other towns. Moreover the percentage of farmers dependent on only 2 lands is higher for Aburi than for any other town. The fact that nearly all Aburi farmers are dependent (or regard themselves as dependent) on 1, 2 or 3 lands is perhaps to be explained by the large area of many of the older Aburi family lands. In the case of Akropong, more than a half of all the farmers were interested in 5 or more lands—such a high proportion partly reflecting the inclusion of so many large creditor-farmers in the 'sample'. In Larteh it is safe to say that most farmers had an interest in 2, 3 or 4 lands, though 22 per cent had an interest in 5 lands or more; the numbers of farmers with interests in fewer than 2 lands is negligible. In Mamfe (where numbers interviewed were much smaller) it is possible that most farmers have an interest in 3, 4, 5 or 6 lands. The Mampong etc. figures are similar to the Larteh figures, except for the lack of farmers owning very long land sequences.

Table III. The table shows that in each of the towns there was a considerable proportion of informants who had acquired no land for themselves—and were thus dependent on lands acquired by their forebears. (As the average age of informants was distinctly high, few of those who had bought no lands for themselves up to date would be likely to do so in future.) The table also shows that if farmers acquire new lands for themselves they usually acquire several; thus, of the 25 Akropong farmers who had bought lands for themselves, only 7 had bought 1 land and only 3 had bought 2 lands.

198

THE AKWAPIM SURVEYS

Of the 38 Larteh farmers who had bought land for themselves, about a half had bought 2 lands and 13 had bought 3 or more lands.

Table IV. Only 10 out of 64 Larteh informants stated that no lands had been acquired by their fathers or grandfathers—and nearly all of them were very old men whose fathers had died before the migration began.

Table V. That virtually all Akwapim lineages have a long history of participation in the migration is indicated by the fact that, excluding the 20 non-cocoa-farmers interviewed in Aburi, only 12 out of 317 informants said that they or their forebears had acquired no land during the pre-lorry age. The proportion of informants who made no mention of lorry-age lands varied very much from town to town, but it is interesting to note that about a third of all informants in Larteh, Aburi and Akropong mentioned no lorry-age acquisitions and were thus entirely dependent on pre-lorry-age lands.

Tables VI and VII. These tables give an indication of the pace of land acquisition during different periods by Aburi and Larteh farmers. In the case of Larteh the most useful key-dates were found to be the influenza epidemic of 1918 (which corresponded with the dawn of the lorry age) and dates of installation of chiefs. With Aburi lands the dates were mainly judged on the basis of information that had been collected earlier, relating to dates of sale in the localities in question. These Aburi figures include lands bought by informants' fathers.

APPENDIX VII. 2
COMPANIES AND THE 'PATRILINEAL SYSTEM'[1]

When inquiries began, in 1957, there was no reason to suspect an association between companies and patrilineal inheritance, if only because the other great means of group migration, the family land system, was not even known to exist. It was noted by chance, in June 1958, that few companies of cocoa-farmers had bought land in the unmapped area between Nsawam and Coaltar and it was only gradually realized that this might be associated with the presence of so many Aburi farmers. An interview with the Adontenhene of Akwapim (the chief of Aburi) at once established the fact that, traditionally, his people had not cared for the idea of migrating by company and many subsequent conversations with elderly Aburi farmers soon confirmed that during the pre-lorry age they had not organized themselves in companies.

The statistical evidence is simple. Ninety-eight people were interviewed in Aburi and associated towns, other than Berekuso: of all the cocoa-lands they 'mentioned' (see Appendix VII. 1, p. 193), only about 26 had been acquired through companies, as many as 23 of them during the lorry age. The Berekuso people have a curious inheritance system, see Appendix VII. 4 (p. 211) and are often closely associated with Ga farmers; the 34 farmers interviewed there 'mentioned' 36 lands which had been acquired through companies, of which as many as 13 had been acquired during the pre-lorry age.

If, therefore, an association could be postulated between the company and patrilineal systems (and, of course, the innovators of the system, the Krobo, are patrilineal), did this mean that none of the matrilineal Akwapim had migrated by company—what, in particular, had been the position of the matrilineal Akropong? First inquiries in Akropong were not at all conclusive, for the farmers there are inclined to apply the word 'company' to family groups. However, it was finally established that:

[1] See chapters II, III, etc.

199

APPENDIX VII. 2

(a) In the pre-lorry age, very few Akropong farmers had formed or joined companies;

(b) In the lorry age, many Akropong farmers acquired their land through companies;

(c) Large family lands which (like Kofi Pare) support a great many *abusua* members are rarer with Akropong, than with Aburi, farmers—but do exist.

(d) A surprisingly large number of Akropong farmers have always bought land individually, both direct from the land-selling chief and 'second-hand' from other Akwapim.

It is to be presumed that with both Aburi and Akropong farmers there has been a tendency for family lands to develop within the strips acquired through companies during the lorry age (provided they are large enough), but until some satisfactory farm maps come into existence this must remain a presumption, particularly as it may be that ordinary members of the *abusua* prefer to exercise their usufructural rights on the older family lands nearer home, so that the newer family lands support far fewer farmers.

It has not yet been possible to investigate the traditional migratory system of the matrilineal Amanokrom farmers. The Amanokrom group which bought land at Adidiso (see Appendix II. 3, p. 62) closely resembled a company proper,[1] except that portions of strips were given away to sundry relatives, in a manner quite unknown to the patrilineal farmers; on the other hand, the Amanokrom land at Dome (see Appendix III. 11, p. 107) resembled a family land.

The only Anum/Boso lands for which farm maps have been obtained up to date are very small and it is not known whether these matrilineal peoples have ever created family lands on the Aburi or Akropong scale.

Finally, it should be noted that with the patrilineal migrants the farm maps have never revealed the existence of a form of social organization remotely resembling a family land, however large the area acquired.

APPENDIX VII. 3

AKWAPIM CASE HISTORIES

The following 'case histories', which are very abbreviated, represent an attempt at illustrating the operation of the migratory process in terms of land acquisition—the majority of cases relating to patrilineal towns, where the process is easier to follow. They have been arbitrarily selected from a mass of material collected in various of the Akwapim home towns—see Appendix VII. 1 (p. 193). The numbers of cocoa-lands inherited by the informant and acquired by him personally are shown in most cases—the figures being subject to the numerous reservations mentioned in Appendix VII. 1 (p. 196). As far as possible the lands are listed in chronological order of acquisition, naming the locality. Such few acreage figures as are given are based on maps or plans —not on oral information. See Maps 16 and 17.

Abbreviations

Inher. mat.:   inherited from matrilineal forebear. (The informant was not necessarily the inheritor proper, but may have been granted usufructuary rights, been given the land, etc.)

Inher. pat.:   inherited from father or paternal grandfather, gifts being included.

Self: informant acquired cocoa-land for himself.

[1] This land was investigated as early as 1957, and the fact that it so closely resembled a company put the general inquiries rather off scent.

AKWAPIM CASE HISTORIES

NYP: 'not yet planted' (with cocoa). This is noted, in some cases in which it applies, as a reminder that there is often a long delay between the date of acquisition of a land and its planting. (If NYP is not stated it does not follow that the land had ever been planted.)

Second-hand land or farm: A land or farm acquired from another migrant farmer and not direct from an Akim chief.

Akropong, No. 1

Inher. mat. 1, self 3=4

A former civil servant, he is farmer (M) of the Boah family group, see Appendix III. 8 (p. 100). (i) Inher. farms in Boah family land; (ii) he was a member of a group of 17 Akropong farmers who bought a land near Assin-Fosu in 1928 for about £3,000, his share costing £120—the land was 'no good' for cocoa, but they recouped their expenses in full by selling timber; (iii) he bought a small second-hand land in 1946 in the Surum (Asamankese) area, NYP; (iv) he bought a large land, described as '2 ropes by 20', in 1953, west of Kankan, near the Worobon river, the seller being a company member who had held it unplanted for about 20 years; he proposes to clear half for his children and hopes that members of his *abusua* will use the other half so that 'the two sides of the family will get to know one another'.

Akropong, No. 2

Inher. mat. 2, self 10=12 (probably forgot some)

A creditor-farmer aged 83. Original source of wealth was (i) a large land bought by a matrilineal forebear near Yaw Koko, well before 1900, much of which was resold to Ga farmers; (ii) inher. land at Adawso; (iii) 42 acres at Trayo, Appendix II. 5 (p. 65), bought at an auction, 2 sons there as farmers; (iv) 11 acres at near-by Obomofo-Densua bought from a Shai farmer, Appendix II. 7 (p. 69); (v)–(vii) 3 lands near Kraboa-Coaltar bought second-hand from Akropong and Mampong farmers; (viii) Kokoso, west of Suhum, bought second-hand from Akropong farmer; (ix) Ayiribe, north-west of Oda, bought large land alone direct from chief for £600, resold much to others, no good for cocoa; (x)–(xii) Oworam area (near Asamankese), all bought as farms from Akim farmers, one cost £700. He said that he had wives living on most of his lands, but that he had divorced one of them because she had refused to go and live at Oworam. In the old days, before swollen shoot, many more farms had been pledged to him; when the swollen shoot came he had, unsuccessfully, resorted to litigation to reclaim the money owing to him.

Akropong, No. 3

Probably more than 24 lands altogether

At first he insisted on speaking as though he were the owner of one cocoa-land only, this being in the Kabu Hill area, but he then suddenly listed 23 other lands, most of which had been bought second-hand and many of which had never been planted; he then again lost interest. He claimed, quite possibly correctly, that at present he had cocoa on one land only. A very willing, though self-contradictory informant, elderly and much respected by others. His original source of wealth had been trading in blankets from the north. Clearly a creditor-farmer, though this he would not admit.

Akropong, No. 4

Inher. mat. 2, self 5=7 (plus many other second-hand lands which he neglected to list)

Probably a creditor-farmer, though he would not admit this. (i) Inher. Adawso; (ii) inher. Kokoso (Suhum); (iii) land near Akroso, in a company of Akropong, about

201

APPENDIX VII. 3

1919; (iv) a second-hand land near Surum (Asamankese); (v) another land near Kokoso; (vi) in company of Akropong, land at Akankawsu (near Fosu); (vii) in 1936 he proposed going to Papase (Volta Region) in a company, but the others withdrew and he went alone; he has put his land in the care of Ewe labourers who are rewarded with a third of the planted area. He regarded (ii) as the origin of his wealth, saying 'I stand on that'.

Akropong, No. 5
Inher. mat. 2, inher. pat. 2, self 10 = 14

This old man had early started buying land for himself on his return from Obuase where he had worked on the construction of the railway. He inherited lands at Adawso and was given land by his father. He claimed that he had spent much money on buying second-hand lands near Teacher Mante and Amanase (south of Suhum) and that he had bought 6 lands through companies in the lorry age, several of which NYP. If not a creditor, something of a financier; bought land for house-building in several places, including Kraboa-Coaltar and Abiriw.

Akropong, No. 6
Inher. mat. 2, inher. pat. 1, self 1 = 4

He had inherited land from his mother who had joined with her brother to buy (i) near Suhum; (ii) Aduasa (near Oda). He was given land by his father at (iii) Akuase (Nkawkaw). He had been the leader of a company which (iv) had acquired *abusa* land at Kyia, near Nkwaten; he said he had 'formulated' the scheme in Suhum and had been associated with Shai and Amanokrom farmers, each of whom had had 'supporters'.

Akropong, No. 7
Self 22 (and others 'lost through litigation', or forgotten)

'I concentrated my mind on buying lands and the little money that remained I lent to people.' This old man had served as a labourer during the Ashanti wars and had then gone to Sekondi to work on the railway. Most of the lands which he started to acquire on returning from Sekondi were within reach of Suhum, where he had built a house, and most, though not all, of them had been bought second-hand—many from well-known men such as Teacher Mante and Omenako. He prided himself on his famous litigious tendencies. He said that cocoa remained on one land only.

Akropong, No. 8
Inher. mat. 4, inher. pat. 1, self 6 = 11

He is the inheritor (K) of the Boah family group, see Appendix III. 8 (p. 100). (i) Inher. Adawso; (ii) inher. 'Boah'; (iii) inher. Aduasa (near Oda); (iv) inher. near Bosuso, 1909; (v) his father had bought a very big land near Adeiso in 1903; (vi)–(viii) 3 self-acquired lands in the Odumkyere/Sukunu area; (ix) Oda area, in company with Aburi farmers; (x) also Oda area; (xi) Kadjebi, Volta Region, 1957, second-hand land.

Akropong, No. 9
Inher. mat. 2, self 0 = 2

Being the son of a woman who had bought a well-known land near Adeiso in the very early days, he said that the very size of this estate had made it unnecessary for him to buy any land for himself.

AKWAPIM CASE HISTORIES

Akropong, No. 10

Inher. mat. 2, self 5 = 7

This old man's maternal uncle had bought lands at (i) Tinkong; (ii) near Suhum. He himself had been a carpenter who had worked on the Sekondi railway line; on his return he had bought (iii) another land near Suhum, following this up with (iv) land in the Kabu Hill area; (v) near Tafo; (vi) Kokompre, near Nkawkaw (second-hand); (vii) Twifu Praso, about 1925, NYP—'the leader had been unable to gather the company members together to go there'. He did not say that (iv) was a large place, but a chance visit there later revealed that he was indeed a famous farmer, who owned many farms and had employed many labourers. On another occasion he said that the source of his finance had been trading—'money is the main object for me'.

Akropong, No. 11

Inher. mat. 0, self 2 = 2

An extremely old, retired, reverend minister, with a wonderful memory of the eighteen-nineties. 'In about 1901 I became interested in buying a land'—but it was not until 1905 that he 'found' a piece of land near Suhien. In association with another minister he had bought another land near Ekaso in 1928.

Akropong, No. 12

Inher. mat. 2, inher. pat. 1, self 3 = 6

(i) Inher. mat. near Asuoya; (ii) inher. mat. Aborodem; (iii) inher. pat. near Tinkong; (iv) Bosuso, 1907, 'brothers and sisters went with their father and each subscribed'; (v) Nankese, also 1907; (vi) Akuase, near Nkawkaw, bought land through a big company of Akropong, Larteh and Mampong people, NYP—'we don't know whether the land has been stolen away'.

Akropong, No. 13

Inher. mat. 1, self 1 = 2

A retired reverend minister. A maternal uncle had bought land at Abrodiem in 1899. Describing himself as a 'traveller', he said that he had tried to interest Ashanti people in cocoa in 1903–8 when he had been there as a teacher. In 1910 he had bought land near Suhien.

Akropong, No. 14

Inher. mat. 3, inher. pat. 1, self 1 = 5

His father, who had been associated with his brothers, had bought land near Nankese and had given half to his children and half to members of his *abusua*. He himself had bought land in the middle of the Afram Plains, near Odonkawkrom, in 1937, in a big mixed company of Akropong, Adukrom etc. farmers; the land had been shared very recently.

Akropong, No. 15

Inher. mat. 6, self 0 = 6

This woman farmer had, in the absence of a suitable male successor, inherited 6 lands from her brother, who had in turn inherited from his maternal uncle, a former teacher. She lives with her sister on a 65-acre farm near Asafo. She had labourers on each of her lands which are: (i) Tinkong; (ii) Akorabo; (iii) Asuboi; (iv) Asafo; (v) Pankese; (vi) Afram Plains. The sisters' husbands are farming on lands which they inherited near Kukurantumi and Adonkwanta.

APPENDIX VII. 3

Larteh, No. 1

Inher. pat. 5, self 1 = 6

Grandfather bought 4 lands before 1900. (v) His father bought near Dedewa; (vi) he himself bought land near Okyereso (Akim Abuakwa) in 1947 in a company.

Larteh, No. 2

Inher. pat. 4, self 6 = 10

Father was a trader, who travelled to Krakye, Buem etc., selling salt etc. (i) Before 1900 he and his brothers had bought a land at Kukua (where he still usually lives); (ii) Adonkwanta; (iii) about 1919 he bought land at Akwatia, through large company, no good for cocoa; (iv) near Kusi, on central railway line, mixed Shai/Ewe/Larteh company; (v) Asuokyene; (vi) near Anum Apapam (second-hand); (vii) near Twifu-Praso, Larteh company; (viii) near Akroso, 1927, company of Ningo people; (ix) Ashanti-Akim, large company of Larteh and Shai, 1937, much litigation, judgment in his favour; (x) Wasa-Akropong, company of Larteh/Shai/Fanti, 1948, NYP. Apart from (i), (ii), (vii) and (viii) the lands are 'unoccupied'.

Larteh, No. 3

Inher. pat. 5, self 4 = 9

Before about 1907 his father had bought 5 lands, 2 of them trans-Densu; he was a prominent creditor-farmer; (vi) Akoase (south of Nkawkaw), bought through company 1915, started planting 1951; (vii) near Kusi (as Larteh No. 2), NYP; (viii) Ashanti-Akim, litigation, NYP; (ix) Akim-Manso, 'litigation is continuing', NYP.

Larteh, No. 4

Inher. pat. 5, self 1 = 6

A woman farmer whose grandfather was (i) one of the founders of the land called Okorase south of Koforidua; (ii) and (iii) grandfather bought 2 lands near Nankese; (iv) father, near Suhum; (v) father bought a land in her name at Pankese in 1925, when she was about fifteen years old—she cleared this herself many years later; (vi) she herself bought Suhum land at an auction in 1958.

Larteh, No. 5

Inher. pat. 3, self 0 = 3

His grandfather, who was a carpenter, (i) bought land near Asuoya. His father, Elisha Kwadjo, was one of the subscribers to the bridge at Mmetiamu; he bought (ii) a large land at Koransan and later became a cocoa-shipper on his own account; (iii) between Coaltar and Asuboi, a land so large that clearing was never completed.

Larteh, No. 6

Inher. pat. 0, self 4 = 4

This famous farmer-creditor was long deceased and information given by daughter. He had settled in Ayikuma before 1892 where he traded in palm produce. With his profits he bought land (i) at Okorase (and in 1905–6 built his first 'storey-house' in Larteh); (ii) Mmetiamu; (iii) near Nankese; (iv) Asuboi. 'He assisted many other farmers to buy land.' His poverty-stricken daughter said that £1,500 had been owing on his death, but that it had been impossible to collect it.

Larteh, No. 7

Inher. pat. 1, self 0 = 1

Speaking on behalf of the descendants of her grandfather who had been one of

AKWAPIM CASE HISTORIES

those who had acquired land at Mmetiamu and had subscribed towards the building of the bridge, this woman said that he had been a trader in palm produce at Ayikuma and that he had bought the Mmetiamu land only. 'He assisted many other farmers to buy land.' He bought no other land partly because of his aspirations, which were frustrated, to become a mine-owner. He was also (though not for long) a cocoa-shipper.

Larteh, No. 8

Inher. pat. 0, self 4=4

'When I was young I went to school and my mother bought one pig and the pig brought forth six. I sold these six. I used the money to buy 'petty petty' things and I was a hawker. Ayikuma was a good place for selling goods—it was an oil-palm trade centre. Small children acted as carriers. I went to Accra, Prampram and Akuse to buy my goods. With my savings I bought a land at Aboatumpan'—near Koforidua; (ii) second-hand at Okorase; (iii) Asuboi, company; (iv) near Anum Apapam.

Larteh, No. 9

Inher. pat. 3, mat. grandfather 1, self 0=4

He described his maternal grandfather, one of Larteh's most famous and wealthy farmers, as a 'land maniac'. He had bought land for food-growing before 1890. 'One of the first was at Mampong; another was nearer to Tutu; one was at Asuoya near the railway line; one was at Aboabo (near Asuoya); one, a very large land, was at Kyekye-were (north of Nsawam); he had many other lands.' He had given his daughter one land and this had duly passed, though not without litigation, to her son. The informant's father was the famous Teacher Mante, of the Basel Mission, who followed his father-in-law in buying a large land north of Nsawam. He himself had bought no land, being a surveyor.

Larteh, No. 10

Inher. pat. 3, self 2=5

'The Larteh people travelled much before cocoa-time. To Accra, Sekondi, Cape Coast, to the north as carriers, hammock-carriers, load-carriers. They kept half their pay and "ate" half (*abunu*); then they pledged their children and added the money to the *abunu* share; before cocoa they traded in rubber in Akim Abuakwa and Ashanti and there was coffee locally; maize was sold to our neighbours who had none.' His grandfather had bought lands at Kyekyewere, Asuoya and Aboabo. He had bought (iv) Okorase (near Adeiso); (v) Okyereso (Akim Abuakwa).

Larteh, No. 11

Inher. pat. 3, self 0=3

Grandfather was a blacksmith and together with his brother bought (i) near Tin-kong; (ii) a large land at Koransan and divided it between his 4 sons, in 1903 or earlier. He also bought (iii) a land 'behind Kofi Pare', but it was so far away that by the time he was able to get there it had been stolen. His father had been a teacher and was later in business as a produce-buyer for more than ten years. He himself is a blacksmith and fitter and has had no occasion to buy more land.

Larteh, No. 12

Inher. pat. 1, self 3=4

His father bought (i) near Asuoya; (ii) he himself joined with his elder brother, his

205

APPENDIX VII. 3

paternal uncle and with 3 of his father's sister's sons to buy a land near Anum Apapam which, according to a surveyor's plan, had an area of about $2\frac{1}{2}$ square miles, the cost having been about £350; (iii) second-hand land, Bankame, Ashanti-Akim; (iv) Asunafo, near Kankan.

Larteh, No. 13

Inher. pat. 4, self 0 = 4

The daughter of Johannes Awua Sono who—see Appendix VIII. 3 (p. 244)—subscribed at least £50 to the building of the bridge at Mmetiamu. She described her father as the first trader to buy oil and kernels for the merchants in Ayikuma—this being before 1892. On the proceeds of this trading he (i) bought land at Okorase (south of Koforidua); (ii) Mmetiamu; (iii) Adidiso (near Nankese); (iv) Asuboi. She worked for her father and he gave her a land at Okorase. She and her sister are now in charge of all the lands, there being no male successors. He was a creditor.

Larteh, No. 14

Inher. pat. 4, self 0 = 4 (and others, forgotten)

His father bought land (i) at Mmetiamu; (ii) Ntunkum (north of Suhum); (iii) Twifu Praso, Larteh company. The son, who is a storekeeper, said that his father had 'tried' to buy many other lands and had lost much money.

Larteh, No. 15

Inher. 2, self 1 = 3

His father (i) bought land at Panto from Akropong people to grow yams there; (ii) Potroase, company of Larteh; (iii) Kwahu ('beyond Nkawkaw'), 1925—'Nobody bothered to go there; this was really the fault of the leader who is now dead and our names are not known to the seller, who says we have lost our land.'

Larteh, No. 16

Inher. 1, self 2 = 3

The informant, the late Nana Okanta Obrentri II (Benkumhene of Akwapim), said that his father had (i) bought land near Mmetiamu on the east bank. He himself, while a clerk with a commercial firm had (ii) bought land near Kankan in a Larteh company. In 1935 (or before) he (iii) joined a large Mamfe company (see Mamfe, No. 8) to buy land on the Afram Plains from the chief of Bukuruwa, the total cost of which was £1,118. (The chief of Bukuruwa came to live in Mampong to collect the instalments due.) During his lifetime the late Benkumhene was more interested in cultivating (iii) than (ii)—for (ii), being more accessible, would be more suitable for him to cultivate when he was an old man.

Larteh, No. 17

Inher. 2, self 0 = 2

The chief of Okorase (south of Koforidua) spoke of his grandfather, Paul Yaw Kumi, who had been a sawyer at Senchi before buying land at Okorase—from Akropong people. He resold much land to other Larteh people. His father (ii) bought land at Adidiso and had subscribed, see Appendix VIII. 3 (p. 244), to the building of the bridge at Mmetiamu. The Larteh people regarded Okorase as a home from home and built 'storey-houses' there.

206

A migrant cocoa-farmer ready to board a lorry. He is wearing a scarf to protect his head from dust.

The bridge at Mmetiamu.

3. Mr Eugene Ohene Walker on his food-farm at Larteh-Ahenease. The Accra plain can be seen 1200 ft beneath the ridge.

4. Mr Ofosu Appiah, Aburi cocoa-far his family land at Odumkyere. An *ntɔmɛ* used for marking boundaries, is on the

A Shai 'village' near Jumapo. Note the [ston]es to prevent the roof from blowing away [and] the pots made by the farmer's wife.

6. The farm yard on the pinnacle of the mountain Nyanao. The roof of the migrant farmer's house can be seen on the right.

7. A typical 'village' in hilly country, inhabited by Shai farmers.

8. An Ewe 'hoe farmer' cultivating devastated cocoa land owned by an Akropong migrant farmer.

9. An Aburi cocoa-farmer on his replanted farm. Note the manner of growth of cocoa pods.

10. Part of a typical small 'village' in the forest. Note the neat store of maize, with the thatch.

11. A small house in Larteh-Ahenease.

12. An old-style 'storey-house' in Larteh-Ahenease, originally owned by C. E. Otu.

13. Dilapidation in Larteh-Ahenease, following swollen shoot.

14. Sakyikrom.

15. A farmer demonstrating the geometry of strip measurement on tapering lands: see p. 45.

AKWAPIM CASE HISTORIES
Mamfe, No. 1
Inher. pat. 0, self 2=2

(i) Dedewa, second-hand; (ii) in 1917 bought land from Asamankese for £500, but Akantin later claimed it and in about 1933 they were given about 2,000 acres near Asuokaw in substitution, much of which was resold to others; he said that the yield from his portion alone had recently been 1,000 loads and that he was employing 30 labourers. His wealth being (unusually) new, his huge house in Mamfe had been completed but recently.

Mamfe, No. 2
Self 3 (others unknown)

(i) Akorabo; (ii) Betom, near Asamankese, now owns 119 acres, land bought through a company of 4, 1 Akropong, 3 Mamfe; (iii) Assin-Adanse.

Mamfe, No. 3
Inher. pat. 1, self 6=7

(i) Inher. Tinkong; (ii) Dedewa, bought from Akogyram—see Appendix VII. 4 (p. 212); (iii) and (iv) bought land at Trayo through two companies; (v) near Anyinam, bought land in a group of 3 brothers and now has more than 100 loads there; (vi) Tumfa, near Kwabeng, bought through a company of Mamfe and Shai, much cocoa there—'some of the other farmers have not planted there, as they have no money'; (vii) near Dunkwa (western region), company of Amanokrom, bought 'about twenty-five years ago', NYP.

Mamfe, No. 4
Inher. pat. 0, self 3=3

This old man, together with his 'brothers', (i) bought land from Akogyram at Dedewa; (ii) Adeiso, second-hand; (iii) Mokwa (Praso), company of Mamfe. At one time he had 'controlled many lands', having been a large farmer-creditor.

Mamfe, No. 5
Inher. pat. 0, self 6=6

The farmer died about twenty years ago and information given by daughters etc. (i) Land near Tinkong bought with money obtained from carpentry and trading in palm-oil; (ii) Trayo (near Nankese), see Appendix II. 5 (p. 65)—bought share I, 274 acres, resold about half; (iii) bought another vast area near Adakwa (near Suhum), again reselling much to others; (iv) near Potroase; (v) near Twifu Praso, bought through Mamfe company; (vi) another land near Twifu Praso, NYP. A large creditor-farmer—'he assisted the Mamfe farmers with loans.'

Mamfe, No. 6
Inher. pat. 1, self 4=5

Farmer deceased, information given by daughter. (i) Inher. Adawso; (ii) Trayo (near Nankese), bought from proceeds of skin trading, company, very large land; (iii) Suhum, where he gave all the land away to his children; (iv) near Jejeti, company of Mamfe; (v) Twifu Praso, Mamfe company.

Mamfe, No. 7
Inher. pat. 2, self 2=4

His father was the younger brother of Akogyram and had land at (i) Dedewa,

207

APPENDIX VII. 3

(ii) Aborodem. He himself bought (iii) 3 ropes at Tumfa, in 1927, through a Mamfe/ Shai company, total cost £1,241 (£23 7s. 6d. a rope)—the land had been divided in 1954. In the same year (iv) he had also bought 6 ropes at Twifu Praso, being a portion of a company land of some 9 square miles in area; this had been divided recently.

Mamfe, No. 8

Inher. pat. 0, self 3 = 3

This remarkable old man who was probably the oldest male inhabitant of Mamfe, had been in the Ashanti wars and (i) bought land across the Densu, near Nankese, in a company; (ii) Twifu Praso; (iii) Afram Plains, bought from Bukuruwa chief, litigation had prevented planting. Although he did not say so (leaving this to others) he had been the leader of the company which bought (ii).

Mamfe, No. 9

Inher. pat. 0, self 3 = 3

Starting as an oil-palm farmer he (i) bought land at Dedewa from Akogyram; (ii) Ntunkum, between Asafo and Nankese, a large Mamfe company (he said '30' members); (iii) Twifu Praso (as Mamfe No. 8).

Mamfe, No. 10

Inher. pat. 2, self 2 = 4

(i) Inher. Tinkong; (ii) inher. Aborodem, a group of his father's brothers, very early purchase, resold much land to Kyerepon, Larteh and Mamfe farmers, he himself employed 10 labourers there; (iii) Akim Manso, before 1925, mixed Mamfe/Shai company, about 3 square miles: capsid spraying has rendered planting possible recently; (iv) farmer did not know location himself—probably resold.

Mamfe, No. 11

Inher. pat. 3, self 4 = 7

Father's 3 purchases included Aborodem, where he resold much land to Larteh farmers; (iv) Aborodem, he himself bought second-hand; (v) near Pramkese, company; (vi) near Kade, mixed Larteh/Mamfe/Kyerepon company, much litigation successfully concluded 'recently' (about twenty years ago), NYP, timber and diamonds there; (vii) Twifu Praso, bought big land (said 44 ropes) through company, claimed that each of his 21 sons and daughters had land there, as well as 3 sisters, one sister's son and one brother's son; he has installed his daughters at the far end of the land to prevent trespassing; said that as Twifu land (bought over a generation ago) only divided about 1950—no one knows what a big farmer he is, but he will surprise people by building a large house in Mamfe soon.

Mamfe, No. 12

Inher. pat. 2, self 2 = 4

His father (i) bought land at Dedewa from Akogyram, giving part to his sister; (ii) Asamankese—but his father was 'too old' and the land was lost; (iii) near Suhum, second-hand from a Mamfe man; (iv) Twifu Praso (leader was Mamfe No. 8). 'When money came to me [from the Suhum land] I started to run transport, but I soon discovered it was not profitable, so I educated my children instead.' As a producebuyer in Suhum he was assisted by his son, who soon left for London and Cambridge —and who is Mr Kankam Boadu, then Managing Director of the Ghana Cocoa Marketing Company.

AKWAPIM CASE HISTORIES
Mamfe, No. 13
Inher. pat. 2, self 3 = 5

(i) Between 1895 and 1897 his father bought Dedewa land from Akogyram; (ii) father 'inadvertently' joined big company of Aburi, Larteh etc. farmers and bought land near Akwatia: no one ever started farming there; (iii) in about 1936 he bought land from chief of Bukuruwa (Kwahu), who had no right to sell—the members of the mixed Mamfe/Amanokrom company lost much money, 'but it is no good crying over spilt milk'; (iv) Twifu Praso, Mamfe company, very poor land and he wants to resell; (v) second-hand, near Nankese.

Aburi, No. 1
Inher. mat. 2, inher. pat. 1, self 1 = 4

Long ago his father bought a land at Otoase, north of Nsawam, which he divided between his sons and his *abusua*. His mat. relatives bought land west of Aburi and near Adawso. He himself bought land near Begoro, 1932, where he has sub-tenants on *abusa* terms.

Aburi, No. 2
Inher. mat. 2, self 1 = 3

His mother Aku (his large house in Aburi is called 'Aku House'), sold palm-kernels and on the proceeds bought (i) herself a trans-Densu land at Aboatumpan (west of Koforidua) about 1896, second-hand; later she went (ii) to Surum with her brothers. He himself (iii) bought land near Oda.

Aburi, No. 3
Inher. mat. 16 lands (not all bought), self at least 7—total uncertain

This remarkable old man listed 16 lands (some of them near Aburi) which he had inherited from his mat. forebears. He himself started farming before 1890, his acquisitions (most of which were large) including Duaden (south of Pakro); Kuaho (near Dokrokyewa)—'4 brothers worked together, they knew they would inherit each other'; near Kraboa-Coaltar ('I became so used to buying land that the owner would ask me to search for a suitable piece for myself'); Ayesu (west of Dokrokyewa), 4 brothers again; Oworam (near Asamankese); near Axim, in western region—'my nephew, a goldsmith, went there and brought news of the place'.

Aburi, No. 4
Inher. mat. 5, self 0 = 5

One of the most famous cocoa-estates of southern Ghana lies west of Aduasa—west of Akim Oda. Bought in about 1925, its area was about 6·7 square miles—according to one plan which may have related to a portion only. The original purchasers were E. K. Etiemo, produce-buyer of Larteh, and Pastor A. O. Mate of Akropong, both of whom were living at Pakro; they recruited several Aburi farmers to join them, each being the head of a sub-group. This informant said that his brother, who had been a produce-buyer at Nsawam, had given him a large portion of his Aduasa land, other portions going to mat. and pat. relatives, and that he had lived there for thirty-two years.

Aburi, No. 5
Inher. mat. 3, self 2 = 5

This ɔsofo (priest) had inherited land at Adumadum and Mfranta. In 1939 his elder brother had bought 2 family lands in Wasa (Opong Valley) of 1·8 and 0·6

209

APPENDIX VII. 3

square miles. He himself had earlier bought 10 acres near Abobiri (south of Odumase-Akim).

Aburi, No. 6

The great interest of the Aburi people in acquiring land wherever they may be, is illustrated by the career of this well-known Aburi resident who, as a surveyor employed by the Survey Department, had travelled widely undertaking 'development work' and at the same time pursuing his interest in farming. In 1918 he had started large-scale farming about 20 miles from Kumasi on the way to Sunyani: 'I met a local farmer and together we took over about a square mile.' Subsequently he was sent to Nkoranza, Kintampo, Wenchi etc.—acquiring land nearly everywhere. When he moved on he 'lost touch' with nearly all his lands. At Adanse-Fomena a land of 5 square miles was given to him by the chief: 'The chief waited and waited for me to plant, but this I could not do as I had gone away, so in the end Akwapim people were given some of the land by the chief.' At Konongo, in Ashanti, where he also has land, he is soon going to plant cocoa, but none of his other farms exists today.

Berekuso, No. 1

Inher. mat. 2, inher. pat. 2, self 4 = 8

His father bought land at Pampanso and at Mfranta and gave 'half to his nephews and half to his children'. He himself bought at: Mepom; Assin-Fosu, NYP; Fomena-Adanse, NYP; Ashanti (near Kumasi).

Berekuso, No. 2

Inher. pat. 2, self 7 = 9

Father bought (i) near Adeiso; (ii) near Asikasu, divided between sons and mat. nephews. Accompanied by his brothers and sons he himself bought a sequence of 7 lands in the Asamankese area and farther north.

Berekuso, No. 3

Inher. pat. 6, self 1 = 7

The informant's father, Osae Yaw, went to Nigeria to work as a carpenter, returning home about 1903. A year or so later he bought land near Asuboi—'he had money so he never joined companies and always had his own land'; (ii)–(iv) three lands near Mfranta; (v) a very large land west of Asikasu, most of which was given to (or inherited by) his sons, some resold to Krobo farmers; (vi) Twifu Praso, NYP, *abusa* tenants, intends to divide between sons. Informant himself, together with a Larteh man, bought land (vii) near Kade.

Obosomase

Inher. 0, self 5 = 5

After buying (i) and (ii) 2 lands near Pakro, this prominent and wealthy man (iii) led a company (or group of companies) to Kwaboanta, west of Coaltar, where many Obosomase people have land, some of which is rented, see Appendix v. 5 (p. 158), each farmer paying a share of the total; (iv) Abanase (Akim-Kotoku), company of Obosomase; (v) Praso-Adanse, immense Obosomase/Tutu/Mampong/Kyerepon company, of which he was the leader, having 'met many farmers' when he was a produce-buyer; if the members had not got the money to pay for the land he 'used to show them where they could get a loan'; portions of land were allocated to each town. Nowadays some of the farmers there encourage young Akwapim men to clear and plant, rewarding them with a half or a third of the planted area.

NOTES ON AKWAPIM TOWNS

APPENDIX VII. 4

ADDITIONAL NOTES ON CERTAIN AKWAPIM TOWNS

Berekuso

Berekuso, which is situated at the southerly end of the Akwapim ridge, seven miles south of Aburi, falls within the Adonten (Aburi) Division of Akwapim and the chief of Berekuso is the Twafohene of Akwapim. Although the town is said to have been connected by road with the main Aburi to Accra road as long ago as the nineteen-twenties, it remains to this day a remote place, largely detached from Akwapim. For many years the Berekuso people have had much commercial and other contact (including inter-marriage) with their (patrilineal) Ga neighbours. They themselves are unique in Akwapim in having an inheritance system which cannot be denoted as straightforwardly matrilineal or patrilineal. Whether this system is correctly regarded as 'dual' (matrilineal *and* patrilineal) cannot be stated: but the following fragmentary notes are offered in the hope that others will pursue this fascinating question further.

It would be mistaken to assume, without further inquiry, that (in respect of either inheritance or succession) the Berekuso people were at one time 'matrilineal' and are now, owing to their contact with the Ga, moving in the 'patrilineal direction'—especially as some of the evidence rather suggests the contrary. The Adontenhene of Akwapim, who described the Berekuso inheritance system as 'very peculiar', told the present writer that the present chief of Berekuso, Nana Adu Mreku Agyeman II,[1] was the first to succeed to his office in the matrilineal line, and that the 'rule had been changed' during the very long term of office of his predecessor, Kwasi Asamoah Mfoafo IV. Then there is the fact, see Appendix VII. 2 (p. 199), that the adoption of the company system by the Berekuso people is nothing new—that it was in the early days that they resembled the patrilineal Akwapim (proper) in the eagerness with which they adopted this system. Certainly everyone in Berekuso takes patrilineal inheritance in some senses for granted: and that the people are apt, on occasions, 'to think patrilineally', became very clear when it was explained that if a maternal nephew, whose uncle had asked for his assistance, happened not to be his uncle's successor, then his uncle 'might treat him *like a son* and give him some property of his own'. It was also stated that 'when a father is alive, sons are solely responsible for his property and must be treated well or they will not reveal its extent'.

As so often, actual practice and 'official' views about practice diverge considerably. At a meeting in February 1959 with the chief and other prominent townsmen, it was stated that the 'usual' inheritance system was matrilineal—'as at Aburi'. An actual example of how this worked out in practice was given. But when the facts of this particular case were checked in the field, it was found that the sons of the very wealthy farmer in question had taken affairs into their own hands and virtually 'ousted' the matrilineal successor—who, as a teacher, had possibly been thankful to discard his responsibilities. Even a section of a very large land which was said to have passed to matrilineal kin was found to have been owned originally by the deceased's sisters—'because they had helped him'. Possibly the origin of the apparent difference of opinion is that the 'successor', who is a matrilineal kinsman, is a mere 'administrator', or trustee, who has the formal function of handing over responsibility for farming to the sons of the deceased—who are, in any case, already 'in charge'.

At the same time it must be recorded that there appears to be nothing 'automatic' about the rights of sons (in general) to take over their father's property. At the same

---

[1] To whom the present writer is much indebted.

211

APPENDIX VII. 4

meeting it was insisted that 'a son who did not serve his father would get nothing'—it being added that if the right of sons to take over their father's property were not 'obvious', then 'delegates would be sent to inspect the land', the sons paying their transport expenses.

The Berekuso farmers have been outstandingly enterprising. They have perhaps tended to congregate in certain areas, such as Mfranta (west of Suhum) where 15 out of 34 Berekuso informants claimed that they owned land. Sometimes they have migrated in company with Ga and other farmers; more usually, perhaps, they formed their own Berekuso groups.

Although Berekuso, like another Aburi town, Nsakye, has failed (perhaps because of its remoteness) to retain the same degree of economic hold over its people as most Akwapim towns (there are no large 'storey-houses' and scarcely any children return home to school), yet the farmers' attachment to it should not be under-rated. Great numbers of them travel long distances to attend the annual festivities there—and there were many of them, see Appendix VIII. 4 (p. 248), who did their town the honour of returning there for the purpose of being enumerated in the 1960 Census.[1]

Mamfe

A most interesting bunch of questions is posed by Mamfe, a relatively small, though ancient, Akwapim town. Why were the migrant cocoa-farmers of Mamfe the most prosperous of all Akwapim farmers? Why, half a century or more ago, were some of their lands so large (see Appendix II. 5, p. 65), that they divided them into large blocks, not strips? Why, if their present situation be judged by the splendid condition of their town houses, have they been able (unlike so many others) to retain some part of the prosperity they enjoyed before swollen shoot?

These questions may be asked, but they cannot be answered. Here it is merely noted that Mamfe's early prosperity may[2] have been connected with the large extent of her local lands in relation to her population—as well as with the enterprise of her citizens in establishing oil-palm plantations on them. And then there is the question of Kwabena Akogyram: do the farmers of Mamfe owe as much to this one man as they always imply?

Akogyram's resale of land at Dedewa, across the Densu from Mangoase, is referred to in Chapter VIII, p. 223. He is said to have been the owner of many oil-palm plantations in the direction of Adawso (perhaps he was a creditor and the plantations were pledged to him) and to have been a general trader based on Akuse and also a trader in salt which he sold himself in the far away north. Perhaps he should not be regarded as a farmer, but as a 'moneyed man', who had never intended to live on the Dedewa land which he bought from the chief of Asafo—or on his land at Aborodem farther north. It seems probable that he started reselling land at Dedewa in 1897 (or slightly earlier) and that virtually all the purchasers were citizens of Mamfe—some said they numbered one hundred or more. As many as 10 out of 20 informants in Mamfe claimed that they, or their forebears, had acquired land at Dedewa—nearly all of them from Akogyram. Much emphasis was laid on the fact that Akogyram was prepared to 'exercise patience' when the farmers found difficulty in paying for their land.

Before his death, which is said to have occurred in 1906, Akogyram bought one more large land, at Mankron, north of Asuboi and again he is said to have resold most

---

[1] Their attempt to swell the official population of Berekuso is said to have been much frustrated by the failure of the enumerator to turn up there until after many of them had returned to their farms.

[2] Until land-tenure conditions in Akwapim have been investigated this must remain a hypothesis.

NOTES ON AKWAPIM TOWNS

of this to Mamfe farmers. He is also said to have bought land at Suhum—which was resold by his successor.

There were, of course, many other Mamfe 'land speculators' apart from Akogyram, but they followed the usual Akwapim fashion of reselling land to whomever was best able to afford it. At Saforosua, see Appendix II. 8 (p. 70), 3 of the 6 original purchasers resold nearly 200 acres to many farmers, few of them from Mamfe. Nearly half of the thousand-acre land at Trayo, Appendix II. 5 (p. 65), was resold by the original purchasers, and few of the buyers were Mamfe men. And then there was the Mamfe man who said that his father's brother had bought land at Aborodem and had resold much of it to Kyerepon and Lartch (as well as Mamfe) people.

Tutu and Obosomase

Unless (as is admittedly possible) many Tutu and Obosomase farmers have severed most of their connexions with their home towns, so that inquiries made there gave an altogether wrong impression of the history and present situation of the migrant farmers, it seems justifiable to conclude that farmers from both these towns, and especially from Tutu, were relatively slow off the mark in the eighteen-nineties and were, later on, unusually reluctant to cross the river Densu. Inquiries in Akim Abuakwa, and in the home towns, certainly show that these farmers seldom formed companies of any size in the early days—although the Obosomase companies which acquired land in the Kwaboanta area, west of Coaltar, were exceptional. Only in Tutu (nowhere else in Akwapim) was the impression formed that the migration had to some extent 'petered out' during the pre-lorry age, when (see Appendix VII. 1, p. 198) a significant proportion, though by no means all, of the farmers lost their momentum.

The large extent of the Tutu lands in Akwapim, as well as their fertility, doubtless had something to do with the lack of enterprise in crossing the river. Then there were the numerous disputes that arose because Omanhene Kwasi Akuffo appropriated and resold Tutu lands—see Appendix VIII. 2 (p. 240), etc. Tutu became heavily indebted as a result of the costs of protracted land litigation—in 1913 the elders of the town stated, in a letter to the D.C. at Aburi, that one land dispute alone had cost over £8,000—and the yoke of poverty left its permanent mark.

During the lorry age many Obosomase farmers (and doubtless many Tutu farmers also) have migrated to distant places: the so-called 'Omanhene' of the stranger-farmers in Sefwi-Wiawso (see p. 237) is an Obosomase man—one who had earlier been a store-keeper at Asamankese.

APPENDIX VII. 5

COCOA-FARM LABOURERS

Three chapters in *The Gold Coast Cocoa Farmer* (see Bibliography) relate to the following five types of labourer (a sixth type, seldom found outside the Volta Region, receives a share of the farm *area* he has planted as his reward):

abusa	who is rewarded with a one-third share of the cocoa he harvests.
nkotokuano	who is paid a fixed sum for each load of cocoa he harvests, this sum always being less than one-third of the value of the cocoa.
annual labourer	who is usually concerned with the establishment of new farms, who is fully maintained by the farmer during the period of his employment and who receives his cash remuneration when he leaves—usually after a year, though sometimes six months.
daily labourer	who is paid by the day, but may be employed for a number of days consecutively, especially at certain times of the year.

APPENDIX VII. 5

contract labourer who is paid a sum agreed in advance for clearing, or weeding, or clearing and planting, a certain specified area.

Subsequent research[1] suggests that this classification is basically sound, except for the failure to realize that it was for long standard practice among many migrant farmers to allow the labourer an *abusa* (one-third) share of the cocoa when the trees were young, putting him on to the lower *nkotokuano* rate as the yield of the trees increased. This conversion from one rate to the other was automatic—unless of course the labourer chose to leave, as he sometimes did. Some farmers allowed their labourers to remain on *abusa* terms longer than others—perhaps up to fifteen years. But not all labourers started on *abusa* terms when the farms were young: thus elderly Anum and Boso cocoa-farmers insist that their first connexion with cocoa-growing was as *nkotokuano* men with Akwapim farmers.

As noted in *The Gold Coast Cocoa Farmer*, the *nkotokuano* system probably originated in Akwapim (it certainly existed there before the farmers crossed the Densu) and subsequently spread across the Volta, whence it was transmitted by returning labourers. (It is admittedly conceivable, so prevalent is the system in the Volta Region, that it originated there—though in connection with what crop?—and spread to Akwapim.) Whether it is unique in West Africa is not known. The other four systems, but not *nkotokuano*, are reported by Köbben[2] as existing in the Ivory Coast.

APPENDIX VII. 6

LINGUISTIC ECONOMICS

How literally should the migrant farmers of southern Ghana, in particular the Akwapim, be regarded as *capitalists* engaged in the *business* of cocoa-farming? Certainly these farmers have throughout been functioning within the framework of what an economist might call a 'market economy', an anthropologist a 'money economy': 'It is only when land and labour as well as fabricated goods are organized as available commodities to be bought and sold through the market mechanism that a money economy exists.'[3] The results of the migration in terms of ever-increasing land acquisition, output of cocoa, labour employment, etc. would certainly seem to justify some degree of analogy with capitalism, at any rate during the expansionary period—which was slowed down by the Great Depression before it was shattered by swollen shoot. And the fact that during the last twenty years or so many of the farmers have reverted to a 'near-subsistence' standard of living again draws attention to the fact that they made money because they were enterprising, not because they were obliged to do so in order to survive.

It has recently been argued that:
'Primitive economy is different from market industrialism not in degree but in kind. The absence of machine technology, pervasive market organisation and all-purpose money, plus the fact that economic transactions cannot be understood apart from social obligation, create, as it were, a non-Euclidean universe to which Western economic theory cannot be fruitfully applied.'[4] If the migrant farmers are not capital-

---

[1] See also Polly Hill, 'Systems of Labour Employment on Gold Coast Cocoa Farms', *Proceedings of the 5th Conference of the West African Institute of Social and Economic Research, 1956*.

[2] See A. J. F. Köbben, *Le Planteur Noir* (1956), chapter v. In Akan areas of the Ivory Coast the term *abusa* is used.

[3] George Dalton, 'Economic Theory and Primitive Society', *American Anthropologist*, vol. 63, no. 1, February 1961, p. 15.   [4] *Ibid.*, p. 20.

LINGUISTIC ECONOMICS

ists (certainly they lack a 'machine technology'), at least they appear to provide a bridge between 'the non-Euclidean universe' and 'market organized industrialism'[1]— that essential ingredient of 'economic growth'. It may be true that the ability 'to produce a class of entrepreneurs who are more than traders is a requirement of any society before economic growth can become a continuous process'.[2] But if it is right to regard the Nigerian transport owner as a 'new kind of African entrepreneur',[3] because of his ability to 'invest in fixed capital', then the Ghanaian migrant farmer has an even greater significance, having invested in land for productive purposes so much earlier— and bearing in mind, incidentally, that he was among the first to buy lorries for commercial operation.

But in the eighteen-nineties when the migration was launched, is it likely that the farmers themselves were *thinking* in terms which without any stretch of the imagination might be designated as 'capitalist'? How at that time did the Akwapim *speak* of 'money', 'interest', 'capital' and the rest? Reference to Christaller's dictionary of Twi (1881 edition) suggests that at that date there were Twi equivalents of many of the key words of economic jargon[4]—although it is admittedly possible that it was Christaller himself who stretched the meanings of many words to cover concepts which were unfamiliar but which were necessary for translation purposes. The following fragmentary list, compiled with the help of Mr S. Nyako-Agyakwa, is offered for what it is worth and includes only words and expressions in the 1881 edition of the dictionary:

English word	Akwapim Twi equivalents	Notes
money	*sika*	the original meaning was gold, but by this time it had come to mean 'money in general'
capital	(i) *dwetiri*	literally 'to cut up a head of cowries'—*tiri* being a head (fifty strings) of cowries (*ntrama*); 'a capital or stock of money to begin trade with; a fund employed in business or any undertaking'
	(ii) *sika-mu*	fund, stock (a whole sum of money, enough for a particular job)
	(iii) *sika-dahɔ*	deposit, capital, stock, fund
	(iv) *sika-ten*	principal, loan
	(v) *titiriw*	capital, principal
to invest	*de sika hyɛ mu*	Christaller gives *hyɛ* 41 meanings, one being 'to accumulate treasures'.
to save	(i) *kora*	to hide, store, bury, etc.
	(ii) *sie*	a word of many meanings, some of them similar to *kora*
loan or debt	(i) *bosea*	
	(ii) *ka*	from the verb 'to be wanting', 'to owe', etc.

---

[1] *Ibid.*, p. 21.   [2] E. K. Hawkins, *Road Transport in Nigeria* (1958), p. 4.
[3] *Ibid.*, p. 89.
[4] Words relating to wages are one of the main gaps in the vocabulary. Rattray notes (*Ashanti Law and Constitution*, p. 114) that the idea of work being remunerated by a fixed wage was unknown in Ashanti until recently and the language contained no word corresponding to 'to pay wages'.

215

APPENDIX VII. 6

English word	Akwapim Twi equivalents	Notes
to lend or borrow	(i) *fɛm*	
	(ii) *bɔ bosea*	
interest	(i) *mfɛntom*	derived from *fɛm* and meaning the sum added to borrowed money
	(ii) *nsiho*	presumably derived from *sie*, 'the additional sum required in repayment of a loan'
to spend	(i) *di*	110 (*sic*) applications of this word are listed in Christaller, of which, perhaps, the primary is 'eat'—consume
	(ii) *hwere*	another word of many meanings—spend, consume, waste, squander, etc.
	(iii) *sɛe*	similar meanings to the foregoing; also means 'spoil'
to buy	*tɔ*	
to sell	(i) *tɔn*	
	(ii) *si konko*	to retail, to broke
'to sell and use up the money received'	*tɔn ... di*	
price	*bo*	'a piece or figure of brass or other metal, a stone or seed used for a weight'
profit	*mfaso*	left over
rich man	(i) *osikani*	he who has money
	(ii) *ɔdefo*	literally, 'a man with things'
	(iii) *dwetiwani*	from *dwetiri* (capital), see p. 180n.
poor man	*ohiani*	he who is in need
pawn, pledge, mortgage	*awowa*	
labour contract	*paa*	'a contract or agreement by which the services of a person are engaged for another person'
labourer, carrier, etc.	*ɔpaani*	derived from *paa*
carrier	*ɔsoafo*	from *soa*, to carry
salary, wage	(i) *akatua*	from *tua ka*, to pay a debt
	(ii) *apaabɔde*	derived from *paa*
trade	*gua*	the words for market, trader, goods, etc. all derive from *gua*
to obtain goods on credit	*firi*	to take, receive, or buy goods on trust or credit
business, agricultural work, etc.	*adwuma*	
'to have the usufruct of'	*didi so*	also means 'to make one's livelihood by', 'to make temporary use of'
land	*asase*	can be used in the sense of a 'piece of land'

216

LINGUISTIC ECONOMICS

English word   Akwapim Twi equivalents

'what is given into   (i) *nsim*
the bargain when a   (ii) *ntoso*
large quantity of
anything is bought'

APPENDIX VII. 7

MISCELLANEOUS COCOA STATISTICS

Total Cocoa Exports from Ghana

The value and quantity of exports for each year up to 1913 are given in Appendix VI. 2 (p. 176). The trend of exports since then is indicated by the following table:

Average for 5 years	000 tons
1916–20	106
1921–25	186
1926–30	219
1931–35	243
1936–40	263
1941–45	193
1946–50	232
1951–55	220
1956–60	249

Production by region

Reliable figures of cocoa-production by region did not become available until the setting up of the marketing board system during the second world war.

Estimated production in *Ashanti* rose from about 5,000 tons in 1912 to about 17,000 tons in 1920 and to about 50,000 tons in 1925. Between 1932 and 1947 Ashanti production varied between about 75,000 tons and 100,000 tons.

Production in the *Eastern Province* between 1932 and 1947 varied between about 100,000 tons and 150,000 tons. Thereafter it declined rapidly as a result of swollen shoot:

	(000 tons)[1]	
	1948–9 season	1956–7 season
Ashanti[2]	126	133
Western Province	46	44
Volta Region	26	32
Eastern Province		
Historic Area[3]	46	21
Other	34	34
Total	278	264

[1] Figures from the *Tenth Annual Report* of the Ghana Cocoa Marketing Board, pp. 36–7, based on purchases by buying centres.

[2] The old Ashanti region—now Ashanti and Brong-Ahafo.

[3] The following buying centres are included: Tafo, Nsawam, Nsawam/Coaltar, Nsawam/Suhum and North, Adeiso, Asamankese. (Koforidua is excluded.)

217

APPENDIX VII. 7

Production by migrant cocoa-farmers of southern Ghana

It has never been possible to estimate, even approximately, the proportion of Ghana's cocoa-exports for which the migrant farmers have been responsible. In the earliest days most of the cocoa was exported from Accra—about 500 tons out of a total of 536 tons in 1900—the other main ports being Ada and Winneba; it is to be presumed that most of the cocoa exported from Accra was produced by the migrants. The railway station at Pakro, an important centre on the route between Akwapim and Akim Abuakwa, was opened in 1911 and, according to P. R. Gould, *Transportation in Ghana*, p. 32, it handled 21,000 tons of cocoa between August and the end of that year—total exports in 1910 were 23,000 tons, in 1911 40,000 tons.

In the nineteen-twenties and -thirties a great proportion (perhaps two-thirds or more) of the 100,000 tons or more produced in the Eastern Province came from the migrants' farms, but there is no means of estimating the proportion of Western Province cocoa for which they were responsible either then or later.

In the 1948–9 season the migrants may have produced between 35,000 and 40,000 tons in the Eastern Province, the corresponding figure for 1956–7 being about 15,000 tons.

Ghana Cocoa Exports. *Average Annual Value/Ton*

Export Values

Years	£ (f.o.b.)	
	High	Low
1900–09	55	37
1910–19	53	27
1920–29	80	33
1930–38	42	17

The table shows the highest and lowest average annual figures during each 10-year period. Thus in the period 1900–9 the highest figure was £55/ton (in 1907), the lowest £37 (in 1905 and 1906).

Between 1947–8 and 1956–7 the average f.o.b. price realized per ton by the Ghana Cocoa Marketing Board exceeded £200 in each season except 1948–9 and 1949–50 and reached £359 in 1953–4 and £355 in 1954–5.

The farmers' receipts

The price received by the farmer *net of transport costs* has always fallen far short of the values shown in the preceding table, and this was especially true in 1900–9 before the opening of the Accra railway. In 1919 when world cocoa-prices were rising the producer received a lower proportion of the world price than in 1930 when they were falling—between the wars the average 'producer price' probably fluctuated between 40 per cent and 80 per cent of the average f.o.b. price.

Under the marketing board system the producer's price has been fixed for the season and between 1947–8 and 1958–9 it varied between 37 per cent and 78 per cent of the Ghana f.o.b. price—much of the balance being accounted for by an export duty levied on a sliding scale dependent on the f.o.b. price.

Between 1926–7 and 1935–6 the total cash received by the farmers annually for their cocoa varied (according to one estimate,[1] which may not be very reliable) between about £11 million (1926–7) and £2½ million (1933–4).

In 1955–6 and 1956–7 the farmers' receipts were £38 million and £43 million, based on a 'producer price' of £4 a load of 60 lb.

[1] See Hill, *The Gold Coast Farmer*, p. 133.

218

CHAPTER VIII

AN OUTLINE GEOGRAPHY OF THE MIGRATION[1]

Very early in the eighteen-nineties, Akwapim farmers from a few of the main towns, including Aburi, Mampong, Larteh and Akropong, started planting coffee and cocoa on land away from the immediate vicinity of their home towns and by 1894 this migration was well under way. Adawso, which became the commercial centre of the cocoa-trade from about 1900 and which was the natural gateway to the west for many Akwapim people, was 'founded' in 1894. (An inscription on a monument in Adawso to Abraham Adu, 'the first Christian chief', records that he died in 1909, 'aged 103', having founded the town in 1894.)[2] A Basel Mission station was established at Apasare, a village adjoining Adawso, in that year, as the record book, still preserved there, notes:[3]

This Station was built in the year 1894. Its history runs thus: When the cocoa business was introduced to this country a great majority of Akwapim left their respective towns and repaired to the bush chiefly to Apasare where there was still virgin forest. This place is the centre of the villages bordering from Akropong Bewase[4]. . . The late Rev. Müller then made a journey through the whole district and chose this place. It was then a dense forest belonging to one Yianoma of Mamfe. He bought it for an amount of £3.

Many of the villages in the neighbourhood of Adawso are famous in the memories of present-day cocoa-farmers—though their existence has gone unrecorded in the books. Old Mangoase, on a hill east of the river Densu, some five miles west of Adawso, is one of them.[5] Owing to swollen shoot

[1] This chapter, which relates almost entirely to the period up to 1918, is presented partly as 'evidence' that the migration occurred and partly for record purposes and it is realized that it will be of little interest to those unfamiliar with the geography of southern Akim Abuakwa. On the basis of information provided by countless farmers, the aim has been to provide a straightforward account of the geographical sequence of the migration. It is both tentative and arbitrary—many well-known districts, farmers and company lands receive no mention. As the histories of larger lands and farms are often more interesting and memorable than those of smaller ones, it has been difficult to avoid giving the misleading impression that all the lands that were acquired were 'large'.

[2] In 1958 Mr Adakwa Asare, who had been born in the Adawso area in about 1886, said that his 'grandfather' Abraham Adu, who was an Amanokrom man, had first cultivated the oil-palm there and that, later on, coffee and then cocoa had been introduced.

[3] The author is grateful to Nana Ntow Boafo I, the chief of Adawso, for having drawn her attention to this record in 1958; the catechist thought that it had probably been written in 1896.

[4] Bewase means, according to Christaller, 'a low tract of country at the foot of a mountain'; Adawso lies about a thousand feet below the towns on the ridge.

[5] Three elderly Larteh men who were living in Old Mangoase when it was visited in 1958 insisted that their 'fathers' had started farming there in 1896 on land which they had bought from the chief of Apedwa and that they had 'extended' westward over the river Densu in 1903.

219

AN OUTLINE GEOGRAPHY

many of the old villages have disappeared without trace, which is one reason why the current edition of the one-inch Ghana Survey[1] includes so few of the place-names which the farmers regard as the jumping-off points for their later migration across the Densu. Many Larteh farmers first began farming farther north, near Asuoya, particularly near Okorase, where Paul Yaw Kuma, who had previously been a sawyer at Senchi, bought a large area, much of which he resold to other Larteh men.[2] Then there is the area east of Asuoya known as Panto, where Omanhene Kwame Fori is said to have made a cocoa-farm before his death in 1895.[3] East of Tinkong lies Awbum, another village founded by Akropong people. (No evidence was provided as to when land at Awbum, Pretu, Apesika, Konko, Panto, etc., was first acquired, but this food-growing hinterland bears the same relationship to Akropong as the western slopes of the ridge down to Ahamahama and Nkyenekyene do to Aburi.) Some of the lands which were planted with coffee or cocoa were bought by the farmers from other Akwapim people, some were already owned by those who planted them. There was a tendency for farmers from certain towns to congregate in certain parts of their hinterland: thus half of the farmers who were interviewed in Mampong said that their forebears had started growing cocoa at Pommu (Pum on the map) about three miles west of Adawso, and most Mamfe farmers probably started near Adawso or Tinkong.

The western migratory path of the farmers from Aburi and associated towns (including Berekuso, Nsakye and Ahwerease) lay farther south. Many Aburi farmers first grew cocoa in the area of Deigo, beneath (about six miles west of) the top of the ridge. Other important place-names were Doboro, Obodan, Ahariso, Ahamahama and Nkyenekyene. Many Aburi farmers experimented with cocoa-growing in several parts of the hinterland running down to the river; one of the oldest of all Aburi residents claimed in 1959 that he could remember his father having planted cocoa in nine such localities, which he named, before 1900. One of these

---

[1] Throughout this book and especially in this chapter, the spelling of place-names has presented much difficulty. Many of the renderings on published maps are manifestly absurd to those with any knowledge of the Twi language; some of these, such as 'Kumasi' (for Kumase), have been common currency for so long that in a non-linguistic work of this nature it would be pedantic to reject them. Another difficulty is that if phonetic principles are followed too closely, doubt and confusion may result if the usual printed version is very different. The Bureau of Ghana Languages has been asked to advise on the spelling of place-names for the report of the 1960 Census, but at the time of writing the Census report is unpublished. The present writer has therefore been largely guided by practical considerations of intelligibility and has retained some of the unsatisfactory versions on the one-inch Ghana Survey and other maps: for this reason the familiar 'Akim' and 'Akwapim' have not been discarded in favour of the more scholarly 'Akyem' and 'Akuapem'.

[2] The land is said to have stretched from the 'town' of Okorase (which lies just to the west of the present main road to Koforidua) as far as the river Densu, over a mile to the west. Paul Yaw Kuma was one of those who contributed to the building of the Mmetiamu bridge—see Appendix VIII. 3 (p. 244).

[3] See Appendix VIII. 2 (p. 240).

220

AN OUTLINE GEOGRAPHY

nine areas was Pakro: most Tutu and Obosomase farmers and some Aburi farmers first moved towards Pakro—a well-known centre to which more reference will be made.

There is no evidence that the migrant farmers planted cocoa on trans-Densu (Akim Abuakwa) land before 1897, at the very earliest. A Mampong farmer produced documentary evidence that his father and his two brothers had bought farming land at Dedewa (see p. 223) as early as 1884,[1] but he thought that they had not started planting cocoa there until about 1905. It has been noted in chapter v that the chiefs of Apapam and Apedwa started selling land immediately north of Nsawam in the early eighteen-nineties and Akwapim farms and villages, such as Yaw Koko, Fosu,[2] Okanta and Teacher Mante,[3] are shown on the 1897 map referred to on p. 152n; but the official papers relating to the Apedwa/Apapam land dispute (Appendix v. 2, p. 151) contain no mention of the word 'cocoa'. This 1897 map does not extend as far west as Sakyikrom,[4] the large land surrounding much of the mountain Nyanao (to the west of Nsawam), which had been bought some time earlier, not expressly for cocoa-growing. Possibly Omanhene Kwame Fori had been the first Akwapim to plant cocoa over the river.[5] However this may have been, it is certain that in 1896 or 1897 a few Akwapim farmers became aware that a shortage of cocoa-land was developing east of the river and that this prompted them to cross over to the other bank and to acquire land—which they did not necessarily start to plant until some time later. Running from north to south, Aboatumpan, Aborodem, Mmetiamu, Koransan, Dedewa, Abrodiem and Pampanso are some of the best-known trans-Densu localities where these pioneering farmers subsequently made their fortunes. But before following the farmers across the river, further mention must be made of the Pakro, Agyinase, Duaden strip of land east of the Densu and just north of Nsawam, where a few of the lands that were acquired were as large as they commonly were farther west.

The individual who bought the largest land in the Pakro area was William Adjabeng Quansah Solomon from Accra, a remarkable farmer.[6] The seller was Omanhene Kwasi Akuffo, but whether the transaction occurred before or after he was installed as Omanhene in 1895 could not be determined. Solomon resold much land to Shai[7] and other farmers, but retained a vast area for his own use, which centred on a 'storey-house' which he built at Agyinase—now on the railway line. When Capt William

---

[1] Under the heading 'Dedewa 1884' an entry, written in Twi, in an old notebook, recorded that the land had been sold by Asafo people to three brothers for the sum of 55 *dare* —the *dare* being a silver coin, or dollar. It was laid down that if, later on, the seller should refuse to sell, he should pay double the purchase-money to the purchaser as compensation.

[2] Presumably the village belonging to Kwadjo Ofosu of Akropong.

[3] Shown on the map as 'Teacher Kufo of Late'.   [4] See Appendix III. 1 (p. 86).

[5] See Appendix VIII. 2 (p. 240).   [6] See Appendix VIII. 1 (p. 238).

[7] The Shai purchasers had previously been labourers.

221

AN OUTLINE GEOGRAPHY

Price-Jones investigated Solomon's affairs following his death in 1936, he reported that this land had a radius of about a mile and a half and contained twenty-seven farms; it was not until he had 'been walking steadily for three days' that he had become familiar with all Solomon's property there.

A year or so before Solomon bought his land, an Aburi farmer called Akoanankran (better known as the father of Kofi Pare[1]) also bought land in the Pakro area from Akuffo. Akuffo's right to sell the land was subsequently challenged by certain Tutu people who claimed that the land was theirs. A judgment in Solomon's (and Akuffo's) favour in 1905[2] provoked Akuffo to claim more land in the area and the well-remembered Battle of Ankwasu[3] (a village about three miles east of Pakro) resulted in 1906, being followed by Akuffo's destoolment in 1907. Later on Chief Justice Sir William Brandford Griffith pronounced two judgments which were opposed in principle to that of 1905; he had come to doubt the validity, especially in relation to Akwapim, of Sarbah's[4] contention, in the 1905 case, that 'any unoccupied land not being a part of the land of a subordinate stool or family, or a private person, would be attached to the paramount stool'. In a case involving Akoanankran in March 1912,[5] the judge (E. C. Watson) endorsed Sir William Brandford Griffith's revised view:

I am of opinion that the land in dispute was never Akwapim stool land. I hold that Akuffo's assumption that it is so is an arbitrary assumption, unsupported either by record or by evidence and Akuffo had no right whatever, in my opinion, to deal with the Parekro [Pakro] land as part of the Akwapim stool and could not confer any title therein. I think that it was, up to 1899, unowned land adjacent to the Tutu Nyago stool. . .[6]

Today Pakro, which has only recently been connected by road to Nsawam, is a pleasant enough 'retiring station'—to some extent resembling a home town on the ridge. Aburi, Obosomase, Tutu, Mampong, Mamfe, Larteh, Akropong, Kyerepon, Ga, Shai and other people are all to be found there. The first 'chief' was Akoanankran, and his successors, down to the present day, have all been Aburi people. In 1911 the

---

[1] See Appendix III. 4 (p. 92).

[2] See P. A. Renner, *Cases in the Courts of the Gold Coast Colony and Nigeria*, vol. I, part II, p. 406. This was a reversal of an earlier judgment.

[3] See Appendix VIII. 2 (p. 242).

[4] The celebrated J. M. Sarbah had been counsel for Solomon.

[5] *Akuamankra (sic) v. Paul and Kwamin Ajaro*, Supreme Court. The writer is indebted to Mr A. O. Quansah of Aburi for access to his copy of the court proceedings, of which, so far as is known, no abstract has hitherto been published.

[6] Ajare and Paul, who were natives of Mampong, claimed to have bought their land in about 1899 from a Tutu Nyago man for the price of £50, the elders having authorized the sale of this 'ancestral land'. They claimed that Akoanankran was not then in occupation of his land, which he had bought a few years earlier, perhaps in 1896: 'All that there was was a hunter's shed made of sticks and palm branches, the same as any other person would make in the forest. There are no women, cooking pots or other things in the place.'

222

AN OUTLINE GEOGRAPHY

recorded population of Pakro was only 321; it was in that year that Pakro railway station was first opened to traffic so that the town became an important buying centre, the population of which rose to 1,143 in 1921.

There is much evidence, as already noted, that it was in 1896 or 1897 that pioneering farmers from several of the Akwapim towns suddenly started acquiring trans-Densu cocoa-lands. Whether it was then, or somewhat earlier, that Kwabena Akogyram[1] of Mamfe had bought his lands at Dedewa (an area which derives its name from a stream more than six miles long which flows parallel to the Densu) and Aborodem (a trans-Densu area about two miles north of Mmetiamu), could not be ascertained; but around 1897, or slightly later, he was certainly reselling land to Mamfe people on a substantial scale and as many as a half of all those interviewed in Mamfe claimed that they, or their forebears, had bought land from him.[2] In the absence of farm maps it is impossible to ascertain the original extent of Akogyram's Dedewa land: it is unlikely to have been as long as four miles, as one informant suggested,[3] but it may have been over a mile wide. It is generally agreed that Akogyram himself had never lived there (had he bought it as a speculation, or to help the people of Mamfe?); and that there had been no measurement of the portions at the time they were resold. Many other people, especially from Mampong, claim to have bought 'Dedewa land' direct from the chief of Apedwa, and soon the place became a home from home. As a well-known song has it, 'Dedewa is our home-town':[4]

> Come dear friend, I pray you,
> Meet me at Mangoase,
> Do not delay, but come quickly,
> Let us meet together.
> As the river is in flood,
> We need a boat to make our crossing.
> Come then, cross with me to Dedewa,
> For Dedewa is our home town.
> Make haste, hurry one and all,
> Let us cross without delay,
> That we may go to our cocoa-farms,
> There to look and hunt for snails,
> And take them home
> For a sizzling palm-oil soup.

[1] See Appendix VII. 4.

[2] Either at Dedewa, or at Aborodem farther north. It was stated in Mamfe, though this may have been an exaggeration, that 'more than a hundred' Mamfe people had obtained land from Akogyram and that he had been willing to wait for payment so that those who owned no capital could pay for the land from its own proceeds.

[3] Two miles was, perhaps, nearer the mark.

[4] Here rendered in free translation from the Twi by Professor Alex Kwapong. The writer is also indebted to Mr Asa-Anakwa of Mamfe and to his mother, Mrs Ofosua Anakwa, for drawing her attention to the song, which is said to have become very popular following its

AN OUTLINE GEOGRAPHY

North of Dedewa is Koransan,[1] an equally well-known place-name. Among the main purchasers of land there, was a group of Mampong 'brothers', including Charles Badu,[2] Peter Botchway and several others, the date of purchase being 1897.[3] The purchasers divided the land into strips and may have delayed planting until 1904 when Charles Badu is known to have started planting his portion which, after allowing for re-sales, had an area of about 110 acres. Peter Botchway is said to have re-sold the whole of his portion, some of it to Larteh people. Larteh farmers are prominent in this area. The owner of one of the largest houses in Lar-teh (a house which had been built from the proceeds of a Koransan farm), said that his grandfather had divided all his Koransan land between his sons in his lifetime and he had a plan showing that one of them had been given an area of over fifty acres in 1903—for which he had 'paid' £6.

West of the Dedewa stream lie areas known to the farmers as Abrodiem, Awusem and Nananko. The house at present occupied by the chief of Mampong bears the name 'Awusam', showing that it was built from the proceeds of farming there. One very old Mampong man claimed that his father and brothers had bought land at Nananko in about 1902, for about £50, and that he himself had been pawned to raise the money. Charles E. Otu[4] was one of many Larteh farmers who owned land in the Nananko area.

Farther north, a well-known Larteh farmer, William Tetteh, bought a large land west of the river at Bibianiha; another Larteh farmer is said to have bought land at neighbouring Aboatumpan in 1901.

At just the same time as the Larteh, Mamfe and Mampong people were starting to plant their first trans-Densu acquisitions, the Aburi and Akro-pong people were beginning to develop their family lands which lay to the extreme south of the cocoa-area, near Nsawam. That the Aburi (and Ahwerease) people should have crossed the river near Nsawam follows from the geographical position of these towns at the southern end of the ridge; but why there should have been a number of important Akropong lands in the same area is not clear. Among these Akropong lands were: the farm and village denoted as 'Yau Fosu Krom' on the 1897 map;[5] Ofobea, about three miles east of Adeiso (called after an Akropong woman of that name); Obuobisa (some two miles farther east); and Mfodwo-Boaten (south of Adeiso) which was bought by Daniel Boaten of Akropong in about 1904.

---

recording on a disc. Fallen trees were used as bridges, except when the river was in flood when boats were necessary.

[1] According to some, the literal translation of this is, 'when you go you do not return', meaning that the place is too distant to go and return in one day.

[2] See W. H. Beckett, *Koransang*, which relates to Charles Badu's portion of the land.

[3] This date was recorded in Charles Badu's diary—information from his son, Mr Philip Badu.

[4] See Appendix VIII. 3 (p. 246).   [5] See p. 152n.

AN OUTLINE GEOGRAPHY

But most of the villages north of the Nsawam to Adeiso road bear the names of farmers from Aburi and associated towns. Sakyikrom[1] is called after Nana Sakyi; Daaman, Duayeden, Akotuakrom ... and many more are all of them based on farmers' names. Ahwerease (called after the Akwapim home town, not the founding farmer) was founded in about 1898.[2] The Rev. Martin Obeng of Aburi thought that his father bought his land at Ayi Bonte (about five miles north-west of Nsawam) about 1896. Daaman was founded somewhat later. From such inquiries as have been made so far, it seems likely that the Aburi farmers had progressed little farther in the direction of Coaltar than Akotuakrom by the end of the second phase of the migration (here arbitrarily put at 1906), though Omanhene Kwasi Akuffo claimed he had bought land near Krabokese as early as 1901.[3]

The farmers proceeded very rapidly northwards from Nsawam in the direction of Suhum. The Rev. Moses Ntow of Nsawam stated that his forebear, Ohene Kwadjo of Aburi, was selling cutlasses in the Asuboi area as early as 1897. Asuboi was a meeting-place of the peoples from all parts of Akwapim—the focal point of the migration until the later development of Suhum—and it may be that nearly all the land was taken up there before 1906. There were some isolated purchases of land for cocoa-growing much farther north in the same direction, associated perhaps with the construction, which began in 1899,[4] of the road from Suhum to Apedwa by the Eastern Akim Goldfields Mining Company. D. P. Hammond, a Ga, is said to have bought his land north of Suhum (it is called 'Niifio', this being his nickname) as early as 1902. It seems that in those early days Ga cocoa-farmers were either prominent individuals like Solomon or Hammond, or smaller farmers who bought land 'second-hand' from Akwapim, though many of them doubtless tried, usually with little success, to establish cocoa on their food-farms south of Nsawam.[5]

Various of the migrant farmers who, for financial or geographical reasons, were late starters in the westward race across the river Densu have received little mention so far. The Krobo people, in particular, were so thoroughly involved in their 'oil-palm migration' that it occurred to few of them to purchase land expressly for cocoa-growing until after 1900. Their usual approach to the trans-Densu area was by way of the Kofori-

---

[1] See Appendix III. 1 (p. 86). Many other Aburi family lands are listed by name in that Appendix.

[2] See Appendix III. 6 (p. 97).

[3] See Appendix VIII. 1 (p. 241) and also Case A.30 in *Cases in Akan Law* for the statement that 'various big farms have been made on the land [west of Kyekyewere] as far back as 1904'.

[4] Information from Dr Peter Gould. According to Dr K. B. Dickson, *Transactions of the Historical Society of Ghana*, vol. v, part I, p. 37, this road was completed in 1905.

[5] The 1907 half-inch map (see p. 227) shows cocoa-growing as far south as Pokuase. (The Ga, even more than the Akwapim, were migrant food-farmers.)

225

AN OUTLINE GEOGRAPHY

dua area, where they had for long been buying land.[1] While many Yilo Krobo (though few Manya Krobo) companies subsequently bought land in southern Akim Abuakwa, there were many Krobo farmers who never moved west of the border country between Akim Abuakwa and Krobo country (the boundary between which remains indeterminate to this day), extending from Koforidua to Begoro and beyond. There are, also, many Shai farmers to be found in parts of this eastern fringe area, for instance in the mountainous district east of Jumapo—see plate 5. Considering their small population at the time of the start of the migration, the Shai are among the most remarkable of all the migrant farmers and their lands are very widely distributed throughout the historic cocoa-growing area. While most present-day Shai farmers claim that they, or more usually their forebears, 'started farming' in the Mangoase or Adawso area, it is doubtful whether, in the earliest days, many of them would have had money to spare for land-purchase (though they were producers of and traders in palm produce) and many of them started as carriers, or labourers, with Akwapim farmers; however, they evolved with great rapidity into farmers in their own right and they were buying trans-Densu land west of Mangoase very soon after 1897.

As remarkable as the Shai are the very widely dispersed Anum and Boso farmers, who, in the early stages, altogether lacked the finance to buy cocoa-land and who were also hampered by the fact that their homeland, east of the river Volta, was more than fifty miles from Adawso. Their first connexion with cocoa was as carriers and labourers with Akwapim farmers. Their evolution from labourer to farmer was sudden and complete—though it was probably delayed until after their great migration to Asamankese in 1907.[2]

The Kyerepon (Akwapim) people resembled the Krobo in approaching southern Akim Abuakwa by way of the Koforidua area—whence some moved west and some north, especially to the Jumapo[3] and Bosuso areas.

It was probably not until after 1906 that any significant number of Fanti, Awutu etc. farmers, from the coastal areas to the south-east, arrived in the Mepom and Asuokaw areas, twenty miles west of Nsawam, where they are now so strongly represented.

Two overlapping phases of the migration have been dealt with so far. During the first of these phases, when most of the lands that were acquired lay east of the Densu, farms were mostly small and many Akwapim, of varying means, participated. During the second phase, which be-

[1] In a case heard by Sir William Brandford Griffith in the Supreme Court in March 1910, evidence was given that land near Koforidua had been bought by Krobo people from the chief of Kukurantumi in about 1890.

[2] See Appendix VIII. 6 (p. 250).

[3] Where there are, also, many Akropong farmers—the neighbours of the Kyerepon.

226

AN OUTLINE GEOGRAPHY

gan in about 1897, prominent farmers from towns such as Larteh and Mampong started planting trans-Densu lands which they had acquired in anticipation of the land shortage which was developing east of the river, and the farmers of Aburi and Akropong began to develop their large southern estates, some of which had been acquired without thought of cocoa. During these first two phases none of the Akwapim farmers migrated in company: the migratory groups, if groups they were, were small sets of closely related kin. During the third phase, which is rather arbitrarily regarded as beginning about 1906, migration by company became the rule for the patrilineal Akwapim and 'the people's migration' was soon in full swing, for under the company system even the most poverty-stricken of Akwapim farmers were able to acquire a 'rope' or two of land. At the same time the network of southern Aburi estates was growing rapidly, the family lands providing a home from home for the majority of Aburi people. Although there are few reliable population figures worth citing, it is clear that between 1901 and 1911 many of the towns on the Akwapim ridge lost much of their population.[1] The Census return for the Birrim District in 1911 was so 'disappointing' (a euphemism for defective) that little is known about the distribution of population in southern Akim country at that time—though 'Akwapim Asuboe' (i.e. Asuboi) had a recorded population of 620. But the report on that Census cautiously observed that 'the centre of gravity of population is beginning to shift from the Coast towns to Inland towns': '. . . owing to a greater sense of security and to the development of agriculture, the tendency is to form small towns and scattered farming villages and . . . the formation of large towns does not in the near future seem probable'.

The first maps on the scale of half-an-inch to the mile, which were prepared under the direction of Major F. G. Guggisberg (Director of Surveys and later Governor) and published in 1907, are of little assistance in tracing the history of the migration, although they represented an attempt to note the areas in which the principal economic crops were grown. That many native Akim cocoa-farmers lagged years behind the migrants is indicated by the fact that the Kibi section of the map shows no cocoa-growing anywhere near Apapam or Apedwa.[2] On the Accra section,[3]

---

[1] See Appendix VIII. 4 (p. 248). In 1906 a Basel missionary, Mohr (see p. 170n), reported as follows: 'The villages situated on the Akwapim range from Aburi northwards to Apirade are gradually emptying themselves and everything withdraws more and more into the plantation district between Akwapim and Akim and into the Densu valley, where these people now build themselves good houses and where new villages arise.' He said that 'the rush into the Akropong Middle School' had 'noticeably slackened, because the parents now prefer to take their sons with them on the farms'.

[2] Though cocoa is recorded as growing north of Akantin, between Kade and Akwatia, south of Asuom and by the bank of the river Pra, near Praso Amuena, in the area between Abomosu and Anyinam and near Jejeti.

[3] This section marks cocoa-growing as far south as Pokuase, half way between Accra and Nsawam.

227

AN OUTLINE GEOGRAPHY

'cocoa and oil palm' are marked as growing on the Akwapim ridge; most of the 'camps' west of the river Densu were unfortunately overlooked, presumably owing to the difficulty of undertaking surveys in dense forest country, although 'Densuano', north-west of Mangoase, and 'Pawpawase' and Kukua farther north are shown. Neither this section nor the 'Komfrodua' (Koforidua) section marks any of the famous place-names such as Dedewa or Koransan;[1] the latter section merely notes that 'dense forest' clothed most of the area to the west of the Densu, except for a few camps near the river, including Krodaso (west of Tinkong) and Adidiso and Nankese—both of which seem to be wrongly located. No village called Suhum was noted, only the stream of that name. Cocoa was recorded as growing south of Asafo, by the Birim river and near Osino and both cocoa and the oil-palm were shown as growing in Krobo and Kyerepon country.

The first companies proper may have bought land in the area southeast of Suhum, but owing to the lack of farm maps there this is not certain. If they did not, then the first company lands in southern Akim country lay mainly to the south and east of Nankese, where all the land was sold by the chiefs of Maase and Asafo to farmers of diverse origin over a very short period from about 1906.[2] There were many farmers who first bought land in the Nankese area and then, a few years later, proceeded slightly farther west, nearer Suhum.

Although the 'assault' on the Suhum area was from two directions, the east and the south, and although Suhum itself has for long been the most remarkable, as well as the most populous, of all the stranger-towns in Akim Abuakwa, it was originally so slow in growing that inhabitants of neighbouring 'towns' (such as Amanase) often suppose, or pretend, that it did not come into existence until long after they had arrived—perhaps not until after 1918.[3] The 'foundation' of the town actually appears to date from the arrival of a group of Amanokrom (Akwapim) farmers who bought land to the west of the present town area from Omanhene Omoako Atta II himself—who is said to have taken over the land because of yet another boundary dispute between the chiefs of Apapam and Apedwa. The exact date of the purchase could not be ascertained, but was almost certainly between 1904 and 1908. As Dr J. M. Hunter considers that the Amanokrom people first started planting cocoa there between

[1] Nor did the Accra section of the next edition of the map, published in 1922, show any of the historic place-names in the forest west of the Densu, except for Metemano, Awusem, Nananko and 'Santrembo' (called Santrama on later editions).

[2] It may be that the land to the south of the area, near the river Mame, was sold slightly earlier than 1906, but dates were unascertainable. The evidence that much of the land nearer Nankese was sold in 1906 and 1907 is exceptionally good. See Appendix II. 3 (p. 62).

[3] A village called Suhum, perhaps an Akim hunter's camp, is shown on the map published by the Basel Missionaries in 1885, see p. 169. Suhum is also marked on two excellent maps of Kwahu and Eastern Akim compiled by F. G. Crowther and published in 1906 (*op. cit.*). (The only other 'stranger-village' shown on these maps is Asuboi.)

228

AN OUTLINE GEOGRAPHY

1908 and 1910 and as Suhum is always said to have been founded after the Mampong people arrived in Amanase to the south (probably in 1906), the nuclear settlement at Suhum may be regarded as dating from about 1908, which would make the recorded population of 135 in 1911 a reasonable figure. (The 1921 Census was so inefficiently conducted that neither Suhum, nor Nankese, were listed at all; in 1931 the recorded population of Suhum was 3,831 and of Nankese 2,655.)

Opinions differ as to whether Teacher Atta (*alias* Atta Sackey) was the first or the second 'chief' of Suhum—he was a twin brother of Attabuom, who is said to have been the leader of the group of Amanokrom kinsmen who bought the land. All the subsequent chiefs, down to the present day, have been members of the *abusua* stemming from the maternal grandmother of these brothers. It is said that in order to encourage other people to come and stay with them the Amanokrom people immediately resold parts of their land to Abonse, Fanti, Ga-Adangme and Ewe peoples. Certainly Suhum soon became the most 'cosmopolitan' of towns, migrant farmers from all the principal towns of origin being strongly represented there.[1]

In the Nankese area, as has been noted, virtually all the land was sold to strangers—and one of the few Akim farmers in the district actually 'bought back' some of the land he farms. But north-east of Suhum, some of the land was retained by Apedwa (Akim) farmers[2] and west of Suhum there are residential clusters inhabited solely by Apapam farmers—who own no more than about $2\frac{1}{2}$ per cent of the land, all their farms being small—just as there are in the Kwesi Komfo Area farther north (see Appendix II. 2, p. 60). A great proportion of all the land in the Ministry of Agriculture's Suhum West Area was bought by companies of Shai cocoa-farmers. Most of the companies in the Suhum area probably bought their land between about 1908 and 1914. At the same time the companies were moving north and west into what are now the Kabu Hill and Kwesi Komfo Areas, where most of the land, other than that retained by Akim farmers, was probably sold before about 1914, as suggested by the fact that many farmers said they owned bearing farms at the time of 'the influenza'—1918. A few individuals bought their land earlier than the companies, among them Omenako,[3] Jonas Kabu (a Ningo trader and produce-buyer, who bought his land about 1910) and Michael G. A. Israel, an

---

[1] Investigations into the history and social organization of Suhum lay outside the scope of the present inquiry—rewarding though they would be.

[2] The Apedwa people were exceptionally enterprising in the extent to which they imitated the strangers by farming on a scale which was larger than that traditional with Akim farmers, on land up to ten miles or more from their home towns. (Dr Hunter reports that many of their devastated farms in the Suhum area are now let off temporarily to Ewe food-farmers.)

[3] See Appendix III. 7 (p. 97). 1907 was suggested·as the date of purchase of his land, though this seems rather early.

AN OUTLINE GEOGRAPHY

Obosomase (Akwapim) man who is said to have resold much of his land, which he bought in 1911, to Krobo, Abiriw and other farmers.

About six miles west of Suhum, in an area only now being opened up by feeder roads, are several villages known as Dome and several more called Mfranta, and most of this land, also, was probably sold before 1914. Mfranta is a great centre for Berekuso farmers who migrated there by company. A Larteh man said that he had bought his land near the Ayensu river, slightly farther south, some time before 1916, when he had gone to live there.[1] Also on the Ayensu river is the locality known as Anum Apapam, where Anum farmers started buying land in about 1912.[2]

Meanwhile the Aburi farmers were working up from the south, Kofi Pare (see Appendix III. 4, p. 92) being perhaps as far north as any of the large family lands proper. In the Krabokese area the first sales may have occurred about 1908, or somewhat earlier; the four Nsakye brothers bought their large tract to the west of the road between Krabokese and Coaltar in 1909 (see Appendix III. 2, p. 89); around Coaltar most of the larger lands were sold at about that time. Although a great variety of farmers bought land in this district, it is a curious fact that no companies were involved; all informants (including those from Larteh) were insistent that their forebears had bought land on their own. (The earliest companies proper were, for some reason, bent on acquiring land in the area of Nankese and Suhum.) Whether any portion of land in the area between Coaltar to the north and Adeiso/Asikaisu/Mepom to the south was sold early or late appears to have been partly a question of which chief considered himself the rightful owner. The chief of Apapam was always in a hurry to sell, but the chief of Asamankese took his time—and this was not only because his boundaries were so exceptionally indeterminate.[3]

For many of the Aburi (and Nsakye) farmers, Sakyikrom (see Appendix III. 1, p. 86) provided a base, or jumping-off ground, for the northern and western migration. In 1960 Sakyikrom residents listed nineteen 'associated' southern lands, many of which had been founded by farmers who were members of one or other of the three 'Sakyikrom *abusua*'. A complex network of kinship in relation to land-ownership developed on

[1] He said that when he went there 'the surrounding lands had already been sold': 'At that time Kwame Mane [the chief of Apapam] was litigating at Accra and was in need of money, so his messengers came in search of people—they came to Asuoya'—where the informant was living.

[2] In 1957 of 23 farmers interviewed in Anum Apapam, 15 were from Anum, 3 were Shai, 3 Larteh, 1 Mampong and 1 Aburi. They claimed that they, or their forebears, had belonged to 7 different companies, most of them of mixed membership—though owing to the lack of farm maps, this could not be checked. The village that is now called Anum Apapam was, until very recently, that curious, but common, type of rural centre, which basically consists of nothing but a school and a market place, all the farmers living on their own lands.

[3] Thus the Kwame Tawiah land at Odumkyere (see Appendix III. 5, p. 96) would not have been sold as late as 1916 had the seller been Apapam, not Asamankese.

AN OUTLINE GEOGRAPHY

these southern lands, which would be hard to unravel satisfactorily today —worth while though the attempt would be. Few reliable dates have been established so far.

Reliable dates are also scanty in the interesting Mepom area where land-tenure conditions are so complex and in part so different from elsewhere in southern Akim Abuakwa.[1] Present-day residents of Mepom, nearly all of whom are strangers, consider the 'father' of the town to have been an Awutu man from Bereku on the coast, who probably reached the district in about 1906, accompanied by his nephew who, in 1958, vividly described their search for good cocoa-land. The Akwapim people usually had no occasion to search for land in this sense, as it was by and large true that up to 1918, during the stage of their migration on foot, all the trans-Densu lands in the historic cocoa-growing area were fit for cocoa,[2] so that the problem was to find a piece of land, rather than a suitable piece of land. This may have been one reason why in the twenties and thirties the Akwapim farmers were such easy victims of the chiefs from the Central Provinces and elsewhere who touted land that was 'no good' for cocoa. But for the Awutu, Fanti etc. farmers who came up from the south, passing through marginal cocoa-areas on the way, the problem was one of selection. The Awutu farmer described how his uncle had gone first to Kwanyaku, where 'he didn't like the land that was offered to him', and then successively to Duakwa, Nyakrom and Akroso, where he was still dissatisfied. Finally they had arrived in the Asamankese area where his uncle 'had tested some of the soil from the roots of a big tree which had been uprooted and found it good'. He had soon been joined by his family and having been given permission by the chief to farm where he liked, he picked out portions of the best farming land over a wide area. At least 39 farms with a total area of 162 acres,[3] were identified as belonging to members of this family in 1958.[4]

About six miles north-west of Asamankese is the well-known Quashie (or Akim-Boso) village,[5] which is situated on a very large tract, bought

[1] See Appendix v. 5 (p. 158).

[2] Except north and west of Asamankese, where much of the land proved to be marginal for cocoa—and where, anyway, the Akwapim bought little land.

[3] These farms were widely dispersed on five of the Ministry of Agriculture's blocks, a single annual rent being paid by the family for the lot.

[4] It is unlikely that any companies proper bought land in the Mepom area until after about 1918. Among other prominent individuals who had earlier bought, or otherwise acquired, land were several Ga: the son of one of them was registered, in 1958, as owning 52 acres from which 12,000 trees had been cut out, owing to swollen shoot; another had been a locomotive driver who had bought land in 1914 on his retirement. The date of the start of the influx of Awutu farmers into the neighbouring Asuokaw area could not be ascertained; most of their farms are to the west of the main road to Asamankese, most of the Akwapim farms being to the east.

[5] The atmosphere of the village, with its huge storey-house dominating the scene, reminded the visitor of southern Italy. (In 1948 the recorded population of Akim-Boso was 729, a figure which doubtless included the inhabitants of many outlying cottages.)

231

AN OUTLINE GEOGRAPHY

partly from the chief of Asamankese in about 1914 and partly, later on, from the chief of Akwatia. The purchasers were several brothers, whose mother (from Boso) had married a Fanti at Saltpond where the sons had been born; it is said that the money for the purchase of the land had been derived from trading. Much of the area proved to be unsuitable for cocoa and, to the brothers' great disappointment, only a small proportion of it was planted successfully—sufficient, however, to give a yield of several hundred loads annually.

About seven miles north-east of Asamankese, beneath the Atewa Range, lies the district known to the farmers as Oworam—a remote place, accessible only by heavy vehicle, and then with difficulty, when it was visited in 1958. (Farther north is Surum, or Suwurum.) This district and that known as Kwaboanta, a little farther south and east, lies at the extreme limit of the migration on foot of the Akwapim farmers who came up from the east. (The strangers who went to the Mepom area approached from a different direction.) In 1911 Asamankese was a populous town, with a recorded population of 3,319 (compared with 1,211 for Kibi and 1,020 for Apedwa) and although there is no evidence that the inhabitants were particularly keen cocoa-farmers at that time,[1] the strangers (as distinct from their 'brothers' the Anum)[2] were at any rate kept at arm's length and allowed to approach little nearer than the Oworam area, until later. Some of the first-comers to Oworam were Larteh farmers; one of them, Okrakwasi Danso,[3] said that he had arrived to inspect the land in 1914 and that there had been no one else farming there at that time so that he had had to buy his food from Akim people at Kwametiakrom, about forty-five minutes away.[4] Farmers from many towns flocked to this area both during the war[5] and afterwards; some were organized in companies, some bought land as individuals—one individual from Mampong bought at least eighty-seven acres; there are, also, a few Akim farmers, most of

[1] In about 1914 a few Asamankese farmers had started farming on a large scale in imitation of the strangers. One of them told the present writer that he had applied to the Asamankese stool for an allocation of land and had cut the boundary, just as though he had been a company of strangers. He had actually succeeded in appropriating as much as about 300 acres of forest land, about five miles from Asamankese. 'All the scholars favoured one area', he explained—meaning by this that educated farmers disliked small dispersed plots. Secure in his boundaries, he had planted 'softly, softly' and some of his land has remained uncleared up to the present day. He put his maximum annual yield in the past at fifty tons of cocoa.

[2] See Appendix VIII. 6 (p. 250).

[3] He said that the chief of Asamankese had demanded the following 'consultation fee': tobacco (five head), umbrella (ordinary black), sandals, chief's underwear (silk and very costly), a print cloth, a case of Schnapps and a big sheep. In addition those who had been deputed by the chief to take them to the land had demanded £24.

[4] As a check on whether a farmer was really the first to arrive in an area, it is often as well to ask where he first obtained his food.

[5] At about this time the chief of Akantin claimed the Oworam land and prolonged litigation ensued, culminating in a recent judgment in favour of Asamankese in the West African Court of Appeal.

232

AN OUTLINE GEOGRAPHY

them 'caretakers' (or their relatives) appointed by the chief.[1] As the remote Kwaboanta area, slightly farther east, is a little nearer Akwapim the farmers arrived there a few years earlier. A Shai letter-writer resident in Kwaboanta-Ada[2] insisted that a company of Shai and Kyerepon farmers had bought land there in 1911 from the chief of Apapam—and that a farmer always called 'James' had arrived there about 1909. Kwaboanta is an important centre for Obosomase[3] farmers, many of whom claim that their cocoa was in bearing there by 1918.

Up to 1918 the migrant farmers did most of their travelling on foot—this is the period called in this book 'the pre-lorry age'. As for the cocoa, man was the only beast of burden and the opening of Nsawam and Pakro railway stations, in 1910 and 1911, represented practical, though belated, recognition of the farmers' achievement—Ghana being from then on the world's largest cocoa-producer. There are, unfortunately, few reliable records relating to prices paid to farmers during the first few decades of the migration,[4] but the introduction of rail transport must have brought about a sudden increase in the net price, after meeting transport costs, received by the farmers. Given rising (net) prices and rising output, the farmers had more money in their pockets available for investment and it was no coincidence that at about this time certain Mamfe, Larteh, Kyerepon and Shai farmers started to make plans to build three foot-bridges across that troublesome barrier, the river Densu, at Mangoase, Mmetiamu (about five miles farther north) and Bibianiha (three miles farther north again). These bridges lay directly on the westward migratory path of the 'company farmers', most of whom by this time owned cocoa-lands on both sides of the river. They were built to enable the farmers to pass more conveniently (especially during the rainy season) between their various lands and their homeland and also to assist in the carrying of the cocoa produced across the river[5] to the nearest point on the railway line.

It would be difficult to exaggerate the symbolic significance of these bridges in relation to the whole story of the migration. Far from representing an old-fashioned form of self-help, they were a newfangled kind of development expenditure, financed by the farmers themselves. Two of the bridges were built by a Swiss engineer called Jacob Isliker—the third, at Bibianiha, was probably built by someone else. The Mmetiamu bridge[6]

---

[1] See Appendix v. 5 (p. 158).   [2] Called after farmers from Ada who bought land.

[3] Obosomase farmers are not found in many parts of southern Akim country, apart from Kwaboanta and Mepom.

[4] The figures in F.A.O., *Cacao*, p. 93, which purport to relate to the 'price paid to the producer' are, at any rate for the earlier days, prices at Accra, including costs of transport to Accra which were always effectively borne by the farmers themselves; depending on where the cocoa was grown, such costs of transport might represent a half or more of the Accra price.

[5] The Twi word for 'the other side of a river' is *asuogya*: thus an Akwapim farmer with a farm on the Akim side might say—*m'fuw no wɔ asuogya* ('my farm is across the river').

[6] See Appendix viii. 3 (p. 243) for a summary of certain documents relating to the building and operation of this bridge and for brief notes on the other bridges.

233

AN OUTLINE GEOGRAPHY

cost the Larteh and Mamfe farmers, who put up the money, about £2,000; opened in 1914, when a three-penny toll was charged to foot-passengers (of whom 25,469 passed over between 24 April and the end of the year) it was business not philanthropy and may, ultimately, have yielded a profit. Although the collection of tolls probably stopped as long ago as about 1937, this bridge still stands sturdily (see plate 2), apparently requiring, unlike so many more modern development works, no maintenance whatsoever. The bridge at Mangoase, which was built at about the same date, is said to have been demolished in 1937 when a road bridge was built by the Public Works Department. The Bibianiha bridge may have been built a few years later—it still stands and like the bridge at Mmetiamu is becoming increasingly useful today as the planting of the devastated trans-Densu lands proceeds. So far as is known, this is the first mention of these bridges in print.[1]

In this summary account of the migration by foot, scarcely any attention has been paid to the north-eastern fringe area of Akim Abuakwa, adjoining Krobo country, which has been neglected mainly owing to the lack of farm maps in most parts of it.[2] It is an area where Krobo farmers greatly predominate. As early as 1907, Nene Mate Kole complained that the chief of Begoro was selling the same land two or three times over and was refusing access to lands he had sold; this chief was subsequently de-stooled for selling the people's land without permission, as was his successor. South-west of Begoro, for instance, between Asafo and Agyapoma and near Adonkwanta, there are also great concentrations of Krobo farmers. The only Akwapim people who had made their way in this direction to any extent before 1918 were the Akropong and the Kyerepon. Akropong farmers acquired land in the Bosuso area as early as 1907, if not earlier, and an Adukrom farmer said that he had purchased land there in 1908. A Ga trader bought an immense land near Bosuso (Adjeikrom) at an early date and resold much of it to a company of Krobo.

A Postscript on the Lorry Age

Soon after 1918 it became the fashion, for those who could afford it, to travel by lorry for most of the way—the lorry age had dawned. A few

---

[1] Apart from Polly Hill, 'The Bridge at Mmetiamu', in *West Africa*, 27 May 1961. The present writer first became aware of the existence of the bridges on reading an unpublished work dated 1938 on the history of Akwapim, by James Lawrence Tete, a Larteh surveyor, and a son of one of the farmers who had subscribed towards the building of the Mmetiamu bridge, which was in the possession of Nana Okanta Obrentri II, the late Benkumhene of Akwapim. She is most grateful to Mr Eugene Ohene Walker, the elder brother of the late Benkumhene, for taking her to see the bridge at Mmetiamu and for introducing her to Mr James Tete Aborah who had preserved the records relating to it; Mr Walker, who is seen in plate 3, also rendered much invaluable help on countless other occasions.

[2] Another 'mapless' area that has, also, been neglected is that part of Akim Kotoku often called 'Akroso' by the farmers—after a large town of that name. There is evidence that Akwapim farmers bought land there at least as early as 1908.

234

AN OUTLINE GEOGRAPHY

lorries had been plying such roads as existed much earlier,[1] but a greatly increased import of vehicles resulted from improved shipping facilities in 1919. In the report on the 1921 Census it was noted that 'it is now quite usual to motor from Sekondi to Accra in one day'; there were said to be 706 miles of motor roads in the Eastern Province; and in Accra alone, in 1921, there were 586 lorries and 214 cars and there were 303 cars and 860 lorries in the rest of the Eastern Province.[2]

As for the availability of land in southern Akim Abuakwa, the position in 1918 was that the chiefs of Apapam and Apedwa had sold nearly all that they had (other than the little retained by their own people)—though much of the land that had been sold remained, as yet, unplanted with cocoa. The chief of Asamankese, on the other hand, had not yet parted with all his unexploited forests and went on doing so throughout the nineteen-twenties—in hilly and mountainous areas sales were made as late as the nineteen-thirties.[3] The chiefs of Asafo and Maase had sold all their more remote land and now, rather curiously, proceeded to sell substantial portions nearer their town areas.[4] The chief of Tafo still had land to sell and in 1925 he was destooled (though subsequently re-enstooled) for 'unlawful sale of stool lands'—in 1927 the chiefs of Apinaman and Abomosu suffered the same fate. But it was clear enough to the more enterprising Akwapim, Krobo, Shai and Ga farmers that a land shortage was fast-developing and in the nineteen-twenties, when the world price of cocoa was still reasonably high, they started 'to buy land forward' (as they sometimes themselves put it) at a greatly increased rate, in more distant areas, whence they travelled by lorry or train. Most of the farmers had no immediate need for the land which they thus acquired—usually through companies. Much of the land proved to be unsuitable for cocoa. In listing the areas in which the farmers bought, or otherwise

[1] Thus it was noted in the report on the 1921 Census that in the Volta River District the first vehicles had been introduced in 1913 when Swanzy's had imported six Ford cars. In 1909, W. S. D. Tudhope noted (*op. cit.*, p. 44) that motors were 'largely utilized in conveying cocoa and trade goods to and from the port of Accra and the trading centres of Nsuam (*sic*) and Dodowah. . .'—this being just before the opening of the Nsawam railway station.

[2] According to *Transportation in Ghana*, p. 66, motor vehicle imports for the first five years after the war averaged 734, of which about 70 per cent came from the United States— 'it was the Ford truck that led the way'. By 1922 much more tar was being used to seal road surfaces.

[3] In April 1959, accompanied by the Rev. Moses Ntow and by two hunters as guides, the present writer ascended the 1,618 ft mountain Nyanao (west of Nsawam), by way of the Aburi family land Duayeden, to the south, and was astonished to find a migrant cocoa-farmer, Otu Addo of Amanokrom, living in a neat and comfortable house, set between huge rocks, on the topmost pinnacle. (See plate 6.) Mr Addo said that his maternal uncle had been one of a company of five (including one Krobo and three Abiriw men), who had bought land on the mountain top from the chief of Asamankese in 1931, but that the others had all since departed, leaving him and his wife there alone. Much of the southern side of the mountain was clothed in thick cocoa-groves—an island of health in an ocean of swollen shoot—and other farmers were encountered in the ascent.

[4] Much to the annoyance, as was said in Asafo, of returning ex-servicemen and others, who soon found that there was no land left.

235

acquired,[1] land in the nineteen-twenties, it is not being suggested that they actually started to plant there at that time.

Following extensive inquiries in Akwapim and elsewhere, a list of the principal districts (outside southern Akim country) in which land was bought in the nineteen-twenties has been compiled, supplementary information being drawn (see Appendix II. 1, p. 55) from the reports of the Reserve Settlement Commissioners. During the twenties mixed companies became more common, groups of people from two or three towns combining together to buy land, each sub-group perhaps subsequently managing its own affairs. The Akwapim surveys suggest that while the geographical pattern of migration during this period did not vary greatly from town to town (obviously the general direction in which the farmers moved was no longer influenced by the exact situation of the town on the ridge), it yet remained true that if one company bought land in a district it tended to attract others from the same home town. The inclusion of a place-name in the list does not necessarily mean that land was sold nearby—places named by farmers are often those where they alight from their lorries. (See map 17.)

(a) The Oda and Kade areas and north-western Akim country generally, including Aduasa, Abenase, Okyereso, Abodum, Adibease, Kyia, Nkwaten, Apoli, Otumi, Nkwatanan;

(b) The Begoro district, including the area now in the Dede Forest Reserve (see Appendix II. 1, p. 59)—this shades into

(c) Kwahu country, in the neighbourhood of the Worobon river;

(d) An area of south-western Kwahu which shades into Akim country, the principal centres listed by the farmers being: Asubone, Kokrompe, Akuase, Pankese and Nwiso (farther west). (Accra and Kumasi had been linked by rail in 1923 and the railway passed through some of these towns.)

(e) The area always known to the farmers as Twifu Praso (or Praso) after the name of the station where the railway crosses the river Pra. (The great rush to buy land here started after 1926 when the Central Railway line reached Oda.)

(f) Other areas in the then Central Provinces approached by the new railway (some of which are in Akim country), e.g. Aperade, Assin-Fosu, Akankawsu;

[1] The Akwapim farmers have always preferred to buy land outright if possible, but as time has gone by they have found vendors in many districts increasingly unwilling to part with their land unconditionally. However, time is usually on the side of the buyer, who seldom finds himself obliged (except in the Asamankese area, see p. 158) to adhere indefinitely to terms agreed originally (such as that of handing over an *abusa* share of the cocoa)—and it often happens that he soon finds himself effectively in the same position as he would have been had he bought the land outright. It must be emphasized that this is not a general survey of tenure conditions in Ghana. There are many other regions and districts, besides Ashanti, where land is seldom sold, but as the Akwapim Case Histories show (Appendix VII. 3, p. 200), Akwapim farmers acquired little land there.

236

AN OUTLINE GEOGRAPHY

(g) Parts of the Abomosu area of northern Akim Abuakwa (where on the whole native Akim farmers predominate), including Ekoso;

(h) Ashanti-Akim, e.g. Gyadem, Bankame;

(i) Wasa and the west generally, isolated pockets in an immense area;

(j) Adanse (Ashanti), e.g. Adanse-Praso, bordering on Akim country.[1]

The world price of cocoa began to fall in 1929 and, never recovering from the great depression, it remained very low throughout the thirties,[2] except in 1936–7. For this reason and also perhaps because the farmers already owned so much unplanted land, the pace of land acquisition slowed down in the thirties as the surveys in Akwapim showed—see also Appendix II. 1 (p. 58). Nor did the southern migrants explore many new districts at this time, though a few of them travelled to newer areas of Ashanti (other than Ashanti-Akim and Adanse, included in the list above); the first moves nortn of the Afram river into the scarcely in-habited Afram plains[3] were made; and, most important, many Akwapim, Ga and Krobo (as well as southern Ewe) farmers acquired land rights in a large new cocoa area north of Jasikan in the Volta Region[4]—two of the best-known centres being Kadjebi and Papase.

Much the most important new area in which the southern migrants have acquired land since the war has been Sefwi-Wiawso and the fact that this district is sometimes vaguely referred to by farmers themselves as 'Ashanti' may be one reason for the erroneous, widespread and persistent belief that the southern farmers have 'gone to Ashanti'. From inquiries made by Miss C. McGlade[5] in Asawinso in 1956, it is clear that most of the principal migrant farmers of southern Ghana are strongly represented there. An Obosomase (Akwapim) man, who spoke of himself as the 'Omanhene' of the stranger-farmers in the Sefwi district, estimated that there were 3,200 of them there in 1956, including (remarkably enough) fifty Akim; he said that he had started farming there in 1942 and that it had been his example that had encouraged so many others to follow. There has been no migration by southerners into Ashanti to compare

[1] An unpublished report on land disputes in the Obuase district of Adanse, by the African Studies Branch of the Colonial Office, 1947, mentions sales of land from 1928 onwards to Akwapim, Krobo, Ga and Ningo cocoa-farmers.

[2] See Appendix VII. 7 (p. 218).

[3] The present-day migration into this 'hunting desert' where there are patches of fertile land, especially in the neighbourhood of remote Odonkawkrom, has many interesting features, not the least of which is the willingness of labourers to be recruited for work there. It is said that Krobo cocoa-farmers bought land at Faso (near Odonkawkrom) as early as 1928: see J. R. Wallis, 'The Kwahus—their connection with the Afram Plain', *Transactions of the Gold Coast and Togoland Historical Society*, vol. I, part III, p. 24.

[4] See Appendix II. 1 (p. 59). The present writer has, so far, given little attention to this very interesting new area, where planting began on a large scale in the late nineteen-thirties.

[5] At that time a Research Fellow of the University College of Ghana. See Cocoa Research Series No. 2, issued by the Economics Research Division, University College of Ghana (cyclostyled).

237

AN OUTLINE GEOGRAPHY

with this (though small pockets of Akwapim and other southerners, including Anum and Boso, do exist in many parts of Ashanti), but an Adukrom farmer who said that he had started 'renting' land near Tepa in 1944 claimed that about a hundred other Kyerepon farmers were also farming there, each on land which he had acquired for himself. There may be a considerable number of Boso, Aburi and Berekuso farmers (as well as others) in the Sunyani area; and southern strangers are scattered about in the Goaso area, though to judge from a report by Mr F. R. Bray[1] most of the farmers now engaged in opening up this important area came from elsewhere in Ashanti.

APPENDIX VIII. 1

WILLIAM ADJABENG QUANSAH SOLOMON

William Adjabeng Quansah Solomon,[2] a famous creditor-farmer, is believed to have been born about 1860. His father, Cobbina Kplee, had been a farmer and was chief of Papase, near Kotoku, south of Nsawam. His mother, Dede, was a member of the well-known Ankrah family of Accra; her brother was Adjabeng the big Accra landowner and trader; he had had an elder brother Ade who had built the large house near the old Kingsway stores, where the family still resides. During his uncle Adjabeng's lifetime Solomon was a clerk; on his uncle's death in 1887 he became a rubber trader, travelling to Ashanti, Cape Coast and Lagos and it is said to have been from the profits of this trading that he bought his first farming lands. The family think a land near Anyinam was the first he acquired, which may be true as he was in possession before 1901;[3] if so, his second purchase, in about 1895, was the immense area at Agyinase, near Pakro, referred to on p. 221. There he retained a vast acreage, not all planted with cocoa, for the use of himself and his family (he is said to have built five houses for his relatives in Pakro), having resold much land, particularly to Shai and Kpone[4] people. In all his farming work he was assisted by his brother, Alfred Asong Solomon, who was said to have died in 1917.

Throughout his life Solomon followed the policy of buying (or having pledged to him) a fresh cocoa-farm whenever he had any money to spare—he bought very little, if any, unplanted land apart from that at Agyinase and Anyinam. A list of the farms he owned at the time of his death in 1936 follows. Obviously the total number of farms is an arbitrary figure—there were said to be 27 farms within the Agyinase estate alone—but, for what it is worth, this total is put at 88. That he was accustomed to managing without cash was shown by the fact that he left none when he died; the

[1] See *Cocoa Development in Ahafo, West Ashanti*, Achimota, 1959 (cyclostyled).

[2] The writer is indebted to Mr Robert Solomon, son of Quansah Solomon, for his assistance during a visit to Pakro in 1959 and to Mr Robert Adjabeng Ankrah, the present head of the family (his paternal grandfather was the brother of Quansah Solomon's mother), for much information including access to the report of Capt. William Price-Jones.

[3] The following record, dated 22 February 1901, happened to be noted among Government Archives: 'All the land after the first stream from Anyinam (River Birrim) up to the point at which the road had been cleared by the people of English [i.e. Nrese] had been sold to one Solomon of Accra for a sum of £100 by the Chief of Mosu.' (ADM 1/839.)

[4] On one visit to Pakro in 1959, 6 out of 15 informants said that their land had been bought from Solomon; one of them, from Kpone, said that his father, who had bought the land, had belonged to a company of about 22 farmers. Many of the purchasers had previously been labourers.

WILLIAM ADJABENG QUANSAH SOLOMON

United Africa Company advanced him such sums as £750 in return for his promise to deliver all his cocoa to them. This system of lending all he had to other farmers, while simultaneously receiving advances from the U.A.C., worked very well until his death when the manager of his estate reported that there were 'no capital or sources of income [apart from rents from a few houses] out of which funds can be got to carry the Estate over the difficult and expensive period of the main crop season'. On 16 November 1936 the manager reported that 100 bags of cocoa had already come from the Agyinase land and that 'a lot more was expected'; present-day informants said that the yield had once been 1,000 bags (over 2,000 loads) and that there had been much other produce besides.

List of Cocoa-Farms (or Land) owned by William Adjabeng Quansah Solomon at the time of his death in 1936[1]

Suhum (1 farm) Five labourers from the Northern Territories were employed on this farm near Okorase which had been bought from an Akropong man. About 200–500 loads of cocoa had been produced on it last season. 'Deceased paid the transport charges from the farm to Nsawam and gave the labourers 2s. each for each load of 75 lbs they brought.' One of Solomon's wives was in charge.

Asuboi (2 farms) Each of these farms had been pledged to Solomon. An *nkotokuano* labourer was employed on each of them: one produced 16 loads and the other 50 bags of cocoa.

Nsawam (1 farm) The farm had been sold by a Ga farmer some seven years previously and lay north of Nsawam. Twenty bags of cocoa were produced. Most of the area was bush.

Suhum (1 farm) No further information.

Kwanyaku (12 farms plus 8 farms) Most of the 12 farms had been bought at an Accra auction. The original owners were working there as *nkotokuano* labourers, for which they were paid 2s. a load; 3 Hausa labourers were also employed. Of the group of 8 farms several had been bought under writ of Fi Fa, the Ohene of Duakwa having won a case in respect of payment of tolls; one had been bought for £72. Some of the farms were recorded as bearing 'very good cocoa'. The Manager considered that the farms in this area were worth at least £3,000.

Agyinase (27 farms) 'At Agyinase the deceased has a very large house and compound. He appears to have made it his more or less permanent place of abode and to have lived there in a sort of feudal state' with his wives and servants. 'The deceased has an enormous piece of land in the neighbourhood of Agyinase, both sides of the railway, more or less round with its centre at the Agyinase House and a radius of about a mile and a half. There are 27 farms on this land. I did not visit the farms as it will take more than a fortnight to go round all the farms...' Later on the Manager returned to the area: 'I was shown round some farms of deceased at the foot of Abrim Hill. These farms border on with farms now cultivated by certain Shai labourers who bought their farms from the deceased some time ago.' The land, he noted, had been bought from the Omanhene of Akropong. There were 5 paid labourers on the farms, but, this number being insufficient, 12 more labourers (at £7 for the year, £8 for the headman) were to be engaged. A number of near-by farms [perhaps not included in the 27] had been pledged to him by Larteh and other

[1] Capt. William Price-Jones of the Supreme Court was appointed temporary manager of Solomon's estate on his death and the list of farms (and other particulars) comes from his report, which also lists certain other property. The manager took up his duties in May 1936 and on 23 November 1936 the court granted probate of the will and the manager was discharged from his duties.

APPENDIX VIII. 1

farmers. 'We have been walking steadily for 3 days—and I think I can say that most, if not all, of deceased's property in the Agyinase-Pakro district is known to me now.' The Manager concluded that the lands were 'very valuable and, if properly administered in the future, capable of becoming more valuable still'.

Asamankese (1 farm) Probably situated near Asuokyene, the farm had been 'bought' from an Accra man and rent was payable under the Asamankese renting system—see Appendix v. 5. Labourers were employed at 2s. 9d. a load, and the farm produced about 190 loads of cocoa.

Marfo (4 farms) Nsawam area. One of the farms was described as 'circular, diameter 350 yds, full of young cocoa in excellent condition and full bearing'. Of the remainder 1 had been sold, 2 pledged, and 3 *nkotokuano* labourers were employed.

Akuffo village (10 farms) All the farms had been pledged. Eighty-five loads were produced on two of them; some of them were considered 'useless'.

Pampanso (1 farm) A large farm with 2 labourers, a headman, cocoa and foodstuffs. 'It originally belonged to [X] of Mampong who mortgaged it to [Y] of Nsawam. The owner mortgaged it for a second time to the deceased. Later the deceased discovered this and took over the first mortgage.'

Anyinam (1 farm) This is the land referred to on p. 238n. It was stated in this report that the land had been a gift in return for some service rendered 'in a matter of litigation some years ago in Accra'. There was no cocoa there.

Asikasu (3 farms) An Awutu man had pledged a farm for between £100 and £150 and the other farms had also been pledged.

Kyerebu (4 farms) West of Nsawam. All 4 farms had been pledged by one man. One of them was 'very large' and had been pledged for about £150. The farms were being looked after by a headman.

Adiembra (2 farms) One of the farms had been bought from a man who had in turn bought it from someone else; it was 'bounded on all sides' by land owned by the famous Mampong man Peter Botchway. With reference to the other, a small farm covered with dense bush, the manager felt sure 'that the deceased could not have seen this property before he lent money on it'.

Sakyikrom (1 farm) The farm had been pledged in about 1931 for £20.

APPENDIX VIII. 2

'OMANHENE THE FARMER'

Kwasi Akuffo was installed Omanhene of Akwapim in 1895 in succession to his maternal uncle Omanhene Kwame Fori; he was destooled in 1907, following the battle of Ankwasu (see below), being ultimately re-enstooled in 1920. He was one of Ghana's pioneer cocoa-farmers and considerable interest therefore attaches to an immensely long letter which he addressed to the Secretary for Native Affairs on 1 March 1915,[1] in which he complained that much of his personal property, including many cocoa farms, had been removed from him and treated as stool property. Whatever allowance may be made for the exaggerations resulting from personal enmity, the list of cocoa-farms provided in the letter is an impressive indication of Kwasi Akuffo's enthusiasm and commercial foresightedness.

Kwasi Akuffo argued in his letter (para. 35) that 'there is no custom in Akwapim for an Omanhene to make farms'—that 'every farm of an Omanhene whether on a stool or on a private land is considered a private property'. Therefore, he had 'suc-

---

[1] The letter was written from his farm-of-exile, situated at Bogyabiyedom ('Akufo' on the present 1-inch Ghana survey) on the main road north of Nsawam.

'OMANHENE THE FARMER'

ceeded to the late Omanhene Quami Fori only in State Emblems'. But his predecessor had been an active land purchaser:

'Quami Fori, when Omanhene, bought a piece of land at Panto in Akwapim and made exchange with part of a stool land at Densu to obtain an additional portion to his Panto land. On this he caused a big village to be built, caused more extensive farms to be made thereon when Omanhene, caused cocoa farms to be made at Amanfo on our family land. He bought two portions of land in Kwabeng and Akoko in Eastern Akim and another two pieces of land in Akwapim between Mamfe and Larte...'

The successors to all these lands, Kwasi Akuffo complained, had been 'the present Omanhene, his mother and brothers'.

Kwasi Akuffo listed twelve pieces of personal property of which he claimed to have been 'uncustomarily deprived'. The list included house property and various local farms, some of which, he claimed, yielded a great deal of cocoa—there was one at Amanprobi (supposed to yield 100 loads) and another between Mampong and Amanokrom, with 600 to 700 loads. More distant farms included one at Tinkong (over 200 loads), one at 'Densu' (over 100 loads) and then there was 'my celebrated cocoa farms, rubber and provision farms and a big village at Atabui,[1] alias Asuabiri, yielding cocoa about 1,000 loads a year, bought and built on it six years before I became Omanhene'—this having 'now fallen into *Sanna*[2] to my great wonder'; adjoining the latter there was also a 'portion of land called Atabui Mmease or Otannurumase land, filled up with cocoa', which again had been bought before he became Omanhene. Finally, he presented an elaborate story as to how he had come into personal possession of land at Akim-Akropong.

Kwasi Akuffo claimed that because of his interest in farming he was mocked at, particularly by the then Omanhene, and nicknamed 'Omanhene the Farmer'. Those who mocked should remember, he said, that many in more 'respectable professions' owed their training to the receipts from his cocoa-farms.

He claimed that he had obtained the land and village on which he was then residing from 'a collection of other people' who looked on him with pity. But he was still insecure, there being the threat of the sale of 'all my belongings by public auction' to meet debts incurred in fighting for his rights.

In the records of the Kibi State Council there are more references to 'Omanhene the farmer'. A case that came before the Omanhene's court on 10 August 1906, related to a dispute between Kwaku Nkansa and Kwadjo Fosu (who said that he had acted throughout on behalf of Kwasi Akuffo) regarding land at Krabokese which each of them claimed to have bought from the stool of Apapam. Kwadjo Fosu claimed that after considering the purchase of a land at Hwereso, which was rejected owing to its proximity to the disputed Apapam/Apedwa boundary, the land at Krabokese had been bought in January 1901. So few records relating to the procedure of land-purchase in the early days exist that it seems worth quoting the following extract from the court records:

'We said that in order to avoid any trouble we don't want to buy any land near the boundary. From Fwereso [*sic*] we went to Krabo Kese [*sic*] with Kwaku Sono [who had been deputed by the elders of Apapam to sell the land]. Kwaku Sono told us that he had sold the land to nobody before. Omanhene Akuffo said that he wants the land extending from Mmensu to Bunkua northern part and from Mmensu to Krabo Kese near Apapam Road; and from Apapam Road to Kuawa stream and from Kuawa

---

[1] To the west of Adawso.

[2] That is it had become stool land, *sannaa* being the stool treasury.

241

APPENDIX VIII. 2

stream to Bonuwa [Bonkua?] road. The bargain was £150, *guaha* was 12s., £8 for cutting boundary and 2 sheep were paid to Kwaku Sono. Omanhene Akuffo said Kwaku Sono should come to him at Akropong for £150. Kwaku Sono went to Akropong and made plan of the land to Omanhene Akuffo. Kwaku Sono's son, by name Abuagye, made the plan[1] on paper for Omanhene Akuffo. Omanhene Akuffo paid £20 each on account to Kwaku Sono. Omanhene Akuffo asked Kwaku Sono to let his son Abuagye go to Accra to Mr. Obuobisa to register the document. He did so. Omanhene Kwasi Akuffo sent me and his nephew Bediako to put boards on the land... We went to the land Krabo Kese and put his name written on board there. We did so on the four corners. Kwame Agyiri, the hunter, came and reported to Omanhene Akuffo that the boards had been taken away from the land. Upon enquiry Omanhene Akuffo heard that Apapam people took away the boards. Apapam people sent messengers to Omanhene Akuffo to inform him that Kwaku Sono stole the land and sold to him. Omanhene Akuffo replied to the messenger that he sent to Amoa Yao, odikro of Apapam, before he bought the land from Kwaku Sono, it was the odikro who sent Kwaku Sono to sell the land to him, therefore it was not a stolen property...'

Later on it was found out that Yao Bosompem, of Apapam, had sold part of the land to Ahwerease people. The Apapam people gave them another land instead. 'We did not know then that Nkansa had bought any land there...' 'Nkansa had sold his land to Akuapim man by name Dareman [Daaman?] living at Nsawam. Omanhene Akuffo, after Nkansa had refused to attend his calling drove him from the land, he uprooted the *ntɔmmɛ*[2] trees from the land...'

That judgment was given for Nkansa is made clear from the abstract of a later, and connected, case given in *Cases in Akan Law*, Case A.30: this later case also mentions a judgment in favour of the chief of Apapam against Kwaku Sono.

An account of the battle of Ankwasu (a village about four miles east of Pakro) is given in Edward Samson's[3] *A Short History of Akuapim and Akropong* (1908). Originally Akuffo had been found guilty of selling land near Pakro which was not his property to Solomon. This judgment had been reversed on appeal by Chief Justice Sir William Brandford Griffith and, in jubilant mood, Akuffo felt entitled to claim all the land in the area. Samson records (p. 18) that it was on 11 January 1907 that Akuffo 'left his capital with some of his chiefs for the purpose of giving each of them a share of Wiapa's land. On the following day he was surrounded by Wiapa and his people, who attacked and in the fight which ensued both sides sustained some considerable losses.' The disturbances continued and the Governor arrived in Akropong, to put a stop to them, on 25 January; Akuffo then admitted that while he had got judgment in respect of the piece of land he had sold to Solomon, this did not apply 'to the whole land of the Tutu people'. Akuffo's destoolment followed.

Although the affairs of Akuffo were attended by so much litigation, the origin of the land-selling activities of his predecessor Kwame Fori (to whom Akuffo acted as court clerk) has never been satisfactorily explained. This Appendix therefore concludes with two extracts from the published papers of the West African Lands Committee, which suggest (if Crowther's understanding was correct) that the situation was

---

[1] The reason for the drawing of a plan and the registration of a document may have been that part of the land was bought as a 'concession'; for reasons which are unclear, a few educated farmers bought 'concession land' for cocoa-farming in the years immediately following the passing of the Concessions Ordinance in 1900.

[2] *Ntɔmmɛ* trees were used then, as they are now, for marking boundaries.

[3] The Aburi minister. (This 'civil war' is well-remembered in Akwapim today.)

'OMANHENE THE FARMER'

much more complex than is generally allowed and that land-selling in the Densu valley by the chiefs of Asafo and Maase started very early. (Although Crowther's inquiries related only to the area north of Mangoase, the chiefs of Maase and Asafo may have sold land farther south; presumably all the land in question lay east of the river Densu.)

'Between 1860 and 1870, Afrim, odikro of Asafo, and his brother, the odikro of Maase, started to sell land in the Densu valley to individuals of Larteh and Shai. This was resented by Ampowa of Kukurantumi, who disputed their right. Atta Obiwom, Omanhene of Akyem-Abuakwa, probably unable to determine the case, declared the land from the Kentenkere Falls [south west of Koforidua] southward as far as the known boundaries of the Akwapim stools, forfeit to his own stool, that is, Kyebi [Kibi]. His successor, Amoako Atta I, apparently doubtful of the propriety of this act, disposed of the disputed land by gift to the stool of Akropong, that is to Asa, Omanhene of Akropong. All the evidence I have taken is clear on the point that it was given to the stool of Akropong and not to the people of Akwapim . . . the stool of Akropong held it by no inherent right of paramountcy. . . Kwamin Fori and Akuffo, particularly the latter, appear to have sold nearly all this land, parting with the fee-simple of large farms to individuals without respect to their tribes and at the present day the greater portion of it is held by private individuals.'[1]

Owusu Ansa, Omanhene of Akwapim, in a letter[2] written from Mangoase and dated 21 July 1913, stated, with what accuracy is not known, that 'nearly all the lands from Kentenkren to Mangoase were sold by ex-Omanhene to private persons contrary to native custom'. He went on to say that there had been two test cases. The second of these was in April 1908 before Sir W. Brandford Griffith:

'. . . after His Honour heard that Akuffo sold 300 or more pieces of stool land, the learned judge suggested a compromise and the Omanhene consented to a judgment that the buyer from Akuffo retains the land for 25 years to reap the benefit of his cocoa trees on payment of £5 a year for ground-rent and the court then thought that it would be an easy matter to get all other such purchasers from Akuffo to consent to such payments, but I have found difficulty from year to year to collect anything from them, and had to sue even the defendant in that test case . . . for arrears of rent, and, in fact, very few of them have acknowledged the title of my stool lands occupied by them since the 1908 test case.'

APPENDIX VIII. 3

THE BRIDGE AT MMETIAMU

(with notes on the Mangoase and Bibianiha bridges and
the access roads to Akwapim)

Mr James Tete Aborah of Larteh, son of James Ashong (see table, p. 244) has, fortunately, preserved some of the account books relating to the building and operation of the footbridge over the river Densu at Mmetiamu (see plate 2 and p. 233) and it seems worth summarizing some of the fragmentary information they contain—adding a few further facts gleaned by oral interview.[3]

---

[1] From a letter from F. G. Crowther, dated 17 October 1913. It was explained in the letter that it was because he had been exploring land-tenure questions in connexion with the building of the railway north of Mangoase that these facts had emerged. (W.A.L.C., *Correspondence and Papers*, p. 110.)

[2] W.A.L.C., *Correspondence and Papers*, p. 112.

[3] The writer is indebted to Mr D. Brokensha for assistance in collecting information.

APPENDIX VIII. 3

It was Mr Eugene Ohene Walker, of Larteh, who introduced the present writer to Mr Aborah in 1958. 'My father,' said Mr Aborah, 'was a farmer and he made pottery and reared pigs and he got an income to buy land at Domeabra [on the eastern bank of the river]; this was in Nana Akrofi's time'—i.e. between 1894 and 1900. He said that the group who bought the land consisted of his paternal grandfather, his father (James Ashong), his father's elder brother (Israel Kwame), together with another Larteh man, Akotey Kofi, who was a friend not a relative. 'The family had one big village and Kofi had another village; they did not resell any of their land. Out of the proceeds from this land they had money to buy another land'—at Koransan, to the west of the river, the purchasing group this time being Israel Kwame, James Ashong and a Larteh friend, Kumi Yirebi. Later on Israel Kwame, again accompanied by James Ashong, bought a third land near Asuboi. Domeabra was said to have been 'the largest place'.

After he had bought the Asuboi land, Israel Kwame 'called a meeting of the whole neighbourhood and told them that owing to floods they often could not get back after they had gone to the other side of the river and that many women and children had lost their lives'. He it was who proposed that they should build a bridge and it was suggested that Jacob Isliker, a Swiss 'building engineer', should be employed for the purpose. (Isliker had originally been employed by the Basel Mission, married successively two Akropong women, the first of whom, Irene Ayesu, bore him seven children, and died in Mangoase, where he is buried, in 1920—his grave being unmarked and overgrown.) The accounts show that Isliker received £10 in 1910 for the 'plan estimate' of the bridge. His employment began on 1 January 1911 at a monthly salary of £20. At about this time, as the table on p. 245 shows, 'the capital' began to be collected in instalments. In 1914 the account book records the 'capital cost of construction' as £2,000, but the records showing how the balance, of nearly £1,000, had been raised could not be found.

According to Jacob Isliker's accounts for 1911–12, he drew his salary for the months of January to May 1911, July to October 1911 and February and March 1912. As the following General Summary of Expenses shows, two of the sponsoring farmers, Israel Kwame and Eliza Kwadjo, also claimed substantial salaries, presumably as managers. The grand total of expenses for 1911–12 fell short of the (doubtless rounded) total of £2,000, and there is no information as to how this balance of over £300 was spent.

General Summary of Expenses for the Bridge at Mmetiamu 1911–12
(Accounts kept by Jacob Isliker)

	£	s.	d.
Salary to building engineer[1]	232	6	6
Tools	11	10	0
Nails, bolts, iron sheets	171	9	6
Stones, sand and transport of same	108	1	0
Cement and transport of same	244	19	0
Timber	271	6	9
Rough timber	9	16	9
Wages to workmen	411	11	5
Wages to messengers and cutting of paths	10	12	11
Subsistence, drams, stationery etc.[2]	21	11	11
	1,493	5	9

[1] and [2]. See next page.

244

THE BRIDGE AT MMETIAMU

By additional payments

For salary claimed by Israel Kwame	102	0	0
For salary claimed by Eliza Kwadjo	76	10	0
For gratification for Mr Benson	7	0	0
	185	10	0
Grand Total	1,678	15	9

[1] Jacob Isliker.
[2] The total included 'a bottle of rum for engaging stonebreakers' (which, according to Mr E. O. Walker, would have been 'Elephant best gin') and 'contractor's drinks'—1s. Isliker's hammockmen to Adawso cost 16s.

The 'Capital'

	Subscribers	£		
1.	Israel Kwami	114	(a)	
		100	(a)	219
		5	(b)	
2.	Johannes Akrofi	102	(a)	
		16	(c)	132
		14	(d)	
3.	James Ashong	100	(a)	125
		25	(b)	
4.	Eliza [Elisha] Kwadjo	103	(a)	103
5.	Salomo Ohene Assah	103	(a)	
		25	(b)	143
		15	(c)	
6.	George Paul Kumi	50	(a)	80
		30	(e)	
7.	Johanes Awua Sono	50	(a)	50
8.	Asamoa Kumah	22	(a)	
		28	(b)	70
		20	(c)	
9.	Asamani and Adjeikrom	16	(a)	
		4	(b)	50
		20	(d)	
		10	(d)	
10.	A loan from Mamfe	100		100
				£1,072

(a) Subscribed before 24 September 1911.
(b) Subscribed on 24 September 1911.
(c) Subscribed on 21 October 1911.
(d) Subscribed on 20 December 1911.
(e) '200 iron sheets, G. P. Kumi'.

Notes on Subscribers (names are spelt as in the account book)

(2) A brother of Israel Kwami's father, said to have a farm in the area.
(3) A younger brother of Israel Kwami—Mr Aborah's father.

APPENDIX VIII. 3

(4) Another brother of Israel Kwami, who also had land on both sides of the river; he was said to be the father of James Lawrence Tete—see p. 234n.

(5) A Mamfe farmer with land to the west of the river at Abrodiem. He was, presumably, the same Ohene Assah as a member of the Mamfe Trayo company, Appendix II. 5 (p. 65), of that name.

(6) A Larteh farmer stated, by Mr Aborah, to be 'the successor of the third chief of Okorase'; he had land west of the river at Adidiso.

(7) Another Larteh farmer who owned land at Okorase and Adidiso.

(8) A Larteh farmer who owned land on the east bank by the bridge—which presumably explains the present-day appellation, 'Asamoah's bridge'.

(9) Asamani and Adjei are said to have been two Mamfe men with land at Abrodiem.

(10) Nothing is known about this loan except that it was negotiated by Israel Kwami and was said to have been paid back in full to Yaw Akortey of Mamfe.

The records suggest, though not conclusively, that the bridge was opened to foot passengers on 24 April 1914, a 3d. toll being charged; from then until the end of 1914 as many as 25,469 passengers paid their toll. The monthly figures of receipts show that four times as many passengers used the bridge in the wet month of June as in the dry months of August and September. Unfortunately records of receipts for nearly all the following years are missing.

The expenses of operating the bridge were considerable. In 1915 the monthly pay of the clerk in charge was £3 10s. and of the watchman £2. The 'secretary', Charles E. Otoo (or Otu), was paid £10 monthly. (He was one of the most prominent Larteh men of his generation. Educated at Mfantsipim, he was at various times government official, court registrar, state secretary and cocoa-shipper on his own account; as a cocoa-farmer he owned land west of the river at Nananko; he is said to have had much to do, after the war, with organizing the building, also by contractors, of the access roads to Larteh; his house, see plate 12, is one of the oldest 'storey-houses' in Larteh.) In 1915, or later, Israel Kwame was paid 6s. a month as treasurer.

The records are so defective that there is no means of telling whether the operation of the bridge yielded a profit, though if passengers continued to flow across at the 1914 rate and if the toll remained for some time at 3d., this may well have been so. (From 24 April 1914 to the end of the year takings were £318.) It is said that there was an annual share-out of proceeds: and perhaps this meant that each of the farmers who had subscribed towards the building of the bridge took a share based on the size of his contribution. There is a gap in the records until 1929 when takings for the year are recorded as only £91 16s. 9d. so that the wages of the clerk in charge and of the watchman had to be reduced. Thereafter takings fell steadily, reaching £32 8s. 1d. in 1934. The toll was lowered to 1d. in July 1935. The main cause of the decline in receipts was, presumably, that the bridge ceased to be on what the farmers called 'the main road between Larteh and Asuboi', owing to increased use of lorry transport; other causes may have been the declining fertility of the lands east of the river and the expanding scope of the migration. The last record relates to May 1937, when 17s. 5d. was collected from a 1d. toll. Perhaps the collection of tolls then ceased, for it was at about this time that a lorry bridge was constructed (at public expense) across the river at Mangoase.

The Mangoase Bridge

The remains of the bridge built by the farmers at Mangoase may be seen about a hundred yards downstream from the present lorry bridge. It is said that the contractor was Jacob Isliker—and it may be that the delay over completing the bridge at

246

THE BRIDGE AT MMETIAMU

Mmetiamu resulted from the fact that the Mangoase bridge was planned later and opened earlier, perhaps before the railway reached Mangoase in May 1913. An unsatisfactory feature of this bridge was that (unlike that at Mmetiamu) it had to be approached by canoe during the rainy season! (Presumably the waters rushed so fast beneath the bridge that it was worth disembarking.) One informant said that the bridge was washed away by heavy floods before the building of the road bridge, at public expense, in 1937.

It is said that tolls of first 6d., then 3d. and finally 1d., were charged to foot-passengers and that there had been a dispute among those who had subscribed the money, so that it was not surprising that no account books relating to its building or operation could be found. The main subscribers were said to be Akwapim and the names of 4 Mamfe, 3 Larteh and 4 Mampong farmers were listed; Shai farmers, also, were said to have subscribed.

The Bibianiha Bridge

A visit to this bridge in March 1960 revealed it to be a much inferior structure to that at Mmetiamu—so it may be true as some (though not all) informants insisted that it had not been built by Jacob Isliker. However, it was still in good condition and a continuous stream of passengers, many of them carrying palm-wine, was observed. An access road to the bridge was then being built, by communal labour, to enable lorries to approach from Koforidua. Just west of the river was a 'village', consisting of little save a building-less school—run by local people. A very old lady was sitting there, having walked from Koforidua that day; she said that her father, William Tete, of Larteh Ahenease, was among those who had bought a large land west of the river; much of the land was owned by Kyerepon farmers and it is probably true, as recorded by J. L. Tete in his book, that the money for the bridge was subscribed by Larteh and Kyerepon farmers.

The Access Roads to Akwapim

James Lawrence Tete, in his typescript book on the history of Akwapim, said that the Akwapim people had spent a total of £47,500 on contractor-built access roads to Akwapim in a period of ten years, which he did not specify—but which would have been around 1916 to 1926. The sum may be of the right order of magnitude, though the book is not in all respects accurate and no complete breakdown of the figure is given. Three of the most important of these access roads were: that from Nsawam to Aburi (financed by Aburi farmers, at a cost, according to Tete, of £8,000—from another source it was learnt that the Aburi farmers had tried, unsuccessfully, to build a road down the scarp to Ayimensah); the Mamfe to Larteh road (recorded cost £3,300[1]); and the spectacularly hair-pinned road down the scarp which joins Larteh with Ayikuma—which, after many vicissitudes, involving changes in contractors, was ceremonially opened in 1926 by Governor Guggisberg, who marked the occasion by presenting the Benkumhene of Akwapim (the chief of Larteh) with a Ford car. (An earlier Governor, Sir Hugh Clifford, had shown so little appreciation of the position that, in *German Colonies*, 1918, he had commented that the roads had been built 'to enable the cultivators to spend their week-end in the bosoms of their families' rather than in their 'cocoa-gardens in the plains (*sic*)'.)

[1] According to J. K. Ansah, *The Centenary History of the Larteh Presbyterian Church*, p. 25, the cost of the road was £4,000 and of the Larteh to Ayikuma road £7,500.

APPENDIX VIII. 4

THE POPULATION OF AKWAPIM, 1891 TO 1960

The recorded population figures for the principal Akwapim towns for the first four Census years, starting with 1891, inspire little confidence—see the following table. The Honorary Secretary of the Census Committee for the 1891 Census (Dr J. Farrell Easmon) regarded the Akwapim figures, as well as those for the principal towns along the littoral, as 'fairly accurate' and while it does appear that this Census may have been much superior to that which followed in 1901, the following description of the procedure should be noted:

'Chiefs were asked to carry out the counting which, in accordance with native custom at the time, was done by heads of families placing in a bowl or other receptacle a cowrie for each female or a grain of corn for each male member of the family. The cowries and grains were counted and the numbers of each communicated to the District Commissioner by the Chief. This practice was gradually discontinued in later years but even in 1921 it was still followed in some of the more out-of-way areas.'[1]

Recorded Population of Principal Akwapim Towns, 1891 to 1960

	1891	1901	1911	1921	1931	1948	1960
(1) Aburi	4,410	10,393	1,609	2,080	3,700	3,142	4,715
(2) Berekuso	1,917	1,452	510	425	558	610	911
(3) Nsakye	1,063	2,364	344	200	242	773	341
(4) Ahwerease	1,183	5,481	308	372	423	684	667
(5) Obosomase	1,667	1,779	1,206	811	1,138	1,773	1,475
(6) Tutu	2,088	3,595	678	905	1,657	1,468	2,066
(7) Mampong	3,978	5,832	2,124	690	1,578	3,781	4,449
(8) Larteh—							
Ahenease }	7,615	8,477	4,886	4,128 }	2,632	3,697 }	6,381
Kubease }		3,434	1,621	1,226 }		1,475 }	
(9) Mamfe	1,428	1,642	1,341	1,095	1,914	2,860	3,082
(10) Amanokrom	918	n.a.	430	563	934	760	1,496
(11) Akropong	6,258	9,013	6,218	1,226	2,743	4,150	5,606
(12) Abiriw	2,130	2,313	664	611	1,673	2,728	1,790
(13) Adukrom	9,720	9,088	5,905	699	929	1,668	2,673
(14) Dawu	2,106	1,598	3,314	536	262	1,288	1,335
(15) Awukugua	2,016	4,756	677	466	176	748	1,606
(16) Abonse	1,996	743	596	558	299	203	362
(17) Aseseeso	1,977	898	700	892	343	1,071	540
(18) Apirede	1,500	4,014	1,535	742	396	883	1,052
(19) Nsawam	n.a.	700	2,596	6,143	8,882	8,642	20,240
(20) Adawso	n.a.	n.a.	1,994	515	1,362	860	762
(21) Mangoase	n.a.	n.a.	790	2,961	2,121	2,453	1,943
(22) Pakro	n.a.	n.a.	321	1,143	1,114	1,041	1,002
(23) Tinkong	n.a.	n.a.	151	621	n.a.	557	574
Total population of Akwapim	57,583	82,135	88,047	79,917	86,380	80,089[2]	n.a.

[1] *Census of Population, 1948*, p. 7.
[2] Akwapim Native Authority. Area smaller than that covered by previous figures.

THE POPULATION OF AKWAPIM

Notes on Table

(a) It is known that the 1960 figures for some of the towns on the ridge, for instance Berekuso, were inflated by the inclusion of some migrant farmers who, out of loyalty to their home town, had returned home for the express purpose of being counted.

(b) Differences in enumeration areas make inter-Censal comparison very hazardous.

(c) *Notes on towns*

(1) The rise and fall indicated by the 1891, 1901 and 1911 figures are obviously absurdly great. While the 1901 figure perhaps includes many of the Aburi villages to the west of the ridge (over 200 such villages are, for instance, shown separately in the 1931 report), the 1911 figure is suspiciously low.

(3) and (4) While the 1901 figures are obviously too high, the 1911 figures are conceivably reasonably accurate.

(8) It would seem improbable that the combined populations of Ahenease and Kubease could have been so low in 1931.

(11) The 1901 figure is suspiciously high, the 1921 figure suspiciously low.

(13) The 1911 and 1921 figures are presumably not comparable.

The 1911 Census was the first for which legal powers had been taken and the first to be conducted by enumerators appointed for the purpose.

The recorded population figures for Akim Abuakwa are virtually useless prior to 1921 (the return for the Birim District was officially 'considered disappointing' in 1911) and the history of the migration cannot be studied demographically. But the recorded increase of 55 per cent in the Akim Abuakwa population between 1921 and 1931 was perhaps of the right order of magnitude, reflecting a great increase in the proportion of non-Akim (Akwapim and others) in the population; it should be contrasted with a rise of only 8 per cent in the population of Akwapim during the same decade. (The decrease in the population of Akwapim in 1921, compared with 1911, was 'ascribed by the District Commissioner partly to migration to the richer lands in the adjoining Akim Abuakwa district'—one of the few references ever made to the migration in census reports.)

APPENDIX VIII. 5

THE POPULATION OF 'STRANGER-TOWNS AND VILLAGES',
AKIM ABUAKWA

The decennial Census reports from 1891 to 1921 are almost worthless so far as concerns the historic cocoa-growing area of southern Akim Abuakwa. Even had these Censuses not been so inefficiently conducted (so that, for instance, towns such as Suhum which had been listed in 1911 were forgotten in 1921), the grouping under place-names of such a widely dispersed farming population, most of whom lived on their own portions of land, would have been bound to have presented insuperable difficulties—and this particularly affected comparability over time, considering that sites and names of villages were constantly changing. In 1931 and 1948 similar difficulties were encountered and the following table is presented, for what it is worth, in the knowledge that some of the figures are much more accurate or meaningful than others.

APPENDIX VIII. 5

'Stranger-towns and villages', Akim Abuakwa

	Recorded Population		Ratio of female to male population
	1931	1948	1948[1]
Suhum	3,831	5,099	100
Adeiso	460	3,098	93
Mepom	n.a.	1,770	83
Asuokaw	57	1,769	101
Nankese	2,655	1,650	97
Asuboi	939	1,423	96
Asikasu	101	1,042	91
Anum Apapam[2]		912	103
Anum Apapam Mfrano[2]		1,079	122
Dokrokyewa[2]		643	107
'Mfranta 2'[2]		974	99
Asuboi Hamlets[2]		534	100
Dome[2]		318	88
Akorabo[2]		1,807	109
Kukua[2]		1,168	94

[1] The figures show the number of females per 100 males.
[2] Each of these places was a 'farming district' and most of the farmers lived in villages on their own land. Owing to doubts about comparability, 1931 figures (where they existed) are not shown.

The table shows that, despite swollen shoot, the populations of the main 'stranger-towns', such as Suhum, were higher in 1948 than in 1931. (Provisional figures for 1960 show the population of Suhum as over 10,000, and Adeiso, Mepom, Asuokaw and Nankese had all grown considerably. Some districts in the Abandoned Area, such as Akorabo, had reduced populations.)

In 7 of the 15 localities listed (1948) the number of females living in the area was greater than (or equal to) the number of males. Only in Mepom and Dome was the number of females per 100 males less than 90. In most of the main Akwapim home towns at that time, there were about 1·2 females to every male, showing that slightly more men than women normally live away from home.

APPENDIX VIII. 6

THE ANUM MIGRATION TO ASAMANKESE

The only 'mass migration' into the historic cocoa-growing area which has occurred since the start of cocoa-growing was that of the Anum people to Asamankese. Between 1907 and about 1912 (when the immigration may have petered out) so many Anum people arrived in Asamankese that the Anum section of the town is of comparable size to the Akim section. Asamankese is a 'home from home' for many Anum people; it is there that they build their 'storey-houses' even if they become embroiled, as so many of them do, in further migration.

It has been noted elsewhere that in the early days of commercial cocoa-growing the Anum (and Boso) peoples lacked the cash to buy land, so that their only means of participating in the migration was by attaching themselves, as labourers, carriers or craftsmen, to the Akwapim. But such a status in life afforded them little satisfaction and they were resolved (and as quickly as possible) to become cocoa-farmers in their

250

THE ANUM MIGRATION TO ASAMANKESE

own right. As the following record[1] makes clear the migration to Asamankese was motivated by both political and economic considerations: the Anum people were attracted by the prospect of free land—and the Asamankese people (who were Akwamu) thought it politically wise to swell their numbers by welcoming their 'brothers' from across the Volta.

'We were there [Old Mangoase] in the year 1906, November 16 . . . when we got two messengers from late sub-chief Kwasi Mensah . . . saying . . . that he has been banished by paramount chief Kwadjo Dei at Volta District, Anum. . . He was brought with the stool to Old Mangoase . . . unto the house of Asare and his apprentices. . . There he stated the way and manner he was banished. . . They were ordered to remove to Nyanawase where our ancestors originally came from. . . "I [Kwasi Mensah] wrote a letter to Kwadjo Dei not to value the land more than myself and people which numbered about 1,000. . . In his reply he said that he values land more than lives.". . . The next day Asare . . . closed work with his apprentices, tried the possible best and collected the whole Anums near by, [with the] exception of those who are at day's journey distance, carpenters, sawyers, matchet workmen to the spot. They found that it is right and noble way to go to Nyanawase . . . rather than to buy land. . . We got to Accra in troop about 70 souls. The late Manche Tackyi's funeral custom was being continued on the very morning. . . Ga Manche and his elders took this case into consideration wisely and found the right way to approach . . . the Colonial Secretary with this statement of our immigration. . . They satisfied him and others that more than a century ago they had resided at Nyanawase. . . Accompanied by two linguists of Ga Manche Tackyi they reached Asamankese on 17th February, 1907. . .'

'On our appearance to the town Asamankese 17/2/1907 continual gun shooting was held with wailing and mourning, drinkables both with Chief Kwaku Amoa and the whole nation sorely grieved, which is the modern general funeral custom performance in both sides concluded with saluting and welcome drinks intoxicated in mourning and drinkables in memory of our lost chiefs and brothers in both sides. These deeds were continued 3 days time. [sic]'

Mr J. D. Adams, who had himself been one of the Anum craftsmen working in Old Mangoase, said that their first idea had been to buy land in Kwahu (near Kwahu Praso) for cocoa-growing, but that it had then seemed better to 'return' to the Asamankese area. He thought that the original group of immigrants numbered about 70; they had later been joined by others who came one by one. First of all they had lived by doing odd jobs in the town and soon they had been invited to appropriate cocoa-land for themselves. Each man had farmed on any suitable vacant land, clearing a fresh portion each year. Krakye, Fanti and Ewe labourers had been employed, on a contract basis, in an effort to assert rights by clearing land quickly. The Anum people did not usually live on their land; first they settled in one quarter of the town and then, in about 1914, they removed to the north-eastern quarter, now their town within a town.

---

[1] From an old record book in the possession of Mr J. D. Adams of Asamankese. The extract has been shortened for the sake of clarity.

BIBLIOGRAPHY

Allott, A. *Essays in African Law* (Butterworth, 1960).

Ampene, Emmanuel. *The Political and Social Organization of a Guan Community* (University of Ghana, unpublished M.A. thesis, 1958).

Ansah, J. K. *The Centenary History of the Larteh Presbyterian Church, 1853–1953* (Larteh Presbyterian Church, 1955).

Baker, G. L. 'Research Notes on the Royal Niger Company—its Predecessors and Successors', *Journal of the Historical Society of Nigeria*, vol. 2, no. 1.

Beckett, W. H. *Akokoaso: A Survey of a Gold Coast Village* (London School of Economics, Monographs on Social Anthropology No. 10, 1944).

—— *Koransang: A Gold Coast Cocoa Farm* (Government Printer, Accra, 1945).

Belfield, H. Conway. *Report on the Legislation governing the Alienation of Native Lands in the Gold Coast Colony and Ashanti*, H.M.S.O., Cd. 6278 (1912).

Bevin, H. J. 'The Gold Coast Economy about 1880', *Transactions of the Gold Coast and Togoland Historical Society*, vol. II, Part II (Achimota, 1956).

Boateng, E. A. *A Geography of Ghana* (Cambridge, 1959).

Bohannan, Paul. *Tiv Farm and Settlement*, H.M.S.O., Colonial Research Studies No. 15 (1954).

Bray, F. R. *Cocoa Development in Ahafo, West Ashanti* (Faculty of Agriculture, University of Ghana, 1959, cyclostyled).

Cardinall, A. W. *The Gold Coast, 1931* (Government Printer, Accra, 1932).

Chalmers, Robert. *A History of Currency in the British Colonies* (H.M.S.O., 1893).

Chevalier, M. A *Le Cacaoyer dans l'Ouest Africain* (Augustin Challamel, Paris, 1908).

Christaller, J. G. *A Dictionary of the Asante and Fante Language called Tshi [Twi]* (Basel Evangelical Missionary Society, Basel, 1933, first edition 1881).

Clifford, Hugh. *German Colonies: A Plea for the Native Races* (Murray, 1918).

The Cocoa, Chocolate and Confectionery Alliance (11 Green St, London, W.1), *Reports* of Cocoa Conferences. (The first Conference was held in 1946, the tenth in 1961.)

Colonial Office. *Bibliography of Published Sources relating to African Land Tenure*, H.M.S.O., Col. 258 (1950).

—— *Report of the Commission on the Marketing of West African Cocoa* (the Nowell Report), H.M.S.O., Cmd. 5845 (1938).

Crowther, F. G. 'Notes on a District of the Gold Coast', *Quarterly Journal of the Institute of Commercial Research*, Liverpool University, vol. I (1906).

Dalton, George. 'Economic Theory and Primitive Society', *American Anthropologist*, vol. 63, no. 1 (February 1961).

Danquah, J. B. *Akan Laws and Customs* (Routledge, London, 1928).

—— *The Akim Abuakwa Handbook* (Forster Groom, London, 1928).

—— *Cases in Akan Law* (Routledge, London, 1928).

—— *An Epistle to the Educated Youngman in Akim Abuakwa* (Accra, 1928).

Dickson, K. B. 'Road Transport in Southern Ghana and Ashanti since 1850', *Transactions of the Historical Society of Ghana*, vol. V, Part I (1961).

Djan, Oheneba Sakyi. *The Sunlight Reference Almanac of the Gold Coast Colony and its Dependencies* (Gold Coast, 1936).

BIBLIOGRAPHY

Economic Society of Ghana. *The Economic Bulletin* (University of Ghana, published monthly 1957 to 1960 and quarterly from mid 1962).

Elias, T. Olawale. *Nigerian Land Law and Custom* (Routledge, London, 1951).

Evans-Pritchard, E. E. *Anthropology and History* (Manchester University Press, 1961).

F.A.O. (Food and Agriculture Organization). Commodity Series, Bulletin No. 27, *Cacao* (Rome, 1955).

Field, M. J. 'The Agricultural System of the Manya-Krobo of the Gold Coast', *Africa*, vol. xiv, no. 2 (April 1943).

—— *Akim-Kotoku: an Oman of the Gold Coast* (Crown Agents, 1948).

—— *Social Organization of the Ga People* (Crown Agents, 1940).

Forde, Daryll, and Scott, Richenda. *The Native Economies of Nigeria*, vol. i of *The Economics of a Tropical Dependency*, ed. M. Perham (Faber, London, 1946).

Fortes, Meyer. 'The Ashanti Social Survey: A Preliminary Report', *The Rhodes-Livingstone Journal*, no. 6 (1948).

Fortes, Meyer, and others. 'Ashanti Survey, 1945–46', *The Geographical Journal* (October–December 1947).

Galletti, R., and others. *Nigerian Cocoa Farmers* (Oxford University Press, 1956).

Garlick, Peter C. *African Traders in Kumasi* (University of Ghana, 1959, cyclostyled).

Ghana, Forestry Department. *Reports* of the Reserve Settlement Commissioners (unpublished).

—— Office of the Government Statistician. *Survey of Population and Budgets of Cocoa Producing Families in the Oda-Swedru-Asamankese Area, 1955–56*, Statistical and Economic Papers No. 6 (Government Printer, Accra, 1958).

—— Office of the Government Statistician. *Survey of Cocoa Producing Families in Ashanti, 1956–57*, Statistical and Economic Papers No. 7 (Government Printer, Accra, 1960).

—— Ministry of Information and Broadcasting. *Voices of Ghana: Literary Contributions to the Ghana Broadcasting System, 1955–57* (Government Printer, Accra, 1958).

—— Ministry of Agriculture. *The Ghana Farmer* (Government Printer, Accra, published quarterly).

Ghana Law Reports, 1959, Parts i and ii (General Legal Council, Accra).

Gold Coast, Department of Agriculture. *The Gold Coast Farmer* (Government Printer, Accra, published periodically up to 1939).

—— *Further Correspondence regarding Affairs of the Gold Coast*, H.M.S.O., Cmd. 3687 (1883).

—— *Report of the Commission on Economic Agriculture in the Gold Coast* (1889, unpublished).

—— *Report upon the Customs relating to the Tenure of Land on the Gold Coast*, Enclosure in *Gold Coast*, no. 412 (12 October 1895).

—— *Report on the Eastern Provinces for 1925–26* (Government Printer, Accra).

—— *Reports* on Population Censuses, 1891, 1901, 1911, 1921, 1931, 1948 (Government Printer, Accra).

Gould, Peter. *The Development of the Transportation Pattern in Ghana*, Northwestern University, U.S.A., Studies in Geography No. 5 (1960).

Green, M. M. *Land Tenure in an Ibo Village* (London School of Economics, Monographs on Social Anthropology, 1941).

Griffith, William Brandford. *The Far Horizon: Portrait of a Colonial Judge* (A. H. Stockwell, Ilfracombe, 1951).

BIBLIOGRAPHY

Guggisberg, F. G. *The Gold Coast: A Review of the Events of 1920–26 and the Prospects of 1927–28* (Government Printer, Accra, 1927).

Hancock, W. K. *Survey of British Commonwealth Affairs*, vol. II, Part II (Oxford, 1940.)

Hawkins, E. K. *Road Transport in Nigeria* (Oxford, 1948).

Hay, J. S. 'On the District of Akem in West Africa', *Journal of the Royal Geographical Society*, 1876.

Higgins, Benjamin. *Economic Development* (Constable, London, 1959).

Hill, Polly. *Cocoa Research Series* Nos. 1 to 19 (Economics Department, University of Ghana, 1957 to 1960, cyclostyled).

—— 'The Fundamental Importance of Social Factors: the Ghanaian Capitalist Cocoa Farmer', *Cocoa Conference, 1961* (Cocoa, Chocolate and Confectionery Alliance, 1962).

—— *The Gold Coast Cocoa Farmer: A Preliminary Survey* (Oxford, 1956).

—— 'The History of the Migration of Ghana Cocoa Farmers', *Transactions of the Historical Society of Ghana*, vol. IV, Part I (1959).

—— 'The Migrant Cocoa Farmers of Southern Ghana', *Africa*, vol. XXX, no. 3 (July 1961).

—— 'Systems of Labour Employment on Gold Coast Cocoa Farms', *Proceedings of the Fifth Conference of the West African Institute of Social and Economic Research* (University College Ibadan, Nigeria, 1956).

Hunter, J. M. 'Akotuakrom: A Case Study of a Devastated Cocoa Village in Ghana', *Transactions of the Institute of British Geographers* (1961).

Johnston, Bruce F. *The Staple Food Economies of Western Tropical Africa* (Stanford University Press, California, 1958).

Kemp, Dennis. *Nine Years at the Gold Coast* (Macmillan, London, 1898).

Kirk-Greene, A. H. M. 'The Major Currencies in Nigerian History', *Journal of the Historical Society of Nigeria*, vol. 2, no. 1.

Köbben, A. J. F. *Le Planteur Noir*, Études Éburnéennes (Institut Français d'Afrique Noire, Tournier, 1956).

Krow, Sampson Yao. *Handbook of Sakyikrom* (unpublished).

La Anyane, S. *Aweso: A Manya Krobo Huza* (Ghana Ministry of Agriculture, based on research carried out in 1956, cyclostyled).

Lewis, W. A. *The Theory of Economic Growth* (Allen and Unwin, London, 1955).

Lloyd, P. C. 'Some Notes on the Yoruba Rules of Succession and on "Family Property",' *Journal of African Law*, vol. 3 (1959).

—— *Yoruba Land Law* (Oxford, 1962).

Loveridge, A. J. 'Wills and the Customary Law in the Gold Coast', *Journal of African Administration* (October 1950).

Maitland, F. W. *Domesday Book and Beyond: Three Essays in the Early History of England* (Fontana, London, 1960).

Manshard, Walther. 'Afrikanische Waldhufen- und Waldstreifenfluren', *Die Erde*, Heft 4 (Berlin, 1961).

Mate Kole, Nene Azu. 'The Historical Backgrounds of Krobo Customs', *Transactions of the Gold Coast and Togoland Historical Society*, vol. I, Part IV (1955).

McPhee, A. *The Economic Revolution in British West Africa* (Routledge, London, 1926).

Meek, C. K., and others. *Europe and West Africa* (Oxford, 1940).

Meek, C. K. *Land Law and Custom in the Colonies* (Oxford, 1946).

—— *Land Tenure and Land Administration in Nigeria and the Cameroons*, Colonial Research Studies No. 22 (1957).

BIBLIOGRAPHY

Meek, C. K. 'Some Social Aspects of Land Tenure in Africa', from 'Land Tenure', a special supplement to *The Journal of African Administration* (October 1952).

Myrdal, Gunnar. *Economic Theory and Under-Developed Regions* (London, 1957).

Newlands, H. S. Award in the Akim Abuakwa/Manya Krobo Boundary Dispute (1922, unpublished).

Nowell Report. See Colonial Office. *Report of the Commission on the Marketing of West African Cocoa.*

O.E.E.C. (Organisation for European Economic Co-operation), *Cocoa* (1956).

Orwin, C. S. and C. S. *The Open Fields* (Oxford, 1938).

Pogucki, R. J. H. *Report on Land Tenure in Adangme Customary Law*, Gold Coast Land Tenure, vol. II (Government Printer, Accra, 1955).

—— *Land Tenure in Ga Customary Law*, Gold Coast Land Tenure, vol. III (Government Printer, Accra, 1955).

Radcliffe-Brown, A. R., and Forde, Daryll, ed. *African Systems of Kinship and Marriage* (Oxford, 1950).

Rattray, R. S. *Ashanti* (Oxford, 1923).

—— *Religion and Art in Ashanti* (Oxford, 1927).

—— *Ashanti Law and Constitution* (Oxford, 1929).

Redwar, H. W. Hayes. *Comments on some Ordinances of the Gold Coast Colony* (Sweet and Maxwell, London, 1909).

Reindorf, C. C. *The History of the Gold Coast and Asante* (Basel, 1895; 2nd edition, Basel Mission, 1950).

Renner, P. A. *Cases in the Courts of the Gold Coast Colony and Nigeria*, vol. I, Part II (Sweet and Maxwell, London, 1915).

Report from the Select Committee on the West Coast of Africa, Part II, Appendix (H.M.S.O., 1842).

Samson, Edward. *A Short History of Akuapim and Akropong* (Accra, 1908).

Sarbah, J. M. *Fanti Customary Laws* (Clowes, London, 1897).

Selected Judgments of the Divisional Courts of the Gold Coast (includes Asamankese Arbitration) (Crown Agents, 1930).

Shephard, C. Y. *Report on the Economics of Peasant Agriculture in the Gold Coast* (Government Printer, Accra, 1936).

Taylor, Stephen. *Good General Practice: a Report of a Survey* (Oxford, 1954).

Tete, James Lawrence. *The History of Akwapim* (1938, unpublished).

Tudhope, W. S. D. 'The Development of the Cocoa Industry in the Gold Coast and Ashanti', *Journal of the Royal African Society*, vol. IX (October 1909).

—— *Enquiry into the Gold Coast Cocoa Industry, Interim* and *Final Reports*, Gold Coast Sessional Papers Nos. II and IV (1918–19).

Vansina, J. 'Recording the Oral History of the Bakuba', *Journal of African History*, vol. I, no. 1 (1960).

Varley, W. J., and White, H. P. *The Geography of Ghana* (Longmans, 1958).

Wallis, J. R. 'The Kwahus—their Connection with the Afram Plain', *Transactions of the Gold Coast and Togoland Historical Society*, vol. I, Part III, p. 24.

Wanner, Gustaf Adolf. *Die Basler Handels-Gesellschaft A.G.*, 1859–1959 (Die Gesellschaft, Basel, 1959).

West African Court of Appeal. *Selected Judgments*, vols. I and II.

West African Lands Committee. *Draft Report*, H.M.S.O., African (West), No. 1046 (1917).

—— *Minutes of Evidence etc.*, H.M.S.O., African (West), No. 1047 (1916).

BIBLIOGRAPHY

West African Lands Committee. *Correspondence and Papers laid before the Committee*, H.M.S.O., African (West), No. 1048 (1916).

The West African Law Reports, vols. I to III (West Africa Law Publishing Co. Ltd, Achimota, Ghana, 1956–8).

Wilks, Ivor. 'The Growth of the Akwapim State: a Study in the Control of Evidence', to be published in the *Proceedings of the Fourth International African Seminar*.

Wills, J. Brian, ed. *Agriculture and Land Use in Ghana* (Oxford, 1962).

INDEX

abandoned area, 24
abasam (Twi), 'arm-stretch', 44
Abonse (Akwapim), 63–5
Aborah, A. H., 243–4
Aburi (Akwapim)
  chief of (Adontenhene of Akwapim), 83n, 124, 135n, 199, 211
  inheritance system, 135–6
  migrant farmers: case histories, 209–10; and the company system, 199; early migration of, 220–1, 224–5, 227; and the family land, 75–86, 122–31; inheritance system of, 122–31, 180; numbers of lands bought by, 193–9; and road-building, 247; and Sakyikrom, 86–9; and their sons, 81–3, 128–9, 136, 197
  villages in Akwapim, 162n
  see also Ahwerease/Akim, Akwapim, Berekuso, Dome/Aburi, Kofi Pare, Nsakye, Sakyikrom, Tawiah (Kwame)
Aburi Gardens, 166, 174–6
abusa (Twi), 'one third'
  labourers, 188–9
  Omanhene's share of produce, 147
  type of renting system, 158–9
abusua (Twi), Akan matrilineage, 76, 81, 82n, 122
  see also family land, matrilineal inheritance
abusua panyin (Twi), senior lineage member, 134, 136
acre, in English manorial records, 46–7
Ada, migrant cocoa-farmers of, 27, 233n
Adams, J. D., 251
Adawso (Akwapim), 77, 219–20
Addo, Otu, 235n
Adidiso/Amanokrom company, 50, 63
Adjeikrom, 234
Adu, Abraham, 219
Adukrom (Akwapim), migrant cocoa-farmers, 193–9
  see also Kyerepon
Afram Plains, 42n, 237
Agriculture, Ministry of
  farm maps, 2, 6, 18, 23–5
  farm ownership, 86
  lack of knowledge of farmers, 179
  lack of knowledge of migration, 18
  and swollen shoot, 1–2, 23–5
agyapade (Twi), inherited property, 116n
Agyinase (Akwapim), 238–40
Ahwerease (Akwapim), *see* Aburi
Ahwerease/Akim family land, 97

Akan inheritance, *see* matrilineal inheritance
Akim cocoa-farmers, 61, 76n, 116, 232n
  and Asamankese renting system, 158–9
  see also Akim Abuakwa, *Akokoaso*, Apapam, Apedwa, Asamankese
Akim Abuakwa
  dispute with Akwapim over jurisdiction, 154–7
  farmers, non-migrant, 162, 169
  land sales: after 1918, 235; and customary law, 138–49; Danquah on, 21–2
  Lands Secretary, 149
  migration into, during lorry-age, 236–7
  Omanhene of: and Asamankese Arbitration, 157; and land sales, 139, 143–9
  population: 1921 and 1931, 249; of stranger-villages, 249–50
  uninhabited southern forests, 169
  see also Akim (cocoa-farmers), *Akokoaso*, Apapam, Apedwa, Asafo, Asamankese, Atta (Omanhene, Sir Ofori), company, Danquah (J. B.), land (sale), Maase
Akim-Boso family land, 231–2
Akogyram, Kwabena, 182, 212–13, 223
Akokoaso, book by W. H. Beckett, 14, 18–19, 76n, 116n, 151
Akotuakrom family land, 7, 83–4, 91–2, 129
Akropong (Akwapim)
  early cocoa-growing experiments in, 171
  gifts of land to stool of, 243
  Governor Griffith's visits to, 173, 174, 176
  inheritance system, 85, 135–6
  migrant farmers: 70–1, 77, 220, 224, 227, 234; and *abusua*-villages, 84; case-histories, 201–3; and company system, 199–200; and the family land, 75–86, 129–31; in Kabu Hill area, 84n; numbers of lands bought by, 193–9; and their sons, 84–6, 136–7, 197
  rubber-traders, 164
  villages in Akwapim, 162
  see also Akropong/Bepoase, Akuffo (Omanhene Kwasi), Akwapim, Boah, Mfodwo-Boaten, Omenako
Akropong/Bepoase family land, 85–6, 104–6, 130–1
Akuffo, Omanhene Kwasi, 169, 221–2, 240–3
Akwamu and Sakyikrom, 86–8
Akwapim
  chiefs, in relation to land, 161
  classlessness of people of, 182
  construction of access roads to 247
  creditor farmers, 186–7

257

INDEX

dispute with Akim Abuakwa over jurisdiction, 154–7
economic conditions in eighteen-nineties,
161–70
history and ethnology of, 27–30
home towns: case-histories collected in,
200–10; surveys of, 193–9
Omanhene of, and land purchase in Akim,
145–6, 154–6
patrilineal inheritance systems of, 109–22
population: 1891, 161; 1901 and 1911,
227; of main towns 1891 to 1960, 248–9
'rope', 44
tribunals in Akim Abuakwa, 146
Twi, economic jargon in, 215–17
see also Aburi, Akropong, Akuffo (Omanhene Kwasi), Amanokrom, Berekuso,
Kyerepon, Larteh, Mamfe, Mampong,
Obosomase, Tutu
Akwatia, 157, 158
see also Asamankese
Allott, A., 160
Amanase, 145, 156, 228–9
Amanokrom (Akwapim) migrant farmers
and Suhum, 228–9
see also Adidiso/Amanokrom, Dome-
Amanokrom
Amoah, Kwaku, chief of Asamankese, 158
Anakwa, Asa, 223n
ancestral land, *see* land, ancestral
Ankrah, R. A., 238n
Ankwasu (Akwapim), battle of, 222, 242
Ansah, J. K., 247n
Anum
and Boso migrant cocoa-farmers, 27, 52,
61–2, 200, 226
inheritance system, 135
migration to Asamankese, 250–1
Anum Apapam, 52, 230
Apapam
Apedwa/Apapam land dispute, 144–5,
151–4
cocoa-farmers of, 60–1, 229
land sales by, 77, 139–49, 241
population 1891, 140n
see also Akim Abuakwa, Akim (cocoa-
farmers), cocoa-farmers, land (sale),
etc.
Apasare, *see* Adawso
Apedwa
cocoa-farmers of, 229
land dispute with Apapam, 144–5, 151–4
land sales by, 139–49
population 1891, 140n
see also Akim Abuakwa, Akim (cocoa-
farmers), cocoa-farmers, land (sale)
Apedwa/Apapam land dispute, 144–5, 151–4
area
farmers' ability to judge, 50

indigenous units and concept of, 43–9
see also company, land, strip-farms
asafo (Twi) companies, 38n
Asafo
boundary with Maase, 140n
cocoa-farmers of, 76n
Krobo land purchase near, 49n
land sales by, 50, 62–3, 77, 139–49, 228,
235, 243
see also Akim Abuakwa, Akim (cocoa-
farmers), cocoa-farmers, land (sale)
Asamankese, 169n, 232
Akim farmers of, 232n
Anum migration to, 250–1
arbitration, 147n, 157, 158
land sales by, 77, 230, 235
renting system of, 158–9
see also Akim Abuakwa, Akim-Boso,
land (sale)
Asarekrom, 84
asase (Twi), land, 116n, 196
aseda (Twi), ceremony, 129, 133, 136
Asesewa, Krobo market, 74
Ashanti
land alienations, 56
migration of southern farmers to, 237–
8
Asikasu, 159
Asuboi, 145, 154–6, 225, 227
Asuokoko River forest reserve, 56, 59
Asuokaw, 159
Asuoya (Akwapim), 220
Atta, Omanhene Sir Ofori, paramount chief
of Akim Abuakwa, 145–6, 148, 154–7
see also Akim Abuakwa, land
Awutu migrant cocoa-farmers, 27, 231
Ayi Bonte, 97n, 225

Badu, Charles, 224
Baker, G. L., 165n
bank
farmers' attitude to, 185
first branch opened, 165
barter, 165–6
Basel Mission, 21n, 164n, 165n, 168, 169,
170n, 170–2, 219, 227n, 228n
Beckett, W. H., 14, 18–19, 76n
Begoro, 73–4, 234, 236
Bell, Sir Hesketh, 175
Bepoase family land, *see* Akropong/Bepoase
Berekuso (Akwapim)
chief of, 211
migrant farmers, and the company system, 199; case-histories, 210, 211–12
notes on, 211–12
see also Aburi, Akwapim
Bevin, H. J., 164n, 165n, 166n, 167n, 170n,
176n, 179n
Bibianiha bridge, 6, 233–4, 247

258

INDEX

Boah family land, 50, 85, 100–4, 129–30
Bohannan, P., 111n
Boso, *see* Anum
Bosuso, 234
Botchway, P., 173n, 224
boundaries
  chiefs' uncertainty about, 139–40, 145, 156
  of company lands, 42, 47n
  see also company, family land, land, nt‌ɔmmɛ, etc.
Bray, F. R., 238
Brokensha, D., 21n, 27–30, 133n, 135n, 190n, 191, 243n

Cadbury, W. A., 179n
capital
  farmers' attitude to, 180
  Rattray on, 184n
  Twi words for, 215
capitalists, migrant farmers as, 214–15
Cardinall, A. W., 19–20, 123n, 171
carriers
  cocoa, 170, 187
  Twi word for, 216
case histories of Akwapim migrant farmers, 200–10
celebrations, farmers' expenditure on, 190
census, *see* population
Chai River forest reserve, 59
Chalmers, R., 165n
Chevalier, M. A., 172n, 179n
chiefs
  Akwapim, and land tenure, 161
  as land sellers, 138–49
  as migrant cocoa-farmers, 40, 181
  and strangers, 154
  see also Akim Abuakwa, Apapam, Apedwa, Asafo, Asamankese, company, land
Christaller, J. G., 38n, 48n, 141n, 162, 165n, 215–17
Christianity
  and the Aburi migration, 81
  and cocoa development, 168–9
  see also Basel Mission
Coaltar, *see* Kraboa-Coaltar
cocoa
  buying firms, 170
  conferences, 23n
  development in Nigeria, 169n
  Ghana exports: 1891–1913, 176–7; 1916–60, 217
  growing, on early maps, 227–8
  introduction into Ghana, 166–7, 170–6
  miscellaneous statistics, 217–18
  poor quality of, 170
  price: export prices 1900–38, 218; farmers', 218, 233; and rate of land purchase, 58, 59, 183

  production: Ashanti, 11; by region, 217; by southern migrants, 11–12; world, 170n
  replanting of devastated areas, 5, 24
  swollen shoot disease of, 1–2, 23–5
  transport, in early days, 179n
  trees, numbers cut out, 24
  see also swollen shoot
cocoa-company, *see* company
cocoa-farms, *see* cocoa-farmers, company, family land, strip-farms
cocoa-farmers
  Akwapim creditor-, 186–7
  Ashanti, 11
  attitude to cutting-out, 2
  conventional attitude to, 18, 19, 20, 22
  and indebtedness, 13
  as informants, 9–10
  Macmillan on, 23
  Ministry of Agriculture's definition of, 86
  native, 11, 19n, 61, 76n
  Nowell report on, 22
  price received for cocoa, 218
  as produce buyers, 190–1
  'size' of, 19
  and trading, 190
  types of, 11
  see also company, family land, migrant cocoa-farmers
cocoa-lands, numbers bought by Akwapim farmers, 193–9, 199–200, 200–10
coffee
  exports, 1886–1913, 176–7
  introduction into Ghana, 166–7, 170–6
coin, introduction of British silver, 165–6, 168
commercial firms, *see* firms
commercial records, lack of early, 165n
company
  of cocoa-farmers: 2–3, 4, 38–54, 182; delay in paying for land, 55–6; leaders of, 39–41; membership of, 39–40, 42, 43, 52–4; names of, 39; resale of land by members of, 40, 42n, 53–4; secretaries of, 41; sub-companies, 51, 67
  lands: acreages of, 50, 51–2, 57; boundaries fixed at time of purchase, 42; conventional shape of, 44; cost of, 50, 57–8; customary rules of inheritance and, 109–22; dates of purchase, 58, 59; delay in dividing, 48; distinguished from family lands, 76; division among farmers, 43–9; failure to plant, 55n; Krobo and Shai, 48, 73–4; in Nankese area, 62–3
  system: 38–54; Berekuso farmers and, 199, 211; and *huza* system, 72; introduction of, 227–8; and market in land, 183; and patrilineal inheritance, 113, 199–200

259

INDEX

usage of word, 38n, 75n
see also huza, land, migrant cocoa-farmers, patrilineal inheritance, strip-farms
concessions
granting of, before 1900, 150
Ordinance 1900, 242
consolidation of land-ownership under matrilineal inheritance, 82, 128, 130
'conspicuous expenditure', land purchase as, 184
consumption expenditure, migrant farmers' attitude to, 181
Cooke, C. H., 55, 56, 148n, 160
cowries, 165, 168n, 215
craftsmen, 166
creditors, Akwapim, 183, 186–7, 197n, 201, 204
see also Solomon, W. A. Q.
cross-cousin marriage, 82n, 124–5
Crowther, F. G., 20–1, 74, 144n, 145n, 147n, 155, 164n, 187n, 228n, 242–3
currency, *see* coin
customary law
Akim Abuakwa land sales and, 138–49
inheritance under, 109–31
misconceptions relating to, 14
see also inheritance, land (sale), matrilineal inheritance, patrilineal inheritance
cutlass-farmers versus hoe-farmers, 187n
'cutting-out', *see* swollen shoot disease

Daaman, 87n, 88
Dalton, G., 214
Danquah, J. B., 21–2, 122n, 139n, 143n, 144n, 146n, 225n, 242
dates of land acquisition, 58, 59, 195, 196, 198
daughters as farm-owners among patrilineal migrants, 117
debtors, *see* creditors, pledging
Dede forest reserve, 55, 56
Dedewa, 212, 221, 223–4
Densu
river: 221, 223, 233–4; bridges over, 243–7
valley, early land sales in, 243
Desiri forest reserve, 56
devastated area, definition of, 24
Dickson, K. B., 225
distribution of foodstuffs, etc., 179n
Djan, O. S., 141n
documentation of land sales, 57n, 160
Dome/Aburi family land, 107–8
Dome/Amanokrom family land, 106–7, 200
dwetiri (Twi), capital, 180
dwetiwani (Twi), 'capitalist', 180n

economic growth
role of individual in, 127

and 'traditional organization', 2n
economic jargon in Twi language, 215–17
economics
in Africa, scope of, 178–9
linguistic, 214–17
and social anthropology, 7–8
and social surveys, 8–9
education
Akwapim, 189n, 168
expenditure on, by farmers, 190–1
standards of, among migrant farmers, 46
Elias, T. O., 109n, 138n
enterprise, individual, and Aburi family land system, 82
esusu, type of savings club, 38n
Evans-Pritchard, E. E., 7n
Ewe
labourers, 190
migrant cocoa-farmers, 27
expatriate firms, *see* firms
exports from Ghana, 1886–1913, 176–7

family land, 2–3, 39n, 75–86, 196–7
and *abusua*-villages, 83–4
composition of original family group, 82, 85
contrasted with native Akim farming system, 76n
and cross-cousin marriage, 124–5
customary rules of inheritance and, 122–31
distinguished from company land, 76
leaders and associate-leaders, 80–2
mosaic pattern of farms, 76
name of, 80
and reconciliation of matrilineal and patrilineal principles, 81–2
table relating to eleven lands, 78
see also Aburi, Akropong, cocoa-farmers, land, matrilineal inheritance
family property, 76n
legal concept of, 131–2
see also lineage property
farm-maps, cocoa, 2, 6, 18, 23–5, 45–6
fekuw (Twi), company, 38n
Field, M. J., 1, 26, 44n, 48n, 73–4, 113n, 122n, 125, 139n, 186n
firms, European produce-buying, 165n, 170, 178–9
food
production and distribution, 179n
wholesalers, 190n
food-farmers, 162, 168, 169
women, 164, 168
food-farming in relation to cocoa-farming, 188
Forde, D., 128n
forest reserves, 59–60
see also reserve settlement commissioners

260

INDEX

Forestry Department, 55
Fori, Kwame, Omanhene of Akwapim, 240–3
Fortes, M., 122, 123, 125n, 135
funerals, expenditure on, by farmers, 190

Ga migrant cocoa-farmers, 26, 159, 187, 199, 225, 231n
see also Berekuso
Ga/Mame company land, 63
Galletti, R., 169n
Garlick, P. C., 190n
geography of the migration, 219–38
geometry, indigenous, 45–6, 47n, 67, 74
Ghana Survey
maps, 1907, 227
spelling of place-names, 220n
Goaso, 238
gold exports, 1886–1913, 176–7
Gold Coast, *see* Ghana
gold dust, demonetization of, 165
Goody, E., 135
Gould, P. R., 218, 225n, 235n
Green, M. M., 41n, 47n
Grey, W. H., 20
Griffith, Governor Sir W. B., 163, 165, 166, 167, 173–6
Griffith, Chief Justice Sir W. B., 20, 109, 138n, 142n, 144–5, 153–4, 173, 175, 222, 226n, 242, 243
guaha (Twi) ceremony, 35, 141–3
Guggisberg, Governor Sir F. G., 172, 227

Hall, R. E., 157
hama (Twi, pl. *nhama*), 'rope', 44
Hammond, D. P., 225
Hancock, Sir W. K., 144n, 151, 178n
Hawkins, E. K., 215n
Hay, J. S., 169n
Higgins, B., 178n
Hill, Polly, 19n, 47n, 186n, 187n, 190n, 213–14, 218n, 234n
hoe-farmers versus cutlass-farmers, 187n
home-towns
Akwapim: case-histories collected in, 200–10; surveys of, 193–9
recruitment of company members in, 42
see also Akwapim
houses
in farming areas, 192
investment in, by farmers, 190–1
'never-to-be-completed', 191
Hull, H. M., 140, 144–5, 151–3
Hunter, J. M., 43n, 45, 79, 84n, 91–2, 187n, 228–9
huza (Krobo), system of land purchase, 21, 26, 38n, 72–4, 168n
see also company, Krobo

Ibadan, 169n
income tax, cocoa-farmers' liability to pay, 185
individual, role of, in expanding property, 127
individual property, 76n, 109–31
see also land, self-acquired property
influenza epidemic 1918 and dating, 199
inheritance
customary rules of, 109–31
and farm acreages, 119–22
systems: Aburi and Akropong, 135–7; Berekuso, 211–12; Larteh, Mamfe and Mampong, 133–5; modification of, as result of migration, 113, 123, 133–5, 135–6
see also matrilineal inheritance, patrilineal inheritance, strip-farms
inheritor
in Aburi and Akropong, 123, 125, 126, 127
in patrilineal Akwapim, 113, 134
instalments, payment for land in, 143, 182–3
interest, Twi words for, 216
investments, cocoa-farms as, 180–1
see also capital, saving
Isliker, Jacob, 233, 244–7
Israel, M. G. A., 229

Josenhans, G., 21
jurisdiction, Akwapim/Akim Abuakwa dispute over, 146, 154–7

Kabu, Jonas, 229
Kadjebi, 237
Kemp, D., 176n
Kibi, *see* Akim Abuakwa
kinship
and company system, 43, 75
and family land system, 75–86
and *huza* system, 74
see also abusua, family land, inheritance, sons
Kirk-Greene, A. H. M., 165
Köbben, A. J. F., 214
Kofi Pare family land, 7, 82, 83, 92–8, 125, 126, 222
Koforidua, 225–6
Koransan, 224
Koransang, by W. H. Beckett, 18–19, 224n
Kraboa-Coaltar, 199, 230
Krabokese, 241
family land, 89–90
Krobo
attitude to land, 74, 186n
company lands, 48
early land purchases of, 139
and employment of labourers, 187
huza system, 72–4
land purchase, use of cowries for, 168n

261

INDEX

migrant cocoa-farmers, 25–6, 38n, 48, 49n, 52, 63, 225–6, 234
oil palm plantations, 163
'rope', 44
strip-farms: divided longitudinally, 65; narrowness of, 48–9, 51, 74
territorial ambitions, 72
Krodua, 159
Krow, Sampson Yao, 87n, 88–9
Kwaboanta, 233
Kwahu
migration to, in lorry age, 236–7
traders, 190n
Kwakye, Kwame, 97n
Kwame, Israel, 244–6
Kwame Tawiah family land
see Tawiah, Kwame
Kwapong, A., 223
Kwesi Komfo area, analysis of farm ownership in, 51, 60–2
Kyerepon (Akwapim) migrant farmers, 42n, 52, 226, 233, 238
see also Akwapim, company
Kyerepon/Nobeso company, 53–4, 63–5, 119–22

La Anyane, S., 72n
labourers, cocoa-farm, 83n, 90, 187–90, 213–14, 239–40
  abusa, 188–9, 213–14
  annual, 189, 213
  contract, 189–90, 214
  daily, 189–90, 213
  evolution of, into farmers, 27, 43n, 190, 226
  Ewe, 190
  finance of, 5
  nkotokuano, 188–9, 213–14
  Twi word for, 216
  wives and children of, 189
land
  Akan attitude to, 185
  ancestral, 112
  cost of, Nankese area, 49–50
  gifts of, 132–3
  'keeping qualities' of, 184
  Krobo attitude to, 74
  lineage, 75n
  market in, 183
  quantification of, 42, 43–9
  purchase: and the company system, 38–54; as 'conspicuous expenditure', 184; and family property 132; farmers' willingness to speak of, 12; payment in instalments, 142, 182–3; rate of, in relation to cocoa price, 183; for sons, 185
  renting of, in Asamankese area, 158–9
  sale: Akwapim, 161–2; belief in impossibility of, 12–13; by chiefs, 38; conditions of, in Akim Abuakwa, 148; under customary law, 14, 109, 138–49; Danquah on, 21–2; documentation of, 57n, 160; early, in Densu valley, 242–3; and guaha ceremony, 141–3; irreversibility of transaction, 142; lawyers' attitude to, 20; Nowell Report on, 22; symbolic process of, 41n; West African Lands Committee and, 20–1
  as a savings bank, 183–5
  'second-hand', 40n
  tenure: Akwapim, 212n; Asamankese, 158–9; Brong-Ahafo, 56; 1895 report on, 150
  see also cocoa-lands, company, concessions, family land, inheritance
Lands Bills, 1894, 1897, 150–1
Lang, J. J., 171
Larteh (Akwapim)
  inheritance system, 133–4
  migrant farmers: 43, 49, 51, 182; case-histories, 204–6; and Densu bridges, 233–4, 243–7; early migration of, 219–20, 224, 227; numbers of lands bought by, 193–9; and road-building, 247
  school-children in, 191
  see also Akwapim, company
length, indigenous units of, 43–9
Lewis, W. A., 2n
lineage property
  desire to create, 180–1
  resistance to drift towards, 180–1
  versus individual property, 109–31
linguistic economics, 214–17
Lloyd, P. C., 110n, 115n
lorries, 235
  investment in, by farmers, 190, 215
lorry age, migration during the, 234–8
Loveridge, A. J., 110
lumber exports, 1886–1913, 176–7

Maamedede, 88
Maase
  boundary with Asafo, 140n
  land sales by, 50, 62–3, 77, 140n, 228, 235, 243
  see also Akim Abuakwa, Akim (cocoa-farmers), cocoa-farmers, land (sale)
McGlade, C., 237
Macmillan, W. M., 23, 144n
McPhee, A., 165n
Maitland, F. W., 46n
Mame, see Ga/Mame
Mame/Prade company land, 63
Mamfe (Akwapim), 212–13, 223
  inheritance system, 133–4
  migrant farmers: 51, 220, 223; case-histories, 207–9; delay in planting land, 54; and Densu bridges, 233–4, 243–6; and inheritance, 117; numbers of lands bought by, 193–9

INDEX

villages in Akwapim, 162
see also Akwapim, company, Mamfe/
Saforosua, Mamfe/Trayo
Mamfe/Saforosua company, 38n, 53–4, 70–
1, 119–22
Mamfe/Trayo company, 50, 53–4, 65–7,
119–22
Mampong (Akwapim)
home of Tetteh Quashie, 172
inheritance system, 135
migrant farmers: 51, 220, 224, 227; and
Amanase, 228–9; and Densu bridge,
243–6; and inheritance, 117; numbers
of lands bought by, 193–9
see also Akwapim, company
Mangoase (Akwapim), 219
bridge, 233–4, 246–7
Manshard, W., 72n, 74
Manya Krobo, *see* Krobo
maps *see* Ghana Survey, farm-maps
marriage, cross-cousin, 124–5
Mate Kole, Nene Azu, 49n, 72n, 74
matrilineal inheritance
and Aburi family lands, 81–4
consolidation of ownership under, 128,
130
no division of farms under, 128, 130
and family lands, 122–31
misconceptions about, 123–4
position of sons, 136–7
see also family land, inheritance
Maxwell, Sir W., 150
measurement, indigenous, 43–9
Meek, C. K., 110, 113, 123n, 149, 150, 160
Mepom, 158–9, 231
Mfodwo-Boaten, 84, 224
Mfranta, 212, 230
migrant cocoa-farmers
Akwapim, and labourers, 187–90
Anum and Boso, 27
attitude to migration, 13–14
attitude to money and banks, 184–5
as capitalists, 214–15
case-histories of Akwapim, 200–10
Christian, 81
Ewe, 27
as farm managers, 186
Ga, 26
Krobo, 25–6
motives of, 181–2
Osudoku, 27
quantity of cocoa produced, 11–12, 218
Shai, 26
see also company, family land
migration of cocoa-farmers
in Ashanti, 11
and development of cocoa-growing, 169n
economic aspects, 178–92
geography of, 219–38

neglect of, in literature, 12–14
slowed down by swollen shoot, 7
treatment of, in publications, 18–23
Mmetiamu bridge, 6, 233–4, 243–6
money
family, and the individual, 132
farmers' attitude to, 184–5
Twi words for, 215–17
see also coin
Myrdal, G., 178n

Nankese area, 77
analysis of farm ownership in, 51
cost of land in, 49–50, 62–3, 228–9
see also Shai/Nankese
Napiers, Sir W., 150
Newlands, H. S., 72n, 73, 146, 148, 157
Niger Company, 165n
Nigeria, development of cocoa-growing in,
169n
Nkotokuano (Twi), labourers, 188–9
Nobeso, *see* Kyerepon/Nobeso
Nowell Report, 22–3, 172n
Nsakye (Akwapim)
migrant farmers and Sakyikrom, 86–9
re-foundation of, 87, 212
see also Aburi, Akotuakrom, Akwapim,
Krabokese, Sakyikrom
Nsawam (Akwapim), 77, 151, 155, 199,
224–5
ntɔmmɛ (Twi), boundary tree, 48
Ntow, Danso, Krontihene of Anum, 135n
Nyako-Agyakwa, S., 215
Nyanao, 235n

Obomofo-Densua company, 50, 53–4, 69–
70, 119–22
Obosomase (Akwapim)
migrant farmers: 51, 233, 237; case-
history: 210; numbers of lands bought
by, 193–9
notes on, 213
see also Akwapim
odiadefo (Twi), inheritor, 134
Odonkawkrom, 237n
Ofori, Yaw, 64–5
oil palm
cultivation in Akwapim, 161, 163–4, 167,
169
and *huza* system, 72
see also palm-oil, palm kernels
Okorase, 220
Omanhene (Twi), paramount chief, and
tribute, 147–9
see also Akim Abuakwa, Akuffo, Akwapim, Atta, land
Omenako family land, 97–100, 130
'one-pound-farm', 47n
open-field system, 46n

263

INDEX

Opoku, A. A., 13n, 30–7
Orwin, C. S., 46n
Osudoku migrant cocoa-farmers, 27, 52
Otu, C. E., 246
Oworam, 232

Pakro (Akwapim), 218, 221–3, 233, 238–40, 242
  see also Agyinase
palm oil and kernels, 163, 166, 167, 174
  exports 1886–1913, 176–7
Papase, 237
Pare, Kofi, see Kofi Pare
patrilineal inheritance
  at Akropong/Bepoase, 85
  Akwapim and Shai, 109–22
  and Berekuso, 211–12
  and company system, 199–200
  modifications in, resulting from migration, 113–15
  see also company, inheritance, land, sons
peasant farmer, myth of, 11, 14
place-names, spelling of Ghanaian, 220n
pledging of cocoa-farms, 186–7
  see also creditors
Pogucki, R. J. H., 26, 114n, 139, 141n
population
  of abusua-villages, 83–4
  Akim: 169, 249; stranger-villages, 249–50
  Akwapim: 1891–1960, 248–9; and land shortage, 168; wholly involved in migration, 181–2, 199
  censuses, 18, 162n, 166n, 220n, 227
Potekhin, I. I., 192n
pre-lorry age, defined, 6, 233
Price-Jones, W., 239n
Property, see family property, individual property, inheritance, lineage, self-acquired property

Quansah, A. O., 222n
quantification of land, see area, company, land
Quashie family land, 231–2
Quashie, Tetteh, 172–3

Radcliffe-Brown, A. R., 122n, 124
railway
  central line, 236
  opening of Nsawam and Pakro stations, 233
Rattray, R. S., 12, 86n, 122, 180n, 184n, 215n
Redwar, H. W. Hayes, 131, 132
Reindorf, C. C., 28n, 171
Renner, P. A., 222n
renting of land
  in Asamankese area, 158–9
  in Ashanti, 56
  in Dede Forest Reserve, 56n

Reserve Settlement Commissioners' Reports, 50, 55–60
residence and land rights, 116, 118
Richards, A. I., 124
roads, migrant farmers' construction of, 247
Rodger, Sir J., 154
'rope', indigenous unit of length, 43–9
rubber, 164–5, 166, 167–8
  exports, 1886–1913, 176–7

Saforosua, see Mamfe/Saforosua
Sakyikrom, 86–9
samansew (Twi), 'deathbed declaration', 132–3
Samson, E., 242
Sarbah, J. M., 109, 222
saving
  by cocoa-farmers, 13, 18, 22
  and finance of labour employment, 188
  land purchase as a form of, 73, 183–5
'second-hand land', 40n, 42n, 183, 186–7, 212–13
Sefwi-Wiawso, 42n, 237
self-acquired property, legal concept of, 131–2
  see also individual property
Shai
  company lands, 48
  inheritance system, 109–22
  migrant cocoa-farmers, 26, 48, 187, 226, 229, 233
  'rope', 44
  strip-farms, 48, 51, 65
  see also inheritance, Obomofo-Densua, Shai/Nankese
Shai/Nankese company, 50, 53–4, 67–9, 119–22
Shephard, C. Y., 18
social anthropology and economists, 7–8
social security and Aburi family lands, 82
social surveys, economists' attitude to, 8–9
Solomon, W. A. Q., 187n, 221–2, 238–40, 242
Sono, Kwaku, 241–2
sons
  Aburi farmers and their, 81–3, 128–9, 136, 197
  Akropong farmers and their, 84–6
  Berekuso farmers and their, 211–12
  as direct inheritors (Akwapim), 113–15, 134
  gifts to, 54, 69, 70, 115
  identification with fathers, 115–16
  as original company members, 40n, 43n
  purchase of land for, 185
  see company, family land, inheritance, strip-farms
statistical approach in African social research, 8–10

264

INDEX

stool, *see* chiefs, land, Omanhene
stranger
  demographic definition of, 13n
  linguistics of word, 14
strip-farms, 39
  areas of, 52–4, 120
  division: following death, 113–14; among grandsons, 116; longitudinal or transverse, 65, 68, 69
  Krobo and Shai, 48–9, 51
  Larteh, 49
  and patrilineal inheritance, 113
  see also company, inheritance
Suhum, 154–6, 225, 228–30
Supreme Court records, 132
Survey, *see* Ghana Survey
surveyors, employment of, by farmers, 74, 160
swollen-shoot disease
  and cutting-out, 1–2, 23–5
  long-term effect on tenure system, 128
  and the migration, 7
  see also cocoa

Tafo, 73–4, 235
Tawiah, Kwame, family land, 96–7
Taylor, S., 9n
Tete, L. J., 234n, 247
traders, Griffith on, 165
trading in relation to cocoa-farming, 190
transport
  of cocoa, in early days, 170, 179n
  farmers as owners of, 190, 215
  see also railway
Trayo, *see* Mamfe/Trayo
Tudhope, W. S. D., 18, 172n, 235n
Tutu (Akwapim), 181
  migrant farmers, 51, 193–9
  notes on, 213
  see also Akwapim
Twi language
  economic jargon in, 215–17

spelling of place-names, 220–1
  see also Christaller
Twifu Praso, 236

under-development
  inter-disciplinary approach to, 3–4
  and 'traditional organization', 2
  writings on, and the migration, 178–9
unit of length, indigenous, 43–9
usufructuary rights
  defined, 111
  Twi word for, 216

Vansina, J., 197n
villages
  abusua, 83–4
  agricultural, 162
  on company lands, 48
Volta region
  dates of purchase of land in, 59
  migration into northern, 237

wages, Twi word for, 215n
Walker, E. O., 134, 234n
Wallis, J. R., 237n
Wanner, G. A., 171
West African Lands Committee, 20–1, 132, 149–51, 172, 242–3
wholesalers, food, 190n
Wilks, Ivor, 28, 29, 87, 167n
wills, written, 109n, 187
  see also samansew
wɔfasε (Twi), sister's son, 123
  see also inheritance
women
  cocoa-farmers, 11, 42n, 65, 116–17
  farmers, 164, 168
  wholesalers, 190n

Yaw Koko, 145, 151, 156
Yilo Krobo, *see* Krobo
Yoruba farmers, mobility of, 169

16   The historic cocoa-growing area, showing places mentioned in the text.

LIST OF PLACE NAMES (Alphabetical)

Aboatumpan, 97
Abobiri, 85
Aborodem, 87
Abrodiem, 54
Adakwa, 101
Adawso, 57
Adeiso, 7
Adidiso, 96
Adiembra, 37
Adonkwanta, 110
Agyinase, 45
Ahamahama, 32
Ahariso, 17
Ahwerease-Akim, 11
Akantin, 84
Akim-Boso, 1
Akorabo, 80
Akotuakrom, 29
Akuffo, 34
Akwadum, 105
Amfaho, 41
Ankwasu, 46
Anoff, 10
Anum Apapam, 66
Apapam, 107
Apedwa, 106
Asafo, 109
Asamankese, 2
Asikasu, 5
Asuabiri, 58
Asuboi, 61
Asudom, 27
Asuokaw, 3
Asuokyene, 6
Asuoya, 75
Awbum, 72
Awusem, 60
Ayi Bonte, 30
Bepoase, 38

Betom, 40
Bibianiha, 98
Bosuso, 115
Daaman, 19
Dedewa, 56
Deigo, 33
Doboro, 14
Dokrokyewa, 62
Dome, 82
Domeabra, 53
Duaden, 31
Duayeden, 9
Fotobi, 15
Hwereso, 51
Jumapo, 112
Kabu Hill, 95
Kibi, 108
Kofi Pare, 64
Koforidua, 99
Kokoso, 67
Konko, 77
Koransan, 73
Kraboa-Coaltar, 50
Krabokese, 42
Kuaho, 55
Kukua, 74
Kwaboanta, 49
Kwesi Komfo, 93
Kyekyewere, 52
Maamedede, 21
Maase, 113
Mafukrom, 36
Mangoase, 59
Mankron, 68
Mepom, 4
Meretuam, 24
Metemano, 70
Mfodwo-Boaten, 8
Mfranta, 83

Mmetiamu, 79
Nananko, 69
Nankese, 100
Niifio, 90
Nkyenekyene, 18
Nsawam, 13
Ntunkum, 104
Obodan, 16
Obomofo-Densua, 89
Obuobisa, 20
Odumase-Akim, 102
Odumkyere, 39
Ofobea, 22
Okanta, 92
Okomso, 28
Okorase
  (south of Koforidua), 78
Okorase
  (south of Suhum), 81
Omenako, 91
Onyamkyere, 25
Otoase, 35
Oworam, 63
Pakro, 47
Pampanso, 43
Panto; 76
Potroase, 103
Pretu, 71
Saforosua, 94
Sakyikrom, 12
Suhien, 111
Suhum, 86
Sukyerema, 26
Suwurum; 65
Tafo, 114
Takorase, 23
Teacher Mante, 48
Trayo, 88
Yaw Koko, 44

LIST OF PLACE NAMES (Numerical)

1, Akim-Boso
2, Asamankese
3, Asuokaw
4, Mepom
5, Asikasu
6, Asuokyene
7, Adeiso
8, Mfodwo-Boaten
9, Duayeden
10, Anoff
11, Ahwerease-Akim
12, Sakyikrom
13, Nsawam
14, Doboro
15, Fotobi
16, Obodan
17, Ahariso
18, Nkyenekyene
19, Daaman
20, Obuobisa
21, Maamedede
22, Ofobea
23, Takorase
24, Meretuam
25, Onyamkyere
26, Sukyerema
27, Asudom
28, Okomso
29, Akotuakrom
30, Ayi Bonte
31, Duaden
32, Ahamahama
33, Deigo
34, Akuffo
35, Otoase
36, Mafukrom
37, Adiembra
38, Bepoase
39, Odumkyere

40, Betom
41, Amfaho
42, Krabokese
43, Pampanso
44, Yaw Koko
45, Agyinase
46, Ankwasu
47, Pakro
48, Teacher Mante
49, Kwaboanta
50, Kraboa-Coaltar
51, Hwereso
52, Kyekyewere
53, Domeabra
54, Abrodiem
55, Kuaho
56, Dedewa
57, Adawso
58, Asuabiri
59, Mangoase
60, Awusem
61, Asuboi
62, Dokrokyewa
63, Oworam
64, Kofi Pare
65, Suwurum
66, Anum Apapam
67, Kokoso
68, Mankron
69, Nananko
70, Metemano
71, Pretu
72, Awbum
73, Koransan
74, Kukua
75, Asuoya
76, Panto
77, Konko
78, Okorase (south of Koforidua)

79, Mmetiamu
80, Akorabo
81, Okorase
  (south of Suhum)
82, Dome
83, Mfranta
84, Akantin
85, Abobiri
86, Suhum
87, Aborodem
88, Trayo
89, Obomofo-Densua
90, Niifio
91, Omenako
92, Okanta
93, Kwesi Komfo
94, Saforosua
95, Kabu Hill
96, Adidiso
97, Aboatumpan
98, Bibianiha
99, Koforidua
100, Nankese
101, Adakwa
102, Odumase-Akim
103, Potroase
104, Ntunkum
105, Akwadum
106, Apedwa
107, Apapam
108, Kibi
109, Asafo
110, Adonkwanta
111, Suhien
112, Jumapo
113, Maase
114, Tafo
115, Bosuso

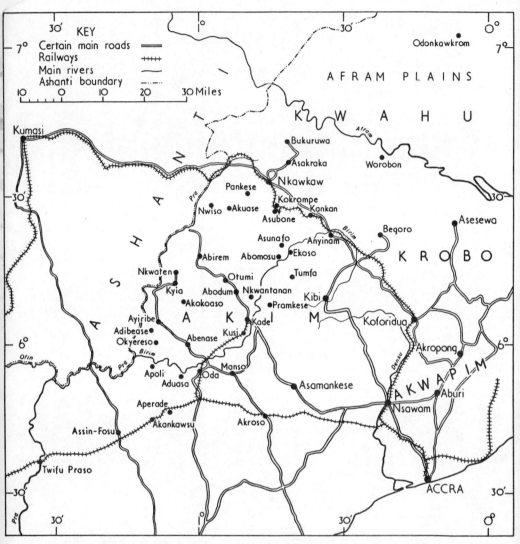

17 The main south-eastern districts in which the migrant farmers acquired land during the lorry age.

THE LIBRARY
ST. MARY'S COLLEGE OF MARYLAND
ST. MARY'S CITY, MARYLAND 20686